The Presidency in Times of Crisis and Disaster

The Presidency in Times of Crisis and Disaster

Primary Documents in Context

Brian M. Harward, Editor

An Imprint of ABC-CLIO, LLC

Santa Barbara, California • Denver, Colorado

Copyright © 2020 by ABC-CLIO, LLC

All rights reserved. No part of this publication may be reproduced, stored in a retrieval system, or transmitted, in any form or by any means, electronic, mechanical, photocopying, recording, or otherwise, except for the inclusion of brief quotations in a review, without prior permission in writing from the publisher.

Library of Congress Cataloging-in-Publication Data

Names: Harward, Brian M., editor.
Title: The presidency in times of crisis and disaster : primary documents in context / Brian M. Harward, editor.
Description: Santa Barbara, California : ABC-CLIO, 2020. | Includes bibliographical references and index.
Identifiers: LCCN 2019026695 (print) | LCCN 2019026696 (ebook) | ISBN 9781440870880 (hardcover) | ISBN 9781440870897 (ebook)
Subjects: LCSH: Executive power—United States—History—Sources. | Crisis management in government—United States—History—Sources. | Political leadership—United States—History—Sources. | Presidents—United States—History—Sources.
Classification: LCC JK516 .P6527 2020 (print) | LCC JK516 (ebook) | DDC 973.09/9—dc23
LC record available at https://lccn.loc.gov/2019026695
LC ebook record available at https://lccn.loc.gov/2019026696

ISBN: 978-1-4408-7088-0 (print)
       978-1-4408-7089-7 (ebook)

24 23 22 21 20   1 2 3 4 5

This book is also available as an eBook.

ABC-CLIO
An Imprint of ABC-CLIO, LLC

ABC-CLIO, LLC
147 Castilian Drive
Santa Barbara, California 93117
www.abc-clio.com

This book is printed on acid-free paper ∞

Manufactured in the United States of America

Contents

CHAPTER 2   Economy and Livelihoods

CHAPTER 3   Natural and Technological Disasters

CHAPTER 4   Political Scandals and Tragedies

CHAPTER 5   War and Conflict

Introduction

Americans have long held paradoxical views of presidents and the exercise of presidential power. We seem to venerate strong leaders such as Abraham Lincoln, Thomas Jefferson, Teddy Roosevelt, and Franklin D. Roosevelt, who acted decisively and with swift efficiency in the face of national crises and pressing policy concerns, even as those actions might push the contemporaneous understanding of the boundaries of the president's constitutional authority. As political scientists William Howell and Terry Moe quip, "There are no legislators on Mount Rushmore" (Moe and Howell 2016, 107). Presidents, they point out, are driven by national interests, national constituencies, and their own legacy as a national figure of consequence. Legislators, by contrast, are motivated by more parochial concerns, short-term goals, and more limited policy agendas. Moreover, the vague language of the Constitution's executive article, Article II, permits presidents broad discretion in interpreting the scope of their authority. In addition, Congress has repeatedly granted (and the courts have upheld) broad statutory discretion to the executive branch in many different policy contexts.

But even as we expect decisive action and bold presidential vision, we also want the president to be bound by constitutional and statutory limits. Claims of inherent or exclusive presidential authority to act in the face of a crisis, let alone in more run-of-the-mill domestic policy areas, are often met with criticism from those who fear the subversion of democratic principles that such a consolidation of power could elicit. Franklin Delano Roosevelt's internment of Japanese Americans, Harry Truman's actions during the Korean War, Richard Nixon's impoundment of funds, George W. Bush's warrantless wiretaps, and Barack Obama's drone strikes each prompted expressions of concern in this regard. The importance of these criticisms is heightened when those expressions of presidential power are understood to be generative, or precedential, and "lay about like a loaded weapon ready for the hand of any authority that can bring forward a plausible claim of an urgent need" (Robert H. Jackson dissent in *Korematsu v. U.S.*, 1944).

As we consider these competing perspectives through the events discussed in this volume, it is instructive to recall another admonishment from Justice Jackson: that we must be mindful of the interdependence and dynamism of presidential power. In this passage from his opinion in *Youngstown Sheet and Tube Co. v. Sawyer*

(1952), Jackson expresses support for the Court's ruling, which struck down President Truman's seizure of the nation's steel industry during a time of war:

> The actual art of governing under our Constitution does not, and cannot, conform to judicial definitions of the power of any of its branches based on isolated clauses, or even single Articles torn from context. While the Constitution diffuses power the better to secure liberty, it also contemplates that practice will integrate the dispersed powers into a workable government. It enjoins upon its branches separateness but interdependence, autonomy, but reciprocity. Presidential powers are not fixed but fluctuate depending upon their disjunction or conjunction with those of Congress.

Presidential power, Jackson suggests, is shaped by events, circumstances, political contexts, institutional resistance, and contestation over constitutional authority and the constitutional order that those conditions create. The powers that the presidency has "on paper" provide an incomplete picture of the powers that particular presidents can actually wield.

Jackson's insistence that we understand presidential power as interdependent and reciprocal in a system of separated powers is a key thread through this volume and is a theme to which we will return several times throughout the collection. It is also important to keep in mind that we cannot understand provisions or "even single Articles torn from context" (*Youngstown Sheet and Tube Co. v. Sawyer* 1952). The Constitution does not always provide a clear authorization for any particular action a president would like to take, and Congress has not always specifically granted that authority by statute. In such cases, some presidents have been reluctant to take a particular action they would otherwise want to pursue. Many more, though, have not considered the lack of explicit constitutional or statutory authority an impediment to their actions, if in their judgment events warrant a presidential response. Thus, contextualizing Article II powers is also a primary aim of this volume. And to do that, it is important to explore the "disjunction and conjunction" (*Youngstown Sheet and Tube Co. v. Sawyer* 1952) of the first two articles of the Constitution as a way to introduce key theoretical approaches to executive power. Of particular note in this context is that the set of Article II powers upon which a president may draw is akin to the set of powers afforded the legislative branch in Article I.

Just as Congress has enumerated and implied powers, so too does the president. At the time of the founding, the scope of those Article I powers was unsettled; in determining the contours of congressional authority, President George Washington relied on the perspectives of Secretary of State Thomas Jefferson and Secretary of the Treasury Alexander Hamilton, among others. Specifically, Washington solicited their views on whether Congress had the power to establish a national bank. Because there is no enumerated or expressed authority to do so, if Congress could indeed establish a national bank, it had to come from its implied powers. Jefferson advised Washington that congressional authority derived principally from Article I's explicit enumeration of power including the power to tax, to raise an army, establish post offices, and so on. Article I, Section 8's "necessary and proper" clause (which follows the enumerated powers and grants Congress the authority "to make all laws which shall be necessary and proper for carrying into execution the foregoing powers"), was not a general grant of authority—it was a grant of power to make laws that were *absolutely* necessary to carry into execution the enumerated powers, and not simply *convenient*. He wrote, "The Constitution restrained them to necessary means, [. . .] to those means without which the grant of the power would be nugatory" (Jefferson 1791, in Ford 1898).

Hamilton's view was quite different. By his account, Congress had "a right to employ all the means requisite and fairly applicable to the attainment of the ends of such power, and which are not precluded by restrictions and exceptions specified in the Constitution" (Hamilton 1791, in Ford 1898). The Hamiltonian view prevailed, and it was adopted almost verbatim by Chief Justice Marshall in the 1819 case *McCulloch v. Maryland*, which established the doctrine of implied powers. Marshall writes, "Among the enumerated powers, we do not find that of establishing a national bank or creating a corporation. But there is no phrase in the instrument which . . . excludes incidental or implied powers; and which requires that everything granted shall be expressly and minutely described." He goes on to say, "Let the end be legitimate, let it be within the scope of the constitution, and all means which are appropriate, which are plainly adapted to that end, which are not prohibited, but consist with the letter and spirit of the constitution, are constitutional."

Marshall acknowledges the concerns of Jefferson and other Democratic Republicans who were fearful of the concentration of power in the central government. "The powers of the government are limited, and its limits are not to be transcended," he says. However, the doctrine of implied powers that Marshall developed in *McCulloch* is premised on the idea that in identifying the scope of the powers of the central government, courts must "enable that body to perform the high duties assigned to it, in a manner most beneficial to the people." This broad grant of authority, beyond the literalist or strict interpretation of the text of the Constitution, grants Congress wide authority to legislate in areas where no explicit, "minute description" of the delegated power is given. Consequently, much—though by no means all—of the contemporary congressional authority to legislate in key areas is derived from this doctrine of implied powers.

As one might imagine, given Article II's vague provisions, a similar dynamic has shaped debates about the full scope of presidential power as well. As a result, a simple review of the text of Article II tells us very little about contemporary presidential power. Reference to the Constitution as a guide to the full scope of presidential power is insufficient for several reasons. For one, Article II is rather limited, consisting of four short sections. Much of the attention of Article II is given to presidential selection (Section 1) and impeachment (Section 4). Sections 2 and 3 identify the powers of the office, including the president's role as commander in chief, presidential pardons, treaty-making power, appointment power, and agenda-setting power for Congress.

Beyond those specific grants of power, key passages bestow rather vague and ambiguous levels of authority. For example, Section 1 states that "[t]he executive power shall be vested in a President." And Section 3 requires that the president "shall take care that the laws are faithfully executed." In their imprecision, both of those provisions allow different interpretations. For instance, on one reading, Section 1's vesting of executive power is simply a designation of official duty, identifying the president as the person who has the executive authority derived from explicit language that follows in subsequent sections of Article II. Similarly, Section 3's "take care" clause could be interpreted as obligating the president to enact laws passed by Congress in a manner that is faithful to the intent of Congress. Moreover, given that the enumerated and implied powers are among the powers designated in Article I (the legislative article of the Constitution), it might follow that Article II vests in the presidency only the power to *execute* the laws passed by Congress. This would be consistent with a literalist, or traditionalist, interpretation of the text.

William Howard Taft, the only person to have been both president and Chief Justice of the Supreme Court, typifies this literalist approach to executive power. He wrote:

> The president can exercise no power which cannot be fairly and reasonably traced to some specific grant of power or justly implied and included within such express grant as proper and necessary to its exercise. Such specific grant must be either in the Federal Constitution or in an act of Congress passed in pursuance thereof. There is no undefined residuum of power which he can exercise because it seems to him to be in the public interest. (Taft 1916, 139–140)

Akin to the Jeffersonian view of Article I, Section 8's "necessary and proper" clause, Taft suggests that the president (like Congress in Art. I) has only expressed (or enumerated) powers, augmented by those powers that are necessary to carry into execution the enumerated powers. For Taft, as for Jefferson, implied powers are generated by the absolute necessity (as opposed to usefulness or convenience) that arises from enumerated powers and are not themselves sources of independent authority beyond the expressed powers.

A different perspective, often attributed to President Theodore Roosevelt, recognizes Article II as a grant of broad authority to the president. By this view, the president has explicit, enumerated powers as well as others—implied and inherent—that bestow the presidency with wide discretion to govern as a "steward' of the public interest. Roosevelt writes, "[M]y view was that every Executive officer in high position was a steward of the people bound actively to do all he could for the people and not to content himself with the negative merit of keeping his talents undamaged in a napkin." He continues, "My belief was that it was not only his right but his duty to do anything that the needs of the nation demanded" (Roosevelt 1926, 347–48). The only restraint on particular expressions of executive power that were taken in the public interest, he concludes, would come from constitutional or congressional prohibitions. This stewardship theory of executive power is consistent with the Hamiltonian view of the doctrine of congressional implied powers, to which Jefferson objected. By this logic, like Congress, the president has all those powers explicitly mentioned in Article II, as well as all those powers necessary and proper to protect the public interest. The authority of the president, then, is only limited by explicit prohibitions found in the Constitution or statute.

Sometimes, however, the public good might demand executive action beyond, or even in contravention of the constitutional or statutory power of the president. Seventeenth-century philosopher John Locke recognized that there may be such instances—crises, disasters, and national emergencies—that would warrant the use of emergency executive power. He argues:

> [T]his power to act according to discretion for the public good, without the prescription of the law and sometimes even against it, is that which is called prerogative; for since in some governments the law-making power is not always in being and is usually too numerous, and so too slow for the dispatch requisite to execution, and because, also, it is impossible to foresee and so by laws to provide for all accidents and necessities that may concern the public, or make such laws as will do no harm, . . . therefore there is a latitude left to the executive power to do many things of choice which the laws do not prescribe. (Locke [1689] 1955, 136)

This approach is consistent with what scholars have called the presidential prerogative view of executive power.

The Lockean emergency powers that presidents have claimed—such as Lincoln during the Civil War, Wilson in World War I, and Roosevelt during World War II—were taken in the absence of congressional or constitutional authority. But there was a finite end to those measures. The Appomattox Courthouse, the Treaty of Versailles, and V-J Day marked the cessation of hostilities against identifiable, uniformed adversaries on traditional battlefields. The extraordinary actions the presidents took to meet the challenges of those conflicts ebbed as those conflicts were resolved. But the terror attacks of September 11, 2001, presented new challenges to national security that were distinct from previous military conflicts. The national security emergency cut across policy areas and institutional structures. No longer was the military the principal institution defending the homeland—now immigration officers, FBI, police, the Treasury Department, and others outside the Department of Defense were actively combatting the threat. The president's role as commander in chief expanded to accommodate that shift and, as a result, the new context changed the political dynamic of separate institutions sharing power. In the view of President George W. Bush, he was "the Decider"; the other branches either did not have the jurisdictional authority to interfere with his actions or had implicitly granted him the power to act unilaterally to face the crisis posed by terrorism. In the contemporary context of global terror, and the ongoing, nongeographically defined conflict with nonstate actors, the emergency powers presidents have claimed are unlikely to recede due to the persistent nature of the challenges of national security. This permanent emergency condition gave rise to a new conception of presidential power: the unilateral or unitary presidency.

This view of unfettered presidential power is based on a reading of Article II, Section 1 as an *exclusive* grant of broad unilateral powers to the president. By this broader reading, the president has complete, exclusive executive authority. It refers to *the* executive power—not *some* executive power; the referent is *all power to execute the law*. Congress, insofar as it would interfere in the execution of law, would be encroaching on the president's unilateral, unfettered executive authority. And the "take care" clause might be interpreted as requiring the president to enact laws in a manner consistent with the president's view of the laws' faithfulness to the president's *own* view of constitutional meaning.

In sum, one might consider the literalist approach of Taft as reflective of a philosophy of *negative government*, the absence of regulatory mechanisms structuring free markets, a disinclination to powerfully engage in foreign affairs, the absence of governmental constraints on labor contracts, working conditions, and so forth. A presidency framed by a literalist approach is limited to enumerated powers, and consequently does not generate many moments of swift, effective, decisive executive action. Nor, predictably, did the office attract a great many people inclined to use the office to wield tremendous national power. The stewardship view, however, is predicated on *positive government*. It assumes the purpose of the office is to tackle the problems of the nation and thereby vests the office with the authority to address those problems, even if the particular tools used are not specified in the text. The steward president is an activist president, using the weight of the office (including its moral and political authority) to address critical events and pressing policy needs of the country.

Not surprisingly, activist presidencies generate far more litigation and political contestation of their actions than do the inactions of literalist presidencies. But even more controversial and consequential are the extraconstitutional prerogative or emergency powers that presidents have taken. The prerogative view proposes that the president is permitted (and even has the obligation) to act unilaterally— even perhaps against congressional or constitutional authorization—if the emergency poses a grave threat to national security, for example. The irony, of course, is that prerogative violates the rule of law in order to secure safety. When there is a critical moment of national crisis or disaster (an insurrection or terrorist attack, for example), the public demand for swift, effective, and extralegal executive action is high and political constraints on executive power are low. As Justice Jackson noted, a Congress unwilling to constrain prerogative invites more expressions of emergency powers; it "lays about like a loaded weapon" as an especially potent concentration of power in one branch of government.

These very different perspectives on presidential power—the literalist, stewardship, prerogative, and unilateral perspectives—are worth considering as we explore the events chronicled in this volume. These views, and several variations, have dominated distinct eras of U.S. history and reflected the actions available to and taken by presidents who held office during those eras. Many factors have contributed to the ascendancy of the stewardship approach (with moments of prerogative marking its trajectory) over time. For instance, the emergence of a national—even global—economy, industrialization, and the challenges that arose in the industrial era necessitated national solutions to national problems. Broad congressional grants of delegated authority to the executive to write regulations have regularly been upheld by the courts, as Congress ceded some dimensions of its lawmaking authority to the executive branch agencies in order to address those pressing national problems. In addition, the New Deal coalition and the Civil Rights era gave rise to powerful citizens' claims on central governmental authority and the expectation that the president in particular had a special role to play in securing citizens' well-being. In addition, the twentieth century's two world wars concentrated military power in the executive branch, and the persistent national security challenges of the twenty-first century have further consolidated that power in the Oval Office. Finally, the rise of candidate-centered campaigns and decline of political party control over candidates for office (including, but not limited to, the president) created incentives for presidents to be active, aggressive stewards of executive power in the public interest.

But just as presidential power can be shaped by the constitutional order of the era, key events and crises can create exceptional circumstances in the "disjunction or conjunction" of presidential and congressional power. A president disinclined to exert independent authority over policymaking generally may be called upon, in the face of a national emergency, to act decisively in the absence of congressional action. Meanwhile, an executive with broad views of presidential unilateral authority may be forced to acquiesce to Congress under certain conditions. Thus, many presidencies have been understood to be characterized by the dynamism, contestation, and reciprocity that exists among these positions of literalism (or the traditional theory of presidential power), stewardship (broad, implied powers), and prerogative (unilateralism and emergency) powers of the president.

As we explore the critical events included in this volume, be attentive to the contexts that shape presidential responsiveness at the moment. Under what conditions are emergency powers taken by the president? Do presidents have different approaches to handling crises and disasters that take place during their administrations? Are some presidents ill-equipped to deal with the crises compared to other presidents? Are presidents more likely to take decisive action in foreign affairs as opposed to domestic affairs? Does Congress, the judiciary, the public, or the media tend to constrain or give free rein to executives at these critical moments? In what ways do these focusing events motivate political actors to limit or extend executive power? To what extent do political considerations drive the actions and positions of presidents in troubled times? These questions and many others will help to guide our inquiry into executive power and executive action in times of crisis and disaster. Looking to the political, economic, and social contexts in which these events take place will help us uncover a great deal about the presidency. The preceding review of the constitutional language and theoretical frames for executive power is necessary, but it is not sufficient to understand the presidency in action, as Jackson reminded us in the *Youngstown Sheet and Tube* case. The power any particular president can muster is contingent. It is contested by political opponents and separated powers, and it is conditioned by precedent, contemporary contexts, and, surely, the person holding the office.

We now turn to consideration of each of these elements through the close examination of key, discrete events to which presidents responded (or failed to respond adequately) since the nation's founding. My hope is to convey critical insights about the presidency, its powers, and its limits by using focusing events and primary contemporary documents that illuminate patterns in political behavior and institutional structures and—just as important—deviations from those patterns. Brief introductory essays frame each of the chapters. These overviews will help guide readers through notable exercises and considerations of executive power and the wider political and cultural contexts in which these events took place.

Chronological List of Events

Year	President	Event	Theme
1793	George Washington	Proclamation of Neutrality	War and Conflict
1794	George Washington	Whiskey Rebellion	Domestic Tranquility
1798	John Adams	Alien and Sedition Acts	War and Conflict
1807	Thomas Jefferson	British Provocation on the Sea	War and Conflict
1814	James Madison	Destruction of Washington, D.C.	War and Conflict
1819	James Monroe	Economic Crisis	Economy and Livelihoods
1821	James Monroe	Missouri Compromise	War and Conflict
1830	Andrew Jackson	Indian Removal Act	War and Conflict
1832	Andrew Jackson	The National Bank	Economy and Livelihoods
1837	Martin Van Buren	Economic Panic of 1837	Economy and Livelihoods
1841	John Tyler	The National Bank	Economy and Livelihoods
1846	James Polk	Mexican-American War	War and Conflict
1850	Millard Fillmore	Compromise of 1850	War and Conflict
1856	Franklin Pierce	Bleeding Kansas	War and Conflict
1857	James Buchanan	*Dred Scott v. Sanford* Case	Domestic Tranquility
1858	James Buchanan	Panic of 1857	Economy and Livelihoods
1863	Abraham Lincoln	Emancipation Proclamation	War and Conflict
1863	Abraham Lincoln	Gettysburg Address	War and Conflict
1863	Abraham Lincoln	Slavery and Citizenship	War and Conflict

Year	President	Event	Theme
1867	Andrew Johnson	Reconstruction	Domestic Tranquility
1868	Andrew Johnson	Removal of the Secretary of War	Political Scandals and Tragedies
1871	Ulysses S. Grant	Habeas Corpus	Domestic Tranquility
1875	Ulysses S. Grant	Panic of 1873	Economy and Livelihoods
1886	Grover Cleveland	Chinese Immigration	Domestic Tranquility
1889	Benjamin Harrison	Johnstown Flood	Natural and Technological Disasters
1894	Grover Cleveland	Pullman Strike	Domestic Tranquility
1895	Grover Cleveland	The Gold Standard	Economy and Livelihoods
1898	William McKinley	Occupation of the Philippines	War and Conflict
1901	Theodore Roosevelt	Assassination of William McKinley	Political Scandals and Tragedies
1903	Theodore Roosevelt	Conservation	Domestic Tranquility
1903	Theodore Roosevelt	Anti-Trust Measures	Economy and Livelihoods
1917	Woodrow Wilson	The Red Scare	Political Scandals and Tragedies
1918	Woodrow Wilson	Nineteenth Amendment	Domestic Tranquility
1918	Woodrow Wilson	World War I	War and Conflict
1923	Warren Harding	Prohibition	Domestic Tranquility
1926	Calvin Coolidge	Immigration Regulation	Domestic Tranquility
1927	Calvin Coolidge	Mississippi Flood	Natural and Technological Disasters
1930	Herbert Hoover	Stock Market Crash	Economy and Livelihoods
1932	Herbert Hoover	The Bonus Army	Domestic Tranquility
1932	Herbert Hoover	Labor Disputes	Economy and Livelihoods
1933	Franklin D. Roosevelt	The New Deal	Domestic Tranquility
1936	Franklin D. Roosevelt	The Dust Bowl	Domestic Tranquility
1941	Franklin D. Roosevelt	Attack on Pearl Harbor	War and Conflict
1944	Franklin D. Roosevelt	World War II	War and Conflict

Year	President	Event	Theme
1945	Harry Truman	Dropping the Atomic Bomb	War and Conflict
1951	Harry Truman	Firing of General Douglas MacArthur	Political Scandals and Tragedies
1952	Harry Truman	McCarthyism	Political Scandals and Tragedies
1952	Harry Truman	Seizure of Steel Companies during the Korean War	War and Conflict
1957	Dwight D. Eisenhower	Little Rock Integration Crisis	Domestic Tranquility
1957	Dwight D. Eisenhower	Launch of Sputnik	War and Conflict
1960	Dwight D. Eisenhower	U-2 Plane Incident	War and Conflict
1961	John F. Kennedy	The Occupation of Berlin	War and Conflict
1961	John F. Kennedy	Bay of Pigs	War and Conflict
1962	John F. Kennedy	Cuban Missile Crisis	War and Conflict
1963	John F. Kennedy	Civil Rights Act	Domestic Tranquility
1963	Lyndon B. Johnson	Assassination of John F. Kennedy	Political Scandals and Tragedies
1964	Lyndon B. Johnson	Alaskan Earthquake	Natural and Technological Disasters
1964	Lyndon B. Johnson	Gulf of Tonkin Incident	War and Conflict
1964	Lyndon B. Johnson	Vietnam War	War and Conflict
1968	Lyndon B. Johnson	Assassination of Dr. Martin Luther King Jr.	Political Scandals and Tragedies
1969	Richard Nixon	Launch of *Apollo 11*	Natural and Technological Disasters
1970	Richard Nixon	Kent State University Protest	Domestic Tranquility
1974	Richard Nixon	Watergate Scandal	Political Scandals and Tragedies
1974	Gerald R. Ford	Pardoning Richard Nixon	Political Scandals and Tragedies
1976	Gerald R. Ford	Swine Flu Outbreak	Domestic Tranquility
1979	Jimmy Carter	Energy Crisis	Domestic Tranquility
1979	Jimmy Carter	Three Mile Island Nuclear Plant Meltdown	Natural and Technological Disasters
1979	Jimmy Carter	Iran Hostage Crisis	War and Conflict

Year	President	Event	Theme
1980	Jimmy Carter	Mount St. Helens Eruption	Natural and Technological Disasters
1981	Ronald Reagan	Air Traffic Controllers Strike	Domestic Tranquility
1983	Ronald Reagan	Bombings in Beirut, Lebanon	War and Conflict
1985	Ronald Reagan	AIDS Crisis	Domestic Tranquility
1986	Ronald Reagan	Space Shuttle *Challenger* Disaster	Natural and Technological Disasters
1987	Ronald Reagan	Iran-Contra Scandal	Political Scandals and Tragedies
1989	George H. W. Bush	Savings and Loans Crisis	Economy and Livelihoods
1989	George H. W. Bush	*Exxon Valdez* Oil Spill	Natural and Technological Disasters
1990	George H. W. Bush	Persian Gulf Crisis	War and Conflict
1993	Bill Clinton	Ambush in Mogadishu	War and Conflict
1995	Bill Clinton	Oklahoma City Bombing	Domestic Tranquility
1995	Bill Clinton	Government Shutdown	Economy and Livelihoods
1998	Bill Clinton	Impeachment	Political Scandals and Tragedies
1999	Bill Clinton	Columbine Shooting	Domestic Tranquility
2000	Bill Clinton	USS *Cole* Attack	War and Conflict
2001	George W. Bush	9/11 Terror Attacks	War and Conflict
2003	George W. Bush	Space Shuttle *Columbia* Disaster	Natural and Technological Disasters
2005	George W. Bush	Hurricane Katrina	Natural and Technological Disasters
2009	Barack Obama	Great Recession	Economy and Livelihoods
2010	Barack Obama	Deepwater Horizon Oil Spill	Natural and Technological Disasters
2012	Barack Obama	Sandy Hook Shooting	Domestic Tranquility
2012	Barack Obama	Hurricane Sandy	Natural and Technological Disasters
2012	Barack Obama	Attack in Benghazi, Libya	War and Conflict
2013	Barack Obama	Government Shutdown	Economy and Livelihoods

Year	President	Event	Theme
2014	Barack Obama	Ebola Virus	Domestic Tranquility
2015	Barack Obama	Ferguson Unrest	Domestic Tranquility
2017	Donald Trump	Charlottesville Shooting	Domestic Tranquility
2017	Donald Trump	Opioid Crisis	Domestic Tranquility
2018	Donald Trump	Wildfires in California	Natural and Technological Disasters
2018	Donald Trump	Hurricane Maria	Natural and Technological Disasters
2018	Donald Trump	United States–Russia Summit	Political Scandals and Tragedies
2019	Donald Trump	Government Shutdown	Economy and Livelihoods

1

Challenges to Domestic Tranquility

INTRODUCTION

During the nineteenth century, Congress was generally understood to be the center of U.S. governmental power. Presidents were far less consequential, as reflected in the limited, or traditional, view of executive power articulated by President William H. Taft, among others. Thus, for much of the nation's history, the presidency was rather hidden from public view. In the past century, however, an expansion of presidential power has taken place, driven by public demand for active presidential leadership as well as the efforts of successive presidents to enlarge the powers of the office. As the policy-making roles of the presidency grew during the first half of the twentieth century, so too did its public exposure. Teddy Roosevelt, as one might expect from his activist view of the presidency, sought to harness public support for his policies, as did Woodrow Wilson. But it was Franklin Roosevelt who radically enlarged the president's role in policy making and agenda setting for the nation's domestic and international affairs.

Roosevelt also carefully cultivated—and ultimately fundamentally changed—how the presidency was covered by the media. Franklin Roosevelt was not the first president to hold press conferences, but he held far more than any previous president, offering biweekly meetings for reporters. During those events, organized by the nation's first presidential press secretary, Roosevelt would deliberately make major policy announcements, further cultivating reporters' attention and desire for access. He also took advantage of technological advances by holding "fireside chats," which were broadcast via radio to homes across the country. He would use those broadcasts to speak directly to citizens, to explain and justify particular actions he proposed to take and thereby rally public support for those efforts.

The effects of Roosevelt's public outreach strategy were significant. As presidency scholars George Edwards III and Stephen Wayne describe it:

> [T]he extensive media focus on the president had three principal effects. First, it permanently added a new role to the president's job, that of communicator in chief, and required that skills commensurate with this role be exercised. Second, it

heightened public expectations of presidential performance. Advances in communications have enabled organized groups to promote the desires of their membership more effectively, and the president has become the focal point for many of these increased demands on government. Third, media coverage linked public approval more closely to the exercise of presidential power. Now, more than ever, presidents need to build support outside of government to gain support within it. (Edwards and Wayne 1999, 11)

Every president after Roosevelt crafted a public relations strategy to bolster his support and help achieve their policy goals. Years later, the White House Communications Office became a key instrument of presidential influence, coordinating and staging events; responding to reporters' queries about current events, adverse stories, or critical comments from political opponents; and orchestrating an effective communication strategy to promote a favorable public impression of the president.

As favorable public sentiment became increasingly recognized as a formidable political weapon in its own right, presidents who failed to achieve their policy goals through congressional bargaining increasingly turned directly to the American people for bargaining leverage. Scholars have described this strategy of "going public" to muster public support for the president's agenda as a powerful means by which presidents can gain traction for their policy agendas (Kernell 1997). The decline in partisan identification among voters, the proliferation of interest groups, and the rise of candidate-centered campaigns, among many other shifts, have contributed to the difficulties presidents face as they engage in coordinated legislative strategies. The cumulative effect of these changes has been an ongoing collective action problem, with very few particularized benefits available to bind the individual participants to an agreement. Individual members of Congress act in their specific interests, not in the interest of a group, coalition, or coordinate body. Therefore, any legislative strategy presidents deploy would have to feature individualized incentives for members of Congress in order to sustain that agreement. Moreover, scholarly studies of representatives' voting behavior reveal that the early twenty-first century has experienced the most ideologically polarized Congress since Reconstruction. In an era of heightened political polarization, bargaining, compromise, and accommodating a divided Congress can very often doom presidents' legislative agendas. Going public can be an effective strategy to compel congressional action.

Just how and when presidents have "gone public" to elicit public support to compel congressional action has varied over time. Presidential speeches broadcast by radio and television, public events, and foreign and domestic travel have all been key components of presidents' communication strategies. In recent years, of course, the internet and social media have given presidents unlimited access to the public. President Trump, for instance, has more than 53 million followers on Twitter who have received, on average, eight tweets per day since he took office. It is unclear how effective that strategy has been for him, however. Part of the explanation may be that his tweets do not appear to be part of a policy-specific, coordinated communication strategy, as they are often inaccurate, incoherent, blustery charges of "Fake News!" or sometimes even vulgar, racist, misogynistic, and profane personal attacks. But even the policy-specific messaging may be limited in its effectiveness, especially over time, as the public becomes fatigued by constant appeals. Direct messaging may be subject to diminishing returns—the more a president engages in that strategy, the less efficacious it becomes. It also hardens a president's position on a particular issue, limiting options for policy outcomes. Any resolution that falls short of the president's stated position can be perceived as a policy loss, further eroding the president's bargaining position.

As political scientists have noted, a president's bargaining position is a valuable resource to him or her in achieving his or her policy goals, especially in the domestic context. In the mid-1950s, the general consensus of the scholarship on the presidency understood presidents to have limited formal powers; hence, they were only able to achieve significant policy goals by harnessing their powers of persuasion. Richard Neustadt, a prominent political scientist and advisor to many presidents, states that the office of the president is rather like a "glorified clerkship," endowing its holder with few formal powers upon which executives could rely to achieve their policy goals. Real power, he argues, is exercised not through commands but rather through the president's power to persuade.

> In form all presidents are leaders, nowadays. In fact this guarantees no more than that they will be clerks. Everybody now expects the man inside the White House to do something about everything. Laws and customs now reflect acceptance of him as the Great Initiator. . . . But such acceptance does not signify that all the rest of government is at his feet. It merely signifies that other men have found it practically impossible for them to do *their* jobs without assurance of initiatives from him. Service for themselves, not power for the president, has brought them to accept his leadership in form. They find his actions useful in their business. The transformation of his routine obligations testifies to their dependence on an active White House. A President, these days, is an invaluable clerk. His influence, however, is a very different matter. Laws and customs tell us very little about leadership in fact. (Neustadt 1962, 6)

Neustadt developed an understanding of presidential power based upon a president's ability to persuade—to convince others to support a president's agenda because of their own judgment of their responsibilities, interests, and benefits. "Persuasion is a two-way street," he writes. "The power to persuade is the power to bargain. Status and authority yield bargaining advantages. But in a government of 'separated institutions sharing powers,' they yield them to all sides" (Neustadt 1962, 36). Therefore, he continues, "[t]he essence of a president's persuasive task with congressmen and everybody else, is to induce them to believe that what he wants of them is what their own appraisal of their own responsibilities requires them to do in their interests, not his" (Neustadt 1962, 46).

But this understanding of presidential power stands in sharp contrast to contemporary scholarship, which places greater emphasis on the formal powers the president can wield to achieve policy goals. That is, our understanding of presidential power as an expression of persuasion and the personality of the president has given way to a view that places the source of presidential power in institutional terms. This understanding posits that even though personality and charisma are important, it is ultimately the institutions that really form the foundation of presidential power. The premise of this scholarship is that institutions matter in deeply consequential ways, structuring the decision-making environment of all political actors, including presidents. Institutions can be formal rules, constitutional provisions, statutory law, and formalized procedures. They can also be informal norms and conventions, developed over time and embedded by practice. Well beyond the presidential persuasive power, this scholarship suggests, the institutions that shape executive branch politics set the terms of presidential engagement with Congress, federal agencies, the courts, the states, the public, the media, foreign policy, and so on.

There have been several important dimensions of this scholarship on the institutional power of the presidency. Among them has been a focus on the presidential veto and the legislative influence the president has by exercising or threatening to exercise that power. In addition, scholars have considered the agenda-setting role of the president (as a "first mover") in determining which issues Congress will take up. Also, regulatory authority and the congressional appointment and removal power of the president have been examined as available mechanisms that give presidents advantages in policy making relative to Congress.

One set of scholars has been particularly important in this reconsideration of presidential power by focusing on a rather distinct source of institutional authority: ambiguity. Yes, they argue, presidents have these formal powers like the veto, appointment power, and the like. But in the ambiguities of Article II, presidents—even really unpersuasive ones—have an incentive to push those formal powers "relentlessly, yet strategically and with moderation" and typically without congressional or judicial counteraction (Moe and Howell 1999, 852). In broad language, Article II vests the president with "the executive power" to "take care that the laws be faithfully executed." Those constitutional provisions are not defined with precision. In their ambiguity, they admit of many interpretations, including the authority for the president to pursue actions that were not explicitly granted. The result, Moe and Howell argue, "is a slow but steady shift of the institutional balance of power over time in favor of presidents" (Moe and Howell 1999, 852). Their work has highlighted

> an institutional basis for presidential power that has gone largely unappreciated to this point but that, in our view, has become so pivotal to presidential leadership, and so central to an understanding of presidential power, that it virtually defines what is distinctively modern about the modern American presidency. This is the president's formal capacity for taking unilateral action and thus for making law on his own. Often, presidents do this through executive orders. Sometimes they do it through proclamations or executive agreements or national security directives. But whatever vehicles they may choose, the end result is that presidents can and do make new law—and thus shift the existing status quo—without the explicit consent of Congress. (Moe and Howell 1999, 851)

Whereas Neustadt argued that presidents rely upon their powers of persuasion and require the assistance of members of Congress to achieve presidential policy goals, institutional scholars demonstrate that the ability of presidents to act unilaterally is a defining feature of the contemporary presidency. This is hugely consequential in eras of heightened political polarization in Congress. Heightened polarization means that major legislative action will require supermajorities rather than simple majorities to overcome filibusters (which can be used by a minority in the Senate to stop bills from proceeding to a vote). As a consequence, the likelihood of congressional inaction on any particular policy issue is high, and the likelihood of congressional reaction to presidential unilateralism is low. Ideological polarization in Congress, then, invites presidents to extend executive power through unilateralism (including, for example, executive orders), rather than bargaining and finding compromise solutions to policy disputes.

Indeed, actions by the Obama and Trump administrations on several domestic policy fronts reveal the incentives presidents have for unilateralism, especially in the face of congressional inaction or disapproval. In 2011 President Obama launched the "We Can't Wait" initiative that sought to exercise unilateral powers in the face of Republican stonewalling in Congress. On issues ranging from mortgage and college loan relief to tax credits for veteran job creation and small business regulation changes, Obama went it alone, issuing executive orders and new regulations that did not require action by Congress. In a 2011 *60 Minutes* interview Obama stated, "I'm not going to wait for Congress. So wherever we have an opportunity and I have the executive authority to get things done, we're just going to go ahead and do them." Among other many other unilateral actions throughout his presidency, Obama also established by proclamation new national parks and national monuments in Utah, Nevada, and Maine. His Republican political opponents decried these actions as an unprecedented presidential power grab, but in reality, Obama was following in the footsteps of many of his predecessors. Any presidents, even those in office during the era in which the limited or traditional view of executive power dominated, exercised unilateral authority, typically through executive orders. Jefferson's Louisiana Purchase in 1803, Lincoln's 1863 Emancipation Proclamation, Lyndon Johnson's employment discrimination ban in 1965, and George W. Bush's reorganization of government and the establishment of the Office of Homeland Security in 2001 are all examples of unilateralism at work.

When Trump took office in January 2017, that authority was available to him as well. Within hours of his inauguration, Trump signed an executive order giving agencies the authority to "waive, defer, grant exemptions from, or delay" provisions in the Affordable Care Act, the signature piece of legislation from the Obama administration that Trump had repeatedly pledged to eradicate. Shortly thereafter, he kept another campaign promise, issuing an executive order that barred residents of seven predominantly Muslim countries from entering the United States (the so-called Muslim travel ban). That was soon followed by another order requiring agencies to repeal two regulatory rules for every new rule they adopt. Still other orders targeted financial regulations established under the Dodd-Frank Act and established the short-lived election integrity commission, among many other unilateral actions. By May 2019, more than halfway through his first term, Donald Trump had issued 107 executive orders. In comparison, the previous three presidents issued fewer through the same period: Clinton had issued 41 executive orders, George W. Bush 85, and Obama 74.

Though media and popular accounts of these unilateral actions by presidents are typically couched in the context of electoral strategy and political opportunism, presidential unilateralism is not driven by electoral concerns or campaign promises alone. It is, rather, a distinctive feature of the modern presidency and a defining characteristic of inter-branch relations. The president's proclivity for the swift efficiency of unilateralism, however, can have important limitations. Typically, and in most policy areas affecting statutory law, a president does not have unfettered authority to act unilaterally in ways that have lasting effect or fundamentally alter the policy. Most presidents, most of the time, would prefer to have Congress act. The scope of the president's ability to make significant, lasting changes under a particular statute may be limited. Ultimately, legislation like the Affordable Care Act or Dodd-Frank Act cannot simply be remade by presidential unilateralism. Congress must vote to repeal or redesign such major laws. The regulations established pursuant to the statutes were promulgated under the Administrative Procedures Act and have the full force of law. They cannot be unilaterally removed. Courts also have a role to play in limiting unilateralism. Trump's travel ban, for example, was struck down by the courts as unconstitutional until the administration finally issued a more carefully written order that could pass judicial muster. Nonetheless, as bargaining with an ideologically polarized Congress becomes less likely to achieve policy results that presidents prefer, and as going public to rally support for policy goals is subject to diminishing returns, presidents may have further incentives to attempt to go it alone.

The events discussed in this chapter typify the constant domestic struggles presidents, courts, Congress, and state actors face in crafting laws and taking actions to meet the pressing needs of the public. The powers Eisenhower invoked to send the 101st Airborne to Little Rock, Arkansas; the Department of Justice review of police behavior in the wake of Michael Brown's shooting death in Ferguson, Missouri; and Kennedy and Johnson's efforts to pass the Civil Rights Act of 1964, for example, demonstrate key features of federal authority in the face of challenges to domestic tranquility. Review of these events, and of the actions taken (or not taken) by presidents, will reveal important insights into presidential power, the connection between the president and the public, presidential communication, and bargaining, among many other themes. In reflecting on these moments, consider how the exercise of presidential power has shifted over time via the interplay of factors such as presidential persona, public opinion, and the political context (including congressional, court, or state actions). In light of these events, is our understanding of presidential power best captured through the institutionalist lens, or is Neustadt's behavioral understanding of presidential power also apt?

President George Washington Authorizes Military Intervention to Confront the Whiskey Rebellion, 1794

President George Washington gave the Proclamation—Authorizing Military Intervention to End Violence and Obstruction of Justice in Protest of Liquor Laws—in Pennsylvania on September 25, 1794. The proclamation was a response to national uprisings in protest of federal taxes on whiskey that had been enacted in 1791. Though the taxes were meant to address debt accrued as a result of the United States' Revolutionary War, it angered the small-scale farmers and whiskey makers who felt they were being unfairly targeted to shoulder the country's economic burden. Tension and violence escalated between farmers and tax collectors over time. Local protests strengthened and reached their peak in 1794 as lawmakers and other prominent political figures aligned themselves with the protestors, specifically Anti-Federalists and Republicans. President Washington had first planned to make peace, and he even sent an envoy to the rebels as they convened in Pittsburgh to plan a larger attack, yet the effort was to no avail. Running out of options, Alexander Hamilton, the treasury secretary at the time, then advised President Washington to send in troops. He had also advised the president to enact the whiskey tax in the first place. Thus, the following proclamation was created, which detailed the government's demands—and consequences for those who did not obey. President Washington's eventual decision to send over 10,000 troops to Pennsylvania and its surrounding areas to quell the unrest shocked many as an overuse of force. The rebels backed off following the military's presence, and the entire episode became an early example of the federal government's right and capacity to exercise power over state affairs.

Whereas from a hope that the combinations against the Constitution and laws of the United States in certain of the western counties of Pennsylvania would yield to time and reflection I thought it sufficient in the first instance rather to take measures for calling forth the militia than immediately to embody them, but the moment is now come when the overtures of forgiveness, with no other condition than a submission to law, have been only partially accepted; when every form of conciliation not inconsistent with the being of Government has been adopted without effect; when the well-disposed in those counties are unable by their influence and example to reclaim the wicked from their fury, and are compelled to associate in their own defense; when the proffered lenity has been perversely misinterpreted into an apprehension that the citizens will march with reluctance; when the opportunity of examining the serious consequences of a treasonable opposition has been employed in propagating principles of anarchy, endeavoring through emissaries to alienate the friends of order from its support, and inviting its enemies to perpetrate similar acts of insurrection; when it is manifest that violence would continue to be exercised upon every attempt to enforce the laws; when, therefore, Government is set at defiance, the contest being whether a small portion of the United States shall dictate to the whole Union, and, at the expense of those who desire peace indulge a desperate ambition:

Now, therefore, I, George Washington, President of the United States, in obedience to that high and irresistible duty consigned to me by the Constitution "to take care that the laws be faithfully executed," deploring that the American name should be sullied by the outrages of citizens on their own Government, commiserating such as remain obstinate from delusion, but resolved, in perfect reliance on that gracious Providence which so signally displays its goodness towards this country, to reduce the refractory to a due subordination to the law, do hereby declare and make known that, with a satisfaction which can be equaled only by the merits of the militia summoned into service from the States of New Jersey, Pennsylvania, Maryland, and Virginia, I have received intelligence of their patriotic alacrity in obeying the call of the present, though painful, yet commanding necessity; that a force which, according to every reasonable expectation, is adequate to the exigency is already in motion to the scene of disaffection; that those who have confided or shall confide in the protection of Government shall meet full succor under the standard and from the arms of the United States; that those who, having offended against the laws, have since entitled themselves to indemnity will be treated with the most liberal good faith if they shall not have forfeited their claim by any subsequent conduct, and that instructions are given accordingly.

And I do moreover exhort all individuals, officers, and bodies of men to contemplate with abhorrence the measures leading directly or indirectly to those crimes which produce this resort to military coercion; to check in their respective spheres the efforts of misguided or designing men to substitute their misrepresentation in the place of truth and their discontents in the place of stable government, and to call to mind that, as the people of the United States have been permitted, under the Divine favor, in perfect freedom, after solemn deliberation, and in an enlightened age, to elect their own government, so will their gratitude for this inestimable blessing be best distinguished by firm exertions to maintain the Constitution and the laws.

And, lastly, I again warn all persons whomsoever and wheresoever not to abet, aid, or comfort the insurgents aforesaid, as they will answer the contrary at their peril; and I do also require all officers and other citizens, according to their several duties, as far as may be in their power, to bring under the cognizance of the laws all offenders in the premises.

In testimony whereof I have caused the seal of the United States of America to be affixed to these presents, and signed the same with my hand. Done at the city of Philadelphia, the 25th day of September, 1794, and of the Independence of the United States of America the nineteenth.

Source: *A Compilation of the Messages and Papers of the Presidents.* Prepared under the direction of the Joint Committee on Printing, of the House and Senate, Pursuant to an Act of the Fifty-Second Congress of the United States. New York: Bureau of National Literature, Inc., 1897.

President James Buchanan Alludes to the *Dred Scott* Case in Inaugural Address, 1857

President James Buchanan entered office during tumultuous times for the United States. The strain between those in support of slavery and those who wished to see it abolished seemed to escalate with each passing day. One court case in particular, Dred Scott v. Sanford, *further heightened tensions over this issue. Dred Scott was a slave who attempted to sue for his freedom upon the death of his slaveowner. He had lived in both a free state and a free territory (now Wisconsin) with his slaveowner for a time, and he believed this entitled him to emancipation. The Supreme Court disagreed with Scott, declaring that no black person in the United States was eligible for citizenship regardless of his or her status—which meant that he or she had no standing to be heard before a court of law. In addition, the Court declared that the Missouri Compromise of 1820 was unconstitutional as it allowed the federal government to interfere with the popular sovereignty of a given state on the issues of slavery. The compromise was what had allowed Wisconsin to remain a free territory. The Supreme Court also asserted that the federal government could not prohibit the creation of a slave state in new territories. President Buchanan gave remarks about the principles on which the Supreme Court would make its decision in his inaugural address given on March 4, 1857. The Supreme Court announced its decision on March 6.*

Fellow-Citizens:

I appear before you this day to take the solemn oath "that I will faithfully execute the office of President of the United States and will to the best of my ability preserve, protect, and defend the Constitution of the United States."

In entering upon this great office I must humbly invoke the God of our fathers for wisdom and firmness to execute its high and responsible duties in such a manner as to restore harmony and ancient friendship among the people of the several States and to preserve our free institutions throughout many generations. Convinced that I owe my election to the inherent love for the Constitution and the Union which still animates the hearts of the American people, let me earnestly ask their powerful support in sustaining all just measures calculated to perpetuate these, the richest political blessings which Heaven has ever bestowed upon any nation. Having determined not to become a candidate for reelection, I shall have no motive to influence my conduct in administering the Government except the desire ably and faithfully to serve my country and to live in grateful memory of my countrymen.

We have recently passed through a Presidential contest in which the passions of our fellow-citizens were excited to the highest degree by questions of deep and vital importance; but when the people proclaimed their will the tempest at once subsided and all was calm.

The voice of the majority, speaking in the manner prescribed by the Constitution, was heard, and instant submission followed. Our own country could alone have exhibited so grand and striking a spectacle of the capacity of man for self-government.

What a happy conception, then, was it for Congress to apply this simple rule, that the will of the majority shall govern, to the settlement of the question of domestic slavery in the Territories. Congress is neither "to legislate slavery into any Territory or State nor to exclude it therefrom, but to leave the people thereof perfectly free to form and regulate their domestic institutions in their own way, subject only to the Constitution of the United States."

As a natural consequence, Congress has also prescribed that when the Territory of Kansas shall be admitted as a State it "shall be received into the Union with or without slavery, as their constitution may prescribe at the time of their admission."

A difference of opinion has arisen in regard to the point of time when the people of a Territory shall decide this question for themselves.

This is, happily, a matter of but little practical importance. Besides, it is a judicial question, which legitimately belongs to the Supreme Court of the United States, before whom it is now pending, and will, it is understood, be speedily and finally settled. To their decision, in common with all good citizens, I shall cheerfully submit, whatever this may be, though it has ever been my individual opinion that under the Nebraska-Kansas act the appropriate period will be when the number of actual residents in the Territory shall justify the formation of a constitution with a view to its admission as a State into the Union. But be this as it may, it is the imperative and indispensable duty of the Government of the United States to secure to every resident inhabitant the free and independent expression of his opinion by his vote. This sacred right of each individual must be preserved. That being accomplished, nothing can be fairer than to leave the people of a Territory free from all foreign interference to decide their own destiny for themselves, subject only to the Constitution of the United States.

The whole Territorial question being thus settled upon the principle of popular sovereignty—a principle as ancient as free government itself—everything of a practical nature has been decided. No other question remains for adjustment, because all agree that under the Constitution slavery in the States is beyond the reach of any human power except that of the respective States themselves wherein it exists. May we not, then, hope that the long agitation on this subject is approaching its end, and that the geographical parties to which it has given birth, so much dreaded by the Father of his Country, will speedily become extinct? Most happy will it be for the country when the public mind shall be diverted from this question to others of more pressing and practical importance. Throughout the whole progress of this agitation, which has scarcely known any intermission for more than twenty years, whilst it has been productive of no positive good to any human being it has been the prolific source of great evils to the master, to the slave, and to the whole country. It has alienated and estranged the people of the sister States from each other, and has even seriously endangered the very existence of the Union. Nor has the danger yet entirely ceased. Under our system there is a remedy for all mere political evils in the sound sense and sober judgment of the people. Time is a great corrective. Political subjects which but a few years ago excited and exasperated the public mind have passed away and are now nearly forgotten. But this question of domestic slavery is of far graver importance than any mere political question, because should the agitation continue it may eventually endanger the personal safety of a large portion of our countrymen where the institution exists. In that event no form of government, however admirable in itself and however productive of material benefits, can compensate for the loss of peace and domestic security around the family altar. Let every Union-loving man, therefore, exert his best influence to suppress this agitation, which since the recent legislation of Congress is without any legitimate object.

It is an evil omen of the times that men have undertaken to calculate the mere material value of the Union. Reasoned estimates have been presented of the pecuniary profits and local advantages which would result to different States and sections from its dissolution and of the comparative injuries which such an event would inflict on other States and sections. Even descending to this low and narrow view of the mighty question, all such calculations are at fault. The bare reference to a single consideration will be conclusive on this point. We at present enjoy a free trade throughout our extensive and expanding country such as the world has never witnessed. This trade is conducted on railroads and canals, on noble rivers and arms of the sea, which bind together the North and the South, the East and the West, of our Confederacy. Annihilate this trade, arrest its free progress by the geographical lines of jealous and hostile States, and you destroy the prosperity and onward march of the whole and every part and involve all in one common ruin. But such considerations, important as they are in themselves, sink into insignificance when we reflect on the terrific evils which would result from disunion to every portion of the Confederacy—to the North, not more than to the South, to the East not more than to the West. These I shall not attempt to portray, because I feel an humble confidence that the kind Providence which inspired our fathers with wisdom to frame the most perfect form of government and union ever devised by man will not suffer it to perish until it shall have been peacefully instrumental by its example in the extension of civil and religious liberty throughout the world.

Next in importance to the maintenance of the Constitution and the Union is the duty of preserving the Government free from the taint or even the suspicion of corruption. Public virtue is the vital spirit of republics, and history proves that when this has decayed and the love of money has usurped its place, although the forms of free government may remain for a season, the substance has departed forever.

Our present financial condition is without a parallel in history. No nation has ever before been embarrassed from too large a surplus in its treasury. This almost necessarily gives birth to extravagant legislation. It produces wild schemes of expenditure and begets a race of speculators and jobbers, whose ingenuity is exerted in contriving and promoting expedients to obtain public money. The purity of official agents, whether rightfully or wrongfully, is suspected, and the character of the government suffers in the estimation of the people. This is in itself a very great evil.

The natural mode of relief from this embarrassment is to appropriate the surplus in the Treasury to great national objects for which a clear warrant can be found in the Constitution. Among these I might mention the extinguishment of the public debt, a reasonable increase of the Navy, which is at present inadequate to the protection of our vast tonnage afloat, now greater than that of any other nation, as well as to the defense of our extended seacoast.

It is beyond all question the true principle that no more revenue ought to be collected from the people than the amount necessary to defray the expenses of a wise, economical, and efficient administration of the Government. To reach this point it was necessary to resort to a modification of the tariff, and this has, I trust, been accomplished in such a manner as to do as little injury as may have been practicable to our domestic manufactures, especially those necessary for the defense of the country. Any discrimination against a particular branch for the purpose of benefiting favored corporations, individuals, or interests would have been unjust to the rest of the community and inconsistent with that spirit of fairness and equality which ought to govern in the adjustment of a revenue tariff.

But the squandering of the public money sinks into comparative insignificance as a temptation to corruption when compared with the squandering of the public lands.

No nation in the tide of time has ever been blessed with so rich and noble an inheritance as we enjoy in the public lands. In administering this important trust, whilst it may be wise to grant portions of them for the improvement of the remainder, yet we should never forget that it is our cardinal policy to reserve these lands, as much as may be, for actual settlers, and this at moderate prices. We shall thus not only best promote the prosperity of the new States and Territories, by furnishing them a hardy and independent race of honest and industrious citizens, but shall secure homes for our children and our children's children, as well as for those exiles from foreign shores who may seek in this country to improve their condition and to enjoy the blessings of civil and religious liberty. Such emigrants have done much to promote the growth and prosperity of the country. They have proved faithful both in peace and in war. After becoming citizens they are entitled, under the Constitution and laws, to be placed on a perfect equality with native-born citizens, and in this character they should ever be kindly recognized.

The Federal Constitution is a grant from the States to Congress of certain specific powers, and the question whether this grant should be liberally or strictly construed has more or less divided political parties from the beginning. Without entering into the argument, I desire to state at the commencement of my Administration that long experience and observation have convinced me that a strict construction of the powers of the Government is the only true, as well as the only safe, theory of the Constitution. Whenever in our past history doubtful powers have been exercised by Congress, these have never failed to produce injurious and unhappy consequences. Many such instances might be adduced if this were the proper occasion. Neither is it necessary for the public service to strain the language of the Constitution, because all the great and useful powers required for a successful administration of the Government, both in peace and in war, have been granted, either in express terms or by the plainest implication.

Whilst deeply convinced of these truths, I yet consider it clear that under the war-making power Congress may appropriate money toward the construction of a military road when this is absolutely necessary for the defense of any State or Territory of the Union against foreign invasion. Under the Constitution Congress has power "to declare war," "to raise and support armies," "to provide and maintain a navy," and to call forth the militia to "repel invasions." Thus endowed, in an ample manner, with the war-making power, the corresponding duty is required that "the United States shall protect each of them [the States] against invasion." Now, how is it possible to afford this protection to California and our Pacific possessions except by means of a military road through the Territories of the United States, over which men and munitions of war may be speedily transported from the Atlantic States to meet and to repel the invader? In the event of a war with a naval power much stronger than our own we should then have no other available access to the Pacific Coast, because such a power would instantly close the route across the isthmus of Central America. It is impossible to conceive that whilst the Constitution has expressly required Congress to defend all the States it should yet deny to them, by any fair construction, the only possible means by which one of these States can be defended. Besides, the Government, ever since its origin, has been in the constant practice of constructing military roads. It might also be wise to consider whether the love for the Union which now animates our fellow-citizens on the Pacific Coast may not be impaired by our neglect or refusal to provide for them, in their remote and isolated condition, the only means by which the power of the States on this side of the Rocky Mountains can reach them in sufficient time to "protect" them "against invasion." I forbear for the present from expressing an opinion as to the wisest and most economical mode in which the Government can lend its aid in accomplishing this great and necessary work. I believe that many of the difficulties in the way, which now appear formidable, will in a great degree vanish as soon as the nearest and best route shall have been satisfactorily ascertained.

It may be proper that on this occasion I should make some brief remarks in regard to our rights and duties as a member of the great family of nations. In our intercourse with them there are some plain principles, approved by our own experience, from which we should never depart. We ought to cultivate peace, commerce, and friendship with all nations, and this not merely as the best means of promoting our own material interests, but in a spirit of Christian benevolence toward our fellow-men, wherever their lot may be cast. Our diplomacy should be direct and frank, neither seeking to obtain more nor accepting less than is our due. We ought to cherish a sacred regard for the independence of all nations, and never attempt to interfere in the domestic concerns of any unless this shall be imperatively required by the great law of self-preservation. To avoid entangling alliances has been a maxim of our policy ever since the days of Washington, and its wisdom no one will attempt to dispute. In short, we ought to do justice in a kindly spirit to all nations and require justice from them in return.

It is our glory that whilst other nations have extended their dominions by the sword we have never acquired any territory except by fair purchase or, as in the case of Texas, by the voluntary determination of a brave, kindred, and independent people to blend their destinies with our own. Even our acquisitions from Mexico form no exception. Unwilling to take advantage of the fortune of war against a sister republic, we purchased these possessions under the treaty of peace for a sum which was considered at the time a fair equivalent. Our past history forbids that we shall in the future acquire territory unless this be sanctioned by the laws of justice and honor. Acting on this principle, no nation will have a right to interfere or to complain if in the progress of events we shall still further extend our possessions. Hitherto in all our acquisitions the people, under the protection of the American flag, have enjoyed civil and religious liberty, as well as equal and just laws, and have been contented, prosperous, and happy. Their trade with the rest of the world has rapidly increased, and thus every commercial nation has shared largely in their successful progress.

I shall now proceed to take the oath prescribed by the Constitution, whilst humbly invoking the blessing of Divine Providence on this great people.

Source: Richardson, James D. *A Compilation of the Messages and Papers of the Presidents 1789–1897*. Volume 6. New York: Bureau of National Literature, 1897, 2961–2967.

President Andrew Johnson Vetoes the Second Reconstruction Act, 1867

President Andrew Johnson gave this veto message on March 23, 1867, as he returned the Second Reconstruction Act to Congress. The act would have given the military the power to oversee elections in the South and required that voters in that region take an oath to the Constitution of the federal government. Many in the South believed that this act, and the other reconstruction acts that were presented, infringed on their right to self-govern and compromised the power of state constitutions. The North was largely supportive of the acts, even though they extended the franchise only to black Southerners, leaving black people across the rest of the country without a voice at the ballot box. President Johnson had also vetoed the First Reconstruction Act, which the second act supplemented, but Congress overruled his action. Congress would also overrule this veto on the same day it was presented. The same pattern would continue into the Third Reconstruction Act until the president went through impeachment in 1868. He and Congress found themselves in a notorious gridlock of power, where the interpretation of the Constitution was the point of contention. Even then, the rest of President Johnson's party (Democratic) was not keen on his penchant for vetoes. In the following document, the president speaks on the idea of black enfranchisement and of his fear that "white disenfranchisement" would ensue in the South if black men were able to vote.

To the House of Representatives:
I have considered the bill entitled "An act supplementary to an act entitled 'An act to provide for the more efficient government of the rebel States,' passed March 2, 1867, and to facilitate restoration," and now return it to the House of Representatives with my objections.

This bill provides for elections in the ten States brought under the operation of the original act to which it is supplementary. Its details are principally directed to the elections for the formation of the State constitutions, but by the sixth section of the bill "all elections" in these States occurring while the original act remains in force are brought within its purview. Referring to these details, it will be found that, first of all, there is to be a registration of the voters. No one whose name has not been admitted on the list is to be allowed to vote at any of these elections. To ascertain who is entitled to registration, reference is made necessary, by the express language of the supplement, to the original act and to the pending bill. The fifth section of the original act provides, as to voters, that they shall be "male citizens of the State, 21 years old and upward, of whatever race, color, or previous condition, who have been residents of said State for one year." This is the general qualification, followed, however, by many exceptions. No one can be registered, according to the original act, "who may be disfranchised for participation in the rebellion"—a provision which left undetermined the question as to what amounted to disfranchisement, and whether without a judicial sentence the act itself produced that effect. This supplemental bill superadds an oath, to be taken by every person before his name can be admitted upon the registration, that he has "not been disfranchised for participation in any rebellion or civil war against the United States." It thus imposes upon every person the necessity and responsibility of deciding for himself, under the peril of punishment by a military commission if he makes a mistake, what works disfranchisement by participation in rebellion and what amounts to such participation. Almost every man—the Negro as well as the white—above 21 years of age who was resident in these ten States during the rebellion, voluntarily or involuntarily, at some time and in some way did participate in resistance to the lawful authority of the General Government. The question with the citizen to whom this oath is to be proposed must be a fearful one, for while the bill does not declare that perjury may be assigned for such false swearing nor fix any penalty for the offense, we must not forget that martial law prevails; that every person is answerable to a military commission, without previous presentment by a grand jury, for any charge that may be made against him, and that the supreme authority of the military commander determines the question as to what is an offense and what is to be the measure of punishment.

The fourth section of the bill provides "that the commanding general of each district shall appoint as many boards of registration as may be necessary, consisting of three loyal officers or persons." The only qualification stated for these officers is that they must be "loyal." They may be persons in the military service or civilians, residents of the State or strangers. Yet these persons are to exercise most important duties and are vested with unlimited discretion. They are to decide what names shall be placed upon the register and from their decision there is to be no appeal. They are to superintend the elections and to decide all questions which may arise. They are to have the custody of the ballots and to make return of the persons elected. Whatever frauds or errors they may commit must pass without redress. All that is left for the commanding general is to receive the returns of the elections, open the same, and ascertain who are chosen "according to the returns of the officers who conducted said elections." By such means and with this sort of agency are the conventions of delegates to be constituted.

As the delegates are to speak for the people, common justice would seem to require that they should have authority from the people themselves. No convention so constituted will in any sense represent the wishes of the inhabitants of these States, for under the all-embracing exceptions of these laws, by a construction which the uncertainty of the clause as to disfranchisement leaves open to the board of officers, the great body of the people may be excluded from the polls and from all opportunity of expressing their own wishes or voting for delegates who will faithfully reflect their sentiments.

I do not deem it necessary further to investigate the details of this bill. No consideration could induce me to give my approval to such an election law for any purpose, and especially for the great purpose of framing the constitution of a State. If ever the American citizen should be left to the free exercise of his own judgment it is when he is engaged in the work of forming the fundamental law under which he is to live. That work is his work, and it can not properly be taken out of his hands. All this legislation proceeds upon the contrary assumption that the people of each of these States shall have no constitution except such as may be arbitrarily dictated by Congress and formed under the restraint of military rule. A plain statement of facts makes this evident.

In all these States there are existing constitutions, framed in the accustomed way by the people. Congress, however, declares that these constitutions are not "loyal and republican," and requires the people to form them anew. What, then, in the opinion of Congress, is necessary to make the constitution of a State "loyal and republican"? The original act answers the question: It is universal Negro suffrage—a question which the Federal Constitution leaves exclusively to the States themselves. All this legislative machinery of martial law, military coercion, and political disfranchisement is avowedly for that purpose and none other. The existing constitutions of the ten States conform to the acknowledged standards of loyalty and republicanism. Indeed, if there are degrees in republican forms of government, their constitutions are more republican now than when these States, four of which were members of the original thirteen, first became members of the Union.

Congress does not now demand that a single provision of their constitutions be changed except such as confine suffrage to the white population. It is apparent, therefore, that these provisions do not conform to the standard of republicanism which Congress seeks to establish. That there may be no mistake, it is only necessary that reference should be made to the original act, which declares "such constitution shall provide that the elective franchise shall be enjoyed by all such persons as have the qualifications herein stated for electors of delegates." What class of persons is here meant clearly appears in the same section; that is to say, "the male citizens of said State 21 years old and upward, of whatever race, color, or previous condition, who have been resident in said State for one year previous to the day of such election."

Without these provisions no constitution which can be framed in any one of the ten States will be of any avail with Congress. This, then, is the test of what the constitution of a State of this Union must contain to make it republican. Measured by such a standard, how few of the States now composing the Union have republican constitutions? If in the exercise of the constitutional guaranty that Congress shall secure to every State a republican form of government universal suffrage for blacks as well as whites is a sine qua non, the work of reconstruction may as well begin in Ohio as in Virginia, in Pennsylvania as in North Carolina.

When I contemplate the millions of our fellow-citizens of the South with no alternative left but to impose upon themselves this fearful and untried experiment of complete Negro enfranchisement—and white disfranchisement, it may be, almost as complete—or submit indefinitely to the rigor of martial law, without a single attribute of freemen, deprived of all the sacred guaranties of our Federal Constitution, and threatened with even worse wrongs, if any worse are possible, it seems to me their condition is the most deplorable to which any people can be reduced. It is true that they have been engaged in rebellion and that their object being a separation of the States and a dissolution of the Union there was an obligation resting upon every loyal citizen to treat them as enemies and to wage war against their cause.

Inflexibly opposed to any movement imperiling the integrity of the Government, I did not hesitate to urge the adoption of all measures necessary for the suppression of the insurrection. After a long and terrible struggle the efforts of the Government were triumphantly successful, and the people of the South, submitting to the stern arbitrament, yielded forever the issues of the contest. Hostilities terminated soon after it became my duty to assume the responsibilities of the chief executive officer of the Republic, and I at once endeavored to repress and control the passions which our civil strife had engendered, and, no longer regarding these erring millions as enemies, again acknowledged them as our friends and our countrymen. The war had accomplished its objects. The nation was saved and that seminal principle of mischief which from the birth of the Government had gradually but inevitably brought on the rebellion was totally eradicated. Then, it seemed to me, was the auspicious time to commence the work of reconciliation; then, when these people sought once more our friendship and protection, I considered it our duty generously to meet them in the spirit of charity and forgiveness and to conquer them even more effectually by the magnanimity of the nation than by the force of its arms. I yet believe that if the policy of reconciliation then inaugurated, and which contemplated an early restoration of these people to all their political rights, had received the support of Congress, every one of these ten States and all their people would at this moment be fast anchored in the Union and the great work which gave the war all its sanction and made it just and holy would have been accomplished. Then over all the vast and fruitful regions of the South peace and its blessings would have prevailed, while now millions are deprived of rights guaranteed by the Constitution to every citizen and after nearly two years of legislation find themselves placed under an absolute military despotism. "A military republic, a government rounded on mock elections and supported only by the sword," was nearly a quarter of a century since pronounced by Daniel Webster, when speaking of the South American States, as "a movement, indeed, but a retrograde and disastrous movement, from the regular and old-fashioned monarchical systems;" and he added:

If men would enjoy the blessings of republican government, they must govern themselves by reason, by mutual counsel and consultation, by a sense and feeling of general interest, and by the acquiescence of the minority in the will of the majority, properly expressed; and, above all, the military must be kept, according to the language of our bill of rights, in strict subordination to the civil authority. Wherever this lesson is not both learned and practiced there can be no political freedom. Absurd, preposterous is it, a scoff and a satire on free forms of constitutional liberty, for frames of government to be prescribed by military leaders and the right of suffrage to be exercised at the point of the sword.

I confidently believe that a time will come when these States will again occupy their true positions in the Union. The barriers which now seem so obstinate must yield to the force of an enlightened and just public opinion, and sooner or later unconstitutional and oppressive legislation will be effaced from our statute books. When this shall have been consummated, I pray God that the errors of the past may be forgotten and that once more we shall be a happy, united, and prosperous people, and that at last, after the bitter and eventful experience through which the nation has passed, we shall all come to know that our only safety is in the preservation of our Federal Constitution and in according to every American citizen and to every State the rights which that Constitution secures.

Source: Richardson, James D. *A Compilation of the Messages and Papers of the Presidents 1789–1897.* Volume 9. New York: Bureau of National Literature, 1897, 3729–3733.

President Ulysses S. Grant Suspends Writ of Habeas Corpus in Parts of South Carolina, 1871

To undermine the right to habeas corpus is to undermine a person's right to trial in the case of wrongful detainment, among other rights and principles. In essence, having free will and the body to act upon it is the basis on which people are imbued their habeas corpus rights. Yet in the most extreme circumstances, the president can suspend a person's right to habeas corpus, which is the action that President Ulysses S. Grant took in South Carolina on October 17, 1871, via Proclamation 201 (reprinted below). The Ku Klux Klan (KKK) had come to overpower the state and engaged in rampant, organized, and violent hate crimes against black individuals, families, and communities. Many local authorities in the state were even members of the KKK. President Grant felt he had to intervene with an approach more direct than the enactment of the Enforcement Act, also known as the Ku Klux Klan Act. This law, which had been signed by Grant on April 20, 1871, was an attempt to temper KKK activity by reinforcing black rights to equal protection of the law and to vote, among other provisions. Federal troops were also sent to the area as aid in the effort. Suspending habeas corpus in certain counties of the state allowed the federal government several advantages in prosecuting Klan members, which included the arrest of masses of people at once without taking them right to trial. The suspension was lifted a few weeks later.

Whereas by an act of Congress entitled "An act to enforce the provisions of the fourteenth amendment to the Constitution of the United States, and for other purposes," approved the 20th day of April, A. D. 1871, power is given to the President of the United States, when in his judgment the public safety shall require it, to suspend the privileges of the writ of *habeas corpus* in any State or part of a State whenever combinations and conspiracies exist in such State or part of a State for the purpose of depriving any portion or class of the people of such State of the rights, privileges, immunities, and protection named in the Constitution of the United States and secured by the act of Congress aforesaid; and whenever such combinations and conspiracies do so obstruct and hinder the execution of the laws of any such State and of the United States as to deprive the people aforesaid of the rights, privileges, immunities, and protection aforesaid, and do oppose and obstruct the laws of the United States and their due execution, and impede and obstruct the due course of justice under the same; and whenever such combinations shall be organized and armed, and so numerous and powerful as to be able by violence either to overthrow or to set at defiance the constituted authorities of said State and of the United States within such State; and whenever by reason of said causes the conviction of such offenders and the preservation of the public peace shall become in such State or part of a State impracticable; and

Whereas such unlawful combinations and conspiracies for the purposes aforesaid are declared by the act of Congress aforesaid to be rebellion against the Government of the United States; and

Whereas by said act of Congress it is provided that before the President shall suspend the privileges of the writ of *habeas corpus* he shall first have made proclamation commanding such insurgents to disperse; and

Whereas on the 12th day of the present month of October the President of the United States did issue his proclamation, reciting therein, among other things, that such combinations and conspiracies did then exist in the counties of Spartanburg, York, Marion, Chester, Laurens, Newberry, Fairfield, Lancaster, and Chesterfield, in the State of South Carolina, and commanding thereby all persons composing such unlawful combinations and conspiracies to disperse and retire peaceably to their homes within five days from the date thereof, and to deliver either to the marshal of the United States for the district of South Carolina, or to any of his deputies, or to any military officer of the United States within said counties, all arms, ammunition, uniforms, disguises, and other means and implements used, kept, possessed, or controlled by them for carrying out the unlawful purposes for which the said combinations and conspiracies are organized; and

Whereas the insurgents engaged in such unlawful combinations and conspiracies within the counties aforesaid have not dispersed and retired peaceably to their respective homes, and have not delivered to the marshal of the United States, or to any of his deputies, or to any military officer of the United States within said counties, all arms, ammunition, uniforms, disguises, and other means and implements used, kept, possessed, or controlled by them for carrying out the unlawful purposes for which the combinations and conspiracies are organized, as commanded by said proclamation, but do still persist in the unlawful combinations and conspiracies aforesaid:

Now, therefore, I, Ulysses S. Grant, President of the United States of America, by virtue of the authority vested in me by the Constitution of the United States and the act of Congress aforesaid, do hereby declare that in my judgment the public safety especially requires that the privileges of the writ of *habeas corpus* be suspended, to the end that such rebellion may be overthrown, and do hereby suspend the privileges of the writ of *habeas corpus* within the counties of Spartanburg, York, Marion, Chester, Laurens, Newberry, Fairfield, Lancaster, and Chesterfield, in said State of South Carolina, in respect to all persons arrested by the marshal of the United States for the said district of South Carolina, or by any of his deputies, or by any military officer of the United States, or by any soldier or citizen acting under the orders of said marshal, deputy, or such military officer within any one of said counties, charged with any violation of the act of Congress aforesaid, during the continuance of such rebellion.

In witness whereof I have hereunto set my hand and caused the seal of the United States to be affixed.

Done at the city of Washington, this 17th day of October, A.D. 1871, and of the Independence of the United States of America the ninety-sixth.

Source: Richardson, James D. *A Compilation of the Messages and Papers of the Presidents 1789–1897.* Volume 9. New York: Bureau of National Literature, 1897, 4090–4092.

President Grover Cleveland Takes Action Regarding Violence toward Chinese Immigrants, 1886

Grover Cleveland gave this special message to Congress on March 1, 1886, to condemn the violent racism directed toward Chinese people in the United States. The tension stemmed from the belief that Chinese workers would take over labor jobs in the country held by white men. While previous laws had been passed to halt the immigration of Chinese people to the United States, President Cleveland attempted to search for common ground because he believed that immigrants from China and other nations could contribute to the United States' prosperity. During this address to Congress, Cleveland references a horrific event that had taken place in Rock Springs, Wyoming, on September 2, 1885, in which scores of Chinese miners were massacred by their white counterparts. The offenders were never prosecuted, but the Chinese government did convince the president to pay retribution to Chinese immigrants living in the United States. Despite President Grover's sympathies, little progress was made in improving relations between the two groups, and he grew disheartened and impatient. Two years after he delivered this message to Congress, the president approved the second iteration of the Chinese Exclusion Act, the Scott Act, which barred Chinese people from returning to the states if they left.

To the Senate and House of Representatives:

It is made the constitutional duty of the President to recommend to the consideration of Congress from time to time such measures as he shall judge necessary and expedient. In no matters can the necessity of this be more evident than when the good faith of the United States under the solemn obligation of treaties with foreign powers is concerned.

The question of the treatment of the subjects of China sojourning within the jurisdiction of the United States presents such a matter for the urgent and earnest consideration of the Executive and the Congress.

In my first annual message, upon the assembling of the present Congress, I adverted to this question in the following words:

The harmony of our relations with China is fully sustained.

In the application of the acts lately passed to execute the treaty of 1880, restrictive of the immigration of Chinese laborers into the United States, individual cases of hardship have occurred beyond the power of the Executive to remedy, and calling for judicial determination.

The condition of the Chinese question in the Western States and Territories is, despite this restrictive legislation, far from being satisfactory. The recent outbreak in Wyoming Territory, where numbers of unoffending Chinamen, indisputably within the protection of the treaties and the law, were murdered by a mob, and the still more recent threatened outbreak of the same character in Washington Territory, are fresh in the minds of all, and there is apprehension lest the bitterness of feeling against the Mongolian race on the Pacific Slope may find vent in similar lawless demonstrations. All the power of this Government should be exerted to maintain the amplest good faith toward China in the treatment of these men, and the inflexible sternness of the law in bringing the wrongdoers to justice should be insisted upon.

Every effort has been made by this Government to prevent these violent outbreaks and to aid the representatives of China in their investigation of these outrages; and it is but just to say that they are traceable to the lawlessness of men not citizens of the United States engaged in competition with Chinese laborers.

Race prejudice is the chief factor in originating these disturbances, and it exists in a large part of our domain, jeopardizing our domestic peace and the good relationship we strive to maintain with China.

The admitted right of a government to prevent the influx of elements hostile to its internal peace and security may not be questioned, even where there is no treaty stipulation on the subject. That the exclusion of Chinese labor is demanded in other countries where like conditions prevail is strongly evidenced in the Dominion of Canada, where Chinese immigration is now regulated by laws more exclusive than our own. If existing laws are inadequate to compass the end in view, I shall be prepared to give earnest consideration to any further remedial measures, within the treaty limits, which the wisdom of Congress may devise.

At the time I wrote this the shocking occurrences at Rock Springs, in Wyoming Territory, were fresh in the minds of all, and had been recently presented anew to the attention of this Government by the Chinese minister in a note which, while not unnaturally exhibiting some misconception of our Federal system of administration in the Territories while they as yet are not in the exercise of the full measure of that sovereign self-government pertaining to the States of the Union, presents in truthful terms the main features of the cruel outrage there perpetrated upon inoffensive subjects of China. In the investigation of the Rock Springs outbreak and the ascertainment of the facts on which the Chinese minister's statements rest the Chinese representatives were aided by the agents of the United States, and the reports submitted, having been thus framed and recounting the facts within the knowledge of witnesses on both sides, possess an impartial truthfulness which could not fail to give them great impressiveness.

The facts, which so far are not controverted or affected by any exculpatory or mitigating testimony, show the murder of a number of Chinese subjects in September last at Rock Springs, the wounding of many others, and the spoliation of the property of all when the unhappy survivors had been driven from their habitations. There is no allegation that the victims by any lawless or disorderly act on their part contributed to bring about a collision; on the contrary, it appears that the law-abiding disposition of these people, who were sojourners in our midst under the sanction of hospitality and express treaty obligations, was made the pretext for an attack upon them. This outrage upon law and treaty engagements was committed by a lawless mob. None of the aggressors—happily for the national good fame—appear by the reports to have been citizens of the United States. They were aliens engaged in that remote district as mining laborers, who became excited against the Chinese laborers, as it would seem, because of their refusal to join them in a strike to secure higher wages. The oppression of Chinese subjects by their rivals in the competition for labor does not differ in violence and illegality from that applied to other classes of native or alien labor. All are equally under the protection of law and equally entitled to enjoy the benefits of assured public order.

Were there no treaty in existence referring to the rights of Chinese subjects; did they come hither as all other strangers who voluntarily resort to this land of freedom, of self-government, and of laws, here peaceably to win their bread and to live their lives, there can be no question that they would be entitled still to the same measure of protection from violence and the same free forum for the redress of their grievances as any other aliens.

So far as the treaties between the United States and China stipulate for the treatment of the Chinese subjects actually in the United States as the citizens or subjects of "the most favored nation" are treated, they create no new status for them; they simply recognize and confirm a general and existing rule, applicable to all aliens alike, for none are favored above others by domestic law, and none by foreign treaties unless it be the Chinese themselves in some respects. For by the third article of the treaty of November 17, 1880, between the United States and China it is provided that—

> ART. III. If Chinese laborers, or Chinese of any other class, now either permanently or temporarily residing in the territory of the United States, meet with ill treatment at the hands of any other persons, the Government of the United States will exert all its power to devise measures for their protection and to secure to them the same rights, privileges, immunities, and exemptions as may be enjoyed by the citizens or subjects of the most favored nation, and to which they are entitled by treaty.

This article may be held to constitute a special privilege for Chinese subjects in the United States, as compared with other aliens; not that it creates any peculiar rights which others do not share, but because, in case of ill treatment of the Chinese in the United States, this Government is bound to "exert all its power to devise measures for their protection," by securing to them the rights to which equally with any and all other foreigners they are entitled.

Whether it is now incumbent upon the United States to amend their general laws or devise new measures in this regard I do not consider in the present communication, but confine myself to the particular point raised by the outrage and massacre at Rock Springs.

The note of the Chinese minister and the documents which accompany it give, as I believe, an unexaggerated statement of the lamentable incident, and present impressively the regrettable circumstance that the proceedings, in the name of justice, for the ascertainment of the crime and fixing the responsibility therefor were a ghastly mockery of justice. So long as the Chinese minister, under his instructions, makes this the basis of an appeal to the principles and convictions of mankind, no exception can be taken; but when he goes further, and, taking as his precedent the action of the Chinese Government in past instances where the lives of American citizens and their property in China have been endangered, argues a reciprocal obligation on the part of the United States to indemnify the Chinese subjects who suffered at Rock Springs, it became necessary to meet his argument and to deny most emphatically the conclusions he seeks to draw as to the existence of such a liability and the right of the Chinese Government to insist upon it.

I draw the attention of the Congress to the latter part of the note of the Secretary of State of February 18, 1886, in reply to the Chinese minister's representations, and invite special consideration of the cogent reasons by which he reaches the conclusion that whilst the United States Government is under no obligation, whether by the express terms of its treaties with China or the principles of international law, to indemnify these Chinese subjects for losses caused by such means and under the admitted circumstances, yet that in view of the palpable and discreditable failure of the authorities of Wyoming Territory to bring to justice the guilty parties or to assure to the sufferers an impartial forum in which to seek and obtain compensation for the losses which those subjects have incurred by lack of police protection, and considering further the entire absence of provocation or contribution on the part of the victims, the Executive may be induced to bring the matter to the benevolent consideration of the Congress, in order that that body, in its high discretion, may direct the bounty of the Government in aid of innocent and peaceful strangers whose maltreatment has brought discredit upon the country, with the distinct understanding that such action is in no wise to be held as a precedent, is wholly gratuitous, and is resorted to in a spirit of pure generosity toward those who are otherwise helpless.

The correspondence exchanged is herewith submitted for the information of the Congress, and accompanies a like message to the House of Representatives.

Source: Richardson, James D. *A Compilation of the Messages and Papers of the Presidents 1789–1897.* Volume 11. New York: Bureau of National Literature, 1897, 4968–4971.

President Grover Cleveland Intervenes in Pullman Strike, 1894

In Chicago in the midsummer of 1894, railway workers refused to operate after the Pullman Palace Car Company cut their wages and demanded other workplace concessions. When workers spoke out, they were fired and confronted by armed troops sent from the federal government. The strike soon expanded to the point that railway operations across the country were affected, sending tremors through the wider economy. President Grover Cleveland issued this proclamation as a warning to the strikers in Chicago and elsewhere to cease their activity and return to work. President Cleveland took other notable actions as he attempted to quell the protests, including the creation of a national holiday known as Labor Day on June 28, 1894. He believed this gesture would show his appreciation to the labor force of the country and restore some goodwill (the bill proposing a national Labor Day had actually been presented to the president about a year earlier, but it was not enacted until after the Pullman Strike exploded). While the holiday was a welcomed consolation, it did not stop the riots, and President Cleveland soon lost patience. In the end, after several violent clashes between federal troops and striking union workers, Cleveland and the railroad industry triumphed. Unable to withstand the economic toll of an extended strike—and growing public hostility to the labor unrest—the workers ended their strike on July 20, 1894, and returned to work.

Whereas, by reason of unlawful obstructions, combinations, and assemblages of persons, it has become impracticable, in the judgment of the President, to enforce by the ordinary course of judicial proceedings the laws of the United States within the State of Illinois, and especially in the city of Chicago within said State; and

Whereas, for the purpose of enforcing the faithful execution of the laws of the United States and protecting its property and removing obstructions to the United States mails in the State and city aforesaid, the President has employed a part of the military forces of the United States:

Now, therefore, I, Grover Cleveland, President of the United States, do hereby admonish all good citizens and all persons who may be or may come within the city and State aforesaid against aiding, countenancing, encouraging, or taking any part in such unlawful obstructions, combinations, and assemblages; and I hereby warn all persons engaged in or in any way connected with such unlawful obstructions, combinations, and assemblages to disperse and retire peaceably to their respective abodes on or before 12 o'clock noon on the 9th day of July instant.

Those who disregard this warning and persist in taking part with a riotous mob in forcibly resisting and obstructing the execution of the laws of the United States or interfering with the functions of the Government or destroying or attempting to destroy the property belonging to the United States or under its protection can not be regarded otherwise than as public enemies.

Troops employed against such a riotous mob will act with all the moderation and forbearance consistent with the accomplishment of the desired end, but the stern necessities that confront them will not with certainty permit discrimination between guilty participants and those who are mingled with them from curiosity and without criminal intent. The only safe course, therefore, for those not actually unlawfully participating is to abide at their homes, or at least not to be found in the neighborhood of riotous assemblages.

While there will be no hesitation or vacillation in the decisive treatment of the guilty, this warning is especially intended to protect and save the innocent.

In testimony whereof I have hereunto set my hand and caused the seal of the United States to be hereto affixed.

Done at the city of Washington, this 8th day of July, A. D. 1894, and of the Independence of the United States the one hundred and nineteenth.

Source: Richardson, James D. *A Compilation of the Messages and Papers of the Presidents 1789–1897.* Volume 13. New York: Bureau of National Literature, 1897, 5931–5932.

President Theodore Roosevelt Remarks on the Importance of Conservation, 1903

Theodore Roosevelt was a pioneering figure in the conservation of U.S. land and water resources. A great appreciator of the beauty of the country's mountains, woodlands, and lakes, he also argued for their conservation on practical grounds. He asserted that they harbored finite resources that had to be protected from unsustainable exploitation. During his presidency he established almost 200 national forests, parks, and reserves, and he spearheaded conservation projects specifically crafted to limit commercialization. In total, President Roosevelt created 230 million acres of federal land. The following address was given at the Capitol Building in Sacramento, California, on May 19, 1903, after the president had toured some of California's most spectacular natural areas and landscapes. He peppers his remarks with imagery of the state's natural beauty and expresses his passion for fostering the relationship between people and the natural world.

Mr. Mayor, and You, My Fellow-Citizens:

It is a great pleasure to have the chance of meeting you here in the capital city of your wonderful State. [*Applause*] In greeting all of you I know that the others will not grudge my saying a special word of acknowledgment to those whose mettle rang true on war's red touchstone, to the men to whom we owe it that we have tonight one country or that there is a President to speak to you—[*applause*]—the men of the Grand Army, the veterans of the great war, I wish also to express at this time my acknowledgments to my escort, the National Guard, many of them my comrades in the lesser war of '98. (Laughter and applause.) You see, in '98 we had a difficulty from which you were wholly free in '61, because with us there was not enough war to go around. [*Applause*]

I have enjoyed to the full my visit to California. I have come across the continent from the East to the West, and now beyond the West to California, for California stands by itself. [*Applause*] I have enjoyed every hour of my stay here. I have just come from a four days' rest in the Yosemite, and I wish to say one word to you here in the capital city of California about certain of your great natural resources, your forests and the water supply coming from the streams that find their sources among the forests of the mountains.

California possesses a wonderful climate, a wonderful soil, and throughout the portions that I have visited it is literally astounding to see how the land yields a hundred and a thousand fold when water is put upon it. And where it is possible to irrigate the land the result is, of course, far better than having to depend upon rainfall anywhere, but no small part of the prosperity of California in the hotter and drier agricultural regions depends upon the preservation of her water supply; and the water supply cannot be preserved unless the forests are preserved. [*Applause*] As regards some of the trees, I want them preserved because they are the only things of their kind in the world. Lying out at night under those giant Sequoias was lying in a temple built by no hand of man, a temple grander than any human architect could by any possibility build, and I hope for the preservation of the groves of giant trees simply because it would be a shame to our civilization to let them disappear. They are monuments in themselves, I ask for the preservation of the other forests on grounds of wise and far-sighted economic policy. I do not ask that lumbering be stopped at all. On the contrary, I ask that the forests be kept for use in lumbering, only that they be so used that not only shall we here, this generation, get the benefit for the next few years, but that our children and our children's children shall get the benefit. In California I am impressed by how great the State is, but I am even more impressed by the immensely greater greatness that lies in the future, and I ask that your marvelous natural resources be handed on unimpaired to your posterity. [*Applause*] We are not building this country of ours for a day. It is to last through the ages. We stand on the threshold of a new century. We look into the dim years that rise before us, knowing that if we are true that the generations that succeed us here shall fall heir to a heritage such as has never been known before. I ask that we keep in mind not only our own interests, but the interests of our children. Any generation fit to do its work must work for the future, for the people of the future, as well as for itself. You, men of the Civil War, fought from '61 to '65 for the Union of that day; yes, and for the Union that was to stand while nations stand in the hereafter. [*Applause*] You fought to make the flag that had been rent asunder once more whole and without a seam and to float over you and to float over all who come after you likewise. You fought for the future; you fought for the looming greatness of the republic in the centuries that were to come, and now I ask that we, in fulfilling the duties of citizenship, keep our gaze fixed likewise on the days that are to come after us. You are building here this great State within whose bounds lies an area as great as an Old World empire, a State with a commerce already vast, but with a commerce which within the century that has now opened shall cover and dominate the entire Pacific Ocean. [*Applause*] You are building your factories, you are tilling the fields; business man, professional man, farmer, wage-worker, all here in this State see a future of unknown possibilities opening before them.

I earnestly ask that you see to it that your resources, by use, are perpetuated for the use of the peoples yet unborn. Use them, but in using, keep and preserve them. Keep the waters; keep the forests; use your lands as you use your bays, your harbors, as you use the cities here, so that by the very fact of the use they will become more valuable as possessions.

I have spoken of the material things, of the things which are indispensable as the foundation, the base of national greatness. We must care for the body first. We must see to it that our tremendous industrial development goes on, that the well-being continues; that the soil yields its wealth in the future as it has in the past, aye, and tenfold more. We cannot for one moment afford to underestimate the vital importance of that material well-being, of the prosperity which we so abundantly enjoy, but I ask also that you remember the things of the mind and the soul as well as the body. Nothing has struck me more in going through California than the interest you are paying to the cause of education, than the way in which your citizens evidently realize that upon the proper training of the children, of those who are to be the men and women of a score of years hence, depends the ultimate welfare of the republic. Let me draw a lesson from you, the men of the Civil War. You needed strong bodies, you needed the supplies, the arms, but more than all, you needed the hearts that drove the bodies into battle. What distinguished our men was the spirit that drove them onward to effort and to strife, onward into action, onward through the march, through the long months of waiting in camp, onward through the fiery ordeal of battle, when men's souls were winnowed out as before the judgment seat. You then rose level to the duty that was before you because of the spirit that burned within your breasts, because you had in you the capacity of generous enthusiasm for the lofty ideal, because you realized that there was something above the body and greater than the body. And now, my fellows, men and women of California, men and women of the American Union, I ask throughout this country that our people keep in their hearts the capacity of devotion to what stands above mere bodily welfare, to the welfare of the spirit, of the mind, of the soul. I ask that we have strong bodies, well cared for, well clothed, well housed. I ask for what is better than a strong body, a sane mind. And I ask finally for what counts for more than body, for more than mind, for character; character which in the last analysis tells most in settling the welfare of either a nation or an individual; character into which many elements enter, but three, above all; in the first place, as a foundation, decency, honesty, morality, the quality that makes a man a good husband, a good neighbor, a man who deals fairly and squarely with those about him, who does his duty to those around him and to the State; and that is not enough. Decency and honesty are not enough. Just as in the Civil War you needed patriotism first, but it made no matter how patriotic a man was, if he ran away you could do nothing with him. [*Applause*] So in civic life you must have decency and honesty, for without them ability makes a man only the more dangerous to his fellows, the greater force for evil. Just again as in the Civil War, if the man did not have in him the capacity of loyalty to his fellows, loyalty to his regiment, loyalty to the flag, if he did not have in him that capacity, the abler he was the worse he was to have in the army. So it is now in civil life; the abler a man is, if he has not the root of righteousness in him the more dangerous a foe to decent government he is, and we shall never rise level to the needs of our nation until we make it understood that the scoundrel who succeeds is to be hunted down by public opinion, by the condemnation and scorn of his fellows, exactly as we hunt down the weaker scoundrel who fails. [*Applause*] But that is not enough. Decency and honesty are a basis, but that is all. I do not care how moral a man is, if his morality is only good while he sits at home in his own parlor, you can do nothing with him. Scant is the use we have for the timid good. In the war you needed patriotism, and then you needed the fighting edge. You had to have that. So in civil life we need the spirit of decency, of honesty, and then, in addition, the quality of courage, of hardihood, of manliness, that makes a man fit to go out into the hurly-burly and do a man's work in the world. That must come, too; and that is not enough. I do not care how moral a man is and how brave he is, if he is a natural born fool you can do nothing with him. I ask, then, for decency as the foundation, for courage and manliness thereon, and finally, in addition to both, I ask for common sense as the moderator and guide of both. [*Applause*]

My fellow-countrymen, I believe in you; I believe in your future; I believe in the future of the American republic, because I believe that the average American citizen has in him just those qualities—the quality of honesty, the quality of courage, and the quality of common sense. While we keep in the community the power of adherence to a lofty ideal and at the same time the power to attempt its realization by practical methods, we can be sure that our progress in the future will be even more rapid than our progress has been in the past, and that in the century now opening, in the centuries that succeed it, this country, already the greatest republic upon which the sun has ever shone, will attain a position of prominence in the world's history that will dwarf into insignificance all that has ever been done before. [*Cheers and applause*]

Source: Lewis, Alfred H. *A Compilation of the Messages and Speeches of Theodore Roosevelt, 1901–1905*. New York: Bureau of National Literature and Art, 1906, 409–412.

President Woodrow Wilson Endorses the Nineteenth Amendment, 1918

It may be fitting that the Women's Suffrage Movement finally reached its glory in the midst of World War I, since the movement felt on many occasions that it was engaged in a long war to secure equality at the ballot box. On September 30, 1918, Woodrow Wilson expressed his support for the Nineteenth Amendment to the Senate, which would give any citizen of the United States the right to vote, regardless of sex (his remarks are below). It was the first time the bill had made it far enough to be introduced on the floor. President Wilson had not always supported women's suffrage; he found the movement to be too radical in the early years of his presidency. His thinking changed, though, in part because of his realization that American women were making important contributions to the war effort. Yet despite the president's encouragement, the 1918 bill did not pass. One year later, however, a suffrage bill did gain passage through Congress, and the Nineteenth Amendment was officially ratified on August 18, 1920, after securing approval from the requisite number of states.

Gentlemen of the Senate:

The unusual circumstances of a world war in which we stand and are judged in the view not only of our own people and our own consciences but also in the view of all nations and peoples will, I hope, justify in your thought, as it does in mine, the message I have come to bring to you. I regard the concurrence of the Senate in the constitutional amendment proposing the extension of the suffrage to women as vitally essential to the successful prosecution of the great war of humanity in which we are engaged. I have come to urge upon you the considerations which have led me to that conclusion. It is not only my privilege, it is also my duty to apprise you of every circumstance and element involved in this momentous struggle which seems to me to affect its very processes and outcome. It is my duty to win the war and to ask you to remove every obstacle that stands in the way of winning it.

I had assumed that the Senate would concur in the amendment because no disputable principle is involved but only a question of the method by which the suffrage is to be extended to women. There is and can be no party issue involved in it. Both of our great national parties are pledged, explicitly pledged, to equality of suffrage for the women of the country. Neither party, therefore, it seems to me, can justify hesitation as to the method of obtaining it, can rightfully hesitate to substitute federal initiative for state initiative, if the early adoption of the measure is necessary to the successful persecution of the war and if the method of state action proposed in the party platforms of 1916 is impracticable within any reasonable length of time, if practicable at all. And its adoption is, in my judgment, clearly necessary to the successful prosecution of the war and the successful realization of the objects for which the war is being fought.

That judgment I take the liberty of urging upon you with solemn earnestness for reasons which I shall state very frankly and which I shall hope will seem as conclusive to you as they seem to me.

This is a peoples' war and the peoples' thinking constitutes its atmosphere and morale, not the predilections of the drawing room or the political considerations of the caucus. If we be indeed democrats and wish to lead the world to democracy, we can ask other peoples to accept in proof of our sincerity and our ability to lead them whither they wish to be led nothing less persuasive and convincing than our actions. Our professions will not suffice. Verification must be forthcoming when verification is asked for. And in this case verification is asked for—asked for in this particular matter. You ask by whom? Not through diplomatic channels; not by Foreign Ministers. Not by the intimations of parliaments. It is asked for by the anxious, expectant, suffering peoples with whom we are dealing and who are willing to put their destinies in some measure in our hands, if they are sure that we wish the same things that they do. I do not speak by conjecture. It is not alone the voices of statesmen and of newspapers that reach me, and the voices of foolish and intemperate agitators do not reach me at all. Through many, many channels I have been made aware what the plain, struggling, workaday folk are thinking upon whom the chief terror and suffering of this tragic war falls. They are looking to the great, powerful, famous Democracy of the West to lead them to the new day for which they have so long waited; and they think, in their logical simplicity, that democracy means that women shall play their part in affairs alongside men and upon an equal footing with them. If we reject measures like this, in ignorance or defiance of what a new age has brought forth, of what they have seen but we have not, they will cease to believe in us; they will cease to follow or to trust us. They have seen their own governments accept this interpretation of democracy—seen old governments like that of Great Britain, which did not profess to be democratic, promise readily and as of course this justice to women, though they had long before refused it, the strange revelations of this war having made many things new and plain, to governments as well as to peoples.

Are we alone to refuse to learn the lesson? Are we alone to ask and take the utmost that our women can give—service and sacrifice of every kind—and still say we do not see what title that gives them to stand by our sides in the guidance of the affairs of their nation and ours? We have made partners of the women in this war; shall we admit them only to a partnership of suffering and sacrifice and toil and not to a partnership of privilege and right? This war could not have been fought, either by the other nations engaged or by America, if it had not been for the services of the women—services rendered in every sphere—not merely in the fields of effort in which we have been accustomed to see them work, but wherever men have worked and upon the very skirts and edges of the battle itself. We shall not only be distrusted but shall deserve to be distrusted if we do not enfranchise them with the fullest possible enfranchisement, as it is now certain that the other great free nations will enfranchise them. We cannot isolate our thought or our action in such a matter from the thought of the rest of the world. We must either conform or deliberately reject what they propose and resign the leadership of liberal minds to others.

The women of America are too noble and too intelligent and too devoted to be slackers whether you give or withhold this thing that is mere justice; but I know the magic it will work in their thoughts and spirits if you give it them. I propose it as I would propose to admit soldiers to the suffrage, the men fighting in the field for our liberties and the liberties of the world, were they excluded. The tasks of the women lie at the very heart of the war, and I know how much stronger that heart will beat if you do this just thing and show our women that you trust them as much as you in fact and of necessity depend upon them.

Have I said that the passage of this amendment is a vitally necessary war measure, and do you need further proof? Do you stand in need of the trust of other peoples and of the trust of our own women? Is that trust an asset or is it not? I tell you plainly, as the commander-in-chief of our armies and of the gallant men in our fleets, as the present spokesman of the people in our dealings with the men and women throughout the world who are now our partners, as the responsible head of a great government which stands and is questioned day by day as to its purposes, its principles, its hopes, whether they be serviceable to men everywhere or only to itself, and who must himself answer these questionings or be shamed, as the guide and director of forces caught in the grip of war and by the same token in need of every material and spiritual resource this great nation possesses—I tell you plainly that this measure which I urge upon you is vital to the winning of the war and to the energies alike of preparation and of battle.

And not to the winning of the war only. It is vital to the right solution of the great problems which we must settle, and settle immediately, when the war is over. We shall need them in our vision of affairs, as we have never needed them before, the sympathy and insight and clear moral instinct of the women of the world. The problems of that time will strike to the roots of many things that we have not hitherto questioned, and I for one believe that our safety in those questioning days, as well as our comprehension of matters that touch society to the quick, will depend upon the direct and authoritative participation of women in our counsels. We shall need their moral sense to preserve what is right and fine and worthy in our system of life as well as to discover just what it is that ought to be purified and reformed. Without their counsellings we shall be only half wise.

That is my case. This is my appeal. Many may deny its validity, if they choose, but no one can brush aside or answer the arguments upon which it is based. The executive tasks of this war rest upon me. I ask that you lighten them and place in my hands instruments, spiritual instruments, which I do not now possess, which I sorely need, and which I have daily to apologize for not being able to employ.

Source: *Supplement to the Messages and Papers of the Presidents, Covering the Second Term of Woodrow Wilson.* New York: Bureau of National Literature, 1921, 8600–8603.

President Warren Harding Speaks to the Public about Prohibition, 1923

The Eighteenth Amendment of the United States Constitution was ratified on January 16, 1919, but it was not enforced until the next year. The amendment made it illegal for any United States citizen to purchase, sell, or transport liquor and other beverages containing alcohol across the country. Proponents of Prohibition asserted that the new law would restore the moral values of the American people, which had been destroyed by the negative consequences of alcohol consumption and the exhaustion of World War I. Many other Americans, however, believed that the amendment had gone too far.

President Warren Harding was often accused of drinking in the White House, but in public he urged Americans to temper their growing agitation with the law and emphasized the social ills that stemmed from alcohol. The following is an excerpt from a speech he delivered to the citizens of Denver, Colorado, on June 25, 1923, in which he emphasized that authorities had a duty to enforce all laws—even controversial ones. He died less than two months later of a heart attack.

The general policy of the states to support the prohibition program, and to cooperate with the federal Government regarding it, is attested by the fact that almost unanimously the states have passed enforcement laws of their own. A difficulty, however, arises at this point. A good deal of testimony comes to Washington that some states are disposed to abdicate their own police authority in this matter, and to turn over the burden of prohibition enforcement to the federal authorities. It is a singular fact that some states which successfully enforced their own prohibition statutes before the eighteenth amendment was adopted have latterly gone backwards in this regard.

Communities in which the policy was frankly accepted as productive of highly beneficial results, and in which there was no widespread protest so long as it was merely a state concern, report that since the federal Government became in part responsible there has been a growing laxity on the part of state authorities about enforcing the law. Doubtless this is largely due to a misconceived notion, too widely entertained, that the federal Government has actually taken over the real responsibility. The fact is quite the contrary. The federal Government is not equipped with the instrumentalities to make enforcement locally effective. It does not maintain either a police or a judicial establishment adequate to or designed for such a task. If the burden of enforcement shall continue to be increasingly thrown upon the federal Government, it will be necessary, at large expense, to create a federal police authority which in time will inevitably come to be regarded as an intrusion upon and interference with the right of local authority to manage local conceits. The possibilities of disaster in such a situation hardly need to be suggested. Yet it is something that we must recognize as among the menaces in this situation.

The federal Government ought to perform, in connection with the enforcement of this policy, those functions which are obviously within its proper province. These are compliance in all its aspects as it relates to international commerce, the importation and exportation of liquors, the collection of federal revenue, the prevention of smuggling, and in general the enforcement of the law within the proper realm of federal authority. But the business of local enforcement, by states and cities, ought to be in the hands of the state and local authorities, and it should be executed in all sincerity and good faith, as other laws are presumed to be executed.

What I am saying must not be construed as indicating any relaxation of the national Government's purpose to do its full duty in this matter.

I have no doubt that if the burden is cast, in undue proportion, upon the national authority the federal Government will, not only under this administration but under whatever others may come in the future, assume and discharge the full obligation. But I am pointing out that this ought not to be made necessary. The national policy ought to be supported by the public opinion and the administrative machinery of the whole country. For myself, I am confident that we are passing now through the most difficult stage of this matter, and that as time passes there will be a more and more willing acceptance by authorities everywhere of the unalterable obligation of law enforcement. The country and the nation will not permit the law of the land to be made a byword.

The issue is fast coming to be recognized, not as an issue between wets and drys, not a question between those who believe in prohibition and those who do riot, not a contention between those who want to drink and those who do not; it is fast being raised above all that, to recognition as an issue of whether the laws of this country can be and will be enforced. So far as the federal Government is concerned, and I am very sure also, so far as concerns the very great majority of the state governments and the local governments, it will be enforced. A gratifying, indeed, it may fairly be said an amazing, progress has been made in the last few years toward better enforcement.

It is a curious illustration of loose thinking that some people have proposed, as a means to protecting the fullest rights of the states, that the states should abandon their part in enforcing the prohibitory policy. That means simply an invitation to the federal Government to exercise powers which should be exercised by the states. Instead of being an assertion of state rights, it is an abandonment of them; it is an abdication; it amounts to a confession by the state that it doesn't choose to govern itself but prefers to turn the task, or a considerable part of it, over to the federal authority. There could be no more complete negation of state rights.

The national Government has been uniformly considerate of the sensibilities of the states about their rights and authorities. But when a state deliberately refuses to exercise the powers which the Constitution expressly confers on it, it obviously commits itself to a policy of nullifying state authority, the end of which we are reluctant to conjecture.

The policy of nullification has never appealed strongly to the American people. There are some historical records regarding efforts of states to nullify national policies; but the spectacle of a state nullifying its own authority, and asking the national sovereignty to take over an important part of its powers, is new. When the implications of this strange proposal are fully understood by people and parties devoted to preserving the rights of the states, the new nullificationists, I venture to say, will discover that they have perpetrated what is likely to prove one of the historic blunders in political management.

I am making my appeal in this matter to the broadest and best sentiments of law-abiding Americans everywhere. We must recognize that there are some people on both sides of this question in whose minds it is absolutely paramount. Some would be willing to sacrifice every other consideration of policy in order to have their own way as to this one. This constitutes one of the most demoralizing factors in the situation.

It was very generally believed that the adoption of the Constitutional amendment would take the question but of our politics. Thus far it has not done so, though I venture to predict that neither of the great parties will see the time, within the lives of any who are now voting citizens, when it will declare openly for the repeal of the eighteenth amendment. But despite all that, the question is kept in politics because of the almost fanatical urgency of the minority of extremists on both sides. Unless, through the recognition and acceptance of the situation in its true light, through the effective enforcement of the law by all the constituted authorities, and with the acquiescence of the clearly dominant public opinion of the country, the question is definitely removed from the domain of political action, it will continue a demoralizing element in our whole public life. It will be a permanent bar to the wise determination of many issues utterly unrelated to the liquor question. It will be the means of encouraging disrespect for many laws. It will bring disrepute upon our community, and be pointed to as justifying the charge that we are a nation of hypocrites. There can be no issue in this land paramount to that of enforcement of the law.

It is easy to understand the conditions out of which much unrest has developed, but it is not easy to comprehend so much of complacency amid a developing peril. I want to give warning against that peril.

Many citizens, not teetotalers in their habits, lawfully acquired stores of private stocks in anticipation of Prohibition, pending the ratification of the amendment and the enactment of the regulatory law. Many others have had no scruple in seeking supplies from those who vend in defiance of the law. The latter practice is rather too costly to be indulged by the masses, so there are literally American millions who resent the lawful possessions of the few, the lawless practices of a few more, and rebel against the denial to the vast majority. Universal Prohibition in the United States would occasion far less discontent than partial Prohibition and partial indulgence.

It is the partial indulgence which challenges the majesty of law, but the greater crime is the impairment of the moral fiber of the republic. The resentful millions have the example of law defiance by those who can afford to buy, and are reckless enough to take the risk, and there is inculcated a contempt for law which may some day find expression in far more serious form.

I do not see how any citizen who cherishes the protection of law in organized society may feel himself secure when he himself is the example of contempt for law. Clearly there is call for awakened conscience and awakened realization of true self-interest on the part of the few who will themselves suffer most when reverence for law is forgotten and passion is expressed in destructive lawlessness. Ours must be a law-abiding republic, and reverence and obedience must spring from the influential and the leaders among men, as well as obedience from the humbler citizen, else the temple will collapse.

Whatever satisfaction there may be in indulgence, whatever objection there is to the so-called invasion of personal liberty, neither counts when the supremacy of law and the stability of our institutions are menaced. With all good intention the majority sentiment of the United States has sought by law to remove strong drink as a curse upon the American citizen, but ours is a larger problem now to remove lawless drinking as a menace to the Republic itself.

There is another phase of law-observance to which reference is impelling. I am thinking of the law of the golden rule, a statute from the Man of Nazareth, who brought new peace and new hope to mankind, and proclaimed service to men the highest tribute to God.

Service is both the inspiration and the accomplishment of quite everything worth while which impels us onward and upward. With service which the Nazarene would approve are associated all our ideals and our finer aspirations. We accept the doctrine for ourselves, as we ought, because we must be firmly established and healthfully and hopefully strong ourselves before we can be effectively helpful to others.

But I believe the law of service demands our larger helpfulness to the world. No, I do not mean entanglement in Old World politics or sponsorship for the adjustment of Old World controversies. I do mean the commitment of this nation to the promotion and preservation of international peace, to the judicial settlement of disputes which, unless settled, lead to added irritation, strained relations, and ultimately to war.

I would like the United States to give of our prestige, our influence, and our power to make the International Court of Justice an outstanding and universally accepted agency of judicial determination of justiciable questions and the peaceful way to international settlements. It is too much to say that such a court will give a guaranty against war, but it will prove the longest step toward war prevention and maintained peace since the world began.

In such a thought is concern for our own country no less than anxiety for a world which is finding readjustment difficult. I am thinking of more than our own freedom from conflict, with all its attending burdens and sorrows. I am thinking of our America having a commitment to an exalting enterprise to save us from the reaction to mere sordid existence, and to keep our hearts aglow while we serve as a vanguard in the march of civilization.

The World War was a frightful calamity, from which the earth will not have fully recovered in a century to come. Nearly five years have passed and peace is not yet secure. Our own cost was beyond an understandable appraisal, but I sometimes feel it was worth much of its cost, because it brought an American awakening and revealed the soul of the republic. We experienced the supreme commitment. We saw our America ready to do or die for our concept of civilization and its guaranties. It exalted us and made us a better, a more patriotically devoted people. I would like to go on, with soul aflame in eagerness to aid humankind, while promoting security for ourselves.

This is no under-appraisal of the essentials of material existence. We may rejoice in the flood tides of material good fortune, we may becomingly boast the measureless resources of the republic through God's bounty in creation and man's genius in development, but we aren't living the becoming life unless we are seeking to advance humankind as we achieve for ourselves. I would like the ages of envy and hate, and conquest and pillage, and armed greed and mad ambitions to be followed by understanding and peace, by the rule of law where force had reigned, the decisions of a world court rather than the decrees of national armies, the observance of the golden rule as the law of human righteousness, and the wail of human suffering and sorrow lost in the glad rejoicings of the onward procession of mankind. If we observe the law of service, if we heed our finer impulses, if we keep alive the soul which we revealed in our national defense, we will add to security for ourselves, and give of our strength to this ideal world advancement.

Source: Richardson, James D. *A Compilation of the Messages and Papers of the Presidents.* Volume 10. New York: Bureau of National Literature, 1925, 9271.

President Calvin Coolidge Orders Legislation Requiring Documentation from Immigrants, 1926

The 1920s were a decade fraught with xenophobia and racial tension in the United States. Such sentiments were so prominent that formal legislation reflecting those fears and anxieties became inevitable. President Calvin Coolidge had signed the Immigration Act in 1924 as a response to the public's general wariness of foreign countries after World War I. The act systematized a national immigration quota. No more than 2 percent of the population of a certain group of people living in the United States at present would be allowed in from that group's place of origin. The quota favored white, European countries and altogether banned immigrants who were ineligible for citizenship, including the entire country of Japan. The creation of the act was grounded in large part on fears that immigrants would swoop in and take the jobs of native-born Americans. The following document,

Executive Order 4476, was enacted by President Coolidge on June 29, 1926. It tightened the regulation of immigration in the United States by way of visa limitations and travel restrictions.

By virtue of the authority vested in me by the Act of Congress approved May 22, 1918, entitled, "An Act to Prevent in Time of War Departure from and Entry into the United States Contrary to the Public Safety," as extended by the Act of Congress of March 2, 1921, entitled, "An Act making appropriations for the Diplomatic and Consular Service for the fiscal year ending June 30, 1922," and with reference to the Act of Congress of May 26, 1924, known as the "Immigration Act of 1924," I hereby prescribe the following regulations governing the entry of aliens into the United States:

Immigrants:
They must present immigration visas, quota or non-quota, in accordance with the requirements of the Immigration Act of 1924, except—

(1) Children born subsequent to the issuance of the immigration visa of the accompanying parent. (Sec. 13 (a) (1), Immigration Act of 1924.) Such children are not required to present documents of any kind;

(2) Aliens who have previously been admitted legally into the United States, have departed therefrom and returned within six months, not having proceeded to countries other than Canada, Newfoundland, St. Pierre, Miquelon, Bermuda, Mexico, Cuba, and other islands included in the Bahama and Greater Antilles groups, are not required to present passports, visas, or permits to reenter.

(3) Aliens, other than those specified in (2) above, who have previously been admitted legally into the United States, have departed therefrom, and are returning from a temporary visit abroad, may present, in lieu of immigration visas, permits to reenter, issued pursuant to Section 10 of the Immigration Act of 1924.

With reference to Section 28 (e) of the Immigration Act of 1924, the Executive Secretary of the Panama Canal, Balboa Heights, Canal Zone, is hereby authorized to issue immigration visas to aliens coming to the United States from the Canal Zone; the Collector of Customs of the Philippine Islands is hereby authorized to issue immigration visas to aliens coming to the United States from the Philippine Islands; the Governor of American Samoa is hereby authorized to issue immigration visas to aliens coming to the United States from American Samoa; and the Governor of Guam is hereby authorized to issue immigration visas to aliens coming to the United States from Guam.

II

Non-Immigrants:
With the exceptions hereinafter specified, they must present passports or official documents in the nature of passports issued by the governments of the

countries to which they owe allegiance, duly visaed by consular officers of the United States; Exceptions:

(1) Persons in transit through the United States to a foreign destination. They may present transit certificates according to regulations prescribed by the Secretary of State.

(2) Aliens who are through passengers on vessels touching at ports of the United States. In this connection the term "United States" is to be construed as in Section 1 of the Immigration Act of 1917. They may land temporarily, under regulations prescribed by the Department of Labor, without documents of any kind.

(3) Wives and children under sixteen years of age accompanying their husbands or parents. They are not required to present separate passports if they are mentioned in the passports of their husbands or parents and their photographs are attached thereto.

(4) Citizens of St. Pierre and Miquelon and French citizens domiciled therein; citizens of Canada, Newfoundland, Bermuda, the Bahamas, and British possessions in the Greater Antilles, and British subjects domiciled therein; citizens of Panama, Mexico, Cuba, Haiti, and the Dominican Republic. Such persons may pass in transit through the United States, or enter the United States temporarily, without passports or visas.

(5) Seamen. Masters of vessels of all nationalities sailing for a port of the United States must submit for visa a list of all the alien members of the vessel's crew to the American consular officer at the port from which the vessel commences its voyage. If there is no American consular officer stationed at that port, the crew list should be submitted at the first port of call (if the vessel touches at any other port) where an American consular officer is located. This does not refer to consular agents, who are not authorized to visa crew lists. However, this paragraph has no application to members of crews of vessels sailing between ports of the United States and ports of Canada, Newfoundland, St. Pierre and Miquelon and not touching at ports of other countries. Such persons are not required to be documental.

When a vessel sails from a port where no American Consul is stationed, but which is within a few hours reach by mail of an American Consulate, so that unreasonable delay and serious loss would not result from referring the crew list to such Consulate, it should be referred thereto for visa.

The visa of a Shipping Commissioner in the Canal Zone shall be accepted as equivalent to the visa of an American Consul.

If an alien seaman whose name is not included in a visaed crew list arrives at a port of the United States he shall not be allowed to land except upon the permission of the Secretary of State.

(6) Aliens making round-trip cruises from American ports without transshipment from the original vessel to another one while en route, provided the original contract for passage calls for transportation from

an American port to the ports included in the cruise, and return to either the original or another American port, require no visas for reentry into the United States.

(7) Aliens of no nationality, and those who, when they apply for visas, are outside of the territories of the countries to which they owe allegiance and who, for any reason, are unable to obtain passports or documents in the nature of passports issued by the governments of such countries, and aliens bearing passports issued by governments not recognized by the United States. They may enter the United States with documents showing their origin and identity, visaed by consuls, under regulations prescribed by the Secretary of State.

III

(1) Aliens entering the Philippine Islands, except those referred to in II (2), must present passports or documents in the nature of passports, duly visaed by consular officers of the United States; but seamen on vessels of all nationalities touching at a port of the Philippine Islands are not required to be documented. Masters of such vessels are, therefore, not required to present visaed crew lists.

(2) Aliens entering any other American possessions not included under Section 28 (a) of the Immigration Act of 1924, do not require documents of any kind.

The definitions contained in Section 28 of the Immigration Act of 1924 shall be regarded as applicable to this order, except as herein otherwise specified.

The Secretary of State and the Secretary of Labor are hereby authorized to make such additional rules and regulations, not inconsistent with this order, as may be deemed necessary for carrying out the provisions of this order and the statutes mentioned herein.

This order shall take effect August 1, 1926, and shall supersede the Executive Order of January 12, 1925, entitled, "Documents Required of Aliens Entering the United States," and the Executive Order of March 31, 1925, entitled, "Documents Required of Aliens Entering the Philippine Islands, Guam and American Samoa," but shall not supersede the Executive Order of July 14, 1924, entitled "Documents Required of Aliens Entering the United States on Airships."

Source: Coolidge, Calvin. Executive Order 4476—*Documents Required of Aliens Entering the United States Online* by Gerhard Peters and John T. Woolley, The American Presidency Project. https://www.presidency.ucsb.edu/node/328746.

President Herbert Hoover Comments on the Bonus Army Investigation, 1932

As a consolation for their service and sacrifices, each World War I veteran was awarded a certificate worth $1,000 by Congress that would be redeemable in 1945. As the Great Depression brought economic desperation to the homes of so many Americans, however, many recipients wanted to redeem their certificates *ahead of time. They organized a protest in the nation's capital that drew veterans from all over the country. Up to 20,000 veterans, along with their families and other supporters, congregated on Capitol Hill and demonstrated peacefully. When the Senate finally rejected the certificates' early redemption, much of the so-called "Bonus Army" simply returned home, but a few thousand were determined to stay. President Herbert Hoover and other leaders such as General Douglas MacArthur grew concerned that the protest would devolve into violence. In addition to the police force already present, President Hoover demanded that federal troops be sent to the site in an effort to intimidate protestors. Witness accounts confirm that tanks rolled through the streets of Washington, D.C., and after several skirmishes erupted that resulted in the deaths of two protestors, the Bonus Army occupation came to an end. The American public was outraged at this ill treatment of veterans, however, and as the criticism intensified, Hoover announced an investigation into the army's actions. At the same time, however, he alleged that some of the protestors were criminals, imposters, and communists, and that they had rioted and caused fiery destruction that posed a threat to national security. The following document provides Hoover's remarks from September 10, 1932, on the findings about the investigation conducted by the Justice Department, as well as excerpted sections from the report itself.*

On the 28th of July last I announced that I had directed the Department of Justice to exhaustively investigate and report in full upon the incidents of the so-called bonus riots of that day in Washington and to present the facts, through sworn witnesses, to the grand jury. I further stated that I should make the Attorney General's report public when received by me.

The investigation has been completed. In giving out the report which shows the character of many of the persons assembled, the incidents and character of the instigators of the this, I wish to state emphatically that the extraordinary proportion of criminal, Communist, and nonveteran elements amongst the marchers as shown by this report, should not be taken to reflect upon the many thousands of honest, law-abiding men who came to Washington with full right of presentation of their views to the Congress. This better element and their leaders acted at all times to restrain crime and violence, but after the adjournment of Congress a large portion of them returned to their homes and gradually these better elements lost control. This report should correct the many misstatements of fact as to this incident with which the country has been flooded.

The text of the Attorney General's report, dated September 9, 1932, follows:

The President, The White House.

Sir: Immediately following the riot by the so-called Bonus Army on July 28th, you directed an investigation and report thereon be made in this Department. We have completed it, and I submit herewith a summary of the result. A vast amount of material in the form of reports, affidavits, and documentary evidence has been accumulated. It is only possible here briefly to summarize the conclusions.

1. The entry of the Bonus Army into the District of Columbia. The first contingent of the Bonus Army arrived about May 27th. On June 3rd, information reached the Department that a contingent from Cleveland

led by C. B. Cowan and another from Detroit led by John T. Pace, comprising about 1300 men, gathered I at the Pennsylvania Railroad yards at Cleveland and had held up a mail train and attempted to commandeer transportation to Washington. Cowan, one of these leaders, has a long police record, he has been convicted and sentenced twice for forgery in Ohio and was sentenced to 13 months, for robbing the mails, to the United States Penitentiary at Atlanta in 1928. Pace, a well known Communist leader has an extended police record. By one means and another these groups and others obtained transportation to Washington. By the middle of June they had congregated here in large numbers. They entered into possession of various tracts of Government property, on some of which were old buildings. In some instances permission to do so was given by the police authorities with the acquiescence of the Treasury, with the understanding that the occupancy would be temporary and would be discontinued at request and when Congress adjourned. Other government tracts were seized without permission and occupied by members of the Bonus Army. The number of Bonus Army marchers in Washington at the time of the adjournment of Congress on July 16th has been variously estimated at from 80000 to 15,000. Several thousand left shortly after Congress adjourned, but other groups came in, and at the time of the riot the best estimates are that there were from 6000 to 8000 bonus marchers in the city.

2.   The quality of the Bonus Army.
     To understand the conditions causing the riot it is necessary to know something of the character of the men in the Bonus Army.

(a) Number of marchers who were not ex-service men. A considerable number of the marchers were not in military service during the World War. An approximation of the number is impossible, but two items of reliable information throw some light on this question.
     [. . .]
Prior to June 12th, 3656 of the marchers who were arriving at Washington registered on the muster rolls of the Bonus Army, giving their names, Army numbers, and other data respecting their World War service. These muster rolls came into the hands of the police and ultimately to the Veterans' Bureau, which commenced to check the names to ascertain whether the marchers were ex-service men. Learning what use was being made of the muster rolls, after June 12th the marchers discontinued the practice of registering. These first 3656 registered arrivals had been checked by the War Department and the Veterans' Bureau against their records of World War service men, with the result that of the total of 3656, 877, or a little more than one-fourth, could not be identified in either department as having had World War service. It is possible that some of the 877 were ex-service men and could not be identified because of meagre information, but the bulk of them were evidently imposters. It has been reported in the press that Director Hines of the Veterans' Bureau has said that over 90% of the Bonus Army were ex-service men. General Hines made no such statement. He did make the

statement on July 23 that he believed not more than 8000 veterans had ever been present at any one time, but the 877 men not identified as veterans were part of the 3,656 registered to which I have referred.

(b) Number of bonus marchers with criminal or police records. Two sources of information are available on this subject. Of the 51 arrested men fingerprinted by the police prior to the riot of July 28th and checked in the fingerprint division of this Department, 17, or an even one-third, had been convicted of various offenses, including larceny, assault, sex offenses, forgery, robbery, military offenses, and disorderly conduct. A more striking result is obtained from the check by the criminal identification bureau of this Department of the fingerprints of 4723 of the bonus marchers who were admittedly veterans and applied for and obtained loans from the Veterans' Bureau, after Congress adjourned, for the ostensible purpose of returning to their homes. Of these 4723, 1069 were found to have police records.

829 or nearly 1 in 5 of the World War service men among the bonus marchers who obtained loans, had been convicted for various offenses, including assault, larceny, burglary, embezzlement, robbery, felonious homicide, forgery and counterfeiting, rape, sex offenses, and narcotic drug violations.

A summary of the police and criminal records of these men follows:

SUMMARY OF POLICE RECORDS OF 4723 EX-SERVICE MEN OF THE BONUS ARMY WHO APPLIED FOR LOANS FROM THE VETERANS' BUREAU

	Total	Disposition pending or unknown	Charges dismissed	Convictions
Assault	46	2	7	37
Auto Theft	32	0	6	26
Burglary	88	1	21	66
Carrying Concealed Weapons	9	1	2	6
Disorderly Conduct and Vagrancy	107	3	35	69
Driving while Intoxicated	24	0	0	24
Drunkenness	98	1	2	95
Embezzlement and Fraud	52	1	13	38
Felonious Homicide	13	0	6	7
Forgery and Counterfeiting	48	0	4	44
Gambling	4	0	2	2
Larceny Theft	167	2	27	138
Liquor Laws	61	3	9	49
Military offenses, Desertion, etc.	84	2	2	80
Miscellaneous	41	4	5	32

	Total	Disposition pending or unknown	Charges dismissed	Convictions
Narcotic Drug Laws	12	0	2	10
Offenses against the Family and Children	18	0	2	16
Rape	8	0	2	6
Robbery	63	0	17	46
Sex Offenses (except rape)	27	0	7	20
Suspicion and Investigation	63	0	49	14
Traffic and Motor Vehicle Laws	4	0	0	1
Totals	1069	20	220	829

Total number of bonus marchers (ex-service men) upon whom fingerprints were obtained	4723
Number of bonus marchers with police records as found from fingerprints	1069
Percentage of these bonus marchers having police records	22.6%
Total number of bonus marchers found to have one or more convictions	829
Percentage of marchers convicted to number having police records	76.9%
Percentage of bonus marchers having convictions to total number whose fingerprints were searched	17.4%

[...]

It will be noted that many of them had been repeatedly convicted under various names. When it is realized that the men who applied for loans to go home after Congress adjourned were the most sensible and the least disorderly, that many with criminal records no doubt refrained from disclosing their identity for any purpose, and a considerable portion of the Bonus Army were not ex-service men and included Communists, radicals, and disorderly elements which always congregate under such conditions, it is probable the Bonus Army brought into the City of Washington the largest aggregation of criminals that had ever been assembled in the city at any one time.

[...]

4. The riot and the use of troops.

At the time of resuming possession of the small area on Pennsylvania Avenue on July 28th, it was not planned immediately to attempt to regain possession by the Government of any of the other tracts occupied by the Bonus Army. It was hoped that their evacuation could be gradually accomplished. The small number of bonus marchers occupying this building vacated it, forcible resistance having been offered only by two or three. No one was hurt by this movement, and the persons evicted were given ample opportunity to pack and leave. However, while this was taking place, speeches of an incendiary nature were being made at Camp Marks, an open area across the Anacostia River, on which a large bonus camp had been established. About noon, when the situation on Pennsylvania Avenue was well in hand and entirely peaceful, the bonus marchers from Camp Marks started across the Anacostia River to the Pennsylvania Avenue tract in large numbers by trucks and other means. They gathered in the street area near the property, then in the possession of the Treasury Department, which was being guarded by 75 police-men, and their number increased to 2000 or 3000. Suddenly, during the noon hour, the mob that had come from Camp Marks rushed the policemen and attacked them with bricks and rocks. Some of the police were felled with clubs. The police had revolvers, but had orders not to use them and did not do so. This attack finally subsided. Thousands of persons were attracted to the scene. The crowd of bonus marchers assembled at this point increased to numbers estimated at 4000 to 6000. With the bystanders, the crowd increased to an estimated number of nearly 20,000. The situation became more strained, and many of the Bonus Army were walking about with clubs and bricks in their hands. This continued until the middle of the afternoon, with continuous talk about attacking the police and driving them out. Some lawfully inclined veterans attempted to calm others, but made no impres-sion. Finally the mob of bonus marchers again attacked the police with bricks, lumps of concrete, and iron bars. Two of the bonus marchers were shot by police who had been set upon and were in danger of their lives. The entire mob became hostile and riotous. It was apparent that a pitched battle on a large scale might start at any moment. Practically the entire police force of the city were called from their posts and assembled at this point, but they were outnumbered 10 or 15 to 1. Not-withstanding the large number of irresponsible persons in the city, the rest of the city was stripped of police protection. Many of the policemen had been on duty all night. It was obvious that the situation was entirely out of the control of the police, and that when darkness arrived appalling scenes of disorder would follow, during which the rest of the city would be without substantial police protection, except for a few scout cars.

[. . .]

There is no difference of opinion about the fact that the presence of troops was necessary to and did prevent further disorder and bloodshed. In their absence, further rioting would have occurred with further bloodshed among bonus march-ers and police, and possibly innocent bystanders.

The troops arrived and, with the use of practically no weapons except tear gas, restored order and cleared the area and put an end to the disturbance.

5. Casualties.

Two bonus marchers were killed in the disturbance. They were shot by police in self defense, not by troops. A full investigation by a coroner's jury established that the police shot in necessary self defense to save themselves from threatened fatal injury. After the troops arrived, no serious injuries to anyone followed. A few of the troops were stoned and slightly injured, and one bonus marcher had his ear cut, but no other casualties were suffered after the troops came. Stories published in some quarters that the troops shot or seriously injured bonus marchers are utterly without foundation. The published reports that an infant child of a bonus marcher named Myers died as a result of tear gas are false. The records at the Gallinger Hospital show that the child died of intestinal trouble contracted and diagnosed before the riot.

[. . .]

8. Grand Jury.

Indictments have been returned by the Grand Jury of the District of Columbia against a number of the alleged rioters. The results of this effort to bring to justice the principals who incited this riot have been unsatisfactory. The reason is that on the day of the riot no detective officers were at Camp Marks, where originated the large movement to march over and attack the police. The function of having detectives and crime prevention agents in a position to observe and obtain evidence against those who at the last moment incited the riotous march and attack, belonged to the District police. The inspector in charge of that branch of the police service reports that he had no orders to place men for that purpose, and, on the contrary, on the day of the disturbance was directed to keep his men out of the area. Consequently, in the confusion and absence of this detective service, it has been impossible to identify and bring to justice some of the principal inciters of the disorder. It is always the case under such conditions, that the radicals and disorderly elements who incite such action do so warily and sometimes fade from the scene when the trouble commences.

9. Conclusion.

This experience demonstrates that it is intolerable that organized bodies of men having a grievance or demand upon the Government should be allowed to encamp in the city and attempt to live off the community like soldiers billeted in an enemy country. Attempts by such groups to intimidate or coerce Congress into granting their demands hurt rather than help their cause, and can only end as this one did, in riot and disorder. The available facts demonstrate that the bonus marchers who remained in the city after Congress adjourned represented no fair cross-section of ex-service men. Prior to the adjournment of Congress, law-abiding ex-service men dominated this gathering and preserved order. Afterwards, the proportion of disorderly and criminal elements among these men steadily increased. Such of their leaders as were well-intentioned lost control over them entirely. It is appalling to think of the disorder and bloodshed that would have occurred if darkness had fallen on the city with the police hopelessly overwhelmed at the scene of the disturbance, and the balance of the community without police protection. The prompt use of the military to outnumber and overawe the disturbers prevented a calamity. The principal reason why the Federal Government was given exclusive jurisdiction over the Capital City was m enable it to preserve order at the seat of government and to protect the Congress and other public officials from unlawful interference while in the discharge of their duties. The right peaceably to petition Congress for redress of alleged grievances does not include assemblage of disorderly thousands at the seat of the government for purposes of coercion.

Source: *Public Papers of the Presidents of the United States. Herbert Hoover, 1932–33.* Washington, D.C.: Government Printing Office, 1977, Document 285.

President Franklin D. Roosevelt Discusses the New Deal in Fireside Chat, 1933

The race for president between Republican incumbent Herbert Hoover and Democratic New York Governor Franklin D. Roosevelt in 1932 had been tense, but ultimately the election itself was anticlimactic. President Hoover was seen by most American voters as ineffective in combating the Great Depression—and indifferent to the toll it was taking on countless families—and Roosevelt capitalized on this perception while also promising decisive action to revive the economy. As a result, Roosevelt defeated the incumbent by the millions in the popular vote and by the hundreds in the Electoral College.

Upon taking office, Roosevelt immediately set about implementing what came to be known as the "New Deal." The New Deal would comprise a web of new federal legislation and jobs programs meant to support and reconnect the U.S. economy and return the nation to stability and prosperity. Throughout his tenure in office, President Roosevelt utilized the radio to deliver a series of addresses, dubbed Fireside Chats by reporters, directly to the American people. The following document is the transcript of one such chat, delivered on July 24, 1933, in which Roosevelt outlined his New Deal policy ideas. He told his national audience that his administration had presented 15 bills to Congress related to the economic recovery of the United States, and he urged his listeners to have faith that the programs and policies contained in these bills would, over time, lift the United States out of the economic quicksand in which it was mired.

After the adjournment of the historical special session of the Congress five weeks ago I purposely refrained from addressing you for two very good reasons. First, I think that we all wanted the opportunity of a little quiet thought to examine and assimilate in a mental picture the crowding events of the hundred days which had been devoted to the starting of the wheels of the New Deal.

Secondly, I wanted a few weeks in which to set up the new administrative organization and to see the first fruits of our careful planning.

I think it will interest you if I set forth the fundamentals of this planning for national recovery; and this I am very certain will make it abundantly clear to you that all of the proposals and all of the legislation since the fourth day of March have not been just a collection of haphazard schemes, but rather the orderly component parts of a connected and logical whole.

Long before Inauguration Day I became convinced that individual effort and local effort and even disjointed Federal effort had failed and of necessity would fail and, therefore, that a rounded leadership by the Federal Government had become a necessity both of theory and of fact. Such leadership, however, had its beginning in preserving and strengthening the credit of the United States Government, because without that no leadership was a possibility. For years the Government had not lived within its income. The immediate task was to bring our regular expenses within our revenues. That has been done.

It may seem inconsistent for a government to cut down its regular expenses and at the same time to borrow and to spend billions for an emergency. But it is not inconsistent because a large portion of the emergency money has been paid out in the form of sound loans which will be repaid to the Treasury over a period of years; and to cover the rest of the emergency money we have imposed taxes to pay the interest and the installments on that part of the debt.

So you will see that we have kept our credit good. We have built a granite foundation in a period of confusion. That foundation of the Federal credit stands there broad and sure. It is the base of the whole recovery plan.

Then came the part of the problem that concerned the credit of the individual citizens themselves. You and I know of the banking crisis and of the great danger to the savings of our people. On March sixth every national bank was closed. One month later 90 percent of the deposits in the national banks had been made available to the depositors. Today only about 5 percent of the deposits in national banks are still tied up. The condition relating to State banks, while not quite so good on a percentage basis, is showing a steady reduction in the total of frozen deposits—a result much better than we had expected three months ago.

The problem of the credit of the individual was made more difficult because of another fact. The dollar was a different dollar from the one with which the average debt had been incurred. For this reason large numbers of people were actually losing possession of and title to their farms and homes. All of you know the financial steps which have been taken to correct this inequality. In addition the Home Loan Act, the Farm Loan Act and the Bankruptcy Act were passed.

It was a vital necessity to restore purchasing power by reducing the debt and interest charges upon our people, but while we were helping people to save their credit it was at the same time absolutely essential to do something about the physical needs of hundreds of thousands who were in dire straits at that very moment. Municipal and State aid were being stretched to the limit. We appropriated half a billion dollars to supplement their efforts and in addition, as you know, we have put 300,000 young men into practical and useful work in our forests and to prevent flood and soil erosion. The wages they earn are going in greater part to the support of the nearly one million people who constitute their families.

In this same classification we can properly place the great public works program running to a total of over three billion dollars—to be used for highways and ships and flood prevention and inland navigation and thousands of self-sustaining State and municipal improvements. Two points should be made clear in the allotting and administration of these projects: first, we are using the utmost care to choose labor-creating, quick-acting, useful projects, avoiding the smell of the pork barrel; and second, we are hoping that at least half of the money will come back to the Government from projects which will pay for themselves over a period of years.

Thus far I have spoken primarily of the foundation stones—the measures that were necessary to reestablish credit and to head people in the opposite direction by preventing distress and providing as much work as possible through governmental agencies. Now I come to the links which will build us a more lasting prosperity. I have said that we cannot attain that in a Nation half boom and half broke. If all of our people have work and fair wages and fair profits, they can buy the products of their neighbors, and business is good. But if you take away the wages and the profits of half of them, business is only half as good. It does not help much if the fortunate half is very prosperous; the best way is for everybody to be reasonably prosperous.

For many years the two great barriers to a normal prosperity have been low farm prices and the creeping paralysis of unemployment. These factors have cut the purchasing power of the country in half. I promised action. Congress did its part when it passed the Farm and the Industrial Recovery Acts. Today we are putting these two Acts to work and they will work if people understand their plain objectives.

First, the Farm Act: It is based on the fact that the purchasing power of nearly half our population depends on adequate prices for farm products. We have been producing more of some crops than we consume or can sell in a depressed world market. The cure is not to produce so much. Without our help the farmers cannot get together and cut production, and the Farm Bill gives them a method of bringing their production down to a reasonable level and of obtaining reasonable prices for their crops. I have clearly stated that this method is in a sense experimental, but so far as we have gone we have reason to believe that it will produce good results.

It is obvious that if we can greatly increase the purchasing power of the tens of millions of our people who make a living from farming and the distribution of farm crops, we shall greatly increase the consumption of those goods which are turned out by industry.

That brings me to the final step—bringing back industry along sound lines.

Last Autumn, on several occasions, I expressed my faith that we can make possible by democratic self-discipline in industry general increases in wages and shortening of hours sufficient to enable industry to pay its own workers enough to let those workers buy and use the things that their labor produces. This can be done only if we permit and encourage cooperative action in industry, because it is obvious that without united action a few selfish men in each competitive group will pay starvation wages and insist on long hours of work. Others in that group must either follow suit or close up shop. We have seen the result of action of that kind in the continuing descent into the economic hell of the past four years.

There is a clear way to reverse that process: If all employers in each competitive group agree to pay their workers the same wages—reasonable wages—and require the same hours—reasonable hours—then higher wages and shorter hours will hurt no employer. Moreover, such action is better for the employer than unemployment and low wages, because it makes more buyers for his product. That is the simple idea which is the very heart of the Industrial Recovery Act.

On the basis of this simple principle of everybody doing things together, we are starting out on this nationwide attack on unemployment. It will succeed if our people understand it— in the big industries, in the little shops, in the great cities and in the small villages. There is nothing complicated about it and there is nothing particularly new in the principle. It goes back to the basic idea of society and of the Nation itself that people acting in a group can accomplish things which no individual acting alone could even hope to bring about.

Here is an example. In the Cotton Textile Code and in other agreements already signed, child labor has been abolished. That makes me personally happier than any other one thing with which I have been connected since I came to Washington. In the textile industry—an industry which came to me spontaneously and with a splendid cooperation as soon as the Recovery Act was signed—child labor was an old evil. But no employer acting alone was able to wipe it out. If one employer tried it, or if one State tried it, the costs of operation rose so high that it was impossible to compete with the employers or States which had failed to act.

The moment the Recovery Act was passed, this monstrous thing which neither opinion nor law could reach through years of effort went out in a flash. As a British editorial put it, we did more under a Code in one day than they in England had been able to do under the common law in eighty-five years of effort. I use this incident, my friends, not to boast of what has already been done but to point the way to you for even greater cooperative efforts this summer and autumn.

We are not going through another winter like the last. I doubt if ever any people so bravely and cheerfully endured a season half so bitter. We cannot ask America to continue to face such needless hardships. It is time for courageous action, and the Recovery Bill gives us the means to conquer unemployment with exactly the same weapon that we have used to strike down child labor.

The proposition is simply this:

If all employers will act together to shorten hours and raise wages we can put people back to work. No employer will suffer, because the relative level of competitive cost will advance by the same amount for all. But if any considerable group should lag or shirk, this great opportunity will pass us by and we shall go into another desperate winter. This must not happen.

We have sent out to all employers an agreement which is the result of weeks of consultation. This agreement checks against the voluntary codes of nearly all the large industries which have already been submitted. This blanket agreement carries the unanimous approval of the three boards which I have appointed to advise in this, boards representing the great leaders in labor, in industry, and in social service. The agreement has already brought a flood of approval from every State, and from so wide a cross-section of the common calling of industry that I know it is fair for all. It is a plan—deliberate, reasonable and just—intended to put into effect at once the most important of the broad principles which are being established, industry by industry, through codes. Naturally, it takes a good deal of organizing and a great many hearings and many months, to get these codes perfected and signed, and we cannot wait for all of them to go through. The blanket agreements, however, which I am sending to every employer will start the wheels turning now, and not six months from now.

There are, of course, men, a few men, who might thwart this great common purpose by seeking selfish advantage. There are adequate penalties in the law, but I am now asking the cooperation that comes from opinion and from conscience. These are the only instruments we shall use in this great summer offensive against unemployment. But we shall use them to the limit to protect the willing from the laggard and to make the plan succeed.

In war, in the gloom of night attack, soldiers wear a bright badge on their shoulders to be sure that comrades do not fire on comrades. On that principle, those who cooperate in this program must know each other at a glance. That is why we have provided a badge of honor for this purpose, a simple design with a legend, "We do our part," and I ask that all those who join with me shall display that badge prominently. It is essential to our purpose.

Already all the great, basic industries have come forward willingly with proposed codes, and in these codes they accept the principles leading to mass reemployment. But, important as is this heartening demonstration, the richest field for results is among the small employers, those whose contribution will be to give new work for from one to ten people. These smaller employers are indeed a vital part of the backbone of the country, and the success of our plan lies largely in their hands.

Already the telegrams and letters are pouring into the White House—messages from employers who ask that their names be placed on this special Roll of Honor. They represent great corporations and companies, and partnerships and individuals. I ask that even before the dates set in the agreements which we have sent out, the employers of the country who have not already done so—the big fellows and the little fellows—shall at once write or telegraph to me personally at the White House, expressing their intentions of going through with the plan. And it is my purpose to keep posted in the post office of every town, a Roll of Honor of all those who join with me.

I want to take this occasion to say to the twenty-four Governors who are now in conference in San Francisco, that nothing thus far has helped in strengthening this great movement more than their resolutions adopted at the very outset of their meeting, giving this plan their instant and unanimous approval, and pledging to support it in their States.

To the men and women whose lives have been darkened by the fact or the fear of unemployment, I am justified in saying a word of encouragement because the codes and the agreements already approved, or about to be passed upon, prove that the plan does raise wages, and that it does put people back to work. You can look on every employer who adopts the plan as one who is doing his part, and those employers deserve well of everyone who works for a living. It will be clear to you, as it is to me, that while the shirking employer may undersell his competitor, the saving he thus makes is made at the expense of his country's welfare.

While we are making this great common effort there should be no discord and dispute. This is no time to cavil or to question the standard set by this universal agreement. It is time for patience and understanding and cooperation. The workers of this country have rights under this law which cannot be taken from them, and nobody will be permitted to whittle them away but, on the other hand, no aggression is now necessary to attain those rights. The whole country will be united to get them for you. The principle that applies to the employers applies to the workers as well, and I ask you workers to cooperate in the same spirit.

When Andrew Jackson, "Old Hickory," died, someone asked, "Will he go to Heaven?" and the answer was, "He will if he wants to." If I am asked whether the American people will pull themselves out of this depression, I answer, "They will if they want to." The essence of the plan is a universal limitation of hours of work per week for any individual by common consent, and a universal payment of wages above a minimum, also by common consent. I cannot guarantee the success of this nationwide plan, but the people of this country can guarantee its success. I have no faith in "cure-alls" but I believe that we can greatly influence economic forces. I have no sympathy with the professional economists who insist that things must run their course and that human agencies can have no influence on economic ills. One reason is that I happen to know that professional economists have changed their definition of economic laws every five or ten years for a very long time, but I do have faith, and retain faith, in the strength of the common purpose, and in the strength of unified action taken by the American people.

That is why I am describing to you the simple purposes and the solid foundations upon which our program of recovery is built. That is why I am asking the employers of the Nation to sign this common covenant with me—to sign it in the name of patriotism and humanity. That is why I am asking the workers to go along with us in a spirit of understanding and of helpfulness.

Source: Franklin D. Roosevelt Presidential Library and Museum. Available online at http://docs.fdrlibrary.marist.edu/042433.html.

President Franklin D. Roosevelt Signs Conservation Act amid the Dust Bowl, 1936

The Soil Conservation and Domestic Allotment Act was passed during the Dust Bowl era on March 1, 1936. The act demonstrates President Roosevelt's creative approach to domestic issues. Its provisions would allow farmers to grow grasses and legumes to support the stability of the soil, rather than surplus crops which enabled the proliferation of dust storms. Many farming families in the South and in the Plains were out of work and money and forced to travel in search of a stable wage. Their land was no longer arable due to severe droughts. The government would open an unspecified fund to support the farmers while they worked and eliminate the threat of any losses the farmers may endure while they took a hiatus from their crops. The act was also important because it again justified federal aid in the midst of a stagnant economy during the Great Depression, such as other legislation had as part of the president's New Deal. The following is President Roosevelt's statement upon signing the act into law.

In signing the Soil Conservation and Domestic Allotment Act, I feel that I am approving a measure which helps to safeguard vital public interests not only for today, but for generations to come.

This legislation represents an attempt to develop, out of the far-reaching and partly emergency efforts under the Agricultural Adjustment Act, a long-time program for American agriculture.

The new law has three major objectives which are inseparably and of necessity linked with the national welfare. The first of these aims is conservation of the soil itself through wise and proper land use. The second purpose is the reestablishment and maintenance of farm income at fair levels so that the great gains made by agriculture in the past three years can be preserved and national recovery can continue. The third major objective is the protection of consumers by assuring adequate supplies of food and fibre now and in the future.

The Federal Government, with an annual expenditure far less than the actual yearly wastage of fertility by erosion in the past will make grants of money to farmers, conditioned upon actual evidence of good land use. Thus, in carrying out the soil conservation plan, there will be provided a positive incentive to and protection for those who voluntarily shift from soil-depleting surplus crops, such as cotton, corn, wheat and tobacco, into erosion-preventing and soil-building crops, such as grasses and legumes, of which there is no surplus. This will help to bring about and maintain a healthy supply-and-demand situation from farm commodities, and will have a beneficial effect on farm prices and farm income.

There will be no contracts with farmers. The program does not control individual production of individual farm commodities. The absence of production control may make impracticable the attainment of exact parity prices, as defined in the Agricultural Adjustment Act. Nevertheless, I am confident that the farmers, cooperating with the Government, will work hard within existing legal limitations to achieve the goal of the new law, which is parity not of farm prices, but of farm income. They and we have not abandoned and will not abandon the principle of equality for agriculture.

In general, the new farm act follows the outlines of a longtime policy for agriculture which I recommended in my statement of October 25, 1935. The wise use of land which it seeks to encourage involves sound farm practice and crop rotation as well as soil conservation. The income insurance feature afforded by the conditional payments will help farmers to maintain these beneficial systems of farming without interruption in poor crop years. Long-time adjustments, as I said last October, can be adapted to natural soil advantages of regions and localities.

Sound farming is of direct interest not only to farmers, but to consumers. To the extent that the new plan succeeds in its aim of preserving and improving farm lands, consumers will share substantially in the benefits. In years of surplus, consumers may lightly take for granted the continuance of adequate supplies of food and fibre; but the recurring dust storms and rivers yellow with silt are a warning that Nature's resources will not indefinitely withstand exploitation or negligence. The only permanent protection which can be given consumers must come from conservation practiced by farmers.

For a long time, I have felt that there was need for concerted action to promote good land use. Years ago, as Governor of the State of New York, I took such steps as I could in that direction, and I described them in detail in a speech at French Lick, Indiana, June 2, 1931, on the subject "Acres Fit and Unfit." I said that, having reached a determination as to the best use of land, "we arrive at once at the larger problem of getting men, women and children—in other words, population—to go along with a program and carry it out." I said, "Government itself must take steps, with approval of the governed, to see that plans become realities."

As I made that speech, I was thinking in terms of my State, of other States and of the Nation. Now this new Act incorporates a system of Federal aid to function when State cooperation with the Federal Government can be arranged.

The provision for State-Federal cooperation, beginning not later than January 1, 1938, will mark a further application of the principle of shared responsibility. This is in accord with the strong feature of the agricultural adjustment programs which operated in a democratic manner through cooperation with the State land grant colleges, State committees, county associations and county committees, township committees and individual farmers.

The history of every Nation is eventually written in the way in which it cares for its soil. The United States, as evidenced by the progressive public opinion and vigorous demand which resulted in the enactment of this law, is now emerging from its youthful stage of heedless exploitation and is beginning to realize the supreme importance of treating the soil well.

I do not regard this farm act as a panacea or as a final plan. Rather I consider it a new basis to build and improve upon, as experience discloses its points of weakness and of strength. Aiming at justice for agriculture and self-interest for the Nation, the plan seeks to salvage and conserve the greatest values in human life and resources with which this Nation is endowed.

Source: *Public Papers of the Presidents of the United States. Franklin D. Roosevelt, 1936.* Volume 5. New York: Random House, 1938, Document 28, 95–102.

President Dwight D. Eisenhower Sends Federal Support to Little Rock, Arkansas, 1957

Racial segregation in public schools was found to be unconstitutional in the Supreme Court ruling Brown v. Board of Education of Topeka *on May 17, 1954. Yet many state and local legislators attempted to either ignore the immediate implications of the court ruling or vowed outright defiance of the desegregation ruling. The most famous and momentous of these clashes over school desegregation came in 1957 at Central High School in Little Rock, Arkansas. When nine black students (dubbed the "Little Rock Nine") sought to enroll and take classes at the all-white high school, Arkansas Governor Orval Faubus sent the National Guard to block their entry into the school. While Governor Faubus insisted it was for the students' own protection, Dwight D. Eisenhower saw the action as an inexcusable violation of the law. He subsequently gave the following Executive Order 10730—Providing Assistance for the Removal of an Obstruction of Justice Within the State of Arkansas. This order placed federal troops in command of the Arkansas National Guard. The president's orders were to escort the students to class through any mobs or protestors awaiting them. The students were able to attend class for a time, but Governor Faubus effectively shut down the public high schools in Little Rock amid continuing aggression against the Little Rock Nine. Only one student of the group ultimately graduated from Central High.*

WHEREAS on September 23, 1957, I issued Proclamation No. 3204 reading in part as follows:

> WHEREAS certain persons in the state of Arkansas, individually and in unlawful assemblages, combinations, and conspiracies, have willfully obstructed the enforcement of orders of the United States District Court for the Eastern District of Arkansas with respect to matters relating to enrollment and attendance at public schools, particularly at Central High School, located in Little Rock School District, Little Rock, Arkansas; and

WHEREAS such wilful obstruction of justice hinders the execution of the laws of that State and of the United States, and makes it impracticable to enforce such laws by the ordinary course of judicial proceedings; and

WHEREAS such obstruction of justice constitutes a denial of the equal protection of the laws secured by the Constitution of the United States and impedes the course of justice under those laws:

NOW, THEREFORE, I, DWIGHT D. EISENHOWER, President of the United States, under and by virtue of the authority vested in me by the Constitution and Statutes of the United States, including Chapter 15 of Title 10 of the United States Code, particularly sections 332, 333 and 334 thereof, do command all persons engaged in such obstruction of justice to cease and desist therefrom, and to disperse forthwith; and

WHEREAS the command contained in that Proclamation has not been obeyed and wilful obstruction of enforcement of said court orders still exists and threatens to continue:

NOW, THEREFORE, by virtue of the authority vested in me by the Constitution and Statutes of the United States, including Chapter 15 of Title 10, particularly sections 332, 333 and 334 thereof, and section 301 of Title 3 of the United States Code, it is hereby ordered as follows:

SECTION 1. I hereby authorize and direct the Secretary of Defense to order into the active military service of the United States as he may deem appropriate to carry out the purposes of this Order, any or all of the units of the National Guard of the United States and of the Air National Guard of the United States within the State of Arkansas to serve in the active military service of the United States for an indefinite period and until relieved by appropriate orders.

SEC. 2. The Secretary of Defense is authorized and directed to take all appropriate steps to enforce any orders of the United States District Court for the Eastern District of Arkansas for the removal of obstruction of justice in the State of Arkansas with respect to matters relating to enrollment and attendance at public schools in the Little Rock School District, Little Rock, Arkansas. In carrying out the provisions of this section, the Secretary of Defense is authorized to use the units, and members thereof, ordered into the active military service of the United States pursuant to Section 1 of this Order.

SEC. 3. In furtherance of the enforcement of the aforementioned orders of the United States District Court for the Eastern District of Arkansas, the Secretary of Defense is authorized to use such of the armed forces of the United States as he may deem necessary.

SEC. 4. The Secretary of Defense is authorized to delegate to the Secretary of the Army or the Secretary of the Air Force, or both, any of the authority conferred upon him by this Order.

Source: Executive Order 10730, 3 CFR 89 (Supp. 1957).

President John F. Kennedy Outlines Civil Rights Act in Report, 1963

The following Radio and Television Report to the American People on Civil Rights was a famous speech delivered on June 11, 1963, by President John F. Kennedy on the many disparities between the lives of black and white people in the United States due to factors such as racism, segregation, and the legacy of slavery. The address was prompted by events in Alabama, where Governor George Wallace had earlier that day personally prevented two black students from enrolling in the University of Alabama by blocking the doorway into the student registration office. When Presidency Kennedy was informed of Wallace's actions, he sent troops from the National Guard to the university as the students' escorts so they could enroll. When the troops showed up at the registration office, Wallace stood aside and the students were able to formally enroll—making Alabama the last Southern state to integrate its state colleges.

Kennedy's speech outlined for the first time to the American public many of the policy ideas that he would later propose in his sweeping Civil Rights Act of 1964. That legislation outlawed segregation and discrimination in all places, including the workplace, and was one of the most comprehensive and important pieces of civil rights legislation in U.S. history.

Good evening, my fellow citizens:

This afternoon, following a series of threats and defiant statements, the presence of Alabama National Guardsmen was required on the University of Alabama to carry out the final and unequivocal order of the United States District Court of the Northern District of Alabama. That order called for the admission of two clearly qualified young Alabama residents who happened to have been born Negro.

That they were admitted peacefully on the campus is due in good measure to the conduct of the students of the University of Alabama, who met their responsibilities in a constructive way.

I hope that every American, regardless of where he lives, will stop and examine his conscience about this and other related incidents. This Nation was founded by men of many nations and backgrounds. It was founded on the principle that all men are created equal, and that the rights of every man are diminished when the rights of one man are threatened.

Today we are committed to a worldwide struggle to promote and protect the rights of all who wish to be free. And when Americans are sent to Viet-Nam or West Berlin, we do not ask for whites only. It ought to be possible, therefore, for American students of any color to attend any public institution they select without having to be backed up by troops.

It ought to be possible for American consumers of any color to receive equal service in places of public accommodation, such as hotels and restaurants and theaters and retail stores, without being forced to resort to demonstrations in the street, and it ought to be possible for American citizens of any color to register and to vote in a free election without interference or fear of reprisal.

It ought to be possible, in short, for every American to enjoy the privileges of being American without regard to his race or his color. In short, every American ought to have the right to be treated as he would wish to be treated, as one would wish his children to be treated. But this is not the case.

The Negro baby born in America today, regardless of the section of the Nation in which he is born, has about one-half as much chance of completing high school as a white baby born in the same place on the same day, one-third as much chance of completing college, one-third as much chance of becoming a professional man, twice as much chance of becoming unemployed, about one-seventh as much chance of earning $10,000 a year, a life expectancy which is 7 years shorter, and the prospects of earning only half as much.

This is not a sectional issue. Difficulties over segregation and discrimination exist in every city, in every State of the Union, producing in many cities a rising tide of discontent that threatens the public safety. Nor is this a partisan issue. In a time of domestic crisis men of good will and generosity should be able to unite regardless of party or politics. This is not even a legal or legislative issue alone. It is better to settle these matters in the courts than on the streets, and new laws are needed at every level, but law alone cannot make men see right.

We are confronted primarily with a moral issue. It is as old as the scriptures and is as clear as the American Constitution.

The heart of the question is whether all Americans are to be afforded equal rights and equal opportunities, whether we are going to treat our fellow Americans as we want to be treated. If an American, because his skin is dark, cannot eat lunch in a restaurant open to the public, if he cannot send his children to the best public school available, if he cannot vote for the public officials who represent him, if, in short, he cannot enjoy the full and free life which all of us want, then who among us would be content to have the color of his skin changed and stand in his place? Who among us would then be content with the counsels of patience and delay?

One hundred years of delay have passed since President Lincoln freed the slaves, yet their heirs, their grandsons, are not fully free. They are not yet freed from the bonds of injustice. They are not yet freed from social and economic oppression. And this Nation, for all its hopes and all its boasts, will not be fully free until all its citizens are free.

We preach freedom around the world, and we mean it, and we cherish our freedom here at home, but are we to say to the world, and much more importantly, to each other that this is a land of the free except for the Negroes; that we have no second-class citizens except Negroes; that we have no class or caste system, no ghettoes, no master race except with respect to Negroes?

Now the time has come for this Nation to fulfill its promise. The events in Birmingham and elsewhere have so increased the cries for equality that no city or State or legislative body can prudently choose to ignore them.

The fires of frustration and discord are burning in every city, North and South, where legal remedies are not at hand. Redress is sought in the streets, in demonstrations, parades, and protests which create tensions and threaten violence and threaten lives.

We face, therefore, a moral crisis as a country and as a people. It cannot be met by repressive police action. It cannot be left to increased demonstrations in the streets. It cannot be quieted by token moves or talk. It is a time to act in the Congress, in your State and local legislative body and, above all, in all of our daily lives.

It is not enough to pin the blame on others, to say this is a problem of one section of the country or another, or deplore the fact that we face. A great change is at hand, and our task, our obligation, is to make that revolution, that change, peaceful and constructive for all.

Those who do nothing are inviting shame as well as violence. Those who act boldly are recognizing right as well as reality.

Next week I shall ask the Congress of the United States to act, to make a commitment it has not fully made in this century to the proposition that race has no place in American life or law. The Federal judiciary has upheld that proposition in a series of forthright cases. The executive branch has adopted that proposition in the conduct of its affairs, including the employment of Federal personnel, the use of Federal facilities, and the sale of federally financed housing.

But there are other necessary measures which only the Congress can provide, and they must be provided at this session. The old code of equity law under which we live commands for every wrong a remedy, but in too many communities, in too many parts of the country, wrongs are inflicted on Negro citizens and there are no remedies at law. Unless the Congress acts, their only remedy is in the street.

I am, therefore, asking the Congress to enact legislation giving all Americans the right to be served in facilities which are open to the public—hotels, restaurants, theaters, retail stores, and similar establishments.

This seems to me to be an elementary right. Its denial is an arbitrary indignity that no American in 1963 should have to endure, but many do.

I have recently met with scores of business leaders urging them to take voluntary action to end this discrimination and I have been encouraged by their response, and in the last 2 weeks over 75 cities have seen progress made in desegregating these kinds of facilities. But many are unwilling to act alone, and for this reason, nationwide legislation is needed if we are to move this problem from the streets to the courts.

I am also asking Congress to authorize the Federal Government to participate more fully in lawsuits designed to end segregation in public education. We have succeeded in persuading many districts to de-segregate voluntarily. Dozens have admitted Negroes without violence. Today a Negro is attending a State-supported institution in every one of our 50 States, but the pace is very slow.

Too many Negro children entering segregated grade schools at the time of the Supreme Court's decision 9 years ago will enter segregated high schools this fall, having suffered a loss which can never be restored. The lack of an adequate education denies the Negro a chance to get a decent job.

The orderly implementation of the Supreme Court decision, therefore, cannot be left solely to those who may not have the economic resources to carry the legal action or who may be subject to harassment.

Other features will be also requested, including greater protection for the right to vote. But legislation, I repeat, cannot solve this problem alone. It must be solved in the homes of every American in every community across our country.

In this respect, I want to pay tribute to those citizens North and South who have been working in their communities to make life better for all. They are acting not out of a sense of legal duty but out of a sense of human decency.

Like our soldiers and sailors in all parts of the world they are meeting freedom's challenge on the firing line, and I salute them for their honor and their courage.

My fellow Americans, this is a problem which faces us all—in every city of the North as well as the South. Today there are Negroes unemployed, two or three times as many compared to whites, inadequate in education, moving into the large cities, unable to find work, young people particularly out of work without hope, denied equal rights, denied the opportunity to eat at a restaurant or lunch counter or go to a movie theater, denied the right to a decent education, denied almost today the right to attend a State university even though qualified. It seems to me that these are matters which concern us all, not merely Presidents or Congressmen or Governors, but every citizen of the United States.

This is one country. It has become one country because all of us and all the people who came here had an equal chance to develop their talents.

We cannot say to 10 percent of the population that you can't have that right; that your children can't have the chance to develop whatever talents they have; that the only way that they are going to get their rights is to go into the streets and demonstrate. I think we owe them and we owe ourselves a better country than that.

Therefore, I am asking for your help in making it easier for us to move ahead and to provide the kind of equality of treatment which we would want ourselves; to give a chance for every child to be educated to the limit of his talents.

As I have said before, not every child has an equal talent or an equal ability or an equal motivation, but they should have the equal right to develop their talent and their ability and their motivation, to make something of themselves.

We have a right to expect that the Negro community will be responsible, will uphold the law, but they have a right to expect that the law will be fair, that the Constitution will be color blind, as Justice Harlan said at the turn of the century.

This is what we are talking about and this is a matter which concerns this country and what it stands for, and in meeting it I ask the support of all our citizens.

Thank you very much.

Source: *Public Papers of the Presidents of the United States. John F. Kennedy, 1963.* Washington, D.C.: Government Printing Office, 1964, 468–471.

President Richard Nixon Answers Question about Kent State University Protest, 1970

On May 1, 1970, a student protest against the United States' continued involvement in the Vietnam War erupted on the Kent State University campus in Ohio. Tensions between the protesters and local police continued to escalate for the next few days. The mayor of the city had already declared a state of emergency and called in the state's National Guard in an attempt to bring order to the ensuing chaos. Instead, on May 4, 1970, members of the guard opened fire on the unarmed student protestors, killing four: Allison Krause, Jeffrey Miller, Sandra Scheuer, and William Schroeder. Nine other students were injured as well. Allegedly, more than two dozen members of the guard had participated in the attack, firing approx-imately 70 rounds. The nation was outraged and looked to President Richard Nixon for answers about both the incident and the United States' role in the Viet-nam War. The following document is an excerpt from a press conference in which President Nixon was asked about the tragedy. In his response, he implied that the Guard's actions might have been triggered by concern for their safety, but subse-quent investigations found no evidence that they were in any physical danger.

POLICE AND NATIONAL GUARD CONDUCT

[15.] Q. Mr. President, in the light of the Kent State University incident, could you tell us what, in your judgment, is the proper action and conduct for a police force or a National Guard force when ordered to clear the campus area and faced with a crowd throwing rocks?

THE PRESIDENT. We think we have done a rather good job here in Washing-ton in that respect. As you note, we handled the two demonstrations, October 15 and November 15 of last year, without any significant casualties, and that took a lot of doing because there were some pretty rough people involved—a few were rough; most of them were very peaceful.

I would hope that the experience that we have had in that respect could be shared by the National Guards, which, of course, are not under Federal control but under State control.

Now, what I say is not to be interpreted as a criticism in advance of my getting the facts of the National Guard at Kent State. I want to know what the facts are. I have asked for the facts. When I get them, I will have something to say about it. But I do know when you do have a situation of a crowd throwing rocks and the National Guard is called in, that there is always the chance that it will escalate into the kind of a tragedy that happened at Kent State.

If there is one thing I am personally committed to, it is this: I saw the pictures of those four youngsters in the Evening Star the day after that tragedy, and I vowed then that we were going to find methods that would be more effective to deal with these problems of violence, methods that would deal with those who would use force and violence and endanger others, but, at the same time, would not take the lives of innocent people.

Source: *Public Papers of the Presidents of the United States. Richard M. Nixon, 1970.* Washington, D.C.: Government Printing Office, 1971, 413–426.

President Gerald R. Ford Creates Emergency Immunization Program during Swine Flu Outbreak, 1976

In the spring of 1976, an outbreak of a severe strain of flu infected fewer than 20 people in Fort Dix, New Jersey. Although one person died as a result, this death led tens of millions of Americans to get vaccinated against what the government and other health agencies dubbed a looming health crisis for the country. The U.S. Department of Health, Education, and Welfare (HEW) hypothesized that the strain could be similar to that of the Spanish flu of 1918, which killed over 500,000

Americans and tens of millions of others worldwide in one of the deadliest disease outbreaks in history. This time, the HEW and some other health agencies warned that this new strain could have the potential to kill even more Americans by the fall. This hypothesis was taken with extreme seriousness by the U.S. government, and in April, President Gerald Ford piloted a National Swine Flu Immunization Program with the help of the HEW. Though vaccinations had not yet been created to treat the flu in 1918, by 1976 vaccinations had become more effective. The insistence of the government, along with President Ford's direct involvement with the vaccination campaign, both alarmed and reassured the public that the shot would curb the mortality of the flu in the country. When fall came around, the outbreak had not become inflamed, though several unintended consequences of the vaccine had. Over 400 people developed a rare neurological syndrome called Guillain-Barre syndrome in correlation to the flu shot. Some later cited the media sensationalism surrounding Swine Flu, the government vaccination program that was crafted in response, and the development of the syndrome as contributors to the emergence of today's antivaccination or "antivax" movement. The following document contains President Ford's remarks on signing the program into action on April 15, 1976.

THE MEASURE I am about to sign represents a timely response to my request for prompt congressional action to provide funds for a national influenza immunization program. This program will offer every American the opportunity to be inoculated against a swine-type influenza virus.

This virus was the cause of a pandemic in 1918 and 1919 that resulted in over half a million deaths in the United States, as well as 20 million deaths around the world. I am gratified that the Congress could act promptly prior to its Easter recess on a matter of great importance to every citizen.

This demonstrates quite clearly the Congress can confront rapidly and effectively the issues that are important to all of us. The Secretary of HEW, David Mathews, and his Department are moving ahead rapidly to implement the program objectives.

We will mobilize all the necessary national resources to ensure that we achieve our goal of making the influenza vaccine available to every American by the end of the year. And I thank the Congress, and I thank the Department of HEW for helping in this very important project.

Source: *Public Papers of the Presidents of the United States. Gerald R. Ford, 1976–77*, Book 2. Washington, D.C.: Government Printing Office, 1979, 1131.

President Jimmy Carter Addresses the Nation about Its Crisis of Confidence, 1979

Democratic President Jimmy Carter took office during a tumultuous time in the United States. After the Watergate Scandal (which concluded as President Ford pardoned President Nixon) and the exhausting Vietnam War, the country was disillusioned with both the federal government and the general state of the nation.

Economic troubles further heightened the sense that America was staggering. Unemployment rates were high, inflation continued to grow, oil shortages were creating long lines at gas stations, and U.S. industries were increasingly viewed as falling behind foreign competitors. In an effort to stir the people into action and revive their spirits, President Carter addressed the nation with a speech, later called the Crisis of Confidence Speech, in which he took a "tough love" approach to the socioeconomic issues the American people were facing. Carter believed that being truthful with the American people about how he saw the country, its challenges, and its continued potential for greatness, was of utmost importance. The following document is a transcript of the speech, which President Carter read on television in July 15, 1979.

Good Evening:

This a special night for me. Exactly three years ago, on July 15, 1976, I accepted the nomination of my party to run for President of the United States. I promised you a President who is not isolated from the people, who feels your pain, and who shares your dreams, and who draws his strength and his wisdom from you.

During the past three years I've spoken to you on many occasions about national concerns, the energy crisis, reorganizing the government, our nation's economy, and issues of war and especially peace. But over those years the subjects of the speeches, the talks, and the press conferences have become increasingly narrow, focused more and more on what the isolated world of Washington thinks is important. Gradually, you've heard more and more about what the government thinks or what the government should be doing and less and less about our nation's hopes, our dreams, and our vision of the future.

Ten days ago, I had planned to speak to you again about a very important subject—energy. For the fifth time I would have described the urgency of the problem and laid out a series of legislative recommendations to the Congress. But as I was preparing to speak, I began to ask myself the same question that I now know has been troubling many of you: Why have we not been able to get together as a nation to resolve our serious energy problem?

It's clear that the true problems of our nation are much deeper—deeper than gasoline lines or energy shortages, deeper even than inflation or recession. And I realize more than ever that as President I need your help. So, I decided to reach out and to listen to the voices of America.

I invited to Camp David people from almost every segment of our society—business and labor, teachers and preachers, governors, mayors, and private citizens. And then I left Camp David to listen to other Americans, men and women like you. It has been an extraordinary ten days, and I want to share with you what I've heard.

First of all, I got a lot of personal advice. Let me quote a few of the typical comments that I wrote down.

This from a southern governor: "Mr. President, you are not leading this nation—you're just managing the government."

"You don't see the people enough anymore."

"Some of your Cabinet members don't seem loyal. There is not enough discipline among your disciples."

"Don't talk to us about politics or the mechanics of government, but about an understanding of our common good."

"Mr. President, we're in trouble. Talk to us about blood and sweat and tears."

"If you lead, Mr. President, we will follow."

Many people talked about themselves and about the condition of our nation. This from a young woman in Pennsylvania: "I feel so far from government. I feel like ordinary people are excluded from political power."

And this from a young Chicano: "Some of us have suffered from recession all our lives."

"Some people have wasted energy, but others haven't had anything to waste."

And this from a religious leader: "No material shortage can touch the important things like God's love for us or our love for one another."

And I like this one particularly from a black woman who happens to be the mayor of a small Mississippi town: "The big shots are not the only ones who are important. Remember, you can't sell anything on Wall Street unless someone digs it up somewhere else first."

This kind of summarized a lot of other statements: "Mr. President, we are confronted with a moral and a spiritual crisis."

Several of our discussions were on energy, and I have a notebook full of comments and advice. I'll read just a few.

"We can't go on consuming forty percent more energy than we produce. When we import oil we are also importing inflation plus unemployment."

"We've got to use what we have. The Middle East has only five percent of the world's energy, but the United States has twenty-four percent."

And this is one of the most vivid statements: "Our neck is stretched over the fence and OPEC has a knife."

"There will be other cartels and other shortages. American wisdom and courage right now can set a path to follow in the future."

This was a good one: "Be bold, Mr. President. We may make mistakes, but we are ready to experiment."

And this one from a labor leader got to the heart of it: "The real issue is freedom. We must deal with the energy problem on a war footing."

And the last that I'll read: "When we enter the moral equivalent of war, Mr. President, don't issue us BB guns."

These ten days confirmed my belief in the decency and the strength and the wisdom of the American people, but it also bore out some of my long-standing concerns about our nation's underlying problems.

I know, of course, being President, that government actions and legislation can be very important. That's why I've worked hard to put my campaign promises into law, and I have to admit, with just mixed success. But after listening to the American people, I have been reminded again that all the legislation in the world can't fix what's wrong with America. So, I want to speak to you first tonight about a subject even more serious than energy or inflation. I want to talk to you right now about a fundamental threat to American democracy.

I do not mean our political and civil liberties. They will endure. And I do not refer to the outward strength of America, a nation that is at peace tonight everywhere in the world, with unmatched economic power and military might.

The threat is nearly invisible in ordinary ways.

It is a crisis of confidence.

It is a crisis that strikes at the very heart and soul and spirit of our national will. We can see this crisis in the growing doubt about the meaning of our own lives and in the loss of a unity of purpose for our nation.

The erosion of our confidence in the future is threatening to destroy the social and the political fabric of America.

The confidence that we have always had as a people is not simply some romantic dream or a proverb in a dusty book that we read just on the Fourth of July. It is the idea which founded our nation and has guided our development as a people. Confidence in the future has supported everything else—public institutions and private enterprise, our own families, and the very Constitution of the United States. Confidence has defined our course and has served as a link between generations. We've always believed in something called progress. We've always had a faith that the days of our children would be better than our own.

Our people are losing that faith, not only in government itself but in their ability as citizens to serve as the ultimate rulers and shapers of our democracy. As a people we know our past and we are proud of it. Our progress has been part of the living history of America, even the world. We always believed that we were part of a great movement of humanity itself called democracy, involved in the search for freedom; and that belief has always strengthened us in our purpose. But just as we are losing our confidence in the future, we are also beginning to close the door on our past.

In a nation that was proud of hard work, strong families, close-knit communities, and our faith in God, too many of us now tend to worship self-indulgence and consumption. Human identity is no longer defined by what one does, but by what one owns. But we've discovered that owning things and consuming things does not satisfy our longing for meaning. We've learned that piling up material goods cannot fill the emptiness of lives which have no confidence or purpose.

The symptoms of this crisis of the American spirit are all around us. For the first time in the history of our country a majority of our people believe that the next five years will be worse than the past five years. Two-thirds of our people do not even vote. The productivity of American workers is actually dropping, and the willingness of Americans to save for the future has fallen below that of all other people in the Western world.

As you know, there is a growing disrespect for government and for churches and for schools, the news media, and other institutions. This is not a message of happiness or reassurance, but it is the truth and it is a warning.

These changes did not happen overnight. They've come upon us gradually over the last generation, years that were filled with shocks and tragedy.

We were sure that ours was a nation of the ballot, not the bullet, until the murders of John Kennedy and Robert Kennedy and Martin Luther King, Jr. We were taught that our armies were always invincible and our causes were always just, only to suffer the agony of Vietnam. We respected the Presidency as a place of honor until the shock of Watergate.

We remember when the phrase "sound as a dollar" was an expression of absolute dependability, until ten years of inflation began to shrink our dollar and our savings. We believed that our nation's resources were limitless until 1973 when we had to face a growing dependence on foreign oil.

These wounds are still very deep. They have never been healed.

Looking for a way out of this crisis, our people have turned to the Federal Government and found it isolated from the mainstream of our nation's life. Washington, D.C., has become an island. The gap between our citizens and our government has never been so wide. The people are looking for honest answers, not easy answers; clear leadership, not false claims and evasiveness and politics as usual.

What you see too often in Washington and elsewhere around the country is a system of government that seems incapable of action. You see a Congress twisted and pulled in every direction by hundreds of well-financed and powerful special interests.

You see every extreme position defended to the last vote, almost to the last breath by one unyielding group or another. You often see a balanced and a fair approach that demands sacrifice, a little sacrifice from everyone, abandoned like an orphan without support and without friends.

Often you see paralysis and stagnation and drift. You don't like it, and neither do I. What can we do?

First of all, we must face the truth, and then we can change our course. We simply must have faith in each other, faith in our ability to govern ourselves, and faith in the future of this nation. Restoring that faith and that confidence to America is now the most important task we face. It is a true challenge of this generation of Americans.

One of the visitors to Camp David last week put it this way: "We've got to stop crying and start sweating, stop talking and start walking, stop cursing and start praying. The strength we need will not come from the White House, but from every house in America."

We know the strength of America. We are strong. We can regain our unity. We can regain our confidence. We are the heirs of generations who survived threats much more powerful and awesome than those that challenge us now. Our fathers and mothers were strong men and women who shaped a new society during the Great Depression, who fought world wars and who carved out a new charter of peace for the world.

We ourselves are the same Americans who just ten years ago put a man on the moon. We are the generation that dedicated our society to the pursuit of human rights and equality. And we are the generation that will win the war on the energy problem and in that process, rebuild the unity and confidence of America.

We are at a turning point in our history. There are two paths to choose. One is a path I've warned about tonight, the path that leads to fragmentation and self-interest. Down that road lies a mistaken idea of freedom, the right to grasp for ourselves some advantage over others. That path would be one of constant conflict between narrow interests ending in chaos and immobility. It is a certain route to failure.

All the traditions of our past, all the lessons of our heritage, all the promises of our future point to another path—the path of common purpose and the restoration of American values. That path leads to true freedom for our nation and ourselves. We can take the first steps down that path as we begin to solve our energy problem.

Energy will be the immediate test of our ability to unite this nation, and it can also be the standard around which we rally. On the battlefield of energy we can win for our nation a new confidence, and we can seize control again of our common destiny.

In little more than two decades we've gone from a position of energy independence to one in which almost half the oil we use comes from foreign countries, at prices that are going through the roof. Our excessive dependence on OPEC has already taken a tremendous toll on our economy and our people. This is the direct cause of the long lines which have made millions of you spend aggravating hours waiting for gasoline. It's a cause of the increased inflation and unemployment that we now face. This intolerable dependence on foreign oil threatens our economic independence and the very security of our nation.

The energy crisis is real. It is worldwide. It is a clear and present danger to our nation. These are facts and we simply must face them.

What I have to say to you now about energy is simple and vitally important.

Point one: I am tonight setting a clear goal for the energy policy of the United States. Beginning this moment, this nation will never use more foreign oil than we did in 1977—never. From now on, every new addition to our demand for energy will be met from our own production and our own conservation. The generation-long growth in our dependence on foreign oil will be stopped dead in its tracks right now and then reversed as we move through the 1980s, for I am tonight setting the further goal of cutting our dependence on foreign oil by one-half by the end of the next decade—a saving of over four and a half million barrels of imported oil per day.

Point two: To ensure that we meet these targets, I will use my presidential authority to set import quotas. I'm announcing tonight that for 1979 and 1980, I will forbid the entry into this country of one drop of foreign oil more than these goals allow. These quotas will ensure a reduction in imports even below the ambitious levels we set at the recent Tokyo summit.

Point three: To give us energy security, I am asking for the most massive peacetime commitment of funds and resources in our nation's history to develop America's own alternative sources of fuel—from coal, from oil shale, from plant products for gasohol, from unconventional gas, from the sun.

I propose the creation of an energy security corporation to lead this effort to replace two and a half million barrels of imported oil per day by 1990. The corporation will issue up to five billion dollars in energy bonds, and I especially want them to be in small denominations so average Americans can invest directly in America's energy security.

Just as a similar synthetic rubber corporation helped us win World War II, so will we mobilize American determination and ability to win the energy war. Moreover, I will soon submit legislation to Congress calling for the creation of this nation's first solar bank which will help us achieve the crucial goal of twenty percent of our energy coming from solar power by the year 2000.

These efforts will cost money, a lot of money, and that is why Congress must enact the windfall profits tax without delay. It will be money well spent. Unlike the billions of dollars that we ship to foreign countries to pay for foreign oil, these funds will be paid by Americans, to Americans. These will go to fight, not to increase, inflation and unemployment.

Point four: I'm asking Congress to mandate, to require as a matter of law, that our nation's utility companies cut their massive use of oil by fifty percent within the next decade and switch to other fuels, especially coal, our most abundant energy source.

Point five: To make absolutely certain that nothing stands in the way of achieving these goals, I will urge Congress to create an energy mobilization board which, like the War Production Board in World War II, will have the responsibility and authority to cut through the red tape, the delays, and the endless roadblocks to completing key energy projects.

We will protect our environment. But when this nation critically needs a refinery or a pipeline, we will build it.

Point six: I'm proposing a bold conservation program to involve every state, county, and city and every average American in our energy battle. This effort will permit you to build conservation into your homes and your lives at a cost you can afford.

I ask Congress to give me authority for mandatory conservation and for standby gasoline rationing. To further conserve energy, I'm proposing tonight an extra ten billion dollars over the next decade to strengthen our public transportation systems. And I'm asking you for your good and for your nation's security to take no unnecessary trips, to use carpools or public transportation whenever you can, to park your car one extra day per week, to obey the speed limit, and to set your thermostats to save fuel. Every act of energy conservation like this is more than just common sense, I tell you it is an act of patriotism.

Our nation must be fair to the poorest among us, so we will increase aid to needy Americans to cope with rising energy prices. We often think of conservation only in terms of sacrifice. In fact, it is the most painless and immediate ways of rebuilding our nation's strength. Every gallon of oil each one of us saves is a new form of production. It gives us more freedom, more confidence, that much more control over our own lives.

So, the solution of our energy crisis can also help us to conquer the crisis of the spirit in our country. It can rekindle our sense of unity, our confidence in the future, and give our nation and all of us individually a new sense of purpose.

You know we can do it. We have the natural resources. We have more oil in our shale alone than several Saudi Arabias. We have more coal than any nation on earth. We have the world's highest level of technology. We have the most skilled work force, with innovative genius, and I firmly believe that we have the national will to win this war.

I do not promise you that this struggle for freedom will be easy. I do not promise a quick way out of our nation's problems, when the truth is that the only way out is an all-out effort. What I do promise you is that I will lead our fight, and I will enforce fairness in our struggle, and I will ensure honesty. And above all, I will act.

We can manage the short-term shortages more effectively, and we will; but there are no short-term solutions to our long-range problems. There is simply no way to avoid sacrifice.

Twelve hours from now I will speak again in Kansas City, to expand and to explain further our energy program. Just as the search for solutions to our energy shortages has now led us to a new awareness of our nation's deeper problems, so our willingness to work for those solutions in energy can strengthen us to attack those deeper problems.

I will continue to travel this country, to hear the people of America. You can help me to develop a national agenda for the 1980s. I will listen; and I will act. We will act together.

These were the promises I made three years ago, and I intend to keep them.

Little by little we can and we must rebuild our confidence. We can spend until we empty our treasuries, and we may summon all the wonders of science. But we can succeed only if we tap our greatest resources—America's people, America's values, and America's confidence.

I have seen the strength of America in the inexhaustible resources of our people. In the days to come, let us renew that strength in the struggle for an energy-secure nation.

In closing, let me say this: I will do my best, but I will not do it alone. Let your voice be heard. Whenever you have a chance, say something good about our country. With God's help and for the sake of our nation, it is time for us to join hands in America. Let us commit ourselves together to a rebirth of the American spirit. Working together with our common faith we cannot fail.

Thank you and good night.

Source: *Public Papers of the Presidents of the United States: Jimmy Carter, 1979, Book 2.* Washington, D.C.: Government Printing Office, 1980, 1235–1241.

President Ronald Reagan Fires Air Traffic Controllers on Strike, 1981

On August 3, 1981, air traffic controllers and members of the Professional Air Traffic Controllers Organization (PATCO) went on strike when the Federal Aviation Administration (FAA) refused to agree to a proposed set of workplace changes for workers, including increased wages and shorter work weeks. In total, the union negotiated for close to an $800 million deal, and when the FAA countered with less than $50 million in extra funds, workers decided to take a stand. Over 10,000 workers walked out, forcing the cancellation of thousands of flights and disrupting the entire national economy. President Ronald Reagan responded by giving the workers an ultimatum: return to work by August 5 or be fired with a lifetime ban on their rehire. This was enough of a threat for a few thousand strikers, *who indeed returned to their posts. Most remained out on strike, however. When August 5 arrived, President Reagan kept his word and fired those who had not yet returned to work. Though the strike was illegal due to previous precedents, and President Reagan was allowed by law to intervene in labor disputes when neces-sary, his use of executive power in this case was very controversial. PATCO, which had endorsed President Reagan's campaign the year before, was decerti-fied by the FAA by October, and the government began to accept new hires by the end of the year. The entire episode is frequently mentioned as a landmark in the decline of American labor unions in the second half of the twentieth century. The following document is Reagan's December 9, 1981, statement on the federal employment status of fired air traffic controllers.*

For the past 4 1/2 months we have kept the airways safe and the Nation's air traffic moving despite a strike by members of the Professional Air Traffic Control-lers Organization.

We faced a choice last August: concede to the demands of a union engaged in an illegal strike—or dismiss the controllers who violated their oath and walked off their jobs, and keep the airways operating with the resources available to us.

We made the only choice we could. While we regret the loss of an experienced work force, we have an even greater commitment to the people of America to uphold the principles on which this country is built—principles of law, due pro-cess, and respect for the public trust.

Those principles have been honored, and our commitment to them remains firm. But at the same time there is another principle we honor in America—the tradition that individuals deserve to be treated with compassion. In that spirit, I am today extending to the air traffic controllers discharged because of their actions in striking against the Federal Government, an opportunity to reapply for Federal employment, in departments and agencies other than the Federal Aviation Administration. I do not believe that those who forfeited their jobs as controllers should be foreclosed from other Federal employment. I am sure that many of those who were misled or badly advised regret their action and would welcome an opportunity to return to Federal service.

So, today I am issuing this directive to the Office of Personnel Management.

First, when the Office of Personnel Management receives applications for Fed-eral employment from former FAA controllers terminated by their strike action, it will apply the same suitability standards as it applies to all other candidates for jobs with the Federal Government. This means that each application will be con-sidered fairly and on a case-by-case basis.

Second, because returning the striking controllers to their former positions would adversely affect operational efficiency, damage morale, and perhaps impair safety, the former controllers will be eligible for employment consideration in any Federal agency except the Federal Aviation Administration.

I realize that these conditions prevent the ex-controllers from returning to their former jobs. But in considering an applicant for a position of public responsibility, we must take into account not only the ability to perform that job but the effect that his or her employment may have on others within the agency. This is particularly true where the effectiveness of the nation's air traffic control system and the safety of the airways are at stake.

Source: *Public Papers of the Presidents of the United States: Ronald Reagan, 1981.* Washington, D.C.: Government Printing Office, 1982, 1148–1149.

President Ronald Reagan Acknowledges AIDS Crisis, 1985

At the beginning of Ronald Reagan's tenure as president, the diagnosis of Acquired Immunodeficiency Syndrome (AIDS) had not been established. It wasn't until the fall of 1982, when the Center for Disease Control (CDC) used the term "AIDS" in a report, that an initial diagnosis of the disease was reached. Due to the rapid proliferation of AIDS in such a short span of time, lawmakers began to introduce bills to allocate research funding for the disease, but much of the funding was not approved fast enough to make a great impact. Meanwhile, Reagan and many other public officials and lawmakers refrained from making public remarks about the disease, as AIDS was understood to be most common among gay men (who in the 1980s did not have nearly the same level of public acceptance of their sexual orientation as they do in the 2010s). Despite many activists' efforts to normalize and care for patients with AIDS across the United States and the world, President Reagan did not speak the term "AIDS" until a September 17, 1985, presidential news conference. In the following excerpt, a reporter questions the federal funding set aside for AIDS research.

Q. Mr. President, the Nation's best-known AIDS scientist says the time has come now to boost existing research into what he called a minor moon shot program to attack this AIDS epidemic that has struck fear into the Nation's health workers and even its schoolchildren. Would you support a massive government research program against AIDS like the one that President Nixon launched against cancer?

The President. I have been supporting it for more than 4 years now. It's been one of the top priorities with us, and over the last 4 years, and including what we have in the budget for '86, it will amount to over a half a billion dollars that we have provided for research on AIDS in addition to what I'm sure other medical groups are doing. And we have $100 million in the budget this year; it'll be 126 million next year. So, this is a top priority with us. Yes, there's no question about the seriousness of this and the need to find an answer.

Q. If I could follow up, sir. The scientist who talked about this, who does work for the Government, is in the National Cancer Institute. He was referring to your program and the increase that you proposed as being not nearly enough at this stage to go forward and really attack the problem.

The President. I think with our budgetary constraints and all, it seems to me that $126 million in a single year for research has got to be something of a vital contribution.

Source: *Public Papers of the Presidents of the United States. Ronald Reagan, 1985, Book 2.* Washington, D.C.: Government Printing Office, 1988, 1103–1110.

President Bill Clinton Remembers Oklahoma City Bombing Victims, 1995

On April 19, 1995, 168 people, including 19 children, died in a domestic terrorist attack of the Alfred P. Murrah Federal Building in Oklahoma City, Oklahoma. The building collapsed when a truck full of explosives was detonated outside. The attack was orchestrated by an ex-army soldier named Timothy McVeigh, who was arrested within hours of the explosion. The Federal Bureau of Investigation (FBI) later discovered, after launching an enormous investigation into the attack, that McVeigh had been assisted by a few coconspirators. McVeigh was believed to have extremist ideologies such as those of the Patriot Movement, and he planned the bombing to take revenge on the federal government for its handling of the Waco siege in 1993. McVeigh was executed via lethal injection in 2001, the first federal execution in almost four decades. The Oklahoma City bombing was the deadliest terror attack ever to take place on U.S. soil at the time. President Bill Clinton traveled to Oklahoma City to give remarks at a memorial service for the victims held on April 23. Following is the president's statement at the service.

Thank you very much. Governor Keating and Mrs. Keating, Reverend Graham, to the families of those who have been lost and wounded, to the people of Oklahoma City who have endured so much, and the people of this wonderful State, to all of you who are here as our fellow Americans: I am honored to be here today to represent the American people. But I have to tell you that Hillary and I also come as parents, as husband and wife, as people who were your neighbors for some of the best years of our lives.

Today our Nation joins with you in grief. We mourn with you. We share your hope against hope that some may still survive. We thank all those who have worked so heroically to save lives and to solve this crime, those here in Oklahoma and those who are all across this great land and many who left their own lives to come here to work hand in hand with you.

We pledge to do all we can to help you heal the injured, to rebuild this city, and to bring to justice those who did this evil.

This terrible sin took the lives of our American family: innocent children, in that building only because their parents were trying to be good parents as well as good workers; citizens in the building going about their daily business; and many there who served the rest of us, who worked to help the elderly and the disabled, who worked to support our farmers and our veterans, who worked to enforce our laws and to protect us. Let us say clearly, they served us well, and we are grateful. But for so many of you they were also neighbors and friends. You saw them at church or the PTA meetings, at the civic clubs, at the ball park. You know them in ways that all the rest of America could not.

And to all the members of the families here present who have suffered loss, though we share your grief, your pain is unimaginable, and we know that. We cannot undo it. That is God's work.

Our words seem small beside the loss you have endured. But I found a few I wanted to share today. I've received a lot of letters in these last terrible days. One stood out because it came from a young widow and a mother of three whose own husband was murdered with over 200 other Americans when Pan Am 103 was shot down. Here is what that woman said I should say to you today: "The anger you feel is valid, but you must not allow yourselves to be consumed by it. The hurt you feel must not be allowed to turn into hate but instead into the search for justice. The loss you feel must not paralyze your own lives. Instead, you must try to pay tribute to your loved ones by continuing to do all the things they left undone, thus ensuring they did not die in vain." Wise words from one who also knows.

You have lost too much, but you have not lost everything. And you have certainly not lost America, for we will stand with you for as many tomorrows as it takes.

If ever we needed evidence of that, I could only recall the words of Governor and Mrs. Keating. If anybody thinks that Americans are mostly mean and selfish, they ought to come to Oklahoma. If anybody thinks Americans have lost the capacity for love and caring and courage, they ought to come to Oklahoma.

To all my fellow Americans beyond this hall, I say, one thing we owe those who have sacrificed is the duty to purge ourselves of the dark forces which gave rise to this evil. They are forces that threaten our common peace, our freedom, our way of life.

Let us teach our children that the God of comfort is also the God of righteousness. Those who trouble their own house will inherit the wind. Justice will prevail.

Let us let our own children know that we will stand against the forces of fear. When there is talk of hatred, let us stand up and talk against it. When there is talk of violence, let us stand up and talk against it. In the face of death, let us honor life. As St. Paul admonished us, let us not be overcome by evil but overcome evil with good.

Yesterday Hillary and I had the privilege of speaking with some children of other Federal employees, children like those who were lost here. And one little girl said something we will never forget. She said we should all plant a tree in memory of the children. So this morning before we got on the plane to come here, at the White House, we planted that tree in honor of the children of Oklahoma. It was a dogwood with its wonderful spring flower and its deep, enduring roots. It embodies the lesson of the Psalms that the life of a good person is like a tree whose leaf does not wither.

My fellow Americans, a tree takes a long time to grow, and wounds take a long time to heal. But we must begin. Those who are lost now belong to God. Some day we will be with them. But until that happens, their legacy must be our lives.

Thank you all, and God bless you.

Source: *Public Papers of the Presidents of the United States. William J. Clinton: 1995, Book 1.* Washington, D.C.: Government Printing Office, 1996, 573–574.

President Bill Clinton Calls for Gun Control Legislation following Columbine Shooting, 1999

On April 20, 1999, two students open fired at their school, Columbine High School, in Littleton, Colorado, and killed 13 people—12 students and a teacher—before committing suicide. The students had first planted time bombs in the school cafeteria, which failed to detonate, before they started shooting. At the time, the shooting was the worst of its kind, and it instigated debate and activism about gun control across the United States. Before the shooting, Bill Clinton had been a proponent of gun control, and he passed two major pieces of legislation, the Brady Bill in 1993 and the Federal Assault Weapons Ban in 1994, which sought background checks and limitations to certain people and purchases. In the following document, President Clinton remarks on the shooting on April 30, 1999, and outlines new measures he will take to secure schools nationwide. Violent images on television or in video games, drugs, and poor parental supervision were often blamed for violence in minors at the time, and President Clinton intended to address those issues in his proposals as well. There is also mention of expanding mental health care for children. Yet when the new gun control bill was proposed just weeks after the shooting, it was defeated in the House by a landslide, which prompted further conversation about the role of the National Rifle Association (NRA) and its lobbying efforts in Congress.

Ladies and gentlemen, in the last several days, like most Americans, I have spent an enormous amount of time following the events in Colorado, talking to family and friends and others. And I have some thoughts on that that I want to share with you today.

Let me begin by saying we got some more good news today on the economic front, with the word that our economy expanded by 4.5 percent in the first quarter of this year. This news provides both more evidence that we should stick with our economic strategy and also is a worthwhile reminder that for all the challenges we face at home and abroad, we are indeed a fortunate people. We are strong enough to meet those challenges.

Over the past 10 days our whole Nation has been united in grief with the people of Littleton, Colorado. We have also been profoundly moved by the courage, the common sense, and the fundamental goodness of Littleton students, teachers, parents, and public servants as they have spoken to us of the tragic events there. I have listened carefully to what they have said and to other young people and parents who have been on the townhall meetings and those whom I have met personally.

We should recognize the simple truth that there is no simple, single answer. We should not be fighting about who takes the blame. Instead, we should all be looking for ways to take responsibility, and we should be doing that together.

As we have united in grief, now we should unite in action. If we ask the right question, "What can we do to give your children safe, whole childhoods?" then there will be answers for parents and children, for teachers, communities, and for those who influence the lives and the environment in which our children live, including those of us in government, religious leaders, the entertainment and Internet communities, those who produce explosives and weapons, and those who use them lawfully.

I am inviting representatives of all these groups to come to the White House on May 10th for a strategy session on children, violence, and responsibility. The First Lady, the Vice President, and Mrs. Gore, all of whom have worked for years to give our children the childhoods they deserve, will join me. I ask everyone to come to this meeting with ideas about how we can move forward together.

As Hillary said yesterday, we need nothing less than a grassroots effort to protect our children and turn them away from violence. If citizens, parents and children alike, working together in their communities, can reduce teen pregnancy, reduce drunk driving, make seatbelt use nearly universal, then working together, we can protect our children.

I want to briefly set out a framework for how this challenge can best be addressed. The push and pull of modern life adds incalculable new burdens to the work of parents. We must strive to find ways to bring parents and children together more, to get parents more involved with their children's lives, to get negative influences and guns out of the lives of our children, and to give families the tools to meet these challenges.

First, we must help parents to pass on their values to their children in the face of a blizzard of popular communications that too often undermine those values. For young people who are particularly vulnerable and isolated, the violent video games they play can seem more real than conversations at home or lessons at school. We've been working to give parents stronger tools to protect their children, and we must do more.

The V-chip will be included in half the new televisions sold this year. And together with the voluntary rating system adopted by broadcasters, it will give parents a new ability to screen the images their children see. Meanwhile, we've launched the most ambitious media plan ever to educate our children about the dangers of drugs.

The Vice President and Internet service providers have given parents the ability to block access to violent or otherwise inappropriate websites. The Vice President will continue to work with industry to find ways to help parents guide their children through cyberspace, and we'll have more to say on that in the days ahead.

We have worked to give our parents the tools to protect children from violence and to take guns out of the hands of children. The policy of zero tolerance for guns in schools led to 6,000 expulsions or suspensions in the last year alone.

This week I proposed new measures to keep guns away from criminals and children; requiring background checks for buying guns at gun shows, as they are required at gun stores now, and background checks for the purchase of explosives; banning handgun ownership for people under 21; and restoring the Brady bill's cooling off period; and closing the loopholes in the assault weapons law.

Even on these contentious issues, I believe we can reach across party lines and find common ground. I hope that sportsmen, gun manufacturers, and lawmakers of all parties will see these steps for what they are, commonsense measures to promote the common good. We all love our children. I respect the rights of hunters and sportsmen. Let's bury the hatchet and build a future for our children together.

We must help parents fulfill their most important responsibilities. We all say we want parents to talk to their children more, but we all know that too many families have too little time even to have dinner together.

Because parents too often have too little time, we've passed the Family and Medical Leave Act, and we're working to expand it. Because too many children leave school at 3, with nowhere to go and no adult to talk to, we've giving a quarter-million kids access to after-school and summer school programs, and we're working to triple that number. Because many parents need help in recognizing the signs of illness in their children, we're working to expand access to mental health care for children of all ages. Next month, Mrs. Gore will host the first White House Conference on Mental Health. We are also working to expand counseling, mentoring, and mental health services in our schools.

Most important of all, and perhaps most difficult, parents must be more active participants in their children's lives. It is not for us to pass judgment on how those two young men in Colorado descended into darkness. We may never know what can be or even what could have been done. But this should be a wake-up call for all parents. We can never take our children for granted. We must never let the lines of communication, no matter how frayed, be broken altogether. Our children need us, even if they don't know it sometimes.

This terrible tragedy must not be an occasion for silence. This weekend I ask all parents, if they have not already done so, to sit down and talk to their children about what happened at Littleton and what is happening in their schools and their lives.

If we are not careful, when our children move through their teen years and begin to create their own separate lives, the bustle and burden of our daily lives can cause families to drift too far apart, to ignore the still-strong needs of children for genuine concern and guidance and honest conversation. This is sometimes the hardest thing of all, but it is vital, and lives depend on it.

Finally, I ask students to do more to help each other. Next week, if you have not already done so, I ask every student in America to look for someone at school who is not in your group. You know, there have always been different crowds in schools, and there always will be. This, too, is an inevitable part of growing up and finding your own path through life. But it should not be an occasion for disrespect or hostility in our schools. After all, our children are all on the same journey, even if they're trying to chart different paths. And this can be profoundly important in building a safer future.

The spirit of America can triumph in this troubling moment, and I am convinced it will. But we must build the energy and will and passion of our country and the fundamental goodness of our people into a grassroots movement to turn away from violence and to give all our children the safe and wholesome childhoods they richly deserve.

Thank you very much.

Source: *Public Papers of the Presidents of the United States. William J. Clinton: 1999, Book 1.* Washington, D.C.: Government Printing Office, 2000–2001, 586–588.

President Barack Obama Gives Remarks at Sandy Hook Interfaith Prayer Vigil, 2012

On December 14, 2012, 20 children and six adults were killed at Sandy Hook Elementary School in Newtown, Connecticut. The attack was one of the worst mass shootings in United States history in both the toll of those killed and in its nature, as most victims were children between the ages of six and seven. Before the attack, the shooter had killed his mother in her home with the weapons that she legally purchased, including a semiautomatic gun, and took those weapons to the school. In addition to the grief and heartache that both the families and the nation endured in the aftermath of the attack, many were angry that there were not gun control laws in place that outlawed semiautomatic weapons or high-capacity magazines, as well as the bulk purchasing of ammunition. The outrage sparked a fierce political debate between those who believed such laws would inhibit their Second Amendment rights and those who believed gun control laws could prevent tragedies such as school shootings. Meanwhile, President Barack Obama had the task of both consoling those who were grieving and mourning and considering how to move the nation forward. It is not often that presidents cry in public in the face of a crisis, but in the following speech, given by President Obama at the Sandy Hook Interfaith Prayer Vigil in Newtown, on December 16, 2012, the president was tearful as he spoke. Gun control legislation was indeed drafted and presented as the Assault Weapons Ban of 2013, but it was defeated in Congress.

Thank you, Governor. To all the families, first-responders; to the community of Newtown, clergy, guests—Scripture tells us: "Do not lose heart. Though outwardly we are wasting away, inwardly we are being renewed day by day. For our light and momentary troubles are achieving for us an eternal glory that far outweighs them all. So we fix our eyes not on what is seen, but on what is unseen, since what is seen is temporary, but what is unseen is eternal. For we know that if the earthly tent we live in is destroyed, we have a building from God, an eternal house in heaven, not built by human hands."

We gather here in memory of 20 beautiful children and 6 remarkable adults. They lost their lives in a school that could have been any school, in a quiet town full of good and decent people that could be any town in America.

Here in Newtown, I come to offer the love and prayers of a nation. I am very mindful that mere words cannot match the depths of your sorrow, nor can they heal your wounded hearts. I can only hope it helps for you to know that you're not alone in your grief; that our world too has been torn apart; that all across this land of ours, we have wept with you and we've pulled our children tight. And you must know that whatever measure of comfort we can provide, we will provide; whatever portion of sadness that we can share with you to ease this heavy load, we will gladly bear it. Newtown, you are not alone.

As these difficult days have unfolded, you've also inspired us with stories of strength and resolve and sacrifice. We know that when danger arrived in the halls of Sandy Hook Elementary, the school's staff did not flinch; they did not hesitate. Dawn Hochsprung and Mary Sherlach, Vicki Soto, Lauren Rousseau, Rachel D'Avino, and Anne Marie Murphy—they responded as we all hope we might respond in such terrifying circumstances: with courage and with love, giving their lives to protect the children in their care.

We know that there were other teachers who barricaded themselves inside classrooms and kept steady through it all and reassured their students by saying: "Wait for the good guys; they're coming." "Show me your smile."

And we know that good guys came: the first-responders who raced to the scene, helping to guide those in harm's way to safety and comfort those in need, holding at bay their own shock and their own trauma because they had a job to do and others needed them more.

And then, there were the scenes of the schoolchildren, helping one another, holding each other, dutifully following instructions in the way that young children sometimes do, one child even trying to encourage a grownup by saying: "I know karate. So it's okay. I'll lead the way out." [*Laughter*]

As a community, you've inspired us, Newtown. In the face of indescribable violence, in the face of unconscionable evil, you've looked out for each other, and you've cared for one another, and you've loved one another. This is how Newtown will be remembered. And with time and God's grace, that love will see you through.

But we as a nation, we are left with some hard questions. Someone once described the joy and anxiety of parenthood as the equivalent of having your heart outside of your body all the time, walking around. With their very first cry, this most precious, vital part of ourselves—our child—is suddenly exposed to the world, to possible mishap or malice. And every parent knows there is nothing we will not do to shield our children from harm. And yet we also know that with that child's very first step and each step after that, they're separating from us; that we won't—that we can't—always be there for them. They'll suffer sickness and setbacks and broken hearts and disappointments. And we learn that our most important job is to give them what they need to become self-reliant and capable and resilient, ready to face the world without fear.

And we know we can't do this by ourselves. It comes as a shock at a certain point where you realize, no matter how much you love these kids, you can't do it by yourself; that this job of keeping our children safe and teaching them well is something we can only do together, with the help of friends and neighbors, the help of a community, and the help of a nation. And in that way, we come to realize that we bear a responsibility for every child because we're counting on everybody else to help look after ours; that we're all parents; that they're all our children.

This is our first task: caring for our children. It's our first job. If we don't get that right, we don't get anything right. That's how, as a society, we will be judged.

And by that measure, can we truly say, as a nation, that we're meeting our obligations? Can we honestly say that we're doing enough to keep our children—all of them—safe from harm? Can we claim, as a nation, that we're all together there, letting them know that they are loved and teaching them to love in return? Can we say that we're truly doing enough to give all the children of this country the chance they deserve to live out their lives in happiness and with purpose?

I've been reflecting on this the last few days, and if we're honest with ourselves, the answer is no. We're not doing enough. And we will have to change.

Since I've been President, this is the fourth time we have come together to comfort a grieving community torn apart by mass shootings, the fourth time we've hugged survivors, the fourth time we've consoled the families of victims. And in between, there have been an endless series of deadly shootings across the country, almost daily reports of victims, many of them children, in small towns and big cities all across America, victims whose—much of the time, their only fault was being in the wrong place at the wrong time.

We can't tolerate this anymore. These tragedies must end. And to end them, we must change. We will be told that the causes of such violence are complex, and that is true. No single law—no set of laws—can eliminate evil from the world or prevent every senseless act of violence in our society.

But that can't be an excuse for inaction. Surely, we can do better than this. If there is even one step we can take to save another child or another parent or another town from the grief that's visited Tucson and Aurora and Oak Creek and Newtown and communities from Columbine to Blacksburg before that, then surely we have an obligation to try.

In the coming weeks, I will use whatever power this office holds to engage my fellow citizens—from law enforcement to mental health professionals to parents and educators—in an effort aimed at preventing more tragedies like this. Because what choice do we have? We can't accept events like this as routine. Are we really prepared to say that we're powerless in the face of such carnage, that the politics are too hard? Are we prepared to say that such violence visited on our children year after year after year is somehow the price of our freedom?

All the world's religions—so many of them represented here today—start with a simple question: Why are we here? What gives our life meaning? What gives our acts purpose? We know our time on this Earth is fleeting. We know that we will each have our share of pleasure and pain; that even after we chase after some earthly goal, whether it's wealth or power or fame or just simple comfort, we will in some fashion fall short of what we had hoped. We know that no matter how good our intentions, we'll all stumble sometimes, in some way. We'll make mistakes; we will experience hardships. And even when we're trying to do the right thing, we know that much of our time will be spent groping through the darkness, so often unable to discern God's heavenly plans.

There's only one thing we can be sure of, and that is the love that we have: for our children, for our families, for each other. The warmth of a small child's embrace: That is true. The memories we have of them, the joy that they bring, the wonder we see through their eyes, that fierce and boundless love we feel for them, a love that takes us out of ourselves and binds us to something larger—we know that's what matters. We know we're always doing right when we're taking care of them, when we're teaching them well, when we're showing acts of kindness. We don't go wrong when we do that.

That's what we can be sure of. And that's what you, the people of Newtown, have reminded us. That's how you've inspired us. You remind us what matters. And that's what should drive us forward in everything we do, for as long as God sees fit to keep us on this Earth.

"Let the little children come to me," Jesus said, "and do not hinder them—for to such belongs the Kingdom of Heaven."

Charlotte. Daniel. Olivia. Josephine. Ana. Dylan. Madeleine. Catherine. Chase. Jesse. James. Grace. Emilie. Jack. Noah. Caroline. Jessica. Benjamin. Avielle. Allison.

God has called them all home. For those of us who remain, let us find the strength to carry on and make our country worthy of their memory.

May God bless and keep those we've lost in His heavenly place. May He grace those we still have with His holy comfort. And may He bless and watch over this community and the United States of America.

Source: *Public Papers of the Presidents of the United States. Barack Obama: 2012, Book 2.* Washington, D.C.: Government Printing Office, 2017, 1857–1860.

President Barack Obama Gives Update on the U.S. Response to Ebola Outbreak, 2014

The Ebola virus (EVD) is a deadly disease with the ability to spread rapidly. When an outbreak occurred in Guinea in December 2013, 49 cases had been confirmed, and 29 people had died of EVD in the country by March 2014. The disease quickly infiltrated neighboring countries and more populous areas, which made its containment and tracking difficult. By the fall of 2015, the World Health Organization (WHO) declared a Public Health Emergency of International Concern (PHEIC) which escalated the status of the outbreak. Soon after, the first patient in the United States was diagnosed with EVD after traveling home from West Africa and died about a week later. This case alarmed the U.S. public. Two of the patient's health care providers contracted the contagious disease soon after treatment, though they recovered. This trend would continue overseas, as health care providers were increasingly infected as a result of working with EVD patients. The Center for Disease Control (CDC) and many other medical agencies made an enormous effort to provide aid and education to those areas most affected, and the virus was contained everywhere in 2016. All in all, over 11,000 people died due to the virus, mostly in Guinea, Liberia, and Sierra Leone. President Barack Obama organized treatment, burials, and an outreach and education effort in West Africa to ensure that aid was present, including deploying a Disaster Assistance Response Team (DART). He also implemented international travel coordination to ensure that anyone coming or going from West Africa, including at least 10,000 health care workers, were screened before returning home. The following document outlines President Obama's response to the epidemic during a news conference on October 28, 2014.

The President. Good afternoon, everybody. I just want to offer a quick update on Ebola and a number of the issues that have been raised.

We know that the best way to protect Americans ultimately is going to stop this outbreak at the source. And I just had the privilege of speaking with some of the men and women who are working to do just that: our Disaster Assistance Response Team on the ground in West Africa.

First and foremost, I thanked them for their incredible dedication and compassion. These are the folks that, from the minute that we saw this Ebola outbreak growing larger than we had seen traditionally, were deployed, were on the ground, and were helping to coordinate the countries where the outbreak is happening to make sure that the response was effective.

And it's typical of what America does best: When others are in trouble, when disease or disaster strikes, Americans help. And no other nation is doing as much to make sure that we contain and ultimately eliminate this outbreak than America.

We deployed this DART team to West Africa back in early August. They're now the strategic and operational backbone of America's response. They've increased the number of Ebola treatment units and burial teams. They've expanded the pipeline of medical personnel and equipment and supplies. They've launched an aggressive education campaign in country. The bottom line is, is that they're doing what it takes to make sure that medical personnel and health care workers from all countries have what they need to get the job done.

And the good news is, is that it's starting to have an impact. Based on the conversations that I had today with them, they're starting to see some progress in Liberia, and the infrastructure is beginning to get built out. That's thanks to the incredible work and dedication of folks from the United States who are leading the way in helping Liberia, Guinea, and Sierra Leone.

And it's critical that we maintain that leadership. The truth is that we're going to have to stay vigilant here at home until we stop the epidemic at its source. And for that, we're going to need to make sure that our doctors and our health care professionals here in the United States are properly trained and informed and that they are coordinated if and when an Ebola case crops up here in the United States. But what's also critically important is making sure that all the talent, skill, compassion, professionalism, dedication, and experience of our folks here can be deployed to help those countries deal with this outbreak at the source.

And that's why yesterday the CDC announced that we're going to have new monitoring and movement guidance that is sensible, based in science, and tailored to the unique circumstances of each health worker that may be returning from one of these countries after they have provided the kind of help that they need. In fact, tomorrow I'm going to have a chance to meet with doctors and public health workers who have already returned from fighting this disease in West Africa or who are about to go, not only to say thank you to them and give them encouragement, but to make sure that we're getting input from them based on the science, based on the facts, based on experience, about how the battle to deal with Ebola is going and how our policies can support the incredible heroism that they are showing.

So we don't want to discourage our health care workers from going to the frontlines and dealing with this in an effective way. Our medical teams here are getting better and better prepared and trained for the possibility of an isolated Ebola case here in the United States. But in the meantime, we've got to make sure that we continue to provide the support of health workers who are going overseas to deal with the disease where it really has been raging.

It's also important for the American people to remind themselves that only two people so far have contracted Ebola on American soil: the two Dallas nurses who treated a patient who contracted it in West Africa. Today, both of them are disease-free. I met with one of them, Nina Pham, last week, and she is doing wonderfully. And I just had a chance to get off the phone with Amber Vinson, who is on her way back home and also, as many of you saw in her press statement today, is doing well also.

Of the seven Americans treated for Ebola so far, all have survived. Right now the only American still undergoing treatment is Dr. Craig Spencer, who contracted the disease abroad while working to protect others. And we should be saluting his service. And we are focused on getting him the best care possible as well. And our thoughts and prayers are with him.

Meanwhile, the West African nations of Senegal and Nigeria have now been declared Ebola-free. That's in part because of outstanding work led in many cases by Americans working in coordination with those countries to make sure that we did not see an outbreak there.

So the point is, is that this disease can be contained. It will be defeated. Progress is possible. But we're going to have to stay vigilant, and we've got to make sure that we're working together. We have to keep leading the global response. America cannot look like it is shying away, because other people are watching what we do, and if we don't have a robust international response in West Africa, then we are actually endangering ourselves here back home. In order to do that, we've got to make sure that those workers who are willing and able and dedicated to go over there in a really tough job, that they're applauded, thanked, and supported. That should be our priority.

And we can make sure that when they come back, they are being monitored in a prudent fashion. But we want to make sure that we understand that they are doing God's work over there. And they're doing that to keep us safe. And I want to make sure that every policy we put in place is supportive of their efforts, because if they are successful, then we're not going to have to worry about Ebola here at home.

America, in the end, is not defined by fear. That's not who we are. America is defined by possibility. And when we see a problem and we see a challenge, then we fix it. We don't just react based on our fears. We react based on facts and judgment and making smart decisions. That's how we have built this country and sustained this country and protected this country. That's why America has defined progress, because we're not afraid when challenges come up.

Thanks to our military, our dedicated medical and health care professionals, the men and women who I spoke to today in West Africa, that leadership and progress continues. And we're going to keep on making progress, and we are going to solve this particular problem just like we've solved every other problem.

But it starts with us having the confidence and understanding that, as challenging as this may be, this is something that will get fixed, in large part because we've got extraordinary Americans with experience, talent, dedication, who are willing to put themselves on the front lines to get things done.

I'll have more about—more to say about this tomorrow when I have those workers here. But I just wanted to emphasize how proud I am of the people who are already involved in this effort and how confident I am after speaking to them that in fact we're going to get this problem under control.

All right? Thank you.

Source: *Remarks by the President on Ebola, October 28, 2014.* White House. Available online at https://obamawhitehouse.archives.gov/the-press-office/2014/10 /28/remarks-president-ebola.

President Barack Obama Remembers Michael Brown and Discusses Race, Class, and Criminal Justice Reform in the United States, 2015

On August 8, 2014, unarmed black teenager Michael Brown was shot and killed by a white police officer, Darren Wilson, in his neighborhood of Ferguson, Missouri. Witness descriptions of the confrontation differed from those presented by the officers, which emphasized the divide between officers and residents in the area, and heightened the tension and confusion that followed the shooting. Residents of Ferguson stated that racial biases against black people had been displayed by police officers and the justice system for years. In a Justice Department Investigation that looked into police practices in Ferguson, the investigation confirmed the discriminatory charges against the police by residents. The death of Michael Brown ignited outrage in the suburb as well as across the nation, where Brown came to represent the disproportionate amount of black men killed by police officers in the United States. Rioting and protests ensued and further deteriorated relations between law enforcement officers and African Americans. When Wilson was not indicted on civil rights charges by a grand jury of nine white people and three black people, those protesting on behalf of Brown's death felt despair. President Barack Obama acknowledged those protesting in Ferguson and around the country and recognized the lasting effect that Brown's death would have on the country. In the following document, the president remarks, around one year after Brown's death on August 15, 2015, about what has been done to improve race relations in the United States, especially in terms of criminal justice reform.

President Barack Obama,

Hi, everybody. It's now been a year since the tragic death of Michael Brown in Ferguson, Missouri. His death—along with the events in Cleveland, Staten Island, Baltimore, Cincinnati, and other communities—sparked protests and soul searching all across our country. Over the past year, we've come to see, more clearly than ever, the frustration in many communities of color and the feeling that our laws can be applied unevenly.

After Ferguson, I said that we have to face these issues squarely. I convened a Task Force on community policing to find commonsense steps that can help us drive down crime and build up trust and cooperation between communities and police, who put their lives on the line every single day to help keep us safe. And I've met personally with rank and file officers to hear their ideas.

In May, this Task Force made up of police officers, activists, and academics proposed 59 recommendations: everything from how we can make better use of data and technology, to how we train police officers, to how law enforcement engages with our schools. And we've been working with communities across America to put these ideas into action.

Dozens of police departments are now sharing more data with the public, including on citations, stops and searches, and shootings involving law enforcement. We've brought together leaders from across the country to explore alternatives to incarceration. The Justice Department has begun pilot programs to help police use body cameras and collect data on the use of force. This fall, the Department will award more than $160 million in grants to support law enforcement and community organizations that are working to improve policing. And all across the country—from States like Illinois and Ohio, to cities like Philadelphia, Boston, and Nashville—local leaders are working to implement the Task Force recommendations in a way that works for their communities.

So we've made progress. And we'll keep at it. But let's be clear: The issues raised over the past year aren't new, and they won't be solved by policing alone. We simply can't ask our police to contain and control issues that the rest of us aren't willing to address as a society. That starts with reforming a criminal justice system that too often is a pipeline from inadequate schools to overcrowded jails, wreaking havoc on communities and families all across the country. So we need Congress to reform our Federal sentencing laws for nonviolent drug offenders. We need to keep working to help more prisoners take steps to turn their lives around so they can contribute to their communities after they've served their time.

More broadly, we need to truly invest in our children and our communities so that more young people see a better path for their lives. That means investing in early childhood education, job training, pathways to college. It means dealing honestly with issues of race, poverty, and class that leave too many communities feeling isolated and segregated from greater opportunity. It means expanding that opportunity to every American willing to work for it, no matter what ZIP Code they were born into.

Because, in the end, that's always been the promise of America. And that's what I'll keep working for every single day that I'm President. Thanks, everybody, and have a great weekend.

Source: *Weekly Address: Continuing Work to Improve Community Policing. The White House.* August 15, 2015. Available online at https://obamawhitehouse .archives.gov/the-press-office/2015/08/15/weekly-address-continuing-work -improve-community-policing.

President Donald Trump Takes Executive Action to Combat Opioid Crisis, 2017

On March 29, 2017, President Donald J. Trump signed an executive order establishing the President's Commission on Combating Drug Addiction and the Opioid Crisis. In the late 1990s, opioids for pain relief were being overprescribed, as major pharmaceutical companies assured the public that such drugs were safe to use, without the risk of addiction. Soon, the drugs were being misused, and their proliferation made the illegal production of heroin and other harmful substances easier. As opioid-related deaths continued to rise, the crisis became an epidemic and spread across the United States, affected all races and ethnicities, and also affected a large range of age demographics. Over time, the socioeconomic statuses of those with opioid addictions have become less of a factor in the crisis as well. Regardless, the crisis proved to be expensive; it has cost the government hundreds of billions of dollars since it gained traction in the 2000s. In addition, more people

died to due opioid-related deaths in 2015 than ever before, and the number con-
tinued to increase thereafter. At the end of 2017, the U.S. Department of Health
and Human Services (HHS) declared a public health emergency. The HHS,
together with the commission created here, would research effective treatments to
combat the crisis. The following is the executive order that spurred an even larger
effort on behalf of the government to find a solution to the opioid epidemic.

By the authority vested in me as President by the Constitution and the laws of
the United States of America, it is hereby ordered as follows:

Section 1. Policy. It shall be the policy of the executive branch to combat the
scourge of drug abuse, addiction, and overdose (drug addiction), including opioid
abuse, addiction, and overdose (opioid crisis). This public health crisis was responsible for more than 50,000 deaths in 2015 alone, most of which involved an opioid,
and has caused families and communities across America to endure significant
pain, suffering, and financial harm.

Sec. 2. Establishment of Commission. There is established the President's Commission on Combating Drug Addiction and the Opioid Crisis (Commission).

Sec. 3. Membership of Commission. (a) The Commission shall be composed of
members designated or appointed by the President.

(b) The members of the Commission shall be selected so that membership is
fairly balanced in terms of the points of view represented and the functions to be
performed by the Commission.

(c) The President shall designate the Chair of the Commission (Chair) from
among the Commission's members.

Sec. 4. Mission of Commission. The mission of the Commission shall be to
study the scope and effectiveness of the Federal response to drug addiction and
the opioid crisis described in section 1 of this order and to make recommendations
to the President for improving that response. The Commission shall:

(a) identify and describe existing Federal funding used to combat drug
addiction and the opioid crisis;

(b) assess the availability and accessibility of drug addiction treatment services and overdose reversal throughout the country and identify areas
that are underserved;

(c) identify and report on best practices for addiction prevention, including
healthcare provider education and evaluation of prescription practices,
and the use and effectiveness of State prescription drug monitoring
programs;

(d) review the literature evaluating the effectiveness of educational messages
for youth and adults with respect to prescription and illicit opioids;

(e) identify and evaluate existing Federal programs to prevent and treat
drug addiction for their scope and effectiveness, and make recommendations for improving these programs; and

(f) make recommendations to the President for improving the Federal
response to drug addiction and the opioid crisis.

Sec. 5. Administration of Commission. (a) The Office of National Drug Control
Policy (ONDCP) shall, to the extent permitted by law, provide administrative

support for the Commission. (b) Members of the Commission shall serve without any additional compensation for their work on the Commission. Members of the Commission appointed from among private citizens of the United States, while engaged in the work of the Commission, may be allowed travel expenses, including per diem in lieu of subsistence, to the extent permitted by law for persons serving intermittently in Government service (5 U.S.C. 5701-5707), consistent with the availability of funds.

(c) Insofar as the Federal Advisory Committee Act, as amended (5 U.S.C. App.) (Act), may apply to the Commission, any functions of the President under that Act, except for those in section 6 and section 14 of that Act, shall be performed by the Director of the ONDCP, in accordance with the guidelines that have been issued by the Administrator of General Services.

Sec. 6. Funding of Commission. The ONDCP shall, to the extent permitted by law and consistent with the need for funding determined by the President, make funds appropriated to the ONDCP available to pay the costs of the activities of the Commission.

Sec. 7. Reports of Commission. Within 90 days of the date of this order, the Commission shall submit to the President a report on its interim recommendations regarding how the Federal Government can address drug addiction and the opioid crisis described in section 1 of this order, and shall submit a report containing its final findings and recommendations by October 1, 2017, unless the Chair provides written notice to the President that an extension is necessary.

Sec. 8. Termination of Commission. The Commission shall terminate 30 days after submitting its final report, unless extended by the President prior to that date.

Sec. 9. General Provisions. (a) Nothing in this order shall be construed to impair or otherwise affect:

(i) the authority granted by law to an executive department or agency, or the head thereof; or

(ii) the functions of the Director of the Office of Management and Budget relating to budgetary, administrative, or legislative proposals.

(b) This order shall be implemented consistent with applicable law and subject to the availability of appropriations.

(c) This order is not intended to, and does not, create any right or benefit, substantive or procedural, enforceable at law or in equity by any party against the United States, its departments, agencies, or entities, its officers, employees, or agents, or any other person.

Source: Executive Order 13784. Establishing the President's Commission on Combating Drug Addiction and the Opioid Crisis. 82 Federal Register 16283-16285, Document 2017-06716. March 29, 2017.

President Donald Trump's Remarks on White Supremacist Rally in Charlottesville, Virginia, 2017

On August 12, 2017, white supremacists and other neo-Nazi, alt-right groups gathered at a "Unite the Right" rally in Charlottesville, Virginia, to protest the proposed removal of a statue of Robert E. Lee, the commander of the Confederate

Army during the American Civil War. Though a Virginia law has not allowed the statue's expulsion to occur, and some proponents of maintaining the statue argued that it is important to recognize the history of slavery in the states, the intention of the Unite the Right demonstration was perhaps not to preserve the past, but rather to relive it. Before noon, Charlottesville had declared a local state of emergency. Counter-protestors formed and soon the two sides engaged. The demonstration became fatal when a white supremacist, James Alex Fields, drove his car into a crowd of counterprotestors and killed one woman, Heather Heyer, and injured tens more. Then a police helicopter, piloted by two state troopers, crashed on its way to the protest and killed them both. Many believed that Fields's attack was an act of domestic terrorism, which renewed the debate of the usage of the word. However, the situation as a whole was indicative of emboldened, alt-right ideologies. President Donald J. Trump used the social medium, Twitter, to make his initial remarks about the unfolding situation and deaths of both Heyer and the two state troopers. In his initial remarks, Trump opined that there were "very fine people on both sides," a statement that was roundly criticized for equating neo-Nazis and the counterprotesters. In the following document, the president gives subsequent verbal remarks about Charlottesville on August 14, 2017.

Thank you. I'm in Washington today to meet with my economic team about trade policy and major tax cuts and reform. We are renegotiating trade deals and making them good for the American worker. And it's about time.

Our economy is now strong. The stock market continues to hit record highs, unemployment is at a 16-year low, and businesses are more optimistic than ever before. Companies are moving back to the United States and bringing many thousands of jobs with them. We have already created over 1 million jobs since I took office.

We will be discussing economic issues in greater detail later this afternoon, but based on the events that took place over the weekend in Charlottesville, Virginia, I would like to provide the Nation with an update on the ongoing Federal response to the horrific attack and violence that was witnessed by everyone.

I just met with FBI Director Christopher Wray and Attorney General Jeff Sessions. The Department of Justice has opened a civil rights investigation into the deadly car attack that killed one innocent American and wounded 20 others. To anyone who acted criminally in this weekend's racist violence, you will be held fully accountable. Justice will be delivered.

As I said on Saturday, we condemn in the strongest possible terms this egregious display of hatred, bigotry, and violence. It has no place in America. And as I have said many times before, no matter the color of our skin, we all live under the same laws, we all salute the same great flag, and we are all made by the same almighty God. We must love each other, show affection for each other, and unite together in condemnation of hatred, bigotry, and violence. We must rediscover the bonds of love and loyalty that bring us together as Americans.

Racism is evil. And those who cause violence in its name are criminals and thugs, including the KKK, neo-Nazis, White supremacists, and other hate groups that are repugnant to everything we hold dear as Americans. We are a nation founded on the truth that all of us are created equal. We are equal in the eyes of our Creator, we are equal under the law, and we are equal under our Constitution. Those who spread violence in the name of bigotry strike at the very core of America.

Two days ago, a young American woman, Heather Heyer, was tragically killed. Her death fills us with grief, and we send her family our thoughts, our prayers, and our love. We also mourn the two Virginia State troopers who died in service to their community, their commonwealth, and their country. Troopers Jay Cullen and Berke Bates exemplify the very best of America, and our hearts go out to their families, their friends, and every member of American law enforcement.

These three fallen Americans embody the goodness and decency of our Nation. In times such as these, America has always shown its true character: responding to hate with love, division with unity, and violence with an unwavering resolve for justice.

As a candidate, I promised to restore law and order to our country, and our Federal law enforcement agencies are following through on that pledge. We will spare no resource in fighting so that every American child can grow up free from violence and fear. We will defend and protect the sacred rights of all Americans, and we will work together so that every citizen in this blessed land is free to follow their dreams in their hearts, and to express the love and joy in their souls.

Thank you, God bless you, and God bless America. Thank you very much.

Source: *Compilation of Presidential Documents. Remarks on the Situation in Charlottesville, Virginia.* August 14, 2017. DCPD-201700570. Available online at https://www.govinfo.gov/content/pkg/DCPD-201700570/html/DCPD-2017 00570.htm.

2

Economy and Livelihoods

INTRODUCTION

Recall that Article II of the Constitution grants the president enumerated powers, including the power to make treaties, grant pardons, nominate judges, appoint various public officials, and participate in the legislative process. That set of expressed powers has also been understood to authorize certain implied powers—powers necessary for the president to carry into execution the enumerated powers. The implied authority of the president to remove certain officials, for instance, has been understood to derive from the (enumerated) presidential appointment power. In addition to the office's expressed and implied powers, Article II confers on the president the authority to "take Care that the laws be faithfully executed." This suggests that by constitutional design, the president has the obligation to execute the laws passed by Congress, and by extension, Congress has an interest in providing the executive branch with the means by which to do so. This is the source of what is known as the delegated powers of the president. These are the powers that presidents have in order to fulfill congressional will with respect to specific statutes. For example, when Congress passes a law and the president signs it (or Congress overrides the president's veto), the executive branch is tasked with "faithfully executing" that law—implementing the policy. Very often, Congress cannot know with certainty how best to implement a particular measure, or have the means by which to do so. Some policy areas are highly complex and require the technical expertise of policy experts (regulating food and drug safety, for instance). Other legislation may be less complex, but the scale so large that Congress simply cannot write detailed legislation for every circumstance (the setting of rates for the interstate shipment of goods, for example). In such cases, executive branch agencies—the bureaucracy—has the responsibility to write regulatory law that "fills in the details" and implement the general provisions of legislation.

The fact that Congress can delegate its legislative power to another branch of government seems to be inconsistent with Founding Father James Madison's argument in *Federalist 47*. Madison writes that "[t]he accumulation of powers, legislative, executive, or judiciary, in the same hands, whether of one, a few or many, and whether self-appointed, or elective, may justly be pronounced the very definition of tyranny." He continues, quoting Montesquieu, from whom the Framers borrowed in developing the separation of powers: "'There can be no liberty where the legislative and executive powers are united in the same person, or body of magistrates,' . . . he did not mean that these departments ought to have no partial agency in or no control over, the acts of each other. His meaning . . . can amount to no more than this, that where the whole power of one department is exercised by the same hands which possess the whole power of another department, the fundamental principles of a free constitution are subverted."

The delegation of power also appears to run afoul of the ancient legal maxim, "A power once delegated cannot be redelegated." That legal principle, called the nondelegation doctrine, suggests that in order to maintain democratic accountability, Congress may not cede to the executive branch its rightful legislative power. The idea is that legislators, as the people's representatives, have been given power to be held in trust. If they then redelegate their legislative power to another institution, the accountability for the actions taken pursuant to that power is unclear. Are the legislators responsible? Their designees? Even if those responsible for the policies are identifiable, it is not clear how the people can hold them to account for the actions they take. If sovereignty resides with the people, and their representatives (who have been delegated the power to write law) redelegate to others in the executive branch the power to write law, the people no longer have the means to remove those individuals for failure to respond to citizens' demands. Though the principle of nondelegation is important for democratic governance and accountability, the Constitution is silent on whether Congress is permitted to delegate its powers. In fact, since the New Deal era, the principle of nondelegation has not constrained Congress from ceding its legislative power in key areas of policy.

The nondelegation doctrine, said the U.S. Supreme Court in *Touby v. U.S.* (1991), "does not prevent Congress from seeking assistance, within proper limits, from the coordinate branches. Thus, Congress does not violate the Constitution merely because it delegates in broad terms, leaving a certain degree of discretion to executive or judicial actors." But what are the "proper limits"? The Court has placed few restrictions on Congress as it delegates. Generally, and with few exceptions, the courts have allowed Congress to delegate broad authority to the executive and judicial branches if Congress does so as a means of exercising its own legislative power. That is, if Congress can legislate in a particular area of policy, it can also delegate in that area. As long as Congress "laid down by legislative act an intelligible principle to which the person or body authorized to take such action is directed to conform," the delegation of power is permissible (*J. W. Hampton Jr. and Co. v U.S.*, 1928).

This "intelligible principle" standard that the Court articulated in *Hampton* can be quite capacious, permitting very broad grants of discretion to bureaucratic agencies in the executive branch to implement laws. The enabling legislation (laws that establish agencies like the Food and Drug Administration, or the Federal Communications Commission, for instance) for many executive branch agencies and independent commissions includes broad delegations of legislative power, such as to "set just and reasonable rates, or "regulate in the public interest." Though there have been rumblings on the Court to revive the nondelegation doctrine (including former Chief Justice William Rehnquist in 1980, among others), the New Deal era was the only time the Court actually struck an act of Congress for violating the doctrine. In a series of cases in 1935 and 1936, the Court struck three impermissible delegations of legislative power, but it has not done so again since that time. As a consequence, the president's role in shaping and implementing legislation has grown apace with the broad grants of delegated power. And because Congress derives its power from enumerated, implied, amendment-enforcing, treaty-enforcing, and inherent powers, the full range of areas in which Congress may legislate (and therefore, presumably, delegate) is linked to an expansion of concurrent executive power over those areas as well. Put another way, as congressional power to regulate interstate commerce (as one example) grows, so too does the range of policy areas in which Congress may delegate, with the result that presidential control over those areas expands as well.

It is not immediately apparent, however, why Congress would willingly give up control over policy outcomes to another branch of government. Certainly, members of Congress have an interest in making good policy, taking positions on key issues of the day, and claiming credit for those policies when seeking reelection (Mayhew 1974). Therefore, delegating discretion to agencies to write regulations and implement policies must serve the self-interest of legislators. Political scientists have explored this decision to delegate extensively. A general consensus among scholars is that members of Congress would prefer to write detailed legislation themselves, ensuring that the implementation of that legislation would not "drift" away from members' policy preferences. However, most of the time, members lack the resources, information, and capacity to write such detailed legislation constraining the implementation of policy. Technological advances often require the specialization and expertise that Congress typically lacks, so they must turn to those in the bureaucracy with informational advantages. In addition, because legislators are driven by reelection, the degree to which their constituents care about and pay attention to a particular issue matters. Therefore, issue salience interacts with complexity. When issues are low in salience, politicians are more likely to delegate broad discretionary authority. Conversely, when an issue is high in salience and low in complexity, members' interest in delegating declines due to constituent demand (Gormley 1986). Members of Congress, then, perform a "political transaction cost analysis" to determine the value of delegating broad discretion or writing detailed legislation themselves (Epstein and O'Halloran 1999). The result is a division of labor, shared with the executive branch, in which congressional delegations of discretion can serve the interests of members of Congress under conditions of uncertainty, fluidity, and incomplete information.

As Congress delegates, though, its members have several means by which they can retain some control over the action of the executive branch agencies to whom they granted implementation power. If conditions permit it, Congress can write detailed legislation with substantive controls in the bill itself in order to constrain, *ex ante* (before implementation), actions of the executive branch. Congress also has the "power of the purse," the power to appropriate funds to the executive. In that respect, executive agencies are reliant upon Congress for their reauthorizations and their annual appropriation bills, without which agencies have neither authority nor funding. Congress can also impose "sunset provisions," limiting the longevity of the measure to a predetermined period of time. If the agency with authority to implement the measure is faithful to congressional preference in its implementation, presumably, the delegation would be reauthorized when it would otherwise be due to sunset. Importantly, Congress also has the ability to oversee the agencies charged with implementing policy. Congressional oversight can come in many forms, but it usually involves formal hearings in which members of the House or Senate subcommittees or committees with jurisdiction over the agencies hear from agency leadership about the agent's actions (or inactions), policies, or other key topics of interest to members of Congress. In addition to substantive controls, sunsetting, appropriations, and oversight, the Senate has the authority to withhold or grant their consent to political appointees nominated by the president to lead the agencies.

Along with these controls that Congress has at its disposal when granting discretion to implement law to agencies, Congress also has a relatively unused, but potentially potent tool in the 1996 Congressional Review Act (CRA). The CRA gives Congress the power to—within 60 days—rescind an agency regulation by a majority vote on a Resolution of Disapproval in both chambers. The effect of the Resolution of Disapproval is not only the revocation of the offending rule, but it also prohibits an agency from promulgating a substantially similar rule in the future. This powerful tool of congressional control over agencies lay relatively dormant for several years until the Trump Administration and Republicans in both chambers of Congress deployed it to revoke a series of rules promulgated at the very end of the Obama Administration. Having been used only once since it was signed, Congress used the CRA to strike 13 rules within President Trump's first 60 days in office.

Though all these mechanisms are available to Congress as it competes with the executive branch for control over the implementation of policy, the president and others in the executive branch retain important informational advantages. Ultimately, they, not Congress, are responsible for how the policy is enacted. And the more complex the policy, the more informational advantages the policy experts in the executive retain. This dynamic has led Congress to enact reporting requirements in many pieces of legislation, obligating agencies to update Congress on their regulatory activities and authorizing Congress to veto agency decisions. The constitutionality of these "legislative veto provisions" was successfully challenged in *Immigration and Naturalization Service v. Chadha* (1983), though Congress routinely incorporates reporting requirements in the bills it passes.

Predictably, presidents tend to ignore such provisions and sometimes specifically object to the statutory language through their signing statements, which are statements submitted by presidents when they sign legislation into law. Many signing statements are simply rhetorical devices, used to thank supporters or highlight key components of the measure that reflect the president's policy preferences. Other times, however, presidents raise constitutional concerns that reflect the president's objections to specific provisions of the statute, such as the inclusion of reporting requirements. Such constitutional signing statements sometimes reveal the president's intentions to not comply with specific provisions of the law and indicate that the implementation of the measure will proceed in a manner consistent with the president's own view of presidential power. In a 2018 signing statement attached to an appropriations bill, for instance, President Trump demonstrated his disinclination to permit congressional encroachment into areas of presidential authority. He wrote that two provisions in the appropriations bill "condition the Executive's authority to expend funds on consultation with congressional committees. As I have previously noted with respect to such requirements . . . the separation of powers does not permit a requirement to consult with the Congress in executive decision-making. My Administration will accordingly treat the consultation requirements as advisory" (https://www.whitehouse.gov/briefings-statements/signing-statement-president-donald-j-trump-h-r-6157/).

Though the federal courts have not weighed upon the constitutionality of presidential signing statements, courts have generally deferred to executive branch agencies as they implement congressional statutes. In the 1984 Supreme Court case *Chevron v. National Resources Defense Council*, the Court confirmed that when statutory language is vague or ambiguous, courts will defer to the executive branch's reasonable interpretation of those legislative mandates. This has come to be known as *Chevron* deference and, again, grants broad authority to the executive to construe statutory meaning in a manner that is consistent with agency (executive) preference that might at times diverge from congressional preferences.

Two "steps" constitute the Court's application of *Chevron* deference, according to Justice Stevens: "When a court reviews an agency's construction of the statute which it administers, it is confronted with two questions. First, always, is the question whether Congress has directly spoken to the precise question at issue. If the intent of Congress is clear, that is the end of the matter; for the court, as well as the agency, must give effect to the unambiguously expressed intent of Congress. If, however, the court determines Congress has not directly addressed the precise question at issue, the court does not simply impose its own construction on the statute, as would be necessary in the absence of an administrative interpretation. Rather, if the statute is silent or ambiguous with respect to the specific issue, the question for the court is whether the agency's answer is based on a permissible construction of the statute."

It is important to note that much of this discussion has assumed that presidential preference and bureaucratic preferences are aligned. Given the president's ability to appoint top leadership in the executive branch, there is usually such alignment. But the majority of individuals who populate executive branch agencies are careerists (professional staff), not political appointees, who may have different perspectives than their agency administrators. Thus, incentives and preferences do diverge at times within the executive branch. When the president and presidential appointees exceed their legal authority, the professional bureaucracy can take actions that thwart those efforts. Whistleblower protections, adverse decisions by administrative law judges, professional and ethical commitments, and divergent policy goals can contribute to agency "drift" from presidential preference. In recent years, President Trump and many of his allies have complained of the "Deep State"—a conspiracy of entrenched government agency employees determined to resist his policy agenda. But the existence of employees who have spent their careers working for the same agency or handful of government departments is hardly a conspiracy. Rather, it is a fundamental characteristic of the consequences of bureaucratic discretion, intra-branch diffusion of authority, policy expertise, and the professionalism of public servants. How presidents and their agents in the bureaucracy balance those tensions is a defining feature of policy implementation within the executive branch.

In this chapter, we explore many examples of the consequences and difficulties associated with national economic policies, almost all implicating the congressional legislative authority over economic regulations and executive branch implementation of those national economic policies. The rise of the vast administrative state in the twentieth century coincided with and was linked to the rise in congressional authority to legislate on national economic matters. Much of that increase in regulatory power of the federal government came as a result of significant economic crises, like the Great Depression, sparked by the stock market crash of 1929, and the Great Recession of 2008.

A brief review of the context of the 2008 recession is useful in revealing the broad reach and economic implications of executive and legislative power. When President Obama took office in 2009, the country faced grave economic difficulties. In just seven years, the United States had gone from a budget surplus of roughly $165 billion to a budget deficit of around $1.5 trillion (adjusted for inflation). Part of the explanation for this dramatic economic downturn has to do with Bush administration tax cuts in 2001 and 2003, the costs associated with waging war in Iraq and Afghanistan, and other major expenditures, including entitlement programs. Finally, subprime lending and the mortgage crisis of 2007 and 2008 proved to be a major impetus for the economic downturn, sinking many large lending institutions and triggering the Great Recession. But it was the response to that mortgage crisis and the consequent recession that really exploded the budget deficit. Two key measures formed that response. The first was passed by a Democratic Congress and signed by outgoing Republican President George W. Bush; the second measure was signed by President Obama in 2009. The 2008 bill bailed out banks that held "toxic assets" (at roughly $700 billion) and the U.S. auto industry (at around $25 billion), which suffered huge losses in 2008. Subsequent action by Congress established consumer protections and imposed regulatory restrictions on banks. The second measure, the Economic Recovery and Reinvestment Act of 2009, sought to save jobs and promote economic recovery through targeted governmental spending, the total cost of which was estimated to be over $800 billion. Given the effect such spending had on the annual budget deficit, politicians and economists differed with respect to the goals, propriety, scope, and legacies of the bailout and stimulus bills. President Obama's remarks on the national economy, featured in this chapter, speak to these challenges and demonstrate the scale of remedies available to the national government in times of economic crisis.

As with the other chapters, specific events or crises do not arise in a political or economic vacuum. Congressional action and presidential control over the execution of that legislative action contribute to the nation's ability to meet the challenges posed by the crisis event. In some cases, the coordinated actions of Congress and the president contributed to the crisis—or at least provided a context in which such a crisis could occur. Equally important, the way interbranch competition over possible resolutions to the crisis plays out is critical. As you review the cases included in this chapter, bear in mind the dynamism, institutional checks and balances, and individual incentives and disincentives at work as Congress, courts, presidents, and bureaucrats seek to shape policy outcomes in the face of grave economic crises.

President James Monroe Discusses the Economic Crisis Facing the Nation, 1819

The United States emerged from the War of 1812 with considerable debt, but by the time President James Monroe took office in 1817, some Americans felt that the young nation's fragile economy was stabilizing and improving. In the middle of Monroe's first term, however, both the Bank of the United States and local banks began to falter, and communities everywhere were hit with economic disaster. This challenge, along with an imbalance of prices on agricultural imports and exports, posed further difficulty. The event and its ensuing consequences bred the Panic of 1819, which would shadow the country into 1821. The following document is an excerpt from President Monroe's Third Annual Message, addressed to the Senate and House of Representatives on December 7, 1819. President Monroe details the "embarrassments" of the country's economic struggle but offers little in the way of suggestions for moving forward. As the solution to the crisis was entangled in both domestic and foreign causes, President Monroe was somewhat limited in his actionable response.

Although the pecuniary embarrassments which affected various parts of the Union during the latter part of the preceding year have during the present been considerably augmented, and still continue to exist, the receipts into the Treasury to the 30th of September last have amounted to $19M. After defraying the current expenses of the Government, including the interest and reimbursement of the public debt payable to that period, amounting to $18.2M, there remained in the Treasury on that day more than $2.5M, which, with the sums receivable during the remainder of the year, will exceed the current demands upon the Treasury for the same period.

The causes which have tended to diminish the public receipts could not fail to have a corresponding effect upon the revenue which has accrued upon imposts and tonnage during the three first quarters of the present year. It is, however, ascertained that the duties which have been secured during that period exceed $18M, and those of the whole year will probably amount to $23M.

For the probable receipts of the next year I refer you to the statements which will be transmitted from the Treasury, which will enable you to judge whether further provision be necessary.

The great reduction in the price of the principal articles of domestic growth which has occurred during the present year, and the consequent fall in the price of labor, apparently so favorable to the success of domestic manufactures, have not shielded them against other causes adverse to their prosperity. The pecuniary embarrassments which have so deeply affected the commercial interests of the nation have been no less adverse to our manufacturing establishments in several sections of the Union.

The great reduction of the currency which the banks have been constrained to make in order to continue specie payments, and the vitiated character of it where such reductions have not been attempted, instead of placing within the reach of these establishments the pecuniary aid necessary to avail themselves of the advantages resulting from the reduction in the prices of the raw materials and of labor, have compelled the banks to withdraw from them a portion of the capital heretofore advanced to them. That aid which has been refused by the banks has not been obtained from other sources, owing to the loss of individual confidence from the frequent failures which have recently occurred in some of our principal commercial cities.

An additional cause for the depression of these establishments may probably be found in the pecuniary embarrassments which have recently affected those countries with which our commerce has been principally prosecuted. Their manufactures, for the want of a ready or profitable market at home, have been shipped by the manufacturers to the United States, and in many instances sold at a price below their current value at the place of manufacture. Although this practice may from its nature be considered temporary or contingent, it is not on that account less injurious in its effects. Uniformity in the demand and price of an article is highly desirable to the domestic manufacturer.

It is deemed of great importance to give encouragement to our domestic manufacturers. In what manner the evils which have been adverted to may be remedied, and how far it may be practicable in other respects to afford to them further encouragement, paying due regard to the other great interests of the nation, is submitted to the wisdom of Congress.

Source: Richardson, James D. *A Compilation of the Messages and Papers of the Presidents*. Volume 2, Part 1. New York: Bureau of National Literature, 1897, 623–631.

President Andrew Jackson Vetoes the Re-Charter of the Second National Bank, 1832

The Second National Bank was installed in 1816 by President James Madison when the First National Bank's charter had expired after four years. Though the Second National Bank's charter would expire in 20 years, Congress introduced legislation for a premature recharter of the bank in 1832. Andrew Jackson had questioned the Second National Bank's constitutional merit and its benefit to the general public even before the bill was presented. The bank had worked to reduce some of the debt that had incurred as a result of the War of 1812, and many thought that it helped stabilize the government overall. However, President Jackson believed that it had also collected monopolizing power and catered to foreign interests. State banks, which supported farmers and the working class, struggled as a result, and the wealth that had accrued because of the National Banks remained in private sectors. This included government interests. The Second National Bank would expire without renewal in 1836. In the following veto message of July 10, 1832, President Andrew Jackson struck down the presented recharter of the Second National Bank, claiming that its influence had grown too strong.

To the Senate:

The bill "to modify and continue" the act entitled "An act to incorporate the subscribers to the Bank of the United States" was presented to me on the 4th July instant. Having considered it with that solemn regard to the principles of the Constitution which the day was calculated to inspire, and come to the conclusion that it ought not to become a law, I herewith return it to the Senate, in which it originated, with my objections.

A bank of the United States is in many respects convenient for the Government and useful to the people. Entertaining this opinion, and deeply impressed with the belief that some of the powers and privileges possessed by the existing bank are unauthorized by the Constitution, subversive of the rights of the States, and dangerous to the liberties of the people, I felt it my duty at an early period of my Administration to call the attention of Congress to the practicability of organizing an institution combining all its advantages and obviating these objections. I sincerely regret that in the act before me I can perceive none of those modifications of the bank charter which are necessary, in my opinion, to make it compatible with justice, with sound policy, or with the Constitution of our country.

The present corporate body, denominated the president, directors, and company of the Bank of the United States, will have existed at the time this act is intended to take effect twenty years. It enjoys an exclusive privilege of banking under the authority of the General Government, a monopoly of its favor and support, and, as a necessary consequence, almost a monopoly of the foreign and domestic exchange. The powers privileges, and favors bestowed upon it in the original charter, by increasing the value of the stock far above its par value, operated as a gratuity of many millions to the stockholders.

An apology may be found for the failure to guard against this result in the consideration that the effect of the original act of incorporation could not be certainly foreseen at the time of its passage. The act before me proposes another gratuity to the holders of the same stock, and in many cases to the same men, of at least seven million more. This donation finds no apology in any uncertainty as to the effect of the act. On all hands it is conceded that its passage will increase at least 20 or 30 per cent more the market price of the stock, subject to the payment of the annuity of $200,000 per year secured by the act, thus adding in a moment one-fourth to its par value. It is not our own citizens only who are to receive the bounty of our Government. More than eight million of the stock of this bank are held by foreigners. By this act the American Republic proposes virtually to make them a present of some millions of dollars. For these gratuities to foreigners and to some of our own opulent citizens the act secures no equivalent whatever. They are the certain gains of the present stockholders under the operation of this act, after making full allowance for the payment of the bonus.

Every monopoly and all exclusive privileges are granted at the expense of the public, which ought to receive a fair equivalent. The many millions which this act proposes to bestow on the stockholders of the existing bank must come directly or indirectly out of the earnings of the American people. It is due to them, therefore, if their Government sell monopolies and exclusive privileges, that they should at least exact for them as much as they are worth in open market. The value of the monopoly in this case may be correctly ascertained. The twenty-eight millions of stock would probably be at an advance of 50 per cent, and command in market at least $42,000,000, subject to the payment of the present bonus. The present value of the monopoly, therefore, is $17,000,000, and this the act proposes to sell for three millions, payable in fifteen annual installments of $200,000 each.

It is not conceivable how the present stockholders can have any claim to the special favor of the Government. The present corporation has enjoyed its monopoly during the period stipulated in the original contract. If we must have such a corporation, why should not the Government sell out the whole stock and thus secure to the people the full market value of the privileges granted? Why should not Congress create and sell twenty-eight millions of stock, incorporating the purchasers with all the powers and privileges secured in this act and putting the premium upon the sales into the Treasury?

But this act does not permit competition in the purchase of this monopoly. It seems to be predicated on the erroneous idea that the present stockholders have a prescriptive right not only to the favor but to the bounty of Government. It appears that more than a fourth part of the stock is held by foreigners and the residue is held by a few hundred of our own citizens, chiefly of the richest class. For their benefit does this act exclude the whole American people from competition in the purchase of this monopoly and dispose of it for many millions less than it is worth. This seems the less excusable because some of our citizens not now stockholders petitioned that the door of competition might be opened, and offered to take a charter on terms much more favorable to the Government and country.

But this proposition, although made by men whose aggregate wealth is believed to be equal to all the private stock in the existing bank, has been set aside, and the bounty of our Government is proposed to be again bestowed on the few who have been fortunate enough to secure the stock and at this moment wield the power of the existing institution. I can not perceive the justice or policy of this course. If our Government must sell monopolies, it would seem to be its duty to take nothing less than their full value, and if gratuities must be made once in fifteen or twenty years let them not be bestowed on the subjects of a foreign government nor upon a designated and favored class of men in our own country. It is but justice and good policy, as far as the nature of the case will admit, to confine our favors to our own fellow citizens, and let each in his turn enjoy an opportunity to profit by our bounty. In the bearings of the act before me upon these points I find ample reasons why it should not become a law.

Source: Richardson, James D. *A Compilation of the Messages and Papers of the Presidents 1789–1897.* Volume 3. New York: Bureau of National Literature, 1897, 1139–1154.

President Martin Van Buren Addresses Congress during the Economic Panic of 1837

President Martin Van Buren gave this message to the Senate and House of Representatives on September 4, 1837. The outset of Van Buren's presidency was

*profoundly impacted by economic policies set in motion by his predecessor,
Andrew Jackson. President Jackson had opposed the national bank. He transferred most of its government funds to state banks until the national bank's charter expired in 1836 without plans for renewal. Though he may have empowered
state banks through this process, the state banks faced few restrictions on their
business as a result, and lent out loads of paper money. This severely inflated the
currency. President Jackson then enacted the Specie Circular before he left office.
This executive order required that citizens pay for federal land with specie, or
gold and silver, to maintain the integrity of paper money.*

*As President Van Buren took office in 1837, the consequences of Jackson's
reactionary order were becoming apparent. The people were alarmed, unable to
supplement paper money with specie for their loans and other similar transactions. They subsequently withdrew funds from their banks in droves. Mass unemployment and riots broke out, and a devastating economic downturn persisted
throughout the rest of Van Buren's presidency. This event would come to be known
as the Panic of 1837. President Van Buren had his own gripes with monopolizing
power, and famously refused to give federal aid to desperate citizens as a result of
the poor economy. Though the president was certain he would not renew the
national bank in the following message, he grappled with a viable response to the
panic. The poor economic conditions persisted and acted as an anchor on his
1840 reelection campaign, which ended in defeat.*

The present and visible effects of these circumstances on the operations of the
Government and on the industry of the people point out the objects which call for
your immediate attention.

They are, to regulate by law the safe-keeping, transfer, and disbursement of the
public moneys; to designate the funds to be received and paid by the Government;
to enable the Treasury to meet promptly every demand upon it; to prescribe the
terms of indulgence and the mode of settlement to be adopted, as well in collecting from individuals the revenue that has accrued as in withdrawing it from former
depositories; and to devise and adopt such further measures, within the constitutional competency of Congress, as will be best calculated to revive the enterprise
and to promote the prosperity of the country.

For the deposit, transfer, and disbursement of the revenue national and
State banks have always, with temporary and limited exceptions, been heretofore
employed; but although advocates of each system are still to be found, it is apparent that the events of the last few months have greatly augmented the desire, long
existing among the people of the United States, to separate the fiscal operations of
the Government from those of individuals or corporations.

Again to create a national bank as a fiscal agent would be to disregard the popular will, twice solemnly and unequivocally expressed. On no question of domestic
policy is there stronger evidence that the sentiments of a large majority are deliberately fixed, and I can not concur with those who think they see in recent events
a proof that these sentiments are, or a reason that they should be, changed.

Events similar in their origin and character have heretofore frequently
occurred without producing any such change, and the lessons of experience

must be forgotten if we suppose that the present overthrow of credit would have been prevented by the existence of a national bank. Proneness to excessive issues has ever been the vice of the banking system—a vice as prominent in national as in State institutions. This propensity is as subservient to the advancement of private interests in the one as in the other, and those who direct them both, being principally guided by the same views and influenced by the same motives, will be equally ready to stimulate extravagance of enterprise by improvidence of credit. How strikingly is this conclusion sustained by experience! The Bank of the United States, with the vast powers conferred on it by Congress, did not or could not prevent former and similar embarrassments, nor has the still greater strength it has been said to possess under its present charter enabled it in the existing emergency to check other institutions or even to save itself. In Great Britain, where it has been seen the same causes have been attended with the same effects, a national bank possessing powers far greater than are asked for by the warmest advocates of such an institution here has also proved unable to prevent an undue expansion of credit and the evils that flow from it. Nor can I find any tenable ground for the reestablishment of a national bank in the derangement alleged at present to exist in the domestic exchanges of the country or in the facilities it may be capable of affording them. Although advantages of this sort were anticipated when the first Bank of the United States was created, they were regarded as an incidental accommodation, not one which the Federal Government was bound or could be called upon to furnish. This accommodation is now, indeed, after the lapse of not many years, demanded from it as among its first duties, and an omission to aid and regulate commercial exchange is treated as a ground of loud and serious complaint. Such results only serve to exemplify the constant desire among some of our citizens to enlarge the powers of the Government and extend its control to subjects with which it should not interfere. They can never justify the creation of an institution to promote such objects. On the contrary, they justly excite among the community a more diligent inquiry into the character of those operations of trade toward which it is desired to extend such peculiar favors.

The various transactions which bear the name of domestic exchanges differ essentially in their nature, operation, and utility. One class of them consists of bills of exchange drawn for the purpose of transferring actual capital from one part of the country to another, or to anticipate the proceeds of property actually transmitted. Bills of this description are highly useful in the movements of trade and well deserve all the encouragement which can rightfully be given to them. Another class is made up of bills of exchange not drawn to transfer actual capital nor on the credit of property transmitted, but to create fictitious capital, partaking at once of the character of notes discounted in bank and of bank notes in circulation, and swelling the mass of paper credits to a vast extent in the most objectionable manner. These bills have formed for the last few years a large proportion of what are termed the domestic exchanges of the country, serving as the means of usurious profit and constituting the most unsafe and precarious paper in circulation. This species of traffic, instead of being upheld, ought to be discountenanced by the Government and the people.

In transferring its funds from place to place the Government is on the same footing with the private citizen and may resort to the same legal means. It may do so through the medium of bills drawn by itself or purchased from others; and in these operations it may, in a manner undoubtedly constitutional and legitimate, facilitate and assist exchanges of individuals founded on real transactions of trade. The extent to which this may be done and the best means of effecting it are entitled to the fullest consideration. This has been bestowed by the Secretary of the Treasury, and his views will be submitted to you in his report.

But it was not designed by the Constitution that the Government should assume the management of domestic or foreign exchange. It is indeed authorized to regulate by law the commerce between the States and to provide a general standard of value or medium of exchange in gold and silver, but it is not its province to aid individuals in the transfer of their funds otherwise than through the facilities afforded by the Post-Office Department. As justly might it be called on to provide for the transportation of their merchandise. These are operations of trade. They ought to be conducted by those who are interested in them in the same manner that the incidental difficulties of other pursuits are encountered by other classes of citizens. Such aid has not been deemed necessary in other countries. Throughout Europe the domestic as well as the foreign exchanges are carried on by private houses, often, if not generally, without the assistance of banks; yet they extend throughout distinct sovereignties, and far exceed in amount the real exchanges of the United States. There is no reason why our own may not be conducted in the same manner with equal cheapness and safety. Certainly this might be accomplished if it were favored by those most deeply interested; and few can doubt that their own interest, as well as the general welfare of the country, would be promoted by leaving such a subject in the hands of those to whom it properly belongs. A system founded on private interest, enterprise, and competition, without the aid of legislative grants or regulations by law, would rapidly prosper; it would be free from the influence of political agitation and extend the same exemption to trade itself, and it would put an end to those complaints of neglect, partiality, injustice, and oppression which are the unavoidable results of interference by the Government in the proper concerns of individuals. All former attempts on the part of the Government to carry its legislation in this respect further than was designed by the Constitution have in the end proved injurious, and have served only to convince the great body of the people more and more of the certain dangers of blending private interests with the operations of public business; and there is no reason to suppose that a repetition of them now would be more successful.

It can not be concealed that there exists in our community opinions and feelings on this subject in direct opposition to each other. A large portion of them, combining great intelligence, activity, and influence, are no doubt sincere in their belief that the operations of trade ought to be assisted by such a connection; they regard a national bank as necessary for this purpose, and they are disinclined to every measure that does not tend sooner or later to the establishment of such an institution. On the other hand, a majority of the people are believed to be irreconcilably opposed to that measure; they consider such a concentration of power dangerous to their liberties, and many of them regard it as a violation of the

Constitution. This collision of opinion has doubtless caused much of the embarrassment to which the commercial transactions of the country have lately been exposed. Banking has become a political topic of the highest interest, and trade has suffered in the conflict of parties. A speedy termination of this state of things, however desirable, is scarcely to be expected. We have seen for nearly half a century that those who advocate a national bank, by whatever motive they may be influenced, constitute a portion of our community too numerous to allow us to hope for an early abandonment of their favorite plan. On the other hand, they must indeed form an erroneous estimate of the intelligence and temper of the American people who suppose that they have continued on slight or insufficient grounds their persevering opposition to such an institution, or that they can be induced by pecuniary pressure or by any other combination of circumstances to surrender principles they have so long and so inflexibly maintained.

My own views of the subject are unchanged. They have been repeatedly and unreservedly announced to my fellow-citizens, who with full knowledge of them conferred upon me the two highest offices of the Government. On the last of these occasions I felt it due to the people to apprise them distinctly that in the event of my election I would not be able to cooperate in the reestablishment of a national bank. To these sentiments I have now only to add the expression of an increased conviction that the reestablishment of such a bank in any form, whilst it would not accomplish the beneficial purpose promised by its advocates, would impair the rightful supremacy of the popular will, injure the character and diminish the influence of our political system, and bring once more into existence a concentrated moneyed power, hostile to the spirit and threatening the permanency of our republican institutions.

Local banks have been employed for the deposit and distribution of the revenue at all times partially and on three different occasions exclusively: First, anterior to the establishment of the first Bank of the United States; secondly, in the interval between the termination of that institution and the charter of its successor; and thirdly, during the limited period which has now so abruptly closed. The connection thus repeatedly attempted proved unsatisfactory on each successive occasion, notwithstanding the various measures which were adopted to facilitate or ensure its success. On the last occasion, in the year 1833, the employment of the State banks was guarded especially, in every way which experience and caution could suggest. Personal security was required for the safe-keeping and prompt payment of the moneys to be received, and full returns of their condition were from time to time to be made by the depositories. In the first stages the measure was eminently successful, notwithstanding the violent opposition of the Bank of the United States and the unceasing efforts made to overthrow it. The selected banks performed with fidelity and without any embarrassment to themselves or to the community their engagements to the Government, and the system promised to be permanently useful; but when it became necessary, under the act of June, 1836, to withdraw from them the public money for the purpose of placing it in additional institutions or of transferring it to the States, they found it in many cases inconvenient to comply with the demands of the Treasury, and numerous and pressing applications were made for indulgence or relief. As the installments under the deposit law became payable their own embarrassments and the necessity under which they lay of curtailing their discounts and calling in their debts increased the general distress and contributed, with other causes, to hasten the revulsion in which at length they, in common with the other banks, were fatally involved.

Under these circumstances it becomes our solemn duty to inquire whether there are not in any connection between the Government and banks of issue evils of great magnitude, inherent in its very nature and against which no precautions can effectually guard.

Unforeseen in the organization of the Government and forced on the Treasury by early necessities, the practice of employing banks was in truth from the beginning more a measure of emergency than of sound policy. When we started into existence as a nation, in addition to the burdens of the new Government we assumed all the large but honorable load of debt which was the price of our liberty; but we hesitated to weigh down the infant industry of the country by resorting to adequate taxation for the necessary revenue. The facilities of banks, in return for the privileges they acquired, were promptly offered, and perhaps too readily received by an embarrassed Treasury. During the long continuance of a national debt and the intervening difficulties of a foreign war the connection was continued from motives of convenience; but these causes have long since passed away. We have no emergencies that make banks necessary to aid the wants of the Treasury; we have no load of national debt to provide for, and we have on actual deposit a large surplus. No public interest, therefore, now requires the renewal of a connection that circumstances have dissolved. The complete organization of our Government, the abundance of our resources, the general harmony which prevails between the different States and with foreign powers, all enable us now to select the system most consistent with the Constitution and most conducive to the public welfare. Should we, then, connect the Treasury for a fourth time with the local banks, it can only be under a conviction that past failures have arisen from accidental, not inherent, defects.

A danger difficult, if not impossible, to be avoided in such an arrangement is made strikingly evident in the very event by which it has now been defeated. A sudden act of the banks entrusted with the funds of the people deprives the Treasury, without fault or agency of the Government, of the ability to pay its creditors in the currency they have by law a right to demand. This circumstance no fluctuation of commerce could have produced if the public revenue had been collected in the legal currency and kept in that form by the officers of the Treasury. The citizen whose money was in bank receives it back since the suspension at a sacrifice in its amount, whilst he who kept it in the legal currency of the country and in his own possession pursues without loss the current of his business. The Government, placed in the situation of the former, is involved in embarrassments it could not have suffered had it pursued the course of the latter. These embarrassments are, moreover, augmented by those salutary and just laws which forbid it to use a depreciated currency, and by so doing take from the Government the ability which individuals have of accommodating their transactions to such a catastrophe.

A system which can in a time of profound peace, when there is a large revenue laid by, thus suddenly prevent the application and the use of the money of the people in the manner and for the objects they have directed can not be wise; but who can think without painful reflection that under it the same unforeseen events might have befallen us in the midst of a war and taken from us at the moment when most wanted the use of those very means which were treasured up to promote the national welfare and guard our national rights? To such embarrassments and to such dangers will this Government be always exposed whilst it takes the moneys raised for and necessary to the public service out of the hands of its own officers and converts them into a mere right of action against corporations entrusted with the possession of them. Nor can such results be effectually guarded against in such a system without investing the Executive with a control over the banks themselves, whether State or national, that might with reason be objected to. Ours is probably the only Government in the world that is liable in the management of its fiscal concerns to occurrences like these.

But this imminent risk is not the only danger attendant on the surrender of the public money to the custody and control of local corporations. Though the object is aid to the Treasury, its effect may be to introduce into the operations of the Government influences the most subtle, founded on interests the most selfish.

The use by the banks, for their own benefit, of the money deposited with them has received the sanction of the Government from the commencement of this connection. The money received from the people, instead of being kept till it is needed for their use, is, in consequence of this authority, a fund on which discounts are made for the profit of those who happen to be owners of stock in the banks selected as depositories. The supposed and often exaggerated advantages of such a boon will always cause it to be sought for with avidity. I will not stop to consider on whom the patronage incident to it is to be conferred. Whether the selection and control be trusted to Congress or to the Executive, either will be subjected to appeals made in every form which the sagacity of interest can suggest. The banks under such a system are stimulated to make the most of their fortunate acquisition; the deposits are treated as an increase of capital; loans and circulation are rashly augmented, and when the public exigencies require a return it is attended with embarrassments not provided for nor foreseen. Thus banks that thought themselves most fortunate when the public funds were received find themselves most embarrassed when the season of payment suddenly arrives.

Unfortunately, too, the evils of the system are not limited to the banks. It stimulates a general rashness of enterprise and aggravates the fluctuations of commerce and the currency. This result was strikingly exhibited during the operations of the late deposit system, and especially in the purchases of public lands. The order which ultimately directed the payment of gold and silver in such purchases greatly checked, but could not altogether prevent, the evil. Specie was indeed more difficult to be procured than the notes which the banks could themselves create at pleasure; but still, being obtained from them as a loan and returned as a deposit, which they were again at liberty to use, it only passed round the circle with diminished speed. This operation could not have been performed had the funds of the Government gone into the Treasury to be regularly disbursed, and not into banks to be loaned out for their own profit while they were permitted to substitute for it a credit in account.

In expressing these sentiments I desire not to undervalue the benefits of a salutary credit to any branch of enterprise. The credit bestowed on probity and industry is the just reward of merit and an honorable incentive to further acquisition. None oppose it who love their country and understand its welfare. But when it is unduly encouraged; when it is made to inflame the public mind with the temptations of sudden and unsubstantial wealth; when it turns industry into paths that lead sooner or later to disappointment and distress, it becomes liable to censure and needs correction. Far from helping probity and industry, the ruin to which it leads falls most severely on the great laboring classes, who are thrown suddenly out of employment, and by the failure of magnificent schemes never intended to enrich them are deprived in a moment of their only resource. Abuses of credit and excesses in speculation will happen in despite of the most salutary laws; no government, perhaps, can altogether prevent them, but surely every government can refrain from contributing the stimulus that calls them into life.

Since, therefore, experience has shown that to lend the public money to the local banks is hazardous to the operations of the Government, at least of doubtful benefit to the institutions themselves, and productive of disastrous derangement in the business and currency of the country, is it the part of wisdom again to renew the connection?

Source: Richardson, James D. *A Compilation of the Messages and Papers of the Presidents 1789–1897.* Volume 4. New York: Bureau of National Literature, 1897, 1541–1563.

President John Tyler Vetoes Bill to Create a National Bank, 1841

This veto, given on September 9, 1841, was the catalyst that prompted all but one member of President John Tyler's cabinet to resign. The bills in question concerned the creation of another national bank, which had been a contentious issue for close to a decade. This was the second veto he had issued to Congress on the proposed creation of a national bank (the first version of the bill had crossed his desk one month earlier). Tension was already high in the government, as President John Tyler was originally President William Henry Harrison's vice president and took office by default upon his death. Tyler's presidency was marred with much interparty conflict, despite the fact that both the House and Senate were led by fellow Whigs. The debate about the creation of a national bank would not be resolved with the following message.

It is with extreme regret that I feel myself constrained by the duty faithfully to execute the office of President of the United States and to the best of my ability to "preserve, protect, and defend the Constitution of the United States" to return to the House in which it originated the bill "to provide for the better collection, safe-keeping, and disbursement of the public revenue by means of a corporation to be styled the Fiscal Corporation of the United States," with my written objections.

In my message sent to the Senate on the 16th day of August last, returning the bill "to incorporate the subscribers to the Fiscal Bank of the United States,"

I distinctly declared that my own opinion had been uniformly proclaimed to be against the exercise "of the power of Congress to create a national bank to operate *per se* over the Union," and, entertaining that opinion, my main objection to that bill was based upon the highest moral and religious obligations of conscience and the Constitution. I readily admit that whilst the qualified veto with which the Chief Magistrate is invested should be regarded and was intended by the wise men who made it a part of the Constitution as a great conservative principle of our system, without the exercise of which on important occasions a mere representative majority might urge the Government in its legislation beyond the limits fixed by its framers or might exert its just powers too hastily or oppressively, yet it is a power which ought to be most cautiously exerted, and perhaps never except in a case eminently involving the public interest or one in which the oath of the President, acting under his convictions, both mental and moral, imperiously requires its exercise. In such a case he has no alternative. He must either exert the negative power entrusted to him by the Constitution chiefly for its own preservation, protection, and defense or commit an act of gross moral turpitude. Mere regard to the will of a majority must not in a constitutional republic like ours control this sacred and solemn duty of a sworn officer. The Constitution itself I regard and cherish as the embodied and written will of the whole people of the United States. It is their fixed and fundamental law, which they unanimously prescribe to the public functionaries, their mere trustees and servants. This *their* will and the law which *they* have given us as the rule of our action have no guard, no guaranty of preservation, protection, and defense, but the oaths which it prescribes to the public officers, the sanctity with which they shall religiously observe those oaths, and the patriotism with which the people shall shield it by their own sovereign will, which has made the Constitution supreme. It must be exerted against the will of a mere representative majority or not at all. It is alone in pursuance of that will that any measure can reach the President, and to say that because a majority in Congress have passed a bill he should therefore sanction it is to abrogate the power altogether and to render its insertion in the Constitution a work of absolute supererogation. The duty is to guard the fundamental will of the people themselves from (in this case, I admit, unintentional) change or infraction by a majority in Congress; and in that light alone do I regard the constitutional duty which I now most reluctantly discharge. Is this bill now presented for my approval or disapproval such a bill as I have already declared could not receive my sanction? Is it such a bill as calls for the exercise of the negative power under the Constitution? Does it violate the Constitution by creating a national bank to operate *per se* over the Union? Its title, in the first place, describes its general character. It is "an act to provide for the better collection, safe-keeping, and disbursement of the *public* revenue by means of a *corporation* to be styled the *Fiscal Corporation* of the *United States*." In style, then, it is plainly national in its character. Its powers, functions, and duties are those which pertain to the collecting, keeping, and disbursing the public revenue. The means by which these are to be exerted is a *corporation* to be styled the *Fiscal* Corporation of the United States. It is a corporation created by the Congress of the United States, in its character of a national legislature for the whole Union, to perform the fiscal purposes, meet the *fiscal* wants and exigencies, supply the *fiscal* uses, and exert the *fiscal* agencies of the Treasury of the United States. Such is its own description of itself. Do its provisions contradict its title? They do not. It is true that by its first section it provides that it shall be established in the District of Columbia; but the amount of its capital, the manner in which its stock is to be subscribed for and held, the persons and bodies, corporate and politic, by whom its stock may be held, the appointment of its directors and their powers and duties, its fundamental articles, especially that to establish agencies in any part of the Union, the corporate powers and business of such agencies, the prohibition of Congress to establish any other corporation with similar powers for twenty years, with express reservation in the same clause to modify or create any bank for the District of Columbia, so that the aggregate capital shall not exceed five millions, without enumerating other features which are equally distinctive and characteristic, clearly show that it can not be regarded as other than a bank of the United States, with powers seemingly more limited than have heretofore been granted to such an institution. It operates *per se* over the Union by virtue of the unaided and, in my view, assumed authority of Congress as a national legislature, as distinguishable from a bank created by Congress for the District of Columbia as the local legislature of the District. Every United States bank heretofore created has had power to deal in bills of exchange as well as local discounts. Both were trading privileges conferred, and both were exercised by virtue of the aforesaid power of Congress over the whole Union. The question of power remains unchanged without reference to the extent of privilege granted. If this proposed corporation is to be regarded as a local bank of the District of Columbia, invested by Congress with general powers to operate over the Union, it is obnoxious to still stronger objections. It assumes that Congress may invest a local institution with general or national powers. With the same propriety that it may do this in regard to a bank of the District of Columbia it may as to a State bank. Yet who can indulge the idea that this Government can rightfully, by making a State bank its fiscal agent, invest it with the absolute and unqualified powers conferred by this bill? When I come to look at the details of the bill, they do not recommend it strongly to my adoption. A brief notice of some of its provisions will suffice.

First. It may justify substantially a system of discounts of the most objectionable character. It is to deal in bills of exchange drawn in one State and payable in another without any restraint. The bill of exchange may have an unlimited time to run, and its renewability is nowhere guarded against. It may, in fact, assume the most objectionable form of accommodation paper. It is not required to rest on any actual, real, or substantial exchange basis. A drawer in one place becomes the accepter in another, and so in turn the accepter may become the drawer upon a mutual understanding. It may at the same time indulge in mere local discounts under the name of bills of exchange. A bill drawn at Philadelphia on Camden, N.J., at New York on a border town in New Jersey, at Cincinnati on Newport, in Kentucky, not to multiply other examples, might, for anything in this bill to restrain it, become a mere matter of local accommodation. Cities thus relatively situated would possess advantages Over cities otherwise situated of so decided a character as most justly to excite dissatisfaction.

Second. There is no limit prescribed to the premium in the purchase of bills of exchange, thereby correcting none of the evils under which the community now labors, and operating most injuriously upon the agricultural States, in which the irregularities in the rates of exchange are most severely felt. Nor are these the only consequences. A resumption of specie payments by the banks of those States would be liable to indefinite postponement; for as the operation of the agencies of the interior would chiefly consist in selling bills of exchange, and the purchases could only be made in specie or the notes of banks paying specie, the State banks would either have to continue with their doors closed or exist at the mercy of this national monopoly of brokerage. Nor can it be passed over without remark that whilst the District of Columbia is made the seat of the principal bank, its citizens are excluded from all participation in any benefit it might afford by a positive prohibition on the bank from all discounting within the District.

These are some of the objections which prominently exist against the details of the bill. Others might be urged of much force, but it would be unprofitable to dwell upon them. Suffice it to add that this charter is designed to continue for twenty years without a competitor; that the defects to which I have alluded, being founded on the fundamental law of the corporation, are irrevocable, and that if the objections be well founded it would be over hazardous to pass the bill into a law.

In conclusion I take leave most respectfully to say that I have felt the most anxious solicitude to meet the wishes of Congress in the adoption of a fiscal agent which, avoiding all constitutional objections, should harmonize conflicting opinions. Actuated by this feeling, I have been ready to yield much in a spirit of conciliation to the opinions of others; and it is with great pain that I now feel compelled to differ from Congress a second time in the same session. At the commencement of this session, inclined from choice to defer to the legislative will, I submitted to Congress the propriety of adopting a fiscal agent which, without violating the Constitution, would separate the public money from the Executive control and perform the operations of the Treasury without being burdensome to the people or inconvenient or expensive to the Government. It is deeply to be regretted that this department of the Government can not upon constitutional and other grounds concur with the legislative department in this last measure proposed to attain these desirable objects. Owing to the brief space between the period of the death of my lamented predecessor and my own installation into office, I was, in fact, not left time to prepare and submit a definitive recommendation of my own in my regular message, and since my mind has been wholly occupied in a most anxious attempt to conform my action to the legislative will. In this communication I am confined by the Constitution to my objections simply to this bill, but the period of the regular session will soon arrive, when it will be my duty, under another clause of the Constitution, "to give to Congress information of the state of the Union and recommend to their consideration such measures as" I "shall judge necessary and expedient." And I most respectfully submit, in a spirit of harmony, whether the present differences of opinion should be pressed further at this time, and whether the peculiarity of my situation does not entitle me to a postponement of this subject to a more auspicious period for deliberation. The two Houses of Congress have distinguished themselves at this extraordinary session by the performance of an immense mass of labor at a season very unfavorable both to health and action, and have passed many laws which I trust will prove highly beneficial to the interests of the country and fully answer its just expectations. It has been my good fortune and pleasure to concur with them in all measures except this. And why should our difference on this alone be pushed to extremes? It is my anxious desire that it should not be. I too have been burdened with extraordinary labors of late, and I sincerely desire time for deep and deliberate reflection on this the greatest difficulty of my Administration. May we not now pause until a more favorable time, when, with the most anxious hope that the Executive and Congress may cordially unite, some measure of finance may be deliberately adopted promotive of the good of our common country?

I will take this occasion to declare that the conclusions to which I have brought myself are those of a settled conviction, founded, in my opinion, on a just view of the Constitution; that in arriving at it I have been actuated by no other motive or desire than to uphold the institutions of the country as they have come down to us from the hands of our godlike ancestors, and that I shall esteem my efforts to sustain them, even though I perish, more honorable than to win the applause of men by a sacrifice of my duty and my conscience.

Source: Richardson, James D. *A Compilation of the Messages and Papers of the Presidents 1789–1897.* Volume 4. New York: Bureau of National Literature, 1897, 1916–1921.

President James Buchanan Addresses Congress about the Nation's Economic Struggles, 1858

The Panic of 1857, one of the worst economic downturns in U.S. history, was caused by a multitude of factors. European investors began to pull out of U.S. banks amid war on the continent, and other foreign investors followed suit, believing that the banks were not stable without Europe's contributions. Many European countries began to work overtime to produce agricultural products that could sustain troops and no longer needed to import crops from the United States, a huge source of the country's income at the time. In a dramatic twist, a cargo ship transporting tens of tons of silver and gold from the West Coast to the East Coast was demolished in a hurricane, which was both a hit to the economy and seen by some Americans as perhaps an omen of bad fortune. President James Buchanan took swift action during the panic and repaired many foreign relationships, and the panic ended in 1858. The following document, a message to Congress on the Conditions of the Treasury given on June 12, 1858, demonstrates the seriousness with which President Buchanan viewed the country's fiscal health as well as his plans for keeping the United States from sliding back into economic jeopardy.

I feel it to be an indispensable duty to call your attention to the condition of the Treasury. On the 19th day of May last the Secretary of the Treasury submitted a report to Congress "on the present condition of the finances of the Government." In this report he states that after a call upon the heads of Departments he had received official information that the sum of $37,000,000 would probably be required during the first two quarters of the next fiscal year, from the 1st of July until the 1st of January. "This sum," the Secretary says," does not include such amounts as may be appropriated by Congress over and above the estimates submitted to them by the Departments, and I have no data on which to estimate for such expenditures. Upon this point Congress is better able to form a correct opinion than I am."

The Secretary then estimates that the receipts into the Treasury from all sources between the 1st of July and the 1st of January would amount to $25,000,000, leaving a deficit of $15,000,000, inclusive of the sum of about $3,000,000, the least amount required to be in the Treasury at all times to secure its successful operation. For this amount he recommends a loan. This loan, it will be observed, was required, after a close calculation, to meet the estimates from the different Departments, and not such appropriations as might be made by Congress over and above these estimates.

There was embraced in this sum of $15,000,000 estimates to the amount of about $1,750,000 for the three volunteer regiments authorized by the act of Congress approved April 7, 1858, for two of which, if not for the third, no appropriation will now be required. To this extent a portion of the loan of $15,000,000 may be applied to pay the appropriations made by Congress beyond the estimates from the different Departments, referred to in the report of the Secretary of the Treasury.

To what extent a probable deficiency may exist in the Treasury between the 1st July and the 1st January next can not be ascertained until the appropriation bills, as well as the private bills containing appropriations, shall have finally passed.

Adversity teaches useful lessons to nations as well as individuals. The habit of extravagant expenditures, fostered by a large surplus in the Treasury, must now be corrected or the country will be involved in serious financial difficulties.

Under any form of government extravagance in expenditure must be the natural consequence when those who authorize the expenditure feel no responsibility in providing the means of payment. Such had been for a number of years our condition previously to the late monetary revulsion in the country. Fortunately, at least for the cause of public economy, the case is now reversed, and to the extent of the appropriations, whatever these may be, ingrafted on the different appropriation bills, as well as those made by private bills, over and above the estimates of the different Departments, it will be necessary for Congress to provide the means of payment before their adjournment. Without this the Treasury will be exhausted before the 1st of January and the public credit will be seriously impaired. This disgrace must not fall upon the country.

It is impossible for me, however, now to ascertain this amount, nor does there at present seem to be the least probability that this can be done and the necessary means provided by Congress to meet any deficiency which may exist in the Treasury before Monday next at 12 o'clock, the hour fixed for adjournment, it being now Saturday morning at half-past 11 o'clock. To accomplish this object the appropriation bills, as they shall have finally passed Congress, must be before me, and time must be allowed to ascertain the amount of the moneys appropriated and to enable Congress to provide the necessary means. At this writing it is understood that several of these bills are yet before the committee of conference and the amendments to some of them have not even been printed.

Foreseeing that such a state of things might exist at the close of the session, I stated in the annual message to Congress of December last that—

> From the practice of Congress such an examination of each bill as the Constitution requires has been rendered impossible. The most important business of each session is generally crowded into its last hours, and the alternative presented to the President is either to violate the constitutional duty which he owes to the people and approve bills which for want of time it is impossible he should have examined, or by his refusal to do this subject the country and individuals to great loss and inconvenience.

For my own part, I have deliberately determined that I shall approve no bills which I have not examined, and it will be a case of extreme and most urgent necessity which shall ever induce me to depart from this rule.

The present condition of the Treasury absolutely requires that I should adhere to this resolution on the present occasion, for the reasons which I have heretofore presented.

In former times it was believed to be the true character of an appropriation bill simply to carry into effect existing laws and the established policy of the country. A practice has, however, grown up of late years to ingraft on such bills at the last hours of the session large appropriations for new and important objects not provided for by preexisting laws and when no time is left to the Executive for their examination and investigation. No alternative is thus left to the President but either to approve measures without examination or by vetoing an appropriation bill seriously to embarrass the operations of the Government. This practice could never have prevailed without a surplus in the Treasury sufficiently large to cover an indefinite amount of appropriations. Necessity now compels us to arrest it, at least so far as to afford time to ascertain the amount appropriated and to provide the means of its payment.

For all these reasons I recommend to Congress to postpone the day of adjournment for a brief period. I promise that not an hour shall be lost in ascertaining the amount of appropriations made by them for which it will be necessary to provide. I know it will be inconvenient for the members to attend a called session, and this above all things I desire to avoid.

Source: Richardson, James D. *A Compilation of the Messages and Papers of the Presidents 1789–1897.* Volume 7. New York: Bureau of National Literature, 1897, 3019–3021.

President Ulysses S. Grant Plans to Revitalize a Floundering Economy, 1875

The following excerpt from President Ulysses S. Grant's Seventh Annual Message given on December 7, 1875, outlines President Grant's plan toward financial recovery in the United States in the midst of the Panic of 1873. Inflation was high due to the country's dependence on specie (and penchant for spending it), and banks were closing at rapid speeds. This caused investors both foreign and domestic to recover their cash as quickly as they could. Many Americans were out of work, especially if their work pertained to developments in infrastructure, as major industrial companies shut down. President Grant's plan sought sustainable solutions to the extent that it could, and he attempted to assuage the country's economic condition from multiple sides. His pointed remarks and organized rhetoric portrayed an image of command and action, a trait the president may have honed from his tenure in the army. Yet the crisis did not resolve until after Grant left office in 1879, and a new vision for the country and its economy was welcomed.

Nothing seems to me more certain than that a full, healthy, and permanent reaction can not take place in favor of the industries and financial welfare of the country until we return to a measure of values recognized throughout the civilized world. While we use a currency not equivalent to this standard the world's recognized standard, specie, becomes a commodity like the products of the soil, the surplus seeking a market wherever there is a demand for it.

Under our present system we should want none, nor would we have any, were it not that customs dues must be paid in coin and because of the pledge to pay interest on the public debt in coin. The yield of precious metals would flow out for the purchase of foreign productions and the United States "hewers of wood and drawers of water," because of wiser legislation on the subject of finance by the nations with whom we have dealings. I am not prepared to say that I can suggest the best legislation to secure the end most heartily recommended. It will be a source of great gratification to me to be able to approve any measure of Congress looking effectively toward securing "resumption."

Unlimited inflation would probably bring about specie payments more speedily than any legislation looking to redemption of the legal-tenders in coin; but it would be at the expense of honor. The legal-tenders would have no value beyond settling present liabilities, or, properly speaking, repudiating them. They would buy nothing after debts were all settled.

There are a few measures which seem to me important in this connection and which I commend to your earnest consideration:

First. A repeal of so much of the legal-tender act as makes these notes receivable for debts contracted after a date to be fixed in the act itself, say not later than the 1st of January, 1877. We should then have quotations at real values, not fictitious ones. Gold would no longer be at a premium, but currency at a discount. A healthy reaction would set in at once, and with it a desire to make the currency equal to what it purports to be. The merchants, manufacturers, and tradesmen of every calling could do business on a fair margin of profit, the money to be received having an unvarying value. Laborers and all classes who work for stipulated pay or salary would receive more for their income, because extra profits would no longer be charged by the capitalists to compensate for the risk of a downward fluctuation in the value of the currency.

Second. That the Secretary of the Treasury be authorized to redeem, say, not to exceed $2,000,000 monthly of legal-tender notes, by issuing in their stead a long bond, bearing interest at the rate of 3.65 per cent per annum, of denominations ranging from $50 up to $1,000 each. This would in time reduce the legal-tender notes to a volume that could be kept afloat without demanding redemption in large sums suddenly.

Third. That additional power be given to the Secretary of the Treasury to accumulate gold for final redemption, either by increasing revenue, curtailing expenses, or both (it is preferable to do both); and I recommend that reduction of expenditures be made wherever it can be done without impairing Government obligations or crippling the due execution thereof. One measure for increasing the revenue—and the only one I think of—is the restoration of the duty on tea and coffee. These duties would add probably $18,000,000 to the present amount received from imports, and would in no way increase the prices paid for those articles by the consumers.

These articles are the products of countries collecting revenue from exports, and as we, the largest consumers, reduce the duties they proportionately increase them. With this addition to the revenue, many duties now collected, and which give but an insignificant return for the cost of collection, might be remitted, and to the direct advantage of consumers at home.

I would mention those articles which enter into manufactures of all sorts. All duty paid upon such articles goes directly to the cost of the article when manufactured here, and must be paid for by the consumers. These duties not only come from the consumers at home, but act as a protection to foreign manufacturers of the same completed articles in our own and distant markets.

I will suggest or mention another subject bearing upon the problem of "how to enable the Secretary of the Treasury to accumulate balances." It is to devise some better method of verifying claims against the Government than at present exists through the Court of Claims, especially those claims growing out of the late war. Nothing is more certain than that a very large percentage of the amounts passed and paid are either wholly fraudulent or are far in excess of the real losses sustained. The large amount of losses proven—on good testimony according to existing laws, by affidavits of fictitious or unscrupulous persons—to have been sustained on small farms and plantations are not only far beyond the possible yield of those places for any one year, but, as everyone knows who has had experience in tilling the soil and who has visited the scenes of these spoliations, are in many instances more than the individual claimants were ever worth, including their personal and real estate.

The report of the Attorney-General, which will be submitted to Congress at an early day, will contain a detailed history of awards made and of claim pending of the class here referred to.

Source: Richardson, James D. *A Compilation of the Messages and Papers of the Presidents 1789–1897.* Volume 10. New York: Bureau of National Literature, 1897, 4286–4310.

President Grover Cleveland Promotes Importance of Financial Soundness, 1895

By the time President Grover Cleveland had given this message to Congress on January 28, 1895, the United States had been mired in economic depression for

*over two years. The gold that the country had founded its economic integrity upon
had amassed and depleted in waves over time, but it had now dwindled to fright-
ening low stock. The government issued bonds in an effort to keep the worth of its
currency stable and to forage for more of the precious metal, but in the meantime,
the strength of its paper tender had been compromised. Silver was presented by
some lawmakers and officials as something of a solution to the deepening crisis;
some called for a complete pivot to silver as the country's economic stronghold,
whereas others believed it could act as a supplement. Yet President Cleveland
was insistent on the importance of reacquiring gold as the central component of
the United States economy, as the following document indicates. His strategies
were not favored by the U.S. people, however, and they failed to revive the listing
economy. The U.S. people welcomed president-elect William McKinley as their
leader in 1896, the same year the depression had finally lifted.*

To the Senate and House of Representatives:

In my last annual message I commended to the serious consideration of the Congress the condition of our national finances, and in connection with the subject
indorsed a plan of currency legislation which at that time seemed to furnish protection against impending danger. This plan has not been approved by the Congress. In
the meantime the situation has so changed and the emergency now appears so threatening that I deem it my duty to ask at the hands of the legislative branch of the
Government such prompt and effective action as will restore confidence in our financial soundness and avert business disaster and universal distress among our people.

Whatever may be the merits of the plan outlined in my annual message as a
remedy for ills then existing and as a safeguard against the depletion of the gold
reserve then in the Treasury, I am now convinced that its reception by the Congress and our present advanced stage of financial perplexity necessitate additional
or different legislation.

With natural resources unlimited in variety and productive strength and with a
people whose activity and enterprise seek only a fair opportunity to achieve
national success and greatness, our progress should not be checked by a false
financial policy and a heedless disregard of sound monetary laws, nor should
the timidity and fear which they engender stand in the way of our prosperity.

It is hardly disputed that this predicament confronts us to-day. Therefore no one
in any degree responsible for the making and execution of our laws should fail to
see a patriotic duty in honestly and sincerely attempting to relieve the situation.
Manifestly this effort will not succeed unless it is made untrammeled by the prejudice of partisanship and with a steadfast determination to resist the temptation to
accomplish party advantage. We may well remember that if we are threatened
with financial difficulties all our people in every station of life are concerned; and
surely those who suffer will not receive the promotion of party interests as an
excuse for permitting our present troubles to advance to a disastrous conclusion. It
is also of the utmost importance that we approach the study of the problems presented as free as possible from the tyranny of preconceived opinions, to the end
that in a common danger we may be able to seek with unclouded vision a safe and
reasonable protection.

The real trouble which confronts us consists in a lack of confidence, widespread and constantly increasing, in the continuing ability or disposition of the Government to pay its obligations in gold. This lack of confidence grows to some extent out of the palpable and apparent embarrassment attending the efforts of the Government under existing laws to procure gold and to a greater extent out of the impossibility of either keeping it in the Treasury or canceling obligations by its expenditure after it is obtained.

The only way left open to the Government for procuring gold is by the issue and sale of its bonds. The only bonds that can be so issued were authorized nearly twenty-five years ago and are not well calculated to meet our present needs. Among other disadvantages, they are made payable in coin instead of specifically in gold, which in existing conditions detracts largely and in an increasing ratio from their desirability as investments. It is by no means certain that bonds of this description can much longer be disposed of at a price creditable to the financial character of our Government.

The most dangerous and irritating feature of the situation, however, remains to be mentioned. It is found in the means by which the Treasury is despoiled of the gold thus obtained without canceling a single Government obligation and solely for the benefit of those who find profit in shipping it abroad or whose fears induce them to hoard it at home. We have outstanding about five hundred million of currency notes of the Government for which gold may be demanded, and, curiously enough, the law requires that when presented and, in fact, redeemed and paid in gold they shall be reissued. Thus the same notes may do duty many times in drawing gold from the Treasury; nor can the process be arrested as long as private parties, for profit or otherwise, see an advantage in repeating the operation. More than $300,000,000 in these notes have already been redeemed in gold, and notwithstanding such redemption they are all still outstanding.

Since the 17th day of January, 1894, our bonded interest-bearing debt has been increased $100,000,000 for the purpose of obtaining gold to replenish our coin reserve. Two issues were made amounting to fifty million each, one in January and the other in November. As a result of the first issue there was realized something more than $58,000,000 in gold. Between that issue and the succeeding one in November, comprising a period of about ten months, nearly $103,000,000 in gold were drawn from the Treasury. This made the second issue necessary, and upon that more than fifty-eight million in gold was again realized. Between the date of this second issue and the present time, covering a period of only about two months, more than $69,000,000 in gold have been drawn from the Treasury. These large sums of gold were expended without any cancellation of Government obligations or in any permanent way benefiting our people or improving our pecuniary situation.

The financial events of the past year suggest facts and conditions which should certainly arrest attention.

More than $172,000,000 in gold have been drawn out of the Treasury during the year for the purpose of shipment abroad or hoarding at home.

While nearly $103,000,000 of this amount was drawn out during the first ten months of the year, a sum aggregating more than two-thirds of that amount, being about $69,000,000, was drawn out during the following two months, thus indicating a marked acceleration of the depleting process with the lapse of time.

The obligations upon which this gold has been drawn from the Treasury are still outstanding and are available for use in repeating the exhausting operation with shorter intervals as our perplexities accumulate.

Conditions are certainly supervening tending to make the bonds which may be issued to replenish our gold less useful for that purpose.

An adequate gold reserve is in all circumstances absolutely essential to the upholding of our public credit and to the maintenance of our high national character.

Our gold reserve has again reached such a stage of diminution as to require its speedy reinforcement.

The aggravations that must inevitably follow present conditions and methods will certainly lead to misfortune and loss, not only to our national credit and prosperity and to financial enterprise, but to those of our people who seek employment as a means of livelihood and to those whose only capital is their daily labor.

It will hardly do to say that a simple increase of revenue will cure our troubles. The apprehension now existing and constantly increasing as to our financial ability does not rest upon a calculation of our revenue. The time has passed when the eyes of investors abroad and our people at home were fixed upon the revenues of the Government. Changed conditions have attracted their attention to the gold of the Government. There need be no fear that we can not pay our current expenses with such money as we have. There is now in the Treasury a comfortable surplus of more than $63,000,000, but it is not in gold, and therefore does not meet our difficulty.

I can not see that differences of opinion concerning the extent to which silver ought to be coined or used in our currency should interfere with the counsels of those whose duty it is to rectify evils now apparent in our financial situation. They have to consider the question of national credit and the consequences that will follow from its collapse. Whatever ideas may be insisted upon as to silver or bimetallism, a proper solution of the question now pressing upon us only requires a recognition of gold as well as silver and a concession of its importance, rightfully or wrongfully acquired, as a basis of national credit, a necessity in the honorable discharge of our obligations payable in gold, and a badge of solvency. I do not understand that the real fiends of silver desire a condition that might follow inaction or neglect to appreciate the meaning of the present exigency if it should result in the entire banishment of gold from our financial and currency arrangements.

Besides the Treasury notes, which certainly should be paid in gold, amounting to nearly $500,000,000, there will fall due in 1904 one hundred millions of bonds issued during the last year, for which we have received gold, and in 1907 nearly six hundred millions of 4 per cent bonds issued in 1877. Shall the payment of these obligations in gold be repudiated? If they are to be paid in such a manner as the preservation of our national honor and national solvency demands, we should not destroy or even imperil our ability to supply ourselves with gold for that purpose.

While I am not unfriendly to silver and while I desire to see it recognized to such an extent as is consistent with financial safety and the preservation of national honor and credit, I am not willing to see gold entirely banished from our currency and finances. To avert such a consequence I believe thorough and radical remedial legislation should be promptly passed. I therefore beg the Congress to give the subject immediate attention.

In my opinion the Secretary of the Treasury should be authorized to issue bonds of the Government for the purpose of procuring and maintaining a sufficient gold reserve and the redemption and cancellation of the United States legal-tender notes and the Treasury notes issued for the purchase of silver under the law of July 14, 1890. We should be relieved from the humiliating process of issuing bonds to procure gold to be immediately and repeatedly drawn out on these obligations for purposes not related to the benefit of our Government or our people. The principal and interest of these bonds should be payable on their face in gold, because they should be sold only for gold or its representative, and because there would now probably be difficulty in favorably disposing of bonds not containing this stipulation. I suggest that the bonds be issued in denominations of twenty and fifty dollars and their multiples and that they bear interest at a rate not exceeding 3 per cent per annum. I do not see why they should not be payable fifty years from their date. We of the present generation have large amounts to pay if we meet our obligations, and long bonds are most salable. The Secretary of the Treasury might well be permitted at his discretion to receive on the sale of bonds the legal-tender and Treasury notes to be retired, and of course when they are thus retired or redeemed in gold they should be canceled.

These bonds under existing laws could be deposited by national banks as security for circulation, and such banks should be allowed to issue circulation up to the face value of these or any other bonds so deposited, except bonds outstanding bearing only 2 per cent interest and which sell in the market at less than par. National banks should not be allowed to take out circulating notes of a less denomination than $10, and when such as are now outstanding reach the Treasury, except for redemption and retirement, they should be canceled and notes of the denomination of $10 and upward issued in their stead. Silver certificates of the denomination of $10 and upward should be replaced by certificates of the denominations under $10.

As a constant means for the maintenance of a reasonable supply of gold in the Treasury, our duties on imports should be paid in gold, allowing all other dues to the Government to be paid in any other form of money.

I believe all the provisions I have suggested should be embodied in our laws if we are to enjoy a complete reinstatement of a sound financial condition. They need not interfere with any currency scheme providing for the increase of the circulating medium through the agency of national or State banks that may commend itself to the Congress, since they can easily be adjusted to such a scheme. Objection has been made to the issuance of interest-bearing obligations for the purpose of retiring the noninterest-bearing legal-tender notes. In point of fact, however, these notes have burdened us with a large load of interest, and it is still accumulating. The aggregate interest on the original issue of bonds, the proceeds of which in gold constituted the reserve for the payment of these notes, amounted to $70,326,250 on January 1, 1895, and the annual charge for interest on these bonds and those issued for the same purpose during the last year will be $9,145,000, dating from January 1, 1895.

While the cancellation of these notes would not relieve us from the obligations already incurred on their account, these figures are given by way of suggesting that their existence has not been free from interest charges and that the longer they are outstanding, judging from the experience of the last year, the more expensive they will become.

In conclusion I desire to frankly confess my reluctance to issuing more bonds in present circumstances and with no better results than have lately followed that course. I can not, however, refrain from adding to an assurance of my anxiety to cooperate with the present Congress in any reasonable measure of relief an expression of my determination to leave nothing undone which furnishes a hope for improving the situation or checking a suspicion of our disinclination or disability to meet with the strictest honor every national obligation.

Source: Richardson, James D. *A Compilation of the Messages and Papers of the Presidents 1789–1897.* Volume 13. New York: Bureau of National Literature, 1897, 5993–5997.

President Theodore Roosevelt Endorses Anti-Trust Measures, 1903

Theodore Roosevelt was the youngest president to be sworn into office at the time of his succession in 1901, after President William McKinley's assassination. Roosevelt brought with him a clear vision for strengthening the United States economy and the nation as a whole. Though the U.S. economy was strong and attractive to foreign investors and immigrants in 1901, President Roosevelt believed that too many corporations had accrued too much power through potentially criminal means and without properly giving back to the public—or acting with regard for the public good—in the way that he believed they should. He subsequently created the Department of Commerce and Labor to help regulate and enforce the country's business laws and practices. The president was a fan of antitrust measures, which were already in place with the Sherman Antitrust Act of 1890 and were designed to break up monopolizing businesses. However, Roosevelt believed that the Sherman Act was insufficient to meet the challenge of breaking up the corporate monopolies that had seized strangleholds over important industries. The following document is an excerpt from the president's Third Annual Message to Congress, delivered on December 7, 1903, in which he calls for increased enforcement of antitrust laws and decries the state of U.S. business ethics.

To the Senate and House of Representatives:

The country is to be congratulated on the amount of substantial achievement which has marked the past year both as regards our foreign and as regards our domestic policy.

With a nation as with a man the most important things are those of the household, and therefore the country is especially to be congratulated on what has been accomplished in the direction of providing for the exercise of supervision over the great corporations and combinations of corporations engaged in interstate commerce. The Congress has created the Department of Commerce and Labor, including the Bureau of Corporations, with for the first time authority to secure proper publicity of such proceedings of these great corporations as the public has the right to know. It has provided for the expediting of suits for the enforcement of the Federal anti-trust law; and by another law it has secured equal treatment to all producers in the transportation of their goods, thus taking a long stride forward in making effective the work of the Interstate Commerce Commission.

The establishment of the Department of Commerce and Labor, with the Bureau of Corporations thereunder, marks a real advance in the direction of doing all that is possible for the solution of the questions vitally affecting capitalists and wageworkers. The act creating the Department was approved on February 14, 1903, and two days later the head of the Department was nominated and confirmed by the Senate. Since then the work of organization has been pushed as rapidly as the initial appropriations permitted, and with due regard to thoroughness and the broad purposes which the Department is designed to serve. After the transfer of the various bureaus and branches to the Department at the beginning of the current fiscal year, as provided for in the act, the personnel comprised 1,289 employees in Washington and 8,836 in the country at large. The scope of the Department's duty and authority embraces the commercial and industrial interests of the Nation. It is not designed to restrict or control the fullest liberty of legitimate business action, but to secure exact and authentic information which will aid the Executive in enforcing existing laws, and which will enable the Congress to enact additional legislation, if any should be found necessary, in order to prevent the few from obtaining privileges at the expense of diminished opportunities for the many.

The preliminary work of the Bureau of Corporations in the Department has shown the wisdom of its creation. Publicity in corporate affairs will tend to do away with ignorance, and will afford facts upon which intelligent action may be taken. Systematic, intelligent investigation is already developing facts the knowledge of which is essential to a right understanding of the needs and duties of the business world. The corporation which is honestly and fairly organized, whose managers in the conduct of its business recognize their obligation to deal squarely with their stockholders, their competitors, and the public, has nothing to fear from such supervision. The purpose of this Bureau is not to embarrass or assail legitimate business, but to aid in bringing about a better industrial condition—a condition under which there shall be obedience to law and recognition of public obligation by all corporations, great or small. The Department of Commerce and Labor will be not only the clearing house for information regarding the business transactions of the Nation, but the executive arm of the Government to aid in strengthening our domestic and foreign markets, in perfecting our transportation facilities, in building up our merchant marine, in preventing the entrance of undesirable immigrants, in improving commercial and industrial conditions, and in bringing together on common ground those necessary partners in industrial progress—capital and labor. Commerce between the nations is steadily growing in volume, and the tendency of the times is toward closer trade relations. Constant watchfulness is needed to secure to Americans the chance to participate to the best advantage in foreign trade; and we may confidently expect that the new Department will justify the expectation of its creators by the exercise of this watchfulness, as well as by the businesslike administration of such laws relating to our internal affairs as are entrusted to its care.

In enacting the laws above enumerated the Congress proceeded on sane and conservative lines. Nothing revolutionary was attempted; but a common-sense and successful effort was made in the direction of seeing that corporations are so handled as to subserve the public good. The legislation was moderate. It was characterized throughout by the idea that we were not attacking corporations, but endeavoring to provide for doing away with any evil in them; that we drew the line against misconduct, not against wealth; gladly recognizing the great good done by the capitalist who alone, or in conjunction with his fellows, does his work along proper and legitimate lines. The purpose of the legislation, which purpose will undoubtedly be fulfilled, was to favor such a man when he does well, and to supervise his action only to prevent him from doing ill. Publicity can do no harm to the honest corporation. The only corporation that has cause to dread it is the corporation which shrinks from the light, and about the welfare of such corporations we need not be oversensitive. The work of the Department of Commerce and Labor has been conditioned upon this theory, of securing fair treatment alike for labor and for capital.

The consistent policy of the National Government, so far as it has the power, is to hold in check the unscrupulous man, whether employer or employee; but to refuse to weaken individual initiative or to hamper or cramp the industrial development of the country. We recognize that this is an era of federation and combination, in which great capitalistic corporations and labor unions have become factors of tremendous importance in all industrial centers. Hearty recognition is given the far-reaching, beneficent work which has been accomplished through both corporations and unions, and the line as between different corporations, as between different unions, is drawn as it is between different individuals; that is, it is drawn on conduct, the effort being to treat both organized capital and organized labor alike; asking nothing save that the interest of each shall be brought into harmony with the interest of the general public, and that the conduct of each shall conform to the fundamental rules of obedience to law, of individual freedom, and of justice and fair dealing towards all. Whenever either corporation, labor union, or individual disregards the law or acts in a spirit of arbitrary and tyrannous interference with the rights of others, whether corporations or individuals, then where the Federal Government has jurisdiction, it will see to it that the misconduct is stopped, paying not the slightest heed to the position or power of the corporation, the union or the individual, but only to one vital fact—that is, the question whether or not the conduct of the individual or aggregate of individuals is in accordance with the law of the land. Every man must be guaranteed his liberty and his right to do as he likes with his property or his labor, so long as he does not infringe the rights of others. No man is above the law and no man is below it; nor do we ask any man's permission when we require him to obey it. Obedience to the law is demanded as a right; not asked as a favor.

We have cause as a nation to be thankful for the steps that have been so successfully taken to put these principles into effect. The progress has been by evolution, not by revolution. Nothing radical has been done; the action has been both moderate and resolute. Therefore the work will stand. There shall be no backward step. If in the working of the laws it proves desirable that they shall at any point be expanded or amplified, the amendment can be made as its desirability is shown. Meanwhile they are being administered with judgment, but with insistence upon obedience to them, and their need has been emphasized in signal fashion by the events of the past year.

Source: Richardson, James D. *A Compilation of the Messages and Papers of the Presidents 1789–1897.* Volume 14. New York: Bureau of National Literature, 1897, 6784–6815.

President Herbert Hoover Wrestles with the Stock Market Crash, 1930

On May 1, 1930, President Herbert Hoover gave a widely anticipated address to the Chamber of Commerce of the United States. His appearance came less than a year after the famous stock market crashed of October 1929, the event that triggered the historic Great Depression. President Hoover was famously opposed to spending federal money in aid for those in dire circumstances due to the weak economic conditions, which especially impacted economically vulnerable demographic groups such as African Americans and rural farmers. He skirted around the federal pool with other fundraising efforts. Yet the public was desperate for relief, and President Hoover was criticized for what was perceived to be a passive response to the unfolding economic crisis. The following passage provides insight into the president's economic strategies during this critical moment in the country's history.

Gentlemen of the United States Chamber of Commerce:

We have been passing through one of those great economic storms which periodically bring hardship and suffering upon our people. While the crash only took place 6 months ago, I am convinced we have now passed the worst and with continued unity of effort we shall rapidly recover. There is one certainty in the future of a people of the resources, intelligence, and character of the people of the United States—that is prosperity.

On the occasion of this great storm we have for the first time attempted a great economic experiment, possibly one of the greatest of our history. By cooperation between Government officials and the entire community, business, railways, public utilities, agriculture, labor, the press, our financial institutions and public authorities, we have undertaken to stabilize economic forces; to mitigate the effects of the crash and to shorten its destructive period. I believe I can say with assurance that our joint undertaking has succeeded to a remarkable degree, and that it furnishes a basis of great tribute to our people for unity of action in time of national emergency. To those many business leaders present here I know that I express the gratitude of our countrymen.

It is unfortunate, in a sense, that any useful discussion of the problems behind and before us has to be expressed wholly in the cold language of economics, for I realize as keenly as anyone can that individually they are not problems in science but are the most human questions in the world. They involve the immediate fears of men and women for their daily bread, the well-being of their children, the security of their homes. They are intensely personal questions fraught with living significance to everything they hold dear. The officers of a ship in heavy seas have as deep a consciousness of the human values involved in the passengers and crew whose lives are in their keeping, but they can best serve them by taking counsel of their charts, compass, and barometer, and by devotion to navigation and the boilers. In like manner, the individual welfare can best be served by us if we devote ourselves to the amelioration of destructive forces for thereby we serve millions of our people.

All slumps are the inexorable consequences of the destructive forces of booms. If we inquire into the primary cause of the great boom on the stock exchanges last year we find it rests mainly upon certain forces inherent in human mind. When our Nation has traveled on the high road to prosperity for a considerable term of years, the natural optimism of our people brings into being a spirit of undue speculation against the future. These vast contagions of speculative emotion have hitherto throughout all history proved themselves uncontrollable by any device that the economist, the businessman, or the Government has been able to suggest. The effect of them is to divert capital and energy from healthy enterprise—the only real source of prosperity—to stimulate waste, extravagance, and unsound enterprise, with the inevitable collapse in panic.

Out of the great crashes hitherto there has always come a long train of destructive forces. A vast number of innocent people are directly involved in losses. Optimism swings to deepest pessimism; fear of the future chokes initiative and enterprise; monetary stringencies, security and commodity panics in our exchanges, bankruptcies and other losses all contribute to stifle consumption, decrease production, and finally express themselves in unemployment, decreased wages, strikes, lockouts, and a long period of stagnation. Many have looked upon all this rise and fall as a disease which must run its course and for which nothing could be done either in prevention, or to speed recovery, or to relieve the hardship which wreaks itself especially upon workers, farmers, and smaller business people. I do not accept the fatalistic view that the discovery of the means to restrain destructive speculation is beyond the genius of the American people.

Our immediate problem, however, has been the necessity to mitigate the effect of the recent crash, and to get back onto the road of prosperity as quickly as possible. This is the first time an effort has been made by the united community to this end. The success of this effort is of paramount importance, not only for our immediate needs but the possibilities it opens for the future. The intensity of the speculative boom on this occasion was, in my view, as great as or greater than any of our major manias before. The intensity of the slump has been greatly diminished by the efforts that have been made.

We—and as we, I speak of many men and many institutions—have followed several major lines of action. Our program was one of deliberate purpose to do everything possible to uphold general confidence which lies at the root of maintained initiative and enterprise; to check monetary, security, and commodity panics in our exchanges; to assure an abundance of capital at decreasing rates of interest so as to enable the resumption of business; to accelerate construction work so as to absorb as many employees as possible from industries hit by decreased demand; to hold up the level of wages by voluntary agreement and thus maintain the living standards of the vast majority who remain in employment to avoid accelerating the depression by the hardship and disarrangement of strikes and lockouts; and by upholding consuming power of the wage earners to in turn support agriculture.

We may well inquire into our progress thus far. We have succeeded in maintaining confidence and courage. We have avoided monetary panic and credit stringency. Those dangers are behind us. From the moment of the crash, interest rates have steadily decreased and capital has become steadily more abundant. Our investment markets have absorbed over 2 billions of new securities since the crash. There has been no significant bank or industrial failure. That danger, too, is safely behind us.

The acceleration of construction programs has been successful beyond our hopes. The great utilities, the railways, and the large manufacturers have responded courageously. The Federal Government has not only expedited its current works but Congress has authorized further expenditures. The Governors, mayors, and other authorities have everywhere been doing their full part. The result has been the placing of contracts of this character to the value of about $500 million during the first 4 months of 1930, or nearly three times the amount brought into being in the corresponding 4 months of the last great depression of 8 years ago. All of which contributes not only to direct employment but also a long train of jobs in the material and transportation industries. We are suffering from a decrease in residential construction, but despite this we have reason to believe that the total construction will still further expand, and we should during 1930 witness a larger gross volume of improvement work than normal.

For the first time in the history of great slumps we have had no substantial reductions in wages and we have had no strikes or lockouts which were in any way connected with this situation.

The accelerated construction has naturally not been able to absorb all the unemployment brought by the injuries of the boom and crash. Unfortunately we have no adequate statistics upon the volume of unemployment. The maximum point of depression was about the first of the year, when, severe as the shock was, the unemployment was much less proportionately than in our two last major depressions. A telegraphic canvass of the Governors and mayors who are cooperating so ably with us in organizing public works brings with one exception the unanimous response of continuously decreasing unemployment each month and the assurance of further decreases again in May.

All these widespread activities of our businessmen and our institutions offer sharp contrast with the activities of previous major crashes and our experiences from them. As a consequence, we have attained a stage of recovery within this short period greater than that attained during a whole year or more following previous equally great storms.

While we are today chiefly concerned with continuing the measures we have in process for relief from this storm, and in which we must have no relaxation, we must not neglect the lessons we have had from it, and we must consider the measures which we can undertake both for prevention of such storms and for relief from them. Economic health, like human health, requires prevention of infection as well as cure of it.

I take it that the outstanding problem and the ideal of our economic system is to secure freedom of initiative and to preserve stability in the economic structure in order that the door of opportunity and equality of opportunity may be held open to all our citizens; that every businessman shall go about his affairs with confidence in the future; that it shall give assurance to our people of a job for everyone who wishes to work; that it shall, by steady improvement through research and invention, advance standards of living to the whole of our people. That will constitute the conquest of poverty, which is the great human aspiration of our economic life.

And these economic storms are the most serious interruptions to this progress which we have to face. Some of you will recollect that following the great boom and slump of 8 years ago, as Secretary of Commerce, I initiated a series of conferences and investigations by representative men into the experiences of that occasion and to make therefrom recommendations for the future. It is worth a moment to examine our conclusions at that time as tested in this present crisis.

The first of the conclusions at that time was that our credit machinery should be strengthened to stand the shock of crash; that the adjustment of interest rates through the Federal Reserve System should retard destructive speculation and support enterprise during the depression.

Our credit machinery has proved itself able to stand shock in the commercial field through the Federal Reserve System, in the industrial field through the bond market and the investment houses, in the farm mortgage field to some extent through the Farm Loan System; and in the installment-buying field through the organization of powerful finance corporations.

But if we examine the strains during the past 6 months we shall find one area of credit which is most inadequately organized and which almost ceased to function under the present stress. This is the provision of a steady flow of capital to the home builder.

From a social point of view this is one of the most vital segments of credit and should be placed in such a definitely mobilized and organized form as would assure its continuous and stable flow. The ownership of homes, the improvement of residential conditions to our people, is the first anchor in social stability and social progress. Here is the greatest field for expanded organization of capital and at the same time stimulation to increased standards of living and social service that lies open to our great loan institutions.

The result of the inability to freely secure capital has been a great diminution in home construction and a large segment of unemployment which could have been avoided had there been a more systematic capital supply organized with the adequacy and efficiency of the other segments of finance. We need right now an especial effort of our loan institutions in all parts of the country to increase the capital available for this purpose as a part of the remedy of the present situation.

There can be no doubt of the service of the Federal Reserve System in not only withstanding the shock but also in promoting the supply of capital after the collapse. We have, however, a new experience in the effect of discount rates and other actions of the system in attempts to retard speculation. The system and the banks managed throughout the whole of the speculative period to maintain interest rates on money for commercial use at 5 to 6 percent per annum, and by their efforts they segregated the use of capital for speculation in such fashion that the rates upon such capital ran up to 18 percent per annum. But even these high rates on speculative capital offered little real retardation to the speculative mania of the country. They served, in fact, to attract capital from productive enterprise, and this was one of the secondary factors in producing the crash itself. The alternative, however, of lifting commercial rates still higher in order to check speculation by checking business is also debatable. The whole bearing of interest rates upon speculation and stable production requires exhaustive consideration in view of these new experiences.

One of the subsidiary proposals in our examination 7 years ago, directed to increase stability, was that improved statistical services should be created which would indicate the approach of undue speculation and thereby give advance storm warnings to the business world and the country. Great improvements were made in the statistical services, and by reading the signals thousands of businessmen avoided the maelstrom of speculation and our major industries came through strong and unimpaired—though the people generally did not grasp these warnings, or this crisis would not have happened. We should have even more accurate services in the future and a wider understanding of their use. We need, particularly, a knowledge of employment at all times, if we are intelligently to plan a proper functioning of our economic system. I have interested myself in seeing that the census we are taking today makes for the first time a real determination of unemployment. I have hopes that upon this foundation we can regularly secure information of first importance to daily conduct in our economic world.

In remedial measures we have followed the recommendations of 7 years ago as to the acceleration of construction work, the most practicable remedy for unemployment. It has been organized effectively in most important directions, and the success of organization in certain local communities points the way to even more effective action in the future by definite plans of decentralization.

Another of the byproducts of this experience which has been vividly brought to the front is the whole question of agencies for placing the unemployed in contact with possible jobs. In this field is also the problem of what is termed technological unemployment. The great expansion in scientific and industrial research, the multiplicity of inventions and increasing efficiency of business, is shifting men in industry with a speed we have never hitherto known. The whole subject is one of profound importance.

We have advanced in all these methods of stability in recent years. The development of our credit system, our statistics, our methods of security and relief in depression, all show progress. We have developed further steps during the past 6 months. But the whole range of our experiences from this boom and slump should be placed under accurate examination with a view to broad determination of what can be done to achieve greater stability for the future both in prevention and in remedy. If such an exhaustive examination meets with general approval, I shall, when the situation clears a little, move to organize a body—representative of business, economics, labor, and agriculture—to undertake it.

I do believe that our experience shows that we can produce helpful and wholesome effects in our economic system by voluntary cooperation through the great associations representative of business, industry, labor, and agriculture, both nationally and locally.

And it is my view that in this field of cooperative action outside of government lies the hope of intelligent information and wise planning. The Government can be helpful in emergency, it can be helpful to secure and spread information.

Such action, however, as may be developed must adhere steadfastly to the very bones of our economic system, which are the framework of progress. And that progress must come from individual initiative, and in time of stress it must be mobilized through cooperative action.

The proper constructive activities of the great voluntary organizations in the community provide the highest form of economic self-government. Permanent advance in the Republic will lie in the initiative of the people themselves.

We are not yet entirely through the difficulties of our situation. We have need to maintain every agency and every force that we have placed in motion until we are far along on the road to stable prosperity.

He would be a rash man who would state that we can produce the economic millennium, but there is great assurance that America is finding herself upon the road to secure social satisfaction, with the preservation of private industry, initiative, and a full opportunity for the development of the individual.

It is true that these economic things are not the objective of life itself. If by their steady improvement we shall yet further reduce poverty, shall create and secure more happy homes, we shall have served to make better men and women and a greater nation.

Source: *Public Papers of the Presidents of the United States. Herbert Hoover, 1930.* Washington, D.C.: Government Printing Office, 1976, Document 144.

President Herbert Hoover Signs the Norris-LaGuardia Act, 1932

As the United States economy struggled in the grip of the Great Depression, the movement to unionize became stronger than ever before. The relationship between the federal government and unions, as well as between employer and employee, had long been strained due to union tactics such as striking for better wages and working conditions. Industrialization had brought colossal assets to the economy, though often at the expense of the underserved laborer. While strikes and other forms of protest had sometimes enabled laborers to achieve their goals, employers in Depression-era America simply could not afford for their workers to go on strike while the economy was in such a weak position. Employers thus began to hit workers with court injunctions if they began to protest in any way or form. These injunctions effectively barred them from strike activity at the risk of legal penalties and unemployment. "Yellow-dog" contracts were also created as a tactic against union protests. Under the terms of these contracts, employees had to pledge not to join a union, or to disassociate from any unions they were currently involved with, in order to gain or maintain employment.

In 1932, however, President Herbert Hoover offered unions a break when he signed a Bill to Limit the Use of Injunctions in Labor Disputes, also known as the Norris-LaGuardia Act, on March 23. The legislation was a response to complaints that such injunctions and contracts were unconstitutional or promoted unconstitutional behavior. The following document is an official White House statement about the legislation, which was not popular with the president's big business supporters (Hoover chose not to release any personal statement about the bill).

THE PRESIDENT, in signing the bill limiting the use of injunction in labor disputes, made public the following letter he received from the Attorney General:
Sir:
Under date of March twenty-first you transmitted to me H.R. 5315, an act to amend the Judicial Code and to define and limit the jurisdiction of courts sitting in equity and for other purposes, with the request that I advise you whether there is any objection to its approval. This bill is the one commonly known as the anti-injunction bill.

Objections have been made to this measure because of the alleged unconstitutionality of some of its provisions, among which are those relating to contracts between employers and employees by which the latter agree not to be members of labor organizations and which are commonly called yellow dog contracts.

One of the major purposes of the bill is to prevent the issuance of injunctions to restrain third parties from persuading employees to violate such contracts, the theory of the bill being that such contracts are exacted from employees not with the idea that they will be treated by the employees as binding obligations but as a basis for invoking the old common law rule against malicious interference with contracts by third persons, and in this way to enable employers to secure injunctions against peaceful persuasion directed at their employees.

There are various other aspects of the bill, the unconstitutionality of which has been debated. It seems to me futile to enter into a discussion of these questions. They are of such a controversial nature that they are not susceptible of final decision by the executive branch of the government, and no executive or administrative ruling for or against the validity of any provisions of this measure could be accepted as final. These questions are of such a nature that they can only be set at rest by judicial decision.

Many objections have been made to the supposed effect of various provisions of this bill. In a number of respects it is not as clear as it might be, and its interpretation may involve differences of opinion, but many of these objections are based on extreme interpretations which are not warranted by the text of the bill as it was readjusted in conference.

It is inconceivable that Congress could have intended to protect racketeering and extortion under the guise of labor organization activity, and the anti-trust division of this Department, having carefully considered the measure, has concluded that it does not prevent injunctions in such cases and that it does not prevent the maintenance by the United States of suits to enjoin unlawful conspiracies or combinations under the anti-trust laws to outlaw legitimate articles of interstate commerce. It does not purport to permit interference by violence with workmen who wish to maintain their employment, and, fairly construed, it does not protect such interference by threats of violence or that sort of intimidation which creates fear of violence.

With due regard for all the arguments for and against the measure, and considering its legislative history, I recommend that it receive your approval.

Source: *Public Papers of the Presidents of the United States. Herbert Hoover, 1932–33.* Washington, D.C.: Government Printing Office, 1977, Document 90.

President George H. W. Bush Outlines a Bailout to Address the Savings and Loans Crisis, 1989

Savings and Loans (S&L) banks were created to lend money to potential homeowners to pay their mortgages, as banks at the time did not give out loans for this reason. As S&L banks became more popular during the midtwentieth century, they amassed hundreds of billions of dollars in assets. In the 1980s, however, high inflation rates translated to higher interest rates, and many homeowners could no longer afford to pay their loans. The banks were hit with huge losses, and their insurance carrier, the Federal Savings and Loan Insurance Corporation (FSLIC), could not cover the expenses—it went bankrupt and dissolved, despite efforts to recapitalize it. Though some S&L banks closed, new laws were passed in an effort to keep them open despite their insolvent status. These measures allowed the banks to give out high-risk, high-limit loans with no real securities or regulation. Though this plan worked to an extent, it was not sustainable. By the end of the crisis, both the government and taxpayers were responsible for bailing out billions in S&L losses.

In the following document, President George H. W. Bush discusses the crisis during a news conference on February 6, 1989, and discusses several ideas to address the problem. Many of these ideas for recovery were later incorporated into the Financial Institutions Reform Recovery and Enforcement Act (FIRREA), which sought to clean up the S&L banks' operations by effectively selling insolvent banks' assets.

The President. Well, for the more than half a century, the U.S. has operated a deposit insurance program that provides direct government protection to the savings of our citizens. This program has enabled tens of millions of Americans to save with confidence. In all the time since creation of the deposit insurance, savers have not lost one dollar of insured deposits, and I am determined that they never will.

Deposit insurance has always been intended to be self-funded. And this means that the banks, the savings and loans, and credit unions that are insured pay a small amount of their assets each year into a fund that's used to protect depositors. In every case, these funds are spent to protect the depositors, not the institutions that fail.

For the last 20 years, conditions in our financial markets have grown steadily more complex, and a portion of the savings and loan industry has encountered steadily growing problems. These financial difficulties have led to a continuous erosion of the strength of the Federal Savings and Loan Insurance Corporation, FSLIC. Economic conditions have played a major role in this situation. However, unconscionable risktaking, fraud, and outright criminality have also been factors. Because of the accumulation of losses at hundreds of these thrift institutions, additional resources must be devoted to cleaning up this problem. We intend to restore our entire deposit insurance system to complete health.

While the issues are complex and the difficulties manifold, we will make the hard choices, not run from them. We will see that the guarantee to depositors is forever honored. And we will see to it that the system is reformed comprehensively so that the situation is not repeated again. To do this, I am today announcing a comprehensive and wide-ranging set of proposals. The Secretary of the Treasury, Nicholas Brady, will describe these proposals to you in detail in a few minutes. However, I think it's important to summarize some of the major points. The proposals include four major elements.

First, currently insolvent savings institutions will be placed under the joint management of the FDIC [Federal Deposit Insurance Corporation] and FSLIC pursuant to existing law. This will enable us to control future risktaking and to begin reducing ongoing losses.

Second, the regulatory mechanism will be substantially overhauled to enable it to more effectively limit risktaking. The FDIC would become the insurance agency for both banks and thrifts under this system, although there's no commingling of funds. The insurer will have the authority to set minimum standards for capital and accounting. Uniform disclosure standards will also be implemented. The chartering agency for thrifts would come under the general oversight of the Secretary of the Treasury.

Third, we will create a financing corporation to issue $50 billion in bonds to finance the cost of resolving failed institutions, which will supplement approximately $40 billion that has already been spent. All of the principal of these bonds and a portion of the interest on them will be paid from industry sources. However, the balance would be paid from on-budget outlays of general revenues. Hopefully, some of these revenues will be recovered in the future through sale of assets and recovery of funds from the wrongdoers.

Fourth, we plan to increase the budget of the Justice Department by approximately $50 million to enable it to create a nationwide program to seek out and punish those that have committed wrongdoing in the management of these failed institutions. These funds will result in almost doubling the personnel devoted to the apprehension and prosecution of individuals committing fraud in our financial markets.

As you can see, these proposals are based upon several overriding principles. First, I will not support any new fee on depositors. Second, we should preserve the overall Federal budget structure and not allow the misdeeds and the wrongdoings of savings and loan executives and the inadequacy of their regulation to significantly alter our overall budget priorities. And third, I have concluded that this proposal, if promptly enacted, will enable our system to prevent any repetition of this situation. And fourth, I have decided to attack this problem head-on with every available resource of our government because it is a national problem. I have directed that the combined resources of our Federal agencies be brought together in a team effort to resolve the problem. And fifth, I believe that banks and thrifts should pay the real cost of providing the deposit insurance protection. The price the FDIC charges banks for their insurance has not been increased since 1935. We propose to increase the bank insurance premium by less than 7 cents per $100 of insurance protection that they receive. Every penny collected would be used to strengthen the FDIC so that the taxpayers will not be called on to rescue it a few years from now.

And I make you a solemn pledge that we will make every effort to recover assets diverted from these institutions and to place behind bars those who have caused losses through criminal behavior. Let those who would take advantage of the public trust and put at risk the savings of American families anticipate that we will seek them out, pursue them, and demand the most severe penalties.

In closing, I want to just say a word to the small savers of America. Across this great land, families and individuals work and save, and we hope to encourage even greater rates of savings to promote a brighter future for our children. Your government has stood behind the safety of insured deposits before, it does today, and it will do so at all times in the future. Every insured deposit will be backed by the full faith and credit of the United States of America, which means that it will be absolutely protected.

For the future, we will seek to achieve a safe, sound, and profitable banking system. However, integrity and prudence must share an equal position with competition in our financial markets. Clean markets are an absolute prerequisite to a free economy and to the public confidence that is its most important ingredient.

I've determined to face this problem squarely and to ask for your support in putting it behind us. I have ordered that the resources of the executive branch be brought to bear on cleaning up this problem. I have personally met with the leadership of Congress on this issue. My administration will work cooperatively with Congress as the legislation that we will submit in a few days' time is considered. I call on the Congress to join me in a determined effort to resolve this threat to the American financial system permanently, and to do so without the delay.

Source: *Public Papers of the Presidents of the United States. George Bush, 1989, Book 1.* Washington, D.C.: Government Printing Office, 1990, 60–65.

President Bill Clinton Delivers Remarks on Government Shutdown, 1995

In November 1995, President Bill Clinton vetoed a budget bill proposed by the Republican Speaker of the House, Newt Gingrich. The ensuing budget standoff resulted in a partial shutdown of the federal government on November 14. The Republican Congress believed that government spending was too high and that the United States was in danger of defaulting on its debt. The bill proposed to slash funds from a wide range of initiatives and programs that Democratic President Clinton sought to maintain or expand. The shutdown was unlike any other in that it had been planned by Gingrich to bring President Clinton back to negotiations, though there were also inferences of a personal motivation behind Gingrich's political maneuver.

While the government resumed operation on November 18 after the Republican Congressional leadership grudgingly agreed to a temporary funding agreement, the government shut down once again over the same issues from December 16 to January 5, 1996. This 21-day shutdown was the longest in the country's history at the time. Hundreds of thousands of federal workers were furloughed, and the government lost over $700 million in the first shutdown and over $1 billion in the next. Moreover, Gingrich's gambit did not work. Public sentiment turned firmly against the Republicans, and in the end, they dropped their opposition to many of President Clinton's budget priorities. Here are President Clinton's remarks on the occasion of the first shutdown, on November 14.

Good afternoon. Today, as of noon, almost half of the Federal Government employees are idle. The Government is partially shutting down because Congress has failed to pass the straightforward legislation necessary to keep the Government running without imposing sharp hikes in Medicare premiums and deep cuts in education and the environment.

It is particularly unfortunate that the Republican Congress has brought us to this juncture because, after all, we share a central goal, balancing the Federal budget. We must lift the burden of debt that threatens the future of our children and grandchildren. And we must free up money so that the private sector can invest, create jobs, and our economy can continue its healthy growth.

Since I took office, we have cut the Federal deficit nearly in half. It is important that the people of the United States know that the United States now has proportionately the lowest Government budget deficit of any large industrial nation. We have eliminated 200,000 positions from the Federal bureaucracy since I took office. Our Federal Government is now the smallest percentage of the civilian work force it has been since 1933, before the New Deal. We have made enormous progress, and now we must finish the job.

Let me be clear: We must balance the budget. I proposed to Congress a balanced budget, but Congress refused to enact it. Congress has even refused to give me the line-item veto to help me achieve further deficit reduction. But we must balance this budget without resorting to their priorities, without their unwise cuts in Medicare and Medicaid, in education and the environment.

Five months ago I proposed my balanced budget plan. It balances the budget in the right way. It cuts hundreds of wasteful and outdated programs. But it upholds our fundamental values to provide opportunity, to respect our obligations to our parents and our children, to strengthen families, and to strengthen America because it preserves Medicare and Medicaid, it invests in education and technology, it protects the environment, and it gives the tax cuts to working families for childrearing and for education.

Unfortunately, Republican leaders in Washington have put ideology ahead of common sense and shared values in their pursuit of a budget plan. We can balance the budget without doing what they seek to do. We can balance the budget without the deep cuts in education, without the deep cuts in the environment, without letting Medicare wither on the vine, without imposing tax increases on the hardest pressed working families in America.

I am fighting for a balanced budget that is good for America and consistent with our values. If they'll give me the tools, I'll balance the budget.

I vetoed the spending bill sent to me by Congress last night because America can never accept under pressure what it would not accept in free and open debate. I strongly believe their budget plan is bad for America. I believe it will undermine opportunity, make it harder for families to do the work that they have to do, weaken our obligations to our parents and our children, and make our country more divided. So I will continue to fight for the right kind of balanced budget.

Remember, the Republicans are following a very explicit strategy announced last April by Speaker Gingrich to use the threat of a Government shutdown to force America to accept their cuts in Medicare and Medicaid, to accept their cuts in education and technology and the environment. Yesterday they sent me legislation that said we will only keep the Government going and we will only let it pay its debts if, and only if, we accept their cuts in Medicare, their cuts in education, their cuts in the environment, and their repeal of 25 years of bipartisan commitments to protect the environment and public health.

On behalf of the American people, I said no. If America has to close down access to education, to a clean environment, to affordable health care to keep our Government open, then the price is too high.

My message to Congress is simple: You say you want to balance the budget, so let's say yes to balancing the budget. But let us together say no to these deep and unwise cuts in education, technology, the environment, Medicare, and Medicaid. Let's say no to raising taxes on the hardest pressed working families in America. These things are not necessary to balance the budget. Yes to balancing the budget; no to the cuts.

I know the loss of Government service will cause disruption in the lives of millions of Americans. We will do our very best to minimize this hardship. But there is, after all, a simple solution to the problem. All Congress has to do is to pass a straightforward bill to let Government perform its duties and pay its debts. Then we can get back to work and resolve our differences over the budget in an open, honest, and straightforward manner.

Before I conclude, I'd like to say a word to the hundreds of thousands of Federal employees who will be affected by this partial shutdown. I know, as your fellow citizens know, that the people who are affected by this shutdown are public servants. They're the people who process our Social Security applications, help our veterans apply for benefits, care for the national parks that are our natural heritage. They conduct the medical research that saves people's lives. They are important to America, and they deserve to be treated with dignity and respect. I will do everything I can to see that they receive back pay and that their families do not suffer because of this.

But it is my solemn responsibility to stand against a budget plan that is bad for America and to stand up for a balanced budget that is good for America. And that is exactly what I intend to do.

Thank you very much.

Source: *Public Papers of the Presidents of the United States. William J. Clinton: 1995, Book 2.* Washington, D.C.: Government Printing Office, 1996, 1755–1757.

President Barack Obama Introduces Measures to Pull America Out of the Great Recession, 2009

The Great Recession, as it came to be known, was one of the most severe economic crises in U.S. history. It began at the end of 2007, in the latter stages of President George W. Bush's second term. By the time President Barack Obama took office on January 20, 2009, hundreds of billions in taxpayer money—close to $1 trillion—in addition to other government purchases and funds, had been allocated toward bailing out failing financial institutions. These efforts were funneled through the Troubled Asset Relief Program (TARP). In particular, the funds went toward those institutions that had invested in subprime mortgages, for mass defaults on these mortgages had triggered a cascade of disastrous economic developments. All in all, millions of Americans lost their jobs, homes, and life savings as a result.

In the following document, President Obama addressed the nation on January 31, 2009, just two weeks after taking office. He discussed his plan of action to lift the country out of recession. Many of his proposed measures were passed by the Democratic-led Congress one month later (Republicans were almost universally opposed) as the American Recovery and Reinvestment Act of 2009 (ARRA). Notable provisions provided in the package included $288 billion in tax breaks, extensions of unemployment benefits, reforms to the financial services industry, and billions for new infrastructure development in the areas of education, energy, and transportation. The recession was declared officially over in June of 2009, though it would take years for the economy to rebound as a whole.

This morning I'd like to talk about some good news and some bad news as we confront our economic crisis.

The bad news is well known to Americans across our country as we continue to struggle through unprecedented economic turmoil. Yesterday we learned that our economy shrank by nearly 4 percent from October through December. That decline was the largest in over a quarter century, and it underscores the seriousness of the economic crisis that my administration found when we took office.

Already the slowdown has cost us tens of thousands of jobs in January alone. And the picture is likely to get worse before it gets better.

Make no mistake, these are not just numbers. Behind every statistic there's a story. Many Americans have seen their lives turned upside down. Families have been forced to make painful choices. Parents are struggling to pay the bills. Patients can't afford care. Students can't keep pace with tuition. And workers don't know whether their retirement will be dignified and secure.

The good news is that we are moving forward with a sense of urgency equal to the challenge. This week, the House passed the American recovery and reinvestment plan, which will save or create more than 3 million jobs over the next few years. It puts a tax cut into the pockets of working families and places a down payment on America's future by investing in energy independence and education, affordable health care, and American infrastructure.

Now this recovery plan moves to the Senate. I will continue working with both parties so that the strongest possible bill gets to my desk. With the stakes so high we simply cannot afford the same old gridlock and partisan posturing in Washington. It's time to move in a new direction.

Americans know that our economic recovery will take years, not months. But they will have little patience if we allow politics to get in the way of action, and our economy continues to slide. That's why I am calling on the Senate to pass this plan, so that we can put people back to work and begin the long, hard work of lifting our economy out of this crisis. No one bill, no matter how comprehensive, can cure what ails our economy. So just as we jump-start job creation, we must also ensure that markets are stable, credit is flowing, and families can stay in their homes.

Last year, Congress passed a plan to rescue the financial system. While the package helped avoid a financial collapse, many are frustrated by the results, and rightfully so. Too often taxpayer dollars have been spent without transparency or accountability. Banks have been extended a hand, but homeowners, students, and small businesses that need loans have been left to fend on their own.

And adding to this outrage, we learned this week that even as they petitioned for taxpayer assistance, Wall Street firms shamefully paid out nearly $20 billion in bonuses for 2008. While I'm committed to doing what it takes to maintain the flow of credit, the American people will not excuse or tolerate such arrogance and greed. The road to recovery demands that we all act responsibly, from Main Street to Washington to Wall Street.

Soon my Treasury Secretary, Tim Geithner, will announce a new strategy for reviving our financial system that gets credit flowing to businesses and families. We'll help lower mortgage costs and extend loans to small businesses so they can create jobs. We'll ensure that CEOs are not draining funds that should be advancing our recovery. And we will insist on unprecedented transparency, rigorous oversight, and clear accountability, so taxpayers know how their money is being spent and whether it is achieving results.

Rarely in history has our country faced economic problems as devastating as this crisis. But the strength of the American people compels us to come together. The road ahead will be long, but I promise you that every day that I go to work in the Oval Office, I carry with me your stories, and my administration is dedicated to alleviating your struggles and advancing your dreams. You are calling for action. Now is the time for those of us in Washington to live up to our responsibilities.

Source: *Public Papers of the Presidents of the United States. Barack Obama: 2009, Book 1.* Washington, D.C.: Government Printing Office, 2010, 28–29.

President Barack Obama Gives Remarks on Government Shutdown, 2013

In September of 2013, when the United States was still recovering from the Great Recession, Democratic President Barack Obama and some Republican members of the House of Representatives disagreed on budget plans concerning the Affordable Care Act (ACA) and the debt ceiling, which led to a government shutdown. The Republican members of the House were concerned about the act's individual mandate on health care, and they believed that the ACA's design and principles were not favorable, as its funding would be subsidized in part from taxing private insurers. Yet since the ACA had passed through Congress in 2010, and was set to commence in 2014, its provisions and funding methods were secured, and would not be impacted with the shutdown. The second issue of raising the debt ceiling stemmed from the Republican Party's ideologies of conservative spending. If the debt ceiling were raised, some Republicans believed it would allow the trend of high spending to continue, despite the fact that President Obama had reduced the federal deficit. When the Republican House and Democratic Senate failed to come to an agreement to meet the federal budget's deadline, the government shut down from October 1 to October 15. Hundreds of millions of dollars were lost each day the shutdown lasted, and by its end, tens of billions had been lost in the U.S. economy overall. Though President Obama fronted much of the blame for the shutdown from Republicans, the ACA proceeded as planned, and the debt ceiling was raised. In the following document of October 1, 2013, President Obama remarks on the shutdown, the ACA, and purpose of the debt ceiling.

Good morning, everybody. At midnight last night, for the first time in 17 years, Republicans in Congress chose to shut down the Federal Government. Let me be more specific: One faction of one party in one House of Congress in one branch of Government shut down major parts of the Government, all because they didn't like one law.

This Republican shutdown did not have to happen. But I want every American to understand why it did happen. Republicans in the House of Representatives refused to fund the Government unless we defunded or dismantled the Affordable Care Act. They've shut down the Government over an ideological crusade to deny affordable health insurance to millions of Americans. In other words, they demanded ransom just for doing their job.

And many Representatives, including an increasing number of Republicans, have made it clear that had they been allowed by Speaker Boehner to take a simple up-or-down vote on keeping the Government open, with no partisan strings attached, enough votes from both parties would have kept the American people's Government open and operating.

Now, we may not know the full impact of this Republican shutdown for some time. It will depend on how long it lasts. But we do know a couple of things. We know that the last time Republicans shut down the Government in 1996, it hurt our economy. And unlike 1996, our economy is still recovering from the worst recession in generations.

We know that certain services and benefits that America's seniors and veterans and business owners depend on must be put on hold. Certain offices, along with every national park and monument, must be closed. And while last night, I signed legislation to make sure our 1.4 million Active Duty military are paid through the shutdown, hundreds of thousands of civilian workers—many still on the job, many forced to stay home—aren't being paid, even if they have families to support and local businesses that rely on them. And we know that the longer this shutdown continues, the worse the effects will be. More families will be hurt. More businesses will be harmed.

So, once again, I urge House Republicans to reopen the Government, restart the services Americans depend on, and allow the public servants who have been sent home to return to work. This is only going to happen when Republicans realize they don't get to hold the entire economy hostage over ideological demands.

As I've said repeatedly, I am prepared to work with Democrats and Republicans to do the things we need to do to grow the economy and create jobs and get our fiscal house in order over the long run. Although I should add, this shutdown isn't about deficits or spending or budgets. After all, our deficits are falling at the fastest pace in 50 years. We've cut them in half since I took office. In fact, many of the demands the Republicans are now making would actually raise our deficits.

So no, this shutdown is not about deficits. It's not about budgets. This shutdown is about rolling back our efforts to provide health insurance to folks who don't have it. It's all about rolling back the Affordable Care Act. This, more than anything else, seems to be what the Republican Party stands for these days. I know it's strange that one party would make keeping people uninsured the centerpiece of their agenda, but that apparently is what it is.

And of course, what's stranger still is that shutting down our Government doesn't accomplish their stated goal. The Affordable Care Act is a law that passed the House; it passed the Senate. The Supreme Court ruled it constitutional. It was a central issue in last year's election. It is settled, and it is here to stay. And because of its funding sources, it's not impacted by a Government shutdown.

And these Americans are here with me today because, even though the Government is closed, a big part of the Affordable Care Act is now open for business. And for them, and millions like them, this is a historic day for a good reason. It's been a long time coming, but today, Americans who have been forced to go without insurance can now visit healthcare.gov and enroll in affordable new plans that offer quality coverage. That starts today.

And people will have 6 months to sign up. So over the next 6 months, people are going to have the opportunity—many times—in many cases, for the first time in their lives—to get affordable coverage that they desperately need.

Now, of course, if you're one of the 85 percent of Americans who already have health insurance, you don't need to do a thing. You're already benefiting from new benefits and protections that have been in place for some time under this law. But for the 15 percent of Americans who don't have health insurance, this opportunity is life changing.

Now, let me just tell folks a few stories that are represented here today. A few years ago, Amanda Barrett left her job in New York to take care of her parents. And for a while, she had temporary insurance that covered her multiple sclerosis. But when it expired, many insurers wouldn't cover her because of her MS. And she ended up paying $1,200 a month. That's nowhere near affordable. So starting today, she can get covered for much less, because today's new plan can't use your medical history to charge you more than anybody else.

Sky-high premiums once forced Nancy Beigel to choose between paying her rent or paying for health insurance. She's been uninsured ever since. So she pays all of her medical bills out of pocket, puts some on her credit card, making them even harder to pay. Nancy says: "They talk about those who fall through the cracks. I fell through the cracks 10 years ago, and I've been stuck there ever since." Well, starting today, Nancy can get covered just like everybody else.

Trinace Edwards was laid off from her job a year ago today. Six months ago, she was diagnosed with a brain tumor. She couldn't afford insurance on the individual market, so she hasn't received treatment yet. Her daughter Lenace, a student at the University of Maryland, is considering dropping out of school to help pay her mom's bills. Well, starting today, thanks to the Affordable Care Act, Trinace can get covered without forcing her daughter to give up on her dreams.

So if these stories of hard-working Americans sound familiar to you, well, starting today, you and your friends and your family and your coworkers can get covered too. Just visit healthcare.gov, and there you can compare insurance plans, side by side, the same way you'd shop for a plane ticket on Kayak or a TV on Amazon. You enter some basic information; you'll be presented with a list of quality, affordable plans that are available in your area, with clear descriptions of what each plan covers and what it will cost. You'll find more choices, more competition, and in many cases, lower prices. Most uninsured Americans will find that they can get covered for a hundred dollars or less.

And you don't have to take my word for it. Go on the web site, healthcare.gov, check it out for yourself. And then show it to your family and your friends and help them get covered, just like mayors and churches and community groups and companies are already fanning out to do across the country.

And there's a hotline where you can apply over the phone and get help with the application or just get questions that you have answered by real people in 150 different languages. So let me give you that number. The number is 1-800-318-2596. 1-800-318-2596. Check out healthcare.gov. Call that number. Show your family and friends how to use it. And we can get America covered, once and for all, so that the struggles that these folks have gone through and millions around the country have gone through for years finally get addressed.

And let me just remind people why I think this is so important. I heard a striking statistic yesterday. If you get cancer, you are 70 percent more likely to live another 5 years if you have insurance than if you don't. Think about that. That is what it means to have health insurance.

Set aside the issues of security and finances and how you're impacted by that, the stress involved in not knowing whether or not you're going to have health care. This is life-or-death stuff. Tens of thousands of Americans die each year just because they don't have health insurance. Millions more live with the fear that they'll go broke if they get sick. And today we begin to free millions of our fellow Americans from that fear.

Already, millions of young adults have been able to stay on their parents' plans until they turn 26. Millions of seniors already have gotten a discount on their prescription medicines. Already, millions of families have actually received rebates from insurance companies that didn't spend enough on their health care. So this law means more choice, more competition, lower costs for millions of Americans.

And this law doesn't just mean economic security for our families. It means we're finally addressing the biggest drivers of our long-term deficits. It means a stronger economy.

Remember, most Republicans have made a whole bunch of predictions about this law that haven't come true. There are no "death panels." Costs haven't sky-rocketed, they're growing at the slowest rate in 50 years. The last 3 years since I signed the Affordable Care Act into law are the three slowest rates of health spending growth on record.

And contrary to Republican claims, this law hasn't destroyed our economy. Over the past 3½ years, our businesses have created 7½ million new jobs. Just today we learned that our manufacturers are growing at the fastest rate in 2½ years. They have factored in the Affordable Care Act. They don't think it's a problem. What's weighing on the economy is not the Affordable Care Act, but the constant series of crises and the unwillingness to pass a reasonable budget by a faction of the Republican Party.

Now, like every new law, every new product rollout, there are going to be some glitches in the signup process along the way that we will fix. I've been saying this from the start. For example, we found out that there have been times this morning where the site has been running more slowly than it normally will. The reason is because more than 1 million people visited healthcare.gov before 7 in the morning.

To put that in context, there were five times more users in the marketplace this morning than have ever been on medicare.gov at one time. That gives you a sense of how important this is to millions of Americans around the country, and that's a good thing. And we're going to be speeding things up in the next few hours to handle all this demand that exceeds anything that we had expected.

Consider that just a couple of weeks ago, Apple rolled out a new mobile operating system. And within days, they found a glitch, so they fixed it. I don't remember anybody suggesting Apple should stop selling iPhones or iPads or threatening to shut down the company if they didn't. That's not how we do things in America. We don't actively root for failure. We get to work, we make things happen, we make them better, we keep going.

So in that context, I'll work with anybody who's got a serious idea to make the Affordable Care Act work better. I've said that repeatedly. But as long as I am President, I will not give in to reckless demands by some in the Republican Party to deny affordable health insurance to millions of hard-working Americans.

I want Republicans in Congress to know: These are the Americans you'd hurt if we're—you were allowed to dismantle this law. Americans like Amanda, Nancy, and Trinace, who now finally have the opportunity for basic security and peace of mind of health care just like everybody else, including Members of Congress. The notion that you'd make a condition for reopening the Government that I make sure these folks don't have health care, that doesn't make any sense. It doesn't make any sense.

Now, let me make one closing point. This Republican shutdown threatens our economy at a time when millions of Americans are still looking for work and businesses are starting to get some traction. So the timing is not good. Of course, a lot of the Republicans in the House ran for office 2 years ago promising to shut down the Government, and so, apparently, they've now gotten their wish. But as I've said before, the irony that the House Republicans have to contend with is, they've shut down a whole bunch of parts of the Government, but the Affordable Care Act is still open for business.

And this may be why you've got many Republican Governors and Senators and even a growing number of reasonable Republican Congressmen who are telling the extreme right of their party to knock it off, pass a budget, move on.

And I want to underscore the fact that Congress doesn't just have to end this shutdown and reopen the Government, Congress generally has to stop governing by crisis. They have to break this habit. It is a drag on the economy. It is not worthy of this country.

For example, one of the most important things Congress has to do in the next couple weeks is to raise what's called the debt ceiling. And it's important to understand what this is. This is a routine vote. Congress has taken this vote 45 times to raise the debt ceiling since Ronald Reagan took office. It does not cost taxpayers a single dime. It does not grow our deficits by a single dime. It does not authorize anybody to spend any new money whatsoever. All it does is authorize the Treasury to pay the bills on what Congress has already spent.

Think about that. If you buy a car and you've got a car note, you do not save money by not paying your car note. You're just a deadbeat. If you buy a house, you don't save money by not authorizing yourself to pay the mortgage. You're just going to be foreclosed on your home. That's what this is about.

It is routine. It is what they're supposed to do. This is not a concession to me. It is not some demand that's unreasonable that I'm making. This is what Congress is supposed to do as a routine matter. And they shouldn't wait until the last minute to do it. The last time Republicans even threatened this course of action—many of you remember, back in 2011—our economy staggered, our credit rating was downgraded for the first time. If they go through with it this time and force the United States to default on its obligations for the first time in history, it would be far more dangerous than a Government shutdown, as bad as a shutdown is. It would be an economic shutdown.

So I'll speak more on this in the coming days, but let me repeat: I will not negotiate over Congress's responsibility to pay bills it's already racked up. I'm not going to allow anybody to drag the good name of the United States of America through the mud just to refight a settled election or extract ideological demands. Nobody gets to hurt our economy and millions of hard-working families over a law you don't like.

There are a whole bunch of things that I'd like to see passed through Congress that the House Republicans haven't passed yet, and I'm not out there saying, well, I'm not—I'm going to let America default unless Congress does something that they don't want to do. That's not how adults operate. Certainly, that's not how our Government should operate. And that's true whether there's a Democrat in this office or a Republican in this office. Doesn't matter whether it's a Democratic House of Representatives or a Republican-controlled House of Representatives. There are certain rules that everybody abides by because we don't want to hurt other people just because we have a political disagreement.

So my main—my basic message to Congress is this: Pass a budget. End the Government shutdown. Pay your bills. Prevent an economic shutdown. Don't wait. Don't delay. Don't put our economy or our people through this any longer.

I am more than happy to work with them on all kinds of issues. I want to get back to work on the things that the American people sent us here to work on: creating new jobs, new growth, new security for our middle class.

We're better than this. Certainly, the American people are a lot better than this. And I believe that what we've accomplished for Amanda and Nancy and Trinace and tens of millions of their fellow citizens on this day proves that even when the odds are long and the obstacles are many, we are and always will be a country that can do great things together.

Thank you very much, everybody. God bless you. Thank you, all of you, for the great work that you're doing. And thank you, Kathleen Sebelius, for the outstanding work that she's doing making sure that millions of Americans can get health insurance.

Thank you.

Source: *Public Papers of the Presidents of the United States. Barack Obama: 2013, Book 2.* Washington, D.C.: Government Printing Office, 2019, 1116–1120.

Donald Trump Links Illegal Immigration to Government Shutdown, 2019

On December 22, 2018, the U.S. federal government was shut down after Republican President Donald J. Trump refused to pass any budget bills presented by Congress that did not include a $5.7 billion provision to build a wall on the southern border of the United States. The wall was the president's solution to "illegal immigration," which he had repeatedly described, both during the 2016 presidential campaign and his first two years in office, as a crisis. Despite the fact that Republicans controlled both the House of Representatives and the Senate at the time, Trump could not muster enough votes to move the "Wall money" through

Congress. The New Year began without progress, as Trump continued to threaten to veto any budget bill that did not include $5.7 billion for a border wall.

On January 3, 2019, Democrats took control of the House of Representatives, which meant that it was even more unlikely that Trump would get the $5.7 billion he wanted for wall construction. Trump soon after introduced the idea of declaring a national emergency to build the wall in an effort to evade congressional approval on its funding. All the while, close to one million federal workers were furloughed or working without pay as the shutdown dragged on. The negative economic effects of the workers' absences and their growing outrage over the situation, however, finally forced the Trump White House to reopen the government on January 25, 2019, for three weeks. On February 15, 2019, with yet another shutdown looming, Trump declared a national emergency to appropriate spending for the wall, triggering a blizzard of lawsuits from opponents who asserted that his appropriation was unconstitutional. The following document is an excerpt from President Trump's State of the Union Address, given on February 5, 2019, in which he discusses the importance of the wall. The shutdown lasted for 35 days, the longest ever in U.S. history.

Now, Republicans and Democrats must join forces again to confront an urgent national crisis. Congress has 10 days left to pass a bill that will fund our government, protect our homeland, and secure our very dangerous southern border.

Now is the time for Congress to show the world that America is committed to ending illegal immigration and putting the ruthless coyotes, cartels, drug dealers, and human traffickers out of business. (Applause.)

As we speak, large, organized caravans are on the march to the United States. We have just heard that Mexican cities, in order to remove the illegal immigrants from their communities, are getting trucks and buses to bring them up to our country in areas where there is little border protection. I have ordered another 3,750 troops to our southern border to prepare for this tremendous onslaught.

This is a moral issue. The lawless state of our southern border is a threat to the safety, security, and financial wellbeing of all America. We have a moral duty to create an immigration system that protects the lives and jobs of our citizens. This includes our obligation to the millions of immigrants living here today who followed the rules and respected our laws. Legal immigrants enrich our nation and strengthen our society in countless ways. (Applause.)

I want people to come into our country in the largest numbers ever, but they have to come in legally. (Applause.)

Tonight, I am asking you to defend our very dangerous southern border out of love and devotion to our fellow citizens and to our country.

No issue better illustrates the divide between America's working class and America's political class than illegal immigration. Wealthy politicians and donors push for open borders while living their lives behind walls, and gates, and guards. (Applause.)

Meanwhile, working-class Americans are left to pay the price for mass illegal migration: reduced jobs, lower wages, overburdened schools, hospitals that are so crowded you can't get in, increased crime, and a depleted social safety net.

Tolerance for illegal immigration is not compassionate; it is actually very cruel. (Applause.)

One in three women is sexually assaulted on the long journey north. Smugglers use migrant children as human pawns to exploit our laws and gain access to our country. Human traffickers and sex traffickers take advantage of the wide-open areas between our ports of entry to smuggle thousands of young girls and women into the United States and to sell them into prostitution and modern-day slavery.

Tens of thousands of innocent Americans are killed by lethal drugs that cross our border and flood into our cities, including meth, heroin, cocaine, and fentanyl.

The savage gang, MS-13, now operates in at least 20 different American states, and they almost all come through our southern border. Just yesterday, an MS-13 gang member was taken into custody for a fatal shooting on a subway platform in New York City. We are removing these gang members by the thousands. But until we secure our border, they're going to keep streaming right back in.

Year after year, countless Americans are murdered by criminal illegal aliens. I've gotten to know many wonderful Angel moms and dads, and families. No one should ever have to suffer the horrible heartache that they have had to endure.

Here tonight is Debra Bissell. Just three weeks ago, Debra's parents, Gerald and Sharon, were burglarized and shot to death in their Reno, Nevada home by an illegal alien. They were in their eighties, and are survived by 4 children, 11 grandchildren, and 20 great-grandchildren. Also here tonight are Gerald and Sharon's granddaughter Heather, and great-granddaughter Madison.

To Debra, Heather, Madison, please stand. Few can understand your pain. Thank you. And thank you for being here. Thank you very much. (Applause.)

I will never forget, and I will fight for the memory of Gerald and Sharon that it should never happen again. Not one more American life should be lost because our nation failed to control its very dangerous border.

In the last two years, our brave ICE officers made 266,000 arrests of criminal aliens, including those charged or convicted of nearly 100,000 assaults, 30,000 sex crimes, and 4,000 killings or murders.

We are joined tonight by one of those law enforcement heroes: ICE Special Agent Elvin Hernandez. When Elvin (applause)—thank you.

When Elvin was a boy, he and his family legally immigrated to the United States from the Dominican Republic. At the age of eight, Elvin told his dad he wanted to become a Special Agent. Today, he leads investigations into the scourge of international sex trafficking.

Elvin says that, "If I can make sure these young girls get their justice, I've [really] done my job." Thanks to his work, and that of his incredible colleagues, more than 300 women and girls have been rescued from the horror of this terrible situation, and more than 1,500 sadistic traffickers have been put behind bars. (Applause.) Thank you, Elvin.

We will always support the brave men and women of law enforcement, and I pledge to you tonight that I will never abolish our heroes from ICE. Thank you. (Applause.)

My administration has sent to Congress a commonsense proposal to end the crisis on the southern border. It includes humanitarian assistance, more law enforcement, drug detection at our ports, closing loopholes that enable child smuggling, and plans for a new physical barrier, or wall, to secure the vast areas between our ports of entry.

In the past, most of the people in this room voted for a wall, but the proper wall never got built. I will get it built. (Applause.)

This is a smart, strategic, see-through steel barrier—not just a simple concrete wall. It will be deployed in the areas identified by the border agents as having the greatest need. And these agents will tell you: Where walls go up, illegal crossings go way, way down. (Applause.)

San Diego used to have the most illegal border crossings in our country. In response, a strong security wall was put in place. This powerful barrier almost completely ended illegal crossings.

The border city of El Paso, Texas used to have extremely high rates of violent crime—one of the highest in the entire country, and considered one of our nation's most dangerous cities. Now, immediately upon its building, with a powerful barrier in place, El Paso is one of the safest cities in our country. Simply put: Walls work, and walls save lives. (Applause.)

So let's work together, compromise, and reach a deal that will truly make America safe.

Source: Compilation of Presidential Documents. Address before a Joint Session of the Congress on the State of the Union February 5, 2019. DCPD-201900063. Available online at https://www.govinfo.gov/content/pkg/DCPD-201900063/html/DCPD -201900063.htm.

3

Natural and Technological Disasters

INTRODUCTION

Today, the president is understood to have a central role in the legislative process. The president sets the congressional agenda by developing and proposing legislation, bargains with Congress to get that agenda through, and mobilizes support for legislative bills and administration policies both on Capitol Hill and among the public. How successful the president is in setting the legislative agenda for the country will of course vary by president and political context. Media coverage of an incoming president often judges the early success of a presidency in terms of what they've been able to accomplish in their first hundred days in office, from January 20 (inauguration day) until the end of April. There is nothing especially important about one hundred days; it is simply a holdover from a particularly aggressive agenda-setting start to the Franklin Delano Roosevelt administration in 1933, when the nation was deep in the grip of the Great Depression.

In order to restore consumer confidence and end the panic that had gripped the country as a result of worldwide economic depression, Roosevelt initiated a plan for a "New Deal," much of which was introduced and enacted within the president's first hundred days in office. As a result of the flurry of New Deal legislation passed during those first months, that period is now used as a yardstick for measuring early presidential success or failure. New presidents, then, have an incentive to act swiftly, be perceived to be responsive to public demands, enact their campaign promises, and take advantage of what is typically called their "honeymoon" period, when their political influence is at its height. Generally, presidential priorities have a better chance of legislative success in the first year of a presidential term than at any other point in the presidency. The difficulty, however, is that while their political influence may be at its highest point, flush from electoral victory, their political effectiveness is at its lowest (at least in the first term). They are executive neophytes, as they are adjusting to the office and its powers. Their staffers are similarly struggling to get up to speed. Political learning is happening, but it is a process that one can only accrue through experience.

New presidents, then, face a paradox of executive power: at a time when their political influence is highest, their ability to take advantage of that influence is at its lowest (Light 1991).

Nonetheless, some presidents are better able to overcome that dynamic than others. A more limited agenda, for instance, may be more achievable than an expansive set of new programs. Bill Clinton understood this, proposing a far more restrained agenda for his second term's first hundred days than the long laundry list of items (many of which faltered in Congress) of his first term's first hundred days. In their second term in office, political learning is high, but so too is their influence in their first few months. Scholars have identified this period as one in which presidents can make significant and substantive policy gains in Congress (Light 1991).

But the substance, not just the scope of the agenda, makes a difference in presidential success as well. For instance, a negative governmental (less government) agenda that is based upon eradicating programs, taxes, or benefits of some kind may be far easier to pass than a positive governmental (more government) agenda that creates and distributes benefits, establishes offices, or reorganizes agencies simply because of the complexity of the policy review that is required of positive action. In addition, presidents who come to office with well-developed, complete policy proposals would predictably fare better than those without, as the rapid development, introduction, and passage of complex policy serve no one particularly well.

The electoral coalition that swept the president into office can also affect the policy agenda of that president. For example, a president with a broad, diverse base of support may find it difficult to develop comprehensive policy options and press for legislation on behalf of that diffuse constituency (hence, Bill Clinton's laundry list of policy items in his first term). Another president, brought to power by a more ideologically homogeneous base of support, may be better able to generate policies targeted to that audience (Donald Trump's tax cuts, for instance).

But as political effectiveness and influence tend to follow rather predictable patterns across presidencies, sometimes the political context shifts in abrupt and dramatic ways. Each president is faced with such key moments. How they set up their administration, anticipate emergencies, respond to those emergencies, and learn from those emergencies has implications for their policy agendas, the electoral prospects of their copartisans, as well as their legacies. Political scientists refer to these events as "focusing events," punctuations in the political landscape that have the potential to upend the status quo in a particular policy area. Scholars are very careful about attributing a particular policy change to any one focusing event, however. Most of the time, policy issues (which are the causes of or are implicated by the discrete events) are multilayered and complex, thus limiting the ability to link a particular policy response to a focusing event. Nonetheless, after a punctuation like a hurricane or terror attack, for example, the policy context does shift in important ways and presidential action, like steps taken by other political actors, is implicated.

When disaster strikes, the U.S. people often look to government to take action. Certainly, if the scale of the disaster is sufficiently large, only the federal government is equipped to respond adequately. These disasters can take a multitude of forms, from the terrorist attacks of September 11 to major natural or technological disasters such as Hurricane Katrina (2005), the Three Mile Island partial nuclear meltdown (1979), the *Exxon Valdez* tanker oil spill (1989), and the BP Deepwater Horizon oil spill (2010). Each required rapid governmental response and extensive subsequent governmental review to ascertain the causes, consequences, and policy solutions that needed to be implemented to help affected Americans and limit the devastating effects of similar tragedies in the future. The natural and technological disasters included in this chapter focus attention on the difficulty governments face in dealing with such sudden crises. For students interested in understanding how disaster and crisis shapes the decision-making environment of governmental actors, it is important to explore some key characteristics that many of these event contexts (and policy makers) share.

Punctuations are sharp, dramatic deviations from the status quo. They are typically discrete events that hold the potential for a moment of significant change in policy. After 9/11, for example, Americans experienced substantial changes in airport security protocols. After the 2008 economic recession, new policies and more governmental oversight of the banking industry resulted. As mentioned earlier, though, it is often difficult to draw a direct line from a punctuation or focusing event to significant policy shifts. Even if a line can be drawn, there is usually a significant time "lag" because of the decision-making context in which such momentous and complicated policy decisions are made (recall the difficulty of orchestrating positive policy solutions quickly). Moreover, some disasters—their causes, effects, and mitigation efforts—are so profoundly complex (nuclear reactors or aeronautics, for instance) that reliance on expertise drives policymaking in ways that might not hold for other disasters (acts of terrorism, wildfires, flood events, or farming droughts, for example).

Typically, policy making by governmental officials is marked by standard operating procedures. These procedures have been adopted and routinized because they are typically the most efficient and effective means of achieving the policy, or they serve some other important function, like security, accountability, or transparency. These standard operating procedures are shortcuts, ways of confronting ordinary policy questions. Under crisis circumstances, however, standard procedures are often not sufficient or applicable, and bureaucrats, as policy implementers, have to make quick decisions based upon incomplete information, an absence of good alternatives, and without a clear understanding of what the likely (and unforeseen) consequences will be of those actions. They might only have a few reasonable options available to them; each of them will likely have advantages and disadvantages, and a course of action must be taken quickly.

Under such circumstances of uncertainty, incomplete information, and limited timeframe, risk-averse bureaucrats are "boundedly rational," as economists have called their behavior. They may make good decisions, or they may make what ultimately turn out to be poor decisions, but they had the virtue of being quick and demonstrated responsivity to the critical situation on the part of the executive branch. What we would be willing to give up in the way of the "correctness" of a decision turns on what the costs were for getting it wrong (or, more hopefully, only mostly right). In addition, tradeoffs in policy goals (between public health

and safety and the imposition of financial burdens, for example) become important as the immediate and longer-term policy responses contribute to the public
perception of the government's handling of the critical event.

Of course, muddling through a disaster is no way to respond to tragic circumstances, so preparedness is a watchword for many agencies tasked with emergency response. Investing in preparedness, however, is not among the public's
primary priorities, thereby limiting its value to the reelection goals of members.
Moreover, the individuals whom presidents appoint to lead those agencies may not
be prepared to deal with the crises that they confront—as Michael Brown, President George W. Bush's appointee to the Federal Emergency Management Agency
(FEMA), discovered during Hurricane Katrina.

Ultimately, resolving the crisis and preventing the next one are goals shared by
all of us. The increased public attention a particular disaster generates does not
automatically lead to policy change, however. Increased public awareness of a
critical issue that a focusing event provides is insufficient for policy change to
occur but should, ideally, create the possibility for policy change. How the public,
interest groups, governmental institutions, and others interact to learn key
lessons—and act on those lessons—from the focusing events matters. In some
cases, a crisis or disaster is evidence of the failure of a policy. How governments
interpret that evidence of policy failure, respond to the crisis, learn from it, and
adapt those lessons for policy change is of fundamental importance. As we observe
through the events collected in this volume, moving from evidence of policy failure to adapting new legislation and regulations is not easily accomplished even
within the executive branch, let alone interbranch coordination or cooperation
among states or with other nations.

The federal bureaucracy is largely resistant to change, even in crisis. Part of
this fundamental conservativism has to do with bounded rationality, but also a
behavioral inclination and sometimes statutory requirement for extensive review
of available alternatives to the status quo. A further difficulty that agencies face in
adapting new policy in the wake of disaster is something called the "proximity
bias" or "availability heuristic." When a disaster happens, policy makers and the
public tend to have their attention focused on the most recent case, rather than on
the universe of all cases of that phenomenon. As possible solutions arise, those
solutions are weighed in light of the most recent occurrence, rather than the set of
all similar events. In the moment, policy makers are understandably risk averse,
not wanting to do anything to introduce more uncertainty to an already uncertain
environment. Thus, certain solutions that may be generally appropriate for such
occurrences (but don't fit the most proximate event) are discounted.

Incremental shifts away from the status quo are possible, but only after cau-
tious consideration of those alternatives. Scholars have adopted the term "incrementalism" to describe this theory of policymaking. This approach understands
the policy arena to be governed by a state of equilibrium among competing groups
with particular claims on that policy area—farmers in the case of agriculture policy, or weapons system manufacturers in defense policy, for instance. Because of
their dominance in a particular area of policy, certain interests often become
entrenched "insiders" and are protective of the policy gains they've made over

long term investments in that policy area. As a result, the status quo often—but not always—prevails against all alternatives.

Sometimes, agencies do make incremental policy changes in response to "outside" pressure group mobilization efforts. But that effect is often attenuated. Mobilized outsiders may devote significant resources to challenging the status quo in a policy area, but the privileged insider groups assert themselves, allowing only limited change. As a result, mobilized interests receive diminishing returns from their efforts over time. Their preferred outcomes are delayed, watered down, or thwarted altogether, and their membership and allied groups disengage as policy change, if it happens, does so only incrementally. Thus, the policy incrementalism adopted by agencies often fails to produce the kind of substantial changes sought by outside groups, as agencies will only deviate modestly from the status quo. Mobilized interests may shift the policy system briefly, but ultimately incremental decision-making processes reassert themselves, as a new, modestly different status quo emerges, or reversion to the prior status quo results.

However, crisis has the potential to change this proclivity for incrementalism. Dramatic shifts in governmental policies do occur on occasion, as stable policy agendas can be punctuated by periods of instability and substantial change. Focusing events create windows of opportunity for mobilized groups to upset the stability and inertia of policy subsystems. Issues may become redefined, new dimensions of an issue may emerge, or potential solutions to a policy issue may become more salient to key players. Mobilized interests and policy entrepreneurs (political actors with policy solutions at the ready) take advantage of the new circumstances, mobilize latent support, apply greater pressure for change, and ultimately break the hold that entrenched interests have on a policy issue (Baumgartner and Jones 1993; Kingdon 1995). Mobilization of interests and the deployment of political learning interact to make dramatic alternation to the status quo possible.

As you review the events of this chapter, consider how the crisis generated or failed to generate political learning and policy adoption. What limited or enabled policy learning? How prepared were the president and the administration to respond and initiate relevant changes? What interests were dominant in shaping the public perception of the key issues involved? What effect did the mobilization of interests have on the policy response to the events? Given that the frequency of events and the costs incurred vary, what effect does the likelihood of recurrence of a catastrophic event have on the actions and interests of the president and other policy makers?

President Benjamin Harrison Addresses the Nation about the Johnstown Flood, 1889

Johnstown, Pennsylvania, was not the first of thousands of U.S. and immigrant communities to owe much of its success to the steel industry. Yet on May 31, 1889, it would be the one to bear the brunt of a lesson in the consequences of mass production and neglect. The town of around 30,000 people was prone to floods due to its mountainous geographical location and its proximity to nearby Lake Conemaugh. A dam was built around the lake to keep back excess water and allow for expansion of iron excavation and steel manufacturing. Unfortunately, the organization that owned the dam, the South Fork Fishing and Hunting Club, had neglected proper maintenance. Heavy rain began to fall one day, and the dam, bursting with 20 million tons of water, was approaching a breaking point. Johnstown residents were familiar with floods and did not all heed the warnings of the dam's laborers to evacuate. The dam gave way, and enormous waves swept through the town, destroying stores and homes, killing livestock, and claiming the lives of more than 2,000 Johnstown residents. The event, which wiped out the town in a matter of minutes, marked the largest environmental disaster in the history of the United States at the time. It also became the Red Cross's first major relief effort. The following remarks were given by President Benjamin Harrison on June 5, 1889, while the United States was still reeling in shock and grief over the incident.

My Fellow-Citizens:

Everyone here to-day is distressingly conscious of the circumstances which have convened this meeting. It would be wholly superfluous for me to attempt to set before you more impressively than the newspapers have already done the horrors attending the calamity which has fallen upon the city of Johnstown and the neighboring hamlets in a large section of Pennsylvania situated on the Susquehanna River. The grim pencil of Doré would be inadequate to portray the distress and horrors of this visitation. In such meetings as we have to-day here in the national capital and other like gatherings that are taking place in all the cities of this land, we have the only relief to the distress and darkness of the picture. When such calamitous visitations fall upon any section of our country we can only put about the dark picture the golden border of love and charity. It is in such fires as this that the brotherhood of men is welded. And where more appropriately than here at the national capital can we give expression to that sympathy and brotherhood which is now so strongly appealed to by the distress of large bodies of our fellow-citizens?

I am glad to say that early this morning, from a city not long ago visited with pestilence, and not long ago appealing to the charity of the philanthropic people of the whole land for relief-the city of Jacksonville, Fla.—there came the reflex, the ebb of that tide of charity which flowed toward them, in a telegram from the chairman of the relief association of that city authorizing me to draw upon them for $2,000 for the relief of the sufferers at Johnstown.

But this is no time for speech. While I talk men and women and children are suffering for the relief which we plan to give to-day.

A word or two of practical suggestion and I will place this meeting in the hands of those who have assembled here to give effect to our loving purposes. I have to-day had a dispatch from the governor of Pennsylvania advising me that communication has just been opened with Williamsport, on a branch of the Susquehanna River, and that the losses in that section have been appalling; that thousands of people there are hungry and homeless and penniless, and there is immediate urgency for food to relieve their necessities, and he advises me that any supplies of food that can be hastily gathered here should be sent direct to Williamsport, where they will be distributed. I suggest, therefore-and the occasion is such that bells might be rung in your streets to call the attention of the thoughtless to this great exigency-that a committee should be appointed to speedily collect contributions of food in order that a train loaded with provisions might be dispatched to-night or in the early morning to these sufferers.

I suggest, secondly, that as many of these people have had the entire furniture of their houses swept away, and have now only a temporary shelter, that a committee be appointed to collect from your citizens such articles of clothing, especially bedclothing, as can be spared; and, now that the summer season is on, there can hardly be many households in Washington that can not spare a blanket or a coverlid for the relief of the suffering ones.

I suggest, thirdly, that, of your substantial business people, bankers, and others, there be appointed a committee, who shall collect money; for, after the first exigency has passed, there will be found in those communities very many who have lost their all, who will need aid in the reconstruction of their demolished homes and in furnishing them in order that they may be again inhabited.

Need I say, in conclusion, that as a temporary citizen of Washington it would give me great satisfaction if the national capital should so generously respond to this call of our distressed fellow-citizens as to be conspicuous among the cities of the land for its ample and generous answer.

I feel, as I am calling for subscriptions, that I should say that on Saturday, on being first apprised of the need at Johnstown, I telegraphed to the mayor of that city my subscription. I do not care now or at any time to speak of anything that is so personal as this, but I felt it due to you, as I am placed here to-day to solicit and urge others to give, that I should say so much as that.

Source: *Public Papers and Addresses of Benjamin Harrison.* Washington, D.C.: Government Printing Office, 1893, 274–275.

President Calvin Coolidge Addresses the Red Cross after the Mississippi Flood, 1927

Calvin Coolidge gives this Address at the Annual Meeting of the American Red Cross, Washington, D.C., on October 3, 1927. The remarks were given in large part to thank the agency for its aid after a devastating flood of the Mississippi River earlier that spring and summer. Heavy rains had strained the levee system that facilitated the river for months until it was eventually destroyed, and the water was unleashed. Dozens of feet of water rose above surrounding communities, most of them reliant on their agricultural products, and damaged their infrastructures. Over 15 million acres of land were flooded, over 200 people were killed, and over 600,000 people were displaced across several states. The flood also impacted African Americans more than any other demographic, as sharecrop laborers who made up much of the South's flood victims were moved to refugee camps sponsored by the Red Cross. It is estimated that a few hundred thousand black people were situated in these refugee camps with far fewer white people, and yet they still faced unfair treatment and discrimination when resources were distributed. These circumstances triggered a renewed social and political movement among affected black people in the South. Many of them eventually abandoned the camps and headed north in search of better conditions. In his remarks, President Coolidge went into detail about the damage, lives lost, and the many government agencies that came to the aid of those hit by the flood. He mentions the success of the refugee camps as well but fails to mention the flood's overall disproportionate impact on black people.

Members of the American Red Cross:

The past months have been times of great activity on the part of our organization. For the fiscal year which ended June 30 relief was extended in 20 different disasters which occurred abroad. Nearly $643,000 was devoted to foreign work. In the same year $8,216,893 was expended in relieving about 690,000 people as a result of 77 domestic disasters. In this sum only about $3,000,000 of the Mississippi flood fund is included, but it does cover $4,480,000 used for relief and rehabilitation due to the storm in Florida, which occurred last year. Including the $3,000,000 expended on the Mississippi flood, the aggregate amount used at home and abroad in the charitable work of this organization in the 12 months referred to amounts to about $16,000,000.

The main work of the present season has been caused by the Mississippi flood. While high water in this basin has been of constant recurrence, the rise this year was 2 or 3 feet above any other record from Cairo to the Gulf of Mexico, a distance of over a thousand miles. Dikes were broken down in 145 places, submerging over 20,000 square miles, involving 174 counties in parts of 7 States. The means of communication were entirely interrupted, much livestock was destroyed, and homes of more than 700,000 persons were flooded. It is estimated that about 250 people were drowned.

The Red Cross established its first flood-relief camp in Arkansas on March 28. In April the situation steadily grew worse. When, on April 21, the city of Greenville, Miss., was inundated, it was realized that a serious catastrophe was impending. The following day the full organization of the Red Cross was placed in action. I issued a proclamation asking the people to contribute $5,000,000 for its work. I named a committee of the Cabinet to see that all the resources of the Government were made available. Secretary Hoover, as a member of the central committee of the Red Cross, was placed in charge of operations. Cooperation and coordination were assured through his general direction and leadership, ably assisted by James L. Feiser, acting chairman of the Red Cross in the absence abroad of Judge Payne. Accompanied by Gen. Edgar Jadwin, Chief of Engineers of the War Department, they left for Memphis on April 23. They have made four trips since, spending a total of about 75 days in the flooded area. The Secretary of War has also been on the scene of the disaster.

The story is one of the fine chapters in American history—a record of generous response to a call for funds, of the high devotion to duty by those engaged in saving life and relieving distress, and of endurance and courage shown by the people of the stricken area. The North and the South have been brought closer together in the bonds of sympathy and understanding. The heart of an entire nation has been quickened.

I issued a second call for an additional five million dollars on May 2, and our country quickly responded. Without further request, the Red Cross fund has now reached a total of over $17,000,000. The money in hand is sufficient to carry the relief still required and the reconstruction plans, already under way, well beyond January 1.

There were many deaths from drowning prior to April 22, but so efficiently was the relief extended that less than half a dozen persons lost their lives thereafter, although the perils were very great. The health of the refugees was so well guarded that there were more births than deaths in the concentration camps. A recent medical survey of the districts affected shows that, generally speaking, disease is less prevalent now than in previous years. This affliction may have proved a blessing in disguise. Undoubtedly the people have learned lessons of sanitation and health which will not be forgotten. The lands have been enriched by deposits of river mud, and many of the farmers, supplied with a better quality of seeds than used before, have been astonished by the size of the crops they have been able to grow since the waters subsided. New buildings will be better than the old. The advantages will remain. And, finally, we propose to solve the problem of flood control so such a situation may never again have to be met. In the solution we shall advance our system of inland waterways.

The $17,000,000 contributed to the Red Cross for Mississippi flood relief by no means represents the total expenditures. It is extremely difficult to estimate the value of the services, the equipment, and the supplies given by the Federal Government, but it probably amounted to about $7,000,000. Of course, a great deal of the equipment will be salvaged.

The railroads in the affected area responded superbly. They provided thousands of box car for shelter, gave free transportation for works and materials—all at an approximate cost of $3,000,000. Other large corporations were most generous. In addition there were important contributions from the States affected and from a variety of organizations in various parts of the country and personal services given by thousands of volunteer workers.

Never before have so many governmental departments been used in the disaster relief work. The War Department had former experience in working with the Red Cross and was familiar with the Mississippi through its Engineer Corps. This department not only did what was possible to hold the levees intact but provided tents, cots, blankets, stoves, and clothing from various depots to the value of $3,000,000. Rescue work was organized in four districts, each under an Army engineer. Marine and aerial activity was coordinated in a most effective way. The Army and the Navy furnished more than 50 airplanes. Without the plane and the radio, the fatalities and destruction would have been much greater. They worked together, collecting and transmitting information, scouting for refugees, and transporting rescue workers and placing in needed points in the quickest possible time medicines and other emergency supplies. A fleet of 1,000 boats, large and small, was used. It came from the Navy, the Army Engineers, the Coast Guard, the Lighthouse Service, and the Coast and Geodetic Survey under the supervision of the Department of Commerce, the Mississippi River Commission, the Inland Waterways Corporation, and other sources.

The Navy contributed 21 airplanes, which covered a total of 100,000 miles, 2 tugs, 16 radio sets, some motor boats, 59 officers, and 155 men. In addition to the work of its Coast Guard, the Treasury Department put its Public Health Service to work on the many serious problems. Nineteen medical officers and four sanitary engineers, thoroughly experienced in public health emergency work and familiar with the localities, at once were placed at the service of the State health officers. Nurses were provided, also about $60,000 worth of equipment and medical supplies, including vaccines and serums. A protective sanitary program has been mapped out, in which the Public Health Service is cooperating with the State and local authorities in 19 counties in 7 States for a period of 18 months, until such authorities can assume the full burden. Of an estimated expenditure of $1,000,000 for the fiscal year 1928, the Public Health Service has agreed to pay $262,000, and to furnish about $200,000 more for 1929. The Rockefeller Foundation is helping to finance the balance of the cost. This work will be of lasting benefit to that country.

The Coast Guard, under the supervision of the Treasury, took up its traditional work for those overwhelmed by the waters. It had 128 boats and 647 officers and men in service, and manned and operated 40 additional boats. This force helped other agencies in rescuing victims of the flood, transporting officers and workers, distributing supplies, salvaging livestock and property, and establishing and operating telephone and telegraph and radio communication.

The Farm Loan Board, through its intermediate credit banks, assumed a very important service in the work of reconstruction. It was realized that money was needed to enable the farmers to replant their crops, to assist local industries with working capital, and protect the local banks. An emergency finance corporation with local capital of $500,000 was organized in each of the States of Louisiana, Arkansas, and Mississippi. At my suggestion to Lewis E. Pierson, its president, the Chamber of Commerce of the United States secured the doubling of this capital through the subscriptions of financiers in other States. The intermediate credit banks have undertaken to discount loans made on this capital of $3,000,000 under terms that will provide total credit resources of $12,000,000. As over a considerable area replanting this year has been impossible, it is suggested that the finance corporations be continued to assist in the 1928 crop operations.

The Department of Agriculture cooperated through the extension forces employed jointly by it and the State agricultural colleges. These agents assisted in moving persons and livestock out of the flooded area and aided the Red Cross in determining certain measures of rehabilitation, the kinds of seeds to be bought, and the best methods of planting. The home-demonstration agents were most useful in the refugee camps and in giving advice on home problems to be faced later by the farmers. The Post Office Department had a difficult problem in handling the mail, which it met most acceptably. The Veterans' Bureau was also of great assistance.

In addition to this participation of the National Government we must not fail to remember the services rendered by the States themselves through their militia, health, and other departments, and by the American Legion. To mention all the industries and organizations which played a helpful part would make an almost interminable list.

So well had the situation been composed by July 12 that the flood relief headquarters, originally established at Memphis and later moved to New Orleans, were transferred to national headquarters here in Washington.

Over 600,000 people have been dependent on the Red Cross for food, clothing, and medical assistance. While nearly 280,000 insisted upon remaining in their water-logged homes, where the task of caring for them was tremendous, 330,000 were transferred to the Red Cross refugee camps, one of which contained as many as 20,000 persons.

When the floods receded the refugees were returned to their homes. Then began the no less important work of rehabilitation and reconstruction, with specially constituted State commissions to work in cooperation with the Red Cross. This included furnishing shelter and household goods where necessary, repairs to buildings, livestock, agricultural implements, and seeds. Out of a crop acreage of about 4,500,000 which was flooded, 1,622,000 acres have been replanted through the assistance of the Red Cross. The crops include cotton, corn, oats, soy beans, peas, wheat, sweet potatoes, alfalfa, and garden truck. Over 100,000 families have been rehabilitated. Now, all except 8 per cent of the people affected are able to provide for themselves.

The people of the South are most appreciative of the assistance given to their stricken States. In my capacity as President of the United States, and as head of the American Red Cross, I wish to extend the highest commendation and thanks of the country to the members of the Cabinet, to all Government officials and employees, to the officers and staff of the Red Cross, to the thousands of volunteers, and to other persons and agencies for the unselfish contribution of time and substance to this great humanitarian work in the Mississippi Valley. But, in our admiration for the stupendous work done there, we must not forget that the Red Cross organization has functioned efficiently throughout the year in every emergency call and in all of its regular activities.

Much glory has been added to our Red Cross emblem. More and more it is coming to be recognized universally as the symbol of love, sympathy, and charity for all those in suffering and distress. Its benign influence reaches out to touch and soften our daily lives, dispelling envy and malice, so that we think less of self and more of others, bringing more of peace on earth and good will toward men.

Source: Coolidge, Calvin. Address at the Annual Meeting of the American Red Cross, Washington, D.C. Online by Gerhard Peters and John T. Woolley, The American Presidency Project, https://www.presidency.ucsb.edu/node/267505.

President Lyndon B. Johnson Provides Federal Aid to Alaska after Earthquake, 1964

On March 27, 1964, an extreme earthquake hit Alaska, killing over 100 people and costing tens of millions of dollars in damage and repair efforts. The earthquake was measured at a 9.2 on the Richter scale, which made it the largest earthquake ever recorded in North America, and the second largest ever recorded in the world. The quake lasted for several minutes, setting off tsunamis, landslides, and more. The following document is an executive order set in motion by President Lyndon B. Johnson on April 2, 1964, that provided immediate aid to the people of Alaska by establishing a Federal Reconstruction and Development Planning Commission.

WHEREAS the people of the State of Alaska have experienced death, injury and property loss and damage of staggering proportions as a result of the earthquake of March 27, 1964; and

WHEREAS the President, acting pursuant to authority granted in the Act of September 30, 1950, as amended (42 U.S.C. 1855-1855g), has declared a major disaster in those areas of Alaska adversely affected by the earthquake beginning on March 27, 1964; and

WHEREAS the Federal Government and the State of Alaska desire to cooperate in the prompt reconstruction of the damaged Alaska communities; and

WHEREAS the Federal and State Governments have a common interest in assuring the most effective use of Federal and State programs and funds in advancing reconstruction and the long-range development of the State; and

WHEREAS such effective use is dependent upon coordination of Federal and State programs, including emergency reconstruction activities, which affect general economic development of the State and the long-range conservation and use of natural resources; and

WHEREAS the Governor of Alaska has declared his intention to establish a State commission for reconstruction and development planning:

NOW, THEREFORE, by virtue of the authority vested in me as President of the United States, it is ordered as follows:

Section 1. Establishment of Commission. (a) There is hereby established the Federal Reconstruction and Development Planning Commission for Alaska (hereinafter referred to as the Commission).

(b) The Commission shall be composed of a Chairman, who shall be designated by the President, the Secretary of Defense, the Secretary of the Interior, the Secretary of Agriculture, the Secretary of Commerce, the Secretary of Labor, the Secretary of Health, Education, and Welfare, the Administrator of the Federal Aviation Agency, the Housing and Home Finance Administrator, the Administrator of the Small Business Administration, the Chairman of the Federal Power Commission, and, so long as the President's declaration of a major disaster is in effect, the Director of the Office of Emergency Planning. Each agency head may designate an alternate to represent him at meetings of the Commission which he is unable to attend.

(c) The Chairman may request the head of any Federal executive department or agency who is not a member of the Commission under the provisions of subsection (b), above, to participate in meetings of the Commission concerned with matters of substantial interest to such department or agency head.

(d) The President shall designate an Executive Director of the Commission, whose compensation shall be fixed in accordance with the standards and procedures of the Classification Act of 1949, as amended.

Sec. 2. Functions of the Commission. (a) The Commission shall develop coordinated plans for Federal programs which contribute to reconstruction and to economic and resources development in Alaska and shall recommend appropriate action by the Federal Government to carry out such plans.

(b) When the Governor of Alaska has designated representatives of the State of Alaska for purposes related to this order, the Commission shall cooperate with such representatives in accomplishing the following:

(1) Making or arranging for surveys and studies to provide data for the development of plans and programs for reconstruction and for economic and resources development in Alaska.

(2) Preparing coordinated plans for reconstruction and economic and resources development in Alaska deemed appropriate to carry out existing statutory responsibilities of Federal, State, and local agencies. Such plans shall be designed to promote optimum benefits from the expenditure of Federal, State, and local funds for consistent objectives and purposes.

(3) Preparing recommendations to the President and to the Governor of Alaska with respect to both short-range and long-range programs and projects to be carried out by Federal, State, or local agencies, including recommendations for such additional Federal or State legislation as may be deemed necessary and appropriate to meet reconstruction and development needs.

Sec. 3. Commission procedures. (a) The Commission shall meet at the call of the Chairman.

(b) The Commission may prescribe such regulations as it deems necessary for the conduct of its affairs, and may establish such field committees in Alaska as may be appropriate.

(c) Personnel assigned to the Commission shall be directed and supervised by the Executive Director of the Commission. Activities of the staff shall be carried out, under the general direction and supervision of the Chairman, in accordance with such policies and programs as may be approved by the Commission.

(d) The Chairman of the Commission shall report to the President from time to time on progress and accomplishments.

Sec. 4. Agency cooperation. (a) Each Federal agency represented on the Commission shall, consonant with law, cooperate with the Commission to expedite and facilitate its work. Each such agency shall, as may be necessary, furnish assistance to the Commission in accordance with the provisions of section 214 of the Act of May 3, 1945 (59 Stat. 134; 31 U.S.C. 691).

(h) Other Federal agencies shall, to the extent permitted by law, furnish the Commission such information or advice bearing upon the work of the Commission as the Chairman may from time to time request.

Sec. 5. Construction. Nothing in this order shall be construed as subjecting any Federal agency or officer, or any function vested by law in, or assigned pursuant to law to, any Federal agency or officer, to the authority of the Commission or of any other agency or officer, or as abrogating any such function in any manner.

Source: 29 Federal Register 4789; April 4, 1964.

The White House Prepares a Moon Disaster Speech for President Richard Nixon, 1969

The 1969 Lunar Landing Mission, which sent spacecraft Apollo 11 *to the moon and back with Neil Armstrong, Buzz Aldrin, and Michael Collins on board, was a historic achievement for the United States and for mankind. Armstrong and Aldrin became the first humans to ever set foot on the moon and collect samples to bring back to Earth. The entire journey lasted from July 16, 1969, when* Apollo 11 *launched into orbit, to July 24, 1969, when all three astronauts returned safely.*

As the mission was underway, however, President Richard Nixon and his administration had to consider the possibility that the Apollo 11 *mission might end in tragedy. Just two years prior, on January 27, 1967,* Apollo 1 *caught fire during a standard test and killed three astronauts. The process of space flight was dangerous from beginning to end despite every precaution. It was for this reason that William Safire, President Nixon's speechwriter, opted to prepare a speech in the case of a disaster. The following document, written on July 18, 1969, was intended to be read by Nixon should Aldrin, Armstrong, and Collins not return. As the* Apollo 11 *mission ended in triumph, the speech was never read. In fact, its existence was not made public until July of 1999, when Safire wrote an essay for the* New York Times *on his preparation of the speech. He explained that the last line of the speech was inspired by poet Rupert Brooke, who died while on duty during World War I.*

To H. R. Haldeman
From: Bill Safire July 18, 1969.
IN EVENT OF MOON DISASTER:
Fate has ordained that the men who went to the moon to explore in peace will stay on the moon to rest in peace.

These brave men, Neil Armstrong and Edwin Aldrin, know that there is no hope for their recovery. But they also know that there is hope for mankind in their sacrifice.

These two men are laying down their lives in mankind's most noble goal: the search for truth and understanding.

They will be mourned by their families and friends; they will be mourned by their nation; they will be mourned by the people of the world; they will be mourned by a Mother Earth that dared send two of her sons into the unknown.

In their exploration, they stirred the people of the world to feel as one; in their sacrifice, they bind more tightly the brotherhood of man.

In ancient days, men looked at stars and saw their heroes in the constellations. In modern times, we do much the same, but our heroes are epic men of flesh and blood

Others will follow, and surely find their way home. Man's search will not be denied. But these men were the first, and they will remain the foremost in our hearts.

For every human being who looks up at the moon in the nights to come will know that there is some corner of another world that is forever mankind.

PRIOR TO THE PRESIDENT'S STATEMENT:

The President should telephone each of the widows-to-be.

AFTER THE PRESIDENT'S STATEMENT, AT THE POINT WHEN NASA ENDS COMMUNICATIONS WITH THE MEN:

A clergyman should adopt the same procedure as a burial at sea, commending their souls to "the deepest of the deep, "concluding with the Lord's Prayer.

Source: Richard Nixon Presidential Library and Museum.

President Jimmy Carter Visits Three Mile Island Nuclear Plant Following Meltdown, 1979

Nuclear power was welcomed as an alternative energy source in the United States in the late 1960s and early 1970s, when the Three Mile Island (TMI) nuclear plant was built in southcentral Pennsylvania. President Jimmy Carter had encouraged the states to explore alternative energy options throughout his time in office. This plant in particular was intended to provide emissions-free power to hundreds of thousands of people in surrounding areas. Yet on March 28, 1979, due to an operations error, the cold water that kept the reactor's core at a stable temperature began to drain. The core began to overheat, and nuclear chemicals began to contaminate the plant. Operators had no choice but to declare an emergency—the first of its kind in the United States. As conditions at the plant remained dangerous two days later, thousands of nearby residents were evacuated. The crisis eventually passed due to the frantic work of scientists and engineers, but the close call had a transformative impact on U.S. energy policy. No new nuclear plants have been built in the United States since the incident.

President Carter, in an effort to assuage any remaining fears about the plant and learn more about what happened, visited TMI in person on April 1, 1979. The following document is a transcript of the remarks the president gave to reporters after his visit.

My primary concern in coming here this afternoon has been to learn as much as I possibly can, as President, about the problems at the Three Mile Island nuclear Power plant and to assure the people, of this region that everything possible is being done and will be done to cope with these problems, both at the reactor and in the contingency planning for all eventualities that might occur in the future.

I want to commend Governor Thornburgh and other State and local officials for their leadership. And I would like to express my personal admiration and appreciation for the citizens of this area who, under the most difficult circumstances, have behaved in a calm and a responsible manner.

I would also like to express my thanks and admiration for the civilian and government personnel who continue to devote themselves without reservation to solving the problems at the reactor site.

The working relation among State, local, Federal, and private personnel has been excellent. And it's also been productive.

The primary and overriding concern for all of us is the health and the safety of the people of this entire area. As I've said before, if we make an error, all of us want to err on the side of extra precautions and extra safety.

I've learned that the radiation levels are being very carefully monitored throughout the area, and any trend toward higher levels would immediately be reported to me and to Governor Thornburgh and others. And every effort will be made to keep those radiation levels down to the present state, which is quite safe for all concerned.

The challenge in the future will be to cool down the reactor core itself to a safe level. And at the present time, all those who are involved here, who are highly qualified, tell me that the reactor core is indeed stable.

However, within the next few days, important decisions will be made on how to bring the reactor down to a cold and stable state. As always, in that transition period, careful preparations are being made, every eventuality is being assessed, and, above all, the health and safety of people involved will be paramount.

I would like to say to the people who live around the Three Mile Island plant that if it does become necessary, your Governor, Governor Thornburgh, will ask you and others in this area to take appropriate action to ensure your safety. If he does, I want to urge that these instructions be carried out calmly and exactly, as they have been in the past few days.

This will not indicate that danger is high. It will indicate that a change is being made in the operation of the cooling water system to permanently correct the present state of the reactor, and it's strictly a precautionary measure.

It's too early yet to make judgments about the lessons to be learned from this nuclear incident. Once the job of satisfactorily dealing with the present circumstances is completed, then there will be a thorough inquiry into the original causes and, obviously, into the events that have occurred since the incident, and additional safety precautions will undoubtedly be evolved. Perhaps some design changes will be implemented to make sure that there is no recurrence of this incident or one similar to it.

We will also do everything possible—I will be personally responsible for thoroughly informing the American people about this particular incident and the status of nuclear safety in the future.

I intend to make sure that the investigation is conducted, is conducted thoroughly, and the results are made public.

And now, I would like to have the honor of introducing a man who has done a superlative job in coordinating this entire effort. And because of the trust of the

American people in him, and particularly those who live in this region, potential panic and disturbance has been minimized.

And I again want to congratulate you, Governor Thornburgh, and thank you on behalf of our country for doing such a superb job.

Thank you very much.

Source: *Public Papers of the Presidents of the United States. Jimmy Carter, 1979, Book 1.* Washington, D.C.: Government Printing Office, 1980, 578–579.

President Jimmy Carter Visits Washington after Mount St. Helens Eruption, 1980

On May 18, 1980, Mount St. Helens in Washington erupted in perhaps the largest volcanic eruption recorded in the United States. Scientists had been monitoring the volcano for several months prior. They realized that an eruption was imminent when earthquakes in the vicinity became more frequent and a large bulge appeared on the side of the mountain, indicative of rising magma and pressure underneath its surface. When the mountain finally blew, the destruction was severe—homes and roads were lost, hundreds of tons of ash coated surrounding towns and infrastructures (even in surrounding states) and a total of 57 people were killed (including a number of victims who disregarded calls to evacuate). In addition, the explosion melted glaciers, set off avalanches, and caused a slew of other chain reactions. Congress quickly appropriated close to $1 billion in relief funding, and President Jimmy Carter flew to Portland, Oregon on May 22, 1980, to discuss the calamitous natural disaster with reporters. The following document contains President Carter's remarks after touring the damage in the area and viewing the crater of a mountain left behind.

THE PRESIDENT. First of all I'd like to make a statement that summarizes my own experience during the last few hours and describe the relationship among the Federal, State, and local government officials and agencies and the private people who will be facing the challenge of repairing the damage done by the recent volcanic explosion. And then following that I'll answer a couple questions about the Mount St. Helens explosion and eruption. I might have to call on some of my advisers to help me with the answers.

My overwhelming sense, as President, is to commend the people of the Northwest region of our country for the tremendous courage and presence of mind that has been shown here and the cooperation among the people in dealing with one of the most remarkable and formidable natural phenomena, I guess, of all recorded time. The calmness and the cooperation that's been shown and which must be shown in the future is one of the most important single factors in minimizing the damage that was potentially catastrophic.

This is a natural disaster of unprecedented dimensions, and of course we deeply regret the injury and the loss of life. But it could have been infinitely worse had there not been careful preparation and had there not been an instant and very effective response Sunday morning after the explosion and the eruption took place.

I've just come, along with Governor Ray, Governor Evans, the members of the congressional delegation, and other officials in my Cabinet as well, from traveling up the Columbia or down the Columbia River and observing the Cowlitz and the Toutle River valleys. We approached the Mount St. Helens area where Spirit Lake used to be, and we talked with people at the Cascade Middle School who had been evacuated from their homes. In the process, we have all been able to share experiences and to share plans for the future among the local, State, and Federal officials who will have to work together as a team in the future.

It's very important to realize that I have already responded with the declaration of a national disaster, at the request of Governor Ray, for the State of Washington, and of course, the other States that are impacted heavily, primarily to the west of here, but to some degree to the south of the explosion, will also be accommodated as soon as I receive those requests.

The Federal Emergency Management Agency will be primarily responsible for the coordination of the combined effort. John Macy, the Director of that agency, is here with me, and Bob Stevens will be my representative in this region in the weeks and the months ahead. Obviously there will be a wide range of assistance necessary, and it will be provided by whichever agency is primarily responsible for that service. Funding for all these services will also be provided, a major portion, of course, by individuals who own homes and businesses, by local officials, county and city level, by States involved, and of course by the Federal Government as well.

Our first priority, which has been handled so well, even before I arrived, is to deal with human needs. I met with a group of people who have been evacuated from their home, primarily in the valley region around the Toutle River. They seem to have been well taken care of. The school officials, the local police officials, the Red Cross, and others have done a very good job there, and they will be moving back into their homes as soon as transportation is open for them.

I'm very pleased that the early concerns about severe health consequences and environmental consequences and the threat of an immediate additional flood that could be even more devastating, those concerns have been alleviated to a substantial degree. The ash which is covering an enormous region of the Northwest is benign in nature. It is not toxic. It is not acid. It has about the same acidity as normal rainfall. In the long run, when it has been accommodated into the ground, I understand that it will not be harmful at all to the quality of the soil nor to the crops growing there. We will be closely monitoring its effect on presently growing crops, but the early expectations of serious damage I don't believe will be realized. The damage will be minimal.

Obviously the lack of transportation is causing a problem for farmers and particularly dairy farmers, because they cannot get their products to market. There will be, obviously, some damage economically, as well, to others who are involved in the transportation of goods and the production of food. Damage to fisheries in these particular river areas will be severe. We don't have any idea how long it'll take them to recover.

Many homes have been destroyed or presently isolated. Timber harvest has been interrupted. About 150 square miles of very rich timber region has been destroyed. Some of the trees that have been felled and not covered by ash can be harvested over a period of months, maybe 2 or 3 years at the most. Some of this is on private land, some, Federal forest land, some State land—I think about 40 percent private, 40 percent Federal, 20 percent State. The Secretary of Agriculture is here, responsible for the Federal efforts in forestry, and he will, of course, coordinate our efforts there.

The Corps of Engineers has already started opening up a channel in the Columbia River, which was almost completely closed to seagoing traffic, as you know, by the massive flood of ash, mud, down the Toutle River, Cowlitz, and into the Columbia. Eventually we'll have as many as eight major dredges there removing the material that has been deposited in the channel. That effort will be expedited as much as possible. The Secretary of the Army is here with me, responsible ultimately for the Corps of Engineers, and I think they deserve a great deal of credit in having moved so rapidly and, I think, so successfully.

There is a substantial economic impact on this area around the Columbia River, the port system, because of interrupted transportation of goods that needs to be marketed through seagoing traffic.

The Department of Interior is also represented here; the Forest and the National Park system, of course, are very closely related.

We don't know what will happen in the future. This is one of the most devastating but also one of the most interesting scientific events in recorded history. My own science adviser, Dr. Frank Press, is here. His specialty is in geology. He has made a deep study of earthquakes and volcanic actions, just coincidentally. He will be working with those who've been on the scene here for many years. Governor Ray, Governor Evans, and others will help to set up a special science advisory committee just to deal with the Mount St. Helens phenomenon and what might occur in the future. This will help to increase even further the degree of safety that has been achieved already and, of course, will provide scientific knowledge and experience that might lead to benefits in other areas of the world.

And finally, I'd like to say that I will be going from here to Spokane to see the kind of damage that has been created over large areas of the Northwest by the heavy fallout of ash. The removal of this ash, the adverse consequences of its being incorporated into internal combustion engines, its interruption of transportation by clogged waterways and also by highways is going to take a long time to correct.

There will be an enormous expense involved, and the correction or the repair of damage done by the Mount St. Helens eruption will undoubtedly take years or perhaps even decades before it can be completely corrected or repaired. Soil erosion will be continuous and severe in the river basin areas north and west of Mount St. Helens, and creating some kind of growth on the land to minimize soil erosion will be a challenge that has not yet been addressed.

What we will do in the next few days is to work very closely with Governor Ray, Governor Evans, and others to list all the challenges that face us together and to try to decide how to allot responsibility, how to make arrangements for meeting the heavy financial costs, and how to schedule these efforts with the maximum involvement of the general public, who must take care of their own local home needs on their own as much as possible.

I hope that we will be as fortunate in the future as we presently expect to be by having minimal agriculture, economic, environmental, health, and safety threats. There obviously was a great deal of concern immediately after the explosion and eruption. My belief is, after talking to scientific advisers and others, that there is no major immediate threat to the health or safety of those in this region.

One of the reasons for the loss of life that has occurred is that tourists and other interested people—curious people—refused to comply with the directives issued by the Governor, the local sheriff, the State patrol and others, and slipped around highway barricades and entered the dangerous area when it was well known to be very dangerous. There has been a substantial loss of life; about 70 people, I understand, are still missing. Some are likely never to be found. And I would like to urge everyone who lives in this region or who might visit this region to comply strictly with the directives of public officials and with the safety precautions that have been evolved for one's own benefit.

I think it might be good, now, for me to try to answer just a few questions.

Source: *Public Papers of the Presidents of the United States. Jimmy Carter, 1980, Book 1.* Washington, D.C.: Government Printing Office, 1980, 950–956.

President Ronald Reagan Mourns the Loss of the Space Shuttle *Challenger,* 1986

On the morning of January 28, 1986, at the Kennedy Space Center in Cape Canaveral, Florida, the National Aeronautics and Space Administration (NASA) prepared to launch the Challenger *space shuttle with seven passengers on board: six astronauts and one civilian school teacher, Christa McAuliffe, who would be the first civilian in space. The launch had been postponed for almost a week due to poor weather conditions and other technical tweaks to the spacecraft, and several engineers warned their managers that cold conditions that morning could have an adverse effect on the proper operation of the* Challenger. *One esteemed engineer, Alan McDonald, even refused to sign off on the shuttle's launch the night before. The* Challenger *launched despite this concern, and 73 seconds later, the spacecraft broke apart. The disaster, which was later broadcast across the United States on television, horrified millions and traumatized the nation. The craft's rubber O-rings, which separated parts of the rocket, had become brittle in the cold, and they failed to seal the craft. NASA had not tested their effectiveness in such conditions before, though many engineers and builders were concerned about their performance prior to the launch. The space shuttle program was shut down for years as NASA reevaluated its operations and designs.*

The Challenger *tragedy occurred on the morning of President Ronald Reagan's scheduled State of the Union Address. The following document is an excerpt from a press conference with the president that the Reagan White House hastily arranged so that he could address the tragedy. He then went on and delivered the regularly scheduled State of the Union Address that evening.*

The President. Well, I'm sure we all realize there's a little change in the procedures. I'd looked forward to coming in here and having a little session with you and some briefing, all very carefully sequestered until 9 o'clock tonight on the State of the Union. But in view of the tragedy that has befallen us, I don't think we'll do that. I know that you're interested in keeping up with this, as I am also, to find out the extent of it and what has taken place. So, I just wanted to say hello and appreciate your coming here and maybe we can do the other thing another time.

Q. Mr. President, can you give us your comments on the tragedy so that we can tell the American people your words, your thoughts?

The President. Well, what can you say? It's a horrible thing that all of us have witnessed it and actually seen it take place. And I just can't rid myself of the thought of the sacrifice and the families that have been watching this also, the families of those people on board and what they must be going through at this point. I'm sure all of America is more than saddened, feels the great weight of this, and wishes, as I do, that there was something we could do to make it easier for those who've suffered such a loss.

Q. Mr. President, what is the latest word you've gotten? Have you gotten any definitive word on the condition—

The President. Actually, no. We have no more information than you yourselves have that are going down there. It's a case of having to wait.

Q. Mr. President, do you want to see all systems halted until we find out explicitly what happened in this tragedy?

The President. Well, I'm not a scientist. I do have confidence in the people that have been running this program. And this is the first in, what is it, 56-some flights that something of this kind has happened. I certainly want everything done that can be done to find out how this could have happened and to ensure against its happening again. But there again, I have to say I'm sure that the people that have to do with this program are determined to do that right now. And I'm quite sure, also, when you look at the safety measures that sometimes those of us looking on have gotten a little impatient with when flights have been aborted, and it hasn't seemed as if the situation—well, it seems as if they were taking things too seriously. Now we know they weren't. And so, I'm confident that there will be no flight until they are absolutely as certain as a human being can be that it is safe.

Q. Mr. President, do you think it raises questions about having citizens aboard the space shuttle?

The President. Well, they're all citizens, and I don't think anyone's ever been on there that isn't a volunteer. I know I've heard many times from other people that have tried to give me reasons why they, or someone like them, should be included in flights of this kind. So, no, that is the last frontier and the most important frontier. We have to say that the space program has been most successful, most effective. And I guess we've been so confident of it that it comes as such a tremendous shock when something of this kind happens.

Q. Will you still go ahead, sir, with your message tonight?

The President. What?

Q. Will you go ahead with your message tonight?

The President. Yes, I feel that things like that have to go on.

Q. Mr. President, are you afraid there'll be any public backlash against the space program because of this tragedy?

The President. I shouldn't think so, and I would certainly do everything I could to express an opinion the other way. You know, we have accidents in every line of transportation, and we don't do away with those things. They've probably got a better safety record than we have out on the highways.

Q. Mr. President, will you tell us—

Q. Do you think it was a mistake to put the teacher on board?

The President. What?

Q. Do you think it was a mistake to put the teacher on board?

The President. No. Again, as I say, this is what the whole space program is leading towards—actual use.

Q. Mr. President, will you tell us exactly who brought you the news and exactly what you thought and said at that point?

The President. We were all sitting in there, and I was preparing myself for your questions on the State of the Union Address when the Vice President and [Assistant to the President for National Security Affairs] John Poindexter came into the room. And all they could say at the time was that they had received a flash that the space shuttle had exploded. And we immediately went into the adjoining room where I have a TV set to get on this, because there was no direct word except that word that had been made public also. And there we saw the replaying and saw the thing actually happen. And it just was, as I say, a very traumatic experience.

Q. But how does that affect your State of the Union speech tonight? I mean, we were told you were going to give an upbeat—"the state of the Union is good"— you know, optimistic speech. This has got to cast a pall on it, doesn't it?

The President. Yes, I'm sure it does. And certainly there could be no speech without mentioning this. But you can't stop governing the Nation because of a tragedy of this kind. So, yes, we'll continue.

Q. Philosophically, do you take some solace in the fact that over the years the American space program has been remarkably safe, that we've not lost as many people as we've been led to believe have been lost in the Soviet Union?

The President. Well, I think we've all had a great pride in that. And it is a kind of, well, at least something to cling to right now, although it doesn't lessen our grief at what has just taken place.

Q. Mr. President, the sending of civilians in space was based on the assumption that it was routine to go into space, that it was now safe, even a teacher we could send up. Do you think that notion is now gone?

The President. Well, what could you say, other than that here was a program that had a 100-percent safety record. The only other fatality did not take place in a space shuttle. It took place in an old type of capsule-

Q. Mr. President—

Mr. Buchanan. One question. One more question.

Q. —so many children have, you know, been a part of this particular space shuttle because of the teacher, and they're doing classrooms. Can you say something that would help them to understand how this happened?

The President. I think people closer to them have got to be doing that. But as I say, the world is a hazardous place, always has been. In pioneering we've always known that there are pioneers that give their lives out there on the frontier. And now this has happened. It probably is more of a shock to all of us because of the fact that we see it happen now and—thanks to the media—not just hearing about it as if something that happened miles away. But I think those that have to do with them must, at the same time, make it plain to them that life does go on and you don't back up and quit some worthwhile endeavor because of tragedy.

Q. Do you have any—

Mr. Buchanan. —got some folks in the Oval Office that are waiting—

The President. Oh.

Q. Sir, do you have any special thoughts about Christa McAuliffe, who, I think it was in this room, was named as the first teacher? What are your thoughts about her today?

The President. I can't get out of my mind her husband and her children. But then that's true of the families of the others. Theirs probably more so because the families of the others had been a part of this whole program and knew that they were in a hazardous occupation. But knowing that they were there and watching, this just is-well, your heart goes out to them.

Q. Thanks very much.

Source: *Public Papers of the Presidents of the United States. Ronald Reagan, 1986, Book 1.* Washington, D.C.: Government Printing Office, 1988–1989, 92–94.

President George H. W. Bush Gives Statement on *Exxon Valdez* Oil Spill, 1989

On March 24, 1989, a single-hulled oil tanker called the Exxon Valdez *ran aground on a reef in Prince William Sound in Alaska, spilling over 10 million gallons of oil into the ocean as a result. The oil killed tens of thousands of marine animals, ruined vast expanses of wildlife habitat, and impacted local economies for decades to come. At the time, the spill was the largest to have occurred in the United States and was used an opportunity to study oil-cleanup methods. Exxon owed the state of Alaska and the United States over $1 billion in damages done, though some estimate the total cost of the disaster is over twice that amount. Following are remarks from a press conference held by President George H. W. Bush on April 7, 1989, two weeks after the spill, in which he discussed the disaster and the subsequent government response.*

When an investigation was launched into the event, it was discovered that the ship's captain, Joseph Hazelwood, was negligent of his duties and allowed an unlicensed mate to control the ship as it navigated an area of the sound that was notoriously treacherous. In the months following the spill, the American public demanded new measures to make sure that such a spill never happened again. Congress responded by passing the Oil Pollution Act of 1990, which President George H. W. Bush signed on August 18, 1990. Among other safety and regulatory measures, this legislation required that oil tankers in United States waters be double-hulled, thus decreasing the likelihood of a large spill, and mandated larger financial penalties for oil spills. The Exxon Valdez *was scrapped after another crash a few years later.*

The President. I have a statement, and then would be glad to take a few questions, and then refer them to our experts here.

But virtually every American is familiar with the tragic environmental disaster in Alaskan waters. And more than 10 million gallons of oil have been spilled, with deadly results for wildlife and hardship for local citizens. We all share the sorrow and concern of Alaskans and a determination to mount a sustained cleanup effort. Our ultimate goal must be the complete restoration of the ecology and the economy of Prince William Sound, including all of its fish, marine mammals, birds, and other wildlife.

The Exxon Corporation has acknowledged responsibility for this spill and its liability for the damages. Exxon should remain responsible for both damages and for employing civilian personnel necessary to control further damage. However, Exxon's efforts standing alone are not enough. And after consulting with the congressional delegation—Senator Ted Stevens, Senator Frank Murkowski, Congressman Don Young—I have determined to add additional Federal resources to the cleanup effort, in addition to the considerable Federal personnel and equipment already on the scene. And this new effort will focus on the job of helping recover oil now in the water and restoring beaches and other damaged areas. This effort should not in any way relieve Exxon from any of its responsibilities or its liabilities.

I've asked Sam Skinner, our Secretary of Transportation, to serve as the coordinator of the efforts of all Federal agencies involved in the cleanup and to work with the Alaskan authorities and Exxon. Admiral Paul Yost, the Commandant of the Coast Guard, will return to Alaska to assume the personal oversight of developments. As we all know, the Coast Guard has many assets in place right now. Also at my direction, Defense Secretary Dick Cheney will make available U.S. Armed Forces personnel and equipment to assist in the cleanup. The military will provide personnel for direct cleanup activities, as well as assisting with the needs of logistics related to the cleanup.

And of course, these efforts must be undertaken carefully, so that further damage to fragile areas will not occur. Intensive planning now going on, as well as appropriate cleanup training, will be completed before ground units are actually deployed. In addition to the Department of Defense personnel, I've asked my staff to develop plans to enable volunteers to participate in cleanup activities. By summer we hope to have developed facilities to enable us to accommodate a corps of Alaskan volunteers. And when I say develop facilities, as these gentlemen will tell you, we're dealing with very remote areas in some cases here.

I've asked EPA Administrator Bill Reilly to coordinate the long-range planning to restore the environment of the Sound. EPA will draw on the expert of leading scientists and oil spill experts in this work, and it will also consult with other Federal agencies that are assessing scientific data regarding the effects of the spill.

We'll not forget the residents of Alaska who have suffered extraordinary economic loss. And when you talk to these Congressmen, as I have, and get it brought home on a case-by-case basis, we have to be concerned, and we are concerned. In addition to paying damage claims against it, we encourage Exxon to increase its local hiring for the cleanup efforts. Secretary Skinner will also work with Exxon and appropriate agencies to develop appropriate loan assistance programs to assist those who have suffered economic injury. This situation has demonstrated the inadequacy of existing contingency plans. And consequently, I have directed a nationwide review of contingency plans of this type to determine improvements that may be necessary.

In describing these measures, we should not be under any illusions. The job of cleaning up the oil from both the sea and the affected land areas will be massive, prolonged, and frustrating. Nothing we can do will totally resolve this problem in the short term. Rather, we must be prepared for a long, sustained effort.

Learning from this experience, we also rededicate ourselves to transportation safety and to realistic planning for accidents that do occur. At the same time, our national security interests in the domestic energy supplies should not be forgotten. The excellent safety record that was recorded prior to this incident must be restored and maintained consistently into the future

Source: *Public Papers of the Presidents of the United States. George Bush, 1989, Book 1.* Washington, D.C.: Government Printing Office, 1990, 381–386.

President George W. Bush Gives Remarks on Space Shuttle *Columbia* Disaster, 2003

On February 1, 2003, the Columbia *space shuttle broke apart and disintegrated over Texas with a crew of seven astronauts onboard. During its takeoff two weeks prior, a piece of foam broke from the craft and damaged the shuttle's left wing. Though multiple factors were said to have contributed to the shuttle's demise, the damaged wing foreshadowed the event. The oldest shuttle in the space shuttle fleet, the* Columbia *had been on 27 missions prior to mission STS-107, a research mission dedicated to space science. Though astronauts onboard the* Columbia *were made aware of the damage to the wing, mission managers also erroneously assured the crew that the damage would not affect the shuttle's reentry. When an investigative report was published in December 2008 on the circumstances surrounding the destruction of the* Columbia, *the public was upset to learn that the concerns of lower-level engineers and others at the National Aeronautics and Space Administration (NASA) following the damage were overlooked. As a result of the disaster, all space shuttle flights were postponed until 2005, and in 2011 the program was shut down. In the following document, President George W. Bush gave this message to the nation on the day that the* Columbia *was lost.*

My fellow Americans, this day has brought terrible news and great sadness to our country. At 9 o'clock this morning, Mission Control in Houston lost contact with our space shuttle *Columbia*. A short time later, debris was seen falling from the skies above Texas. The *Columbia* is lost. There are no survivors.

On board was a crew of seven: Col. Rick Husband; Lt. Col. Michael Anderson; Comdr. Laurel Clark; Capt. David Brown; Comdr. William McCool; Dr. Kalpana Chawla; and Ilan Ramon, a colonel in the Israeli Air Force. These men and women assumed great risk in the service to all humanity.

In an age when space flight has come to seem almost routine, it is easy to over-look the dangers of travel by rocket and the difficulties of navigating the fierce outer atmosphere of the Earth. These astronauts knew the dangers, and they faced them willingly, knowing they had a high and noble purpose in life. Because of their courage and daring and idealism, we will miss them all the more.

All Americans today are thinking as well of the families of these men and women who have been given this sudden shock and grief. You're not alone. Our entire Nation grieves with you. And those you loved will always have the respect and gratitude of this country.

The cause in which they died will continue. Mankind is led into the darkness beyond our world by the inspiration of discovery and the longing to understand. Our journey into space will go on.

In the skies today we saw destruction and tragedy. Yet farther than we can see, there is comfort and hope. In the words of the prophet Isaiah, "Lift your eyes and look to the heavens. Who created all these? He who brings out the starry hosts one by one and calls them each by name. Because of His great power and mighty strength, not one of them is missing."

The same Creator who names the stars also knows the names of the seven souls we mourn today. The crew of the shuttle *Columbia* did not return safely to Earth. Yet we can pray that all are safely home.

May God bless the grieving families, and may God continue to bless America.

Source: *Public Papers of the Presidents of the United States. George W. Bush, 2003, Book 1.* Washington, D.C.: Government Printing Office, 2006, 126–127.

President George W. Bush Tours Areas Damaged by Hurricane Katrina, 2005

During the last week of August 2005, Hurricane Katrina smashed into the U.S. Gulf Coast, leaving an incredible trail of devastation in its wake. Born in the Bahamas as a tropical storm, Katrina grew into a Category 5 hurricane as it hooked over southern Florida, gaining strength until its landfall in Louisiana. In the storm's aftermath, public health emergencies were declared in Louisiana and Mississippi, which bore the brunt of the storm, as well as in Alabama and Florida. Millions were evacuated in the state of Louisiana alone, one of the largest evacuations in the history of the United States. New Orleans, one of the largest cities in the storm's path, had been devastated. Yet resources for those affected by the hurricane were scarce, both during and after the storm. Katrina all but pulverized smaller cities, including Biloxi, Mississippi, but in New Orleans, rainfall had overwhelmed the city's levees, which led to a flood that sunk almost a quarter of it. Organized recovery efforts took days and even weeks to get under way, and criticism of federal agencies responsible for providing such assistance, such as the Federal Emergency Management Agency (FEMA), quickly intensified. President George W. Bush also came in for intense criticism of the anemic government response. Many detractors believed that the poor socioeconomic status of New Orleans at the time contributed to the lack of relief effort given to the city and *made recovery efforts harder. The Bush administration defended its response, pointing out that Bush signed a $10 billion relief bill within days of the storm. Nonetheless, the administration's response to the hurricane, which claimed more than 1,800 lives and cost more than $100 billion in damages, has frequently been described as one of the low points in Bush's presidency. The following is an excerpt of an exchange between President Bush and reporters after touring the damage in Mississippi on September 2, 2005.*

The President. I'm proud to be here with the mayor of Biloxi. The reason I'm proud to be here with him and with the Governor and Senators is because in spite of this terrible tragedy, their spirits are high. It's hard to describe the devastation that we have just walked through. I just talked to a fellow who was raised in a house that used to be, and he's got rubble surrounding him, and I said, "Are you doing all right?" and he said, "I'm doing fine. I'm alive, and my mother is alive." I talked to a fellow who runs a wrecking service—I think it's a wrecking service. He said, "I witnessed Camille. We went through Camille, and we'll go through this storm, Katrina."

You know, there's a lot of sadness, of course, but there's also a spirit here in Mississippi that is uplifting. I want to thank the Governor for his strong leadership. He set some clear parameters and has followed through on helping calm everybody's nerves. I want to thank the mayor. Neither of them asked for this when they got elected. Now they're called upon to help solve the problem.

And I've come down here, one, to take a look at the damage first hand—and I'm telling you, it's worse than imaginable—and secondly, to tell the good people of this part of the world that the Federal Government is going to help. Our first job is to save life. And earlier today, I had a chance to meet with some chopper drivers, guys dangling off of cables that are pulling people out of harm's way. And I want to thank them for their hard work.

We're going to stabilize the situation, and then get food and medicine and water. I traveled today with the head of the Red Cross and the Salvation Army, and people here are going to see compassion pour in here. There's a lot of folks in America that want to help. If you want to help, give cash to the Salvation Army and the Red Cross. We can ask for other help later on, but right now we need to get food and clothes and medicine to the people. And we'll do so. And one of the main delivery systems will be the armies of compassion.

We're going to clean all this mess up. The Federal Government is going to—will spend money to clean it up. The first downpayment will be signed tonight by me as a result of the good work of the Senate and the House—$10 1/2 billion. But that's just the beginning.

But the people have got to understand that out of this rubble is going to come a new Biloxi, Mississippi. It's hard to envision it right now. When you're standing amidst all that rubble, it's hard to think about a new city. But when you talk to folks that have been through Camille and have seen what happens and you listen to the spirit of people, you realize, Mr. Mayor, that after a lot of hard work, people are going to be—people will be proud of the effort. And I want to thank you for your leadership here. And Haley, I want to thank you for yours.

Again, I want to thank Trent and Thad. They're going to be very important Members of the—they are important Members of the Senate, and they're going to be an important part of this—making sure that we fund this recovery effort.

I'll answer a couple of questions, then I'm going to go.

Source: *Public Papers of the Presidents of the United States. George W. Bush: 2005, Book 2.* Washington, D.C.: Government Printing Office, 2009, 1386–1389.

President Barack Obama Discusses Status of Deepwater Horizon Oil Spill, 2010

On April 20, 2010, a Deepwater Horizon oil rig leased by British Petroleum and owned by Transocean exploded on the Gulf of Mexico over a large oil well almost 20,000 feet into the seafloor. The well, which workers had attempted to plug that night, could not trap the gas. Instead, the gas ignited and destroyed the rig above it, killing 11 workers and wounding over a dozen more. As the well continued to leak, despite frantic efforts to seal it, more than 3 million barrels of oil spilled into the ocean. It ultimately took close to three months to seal the deep sea well. In an effort to clean up the oil, close to 2 million gallons of oil dispersant was released at the site. In total, those liable for the explosion and spill settled for close to $15 billion in legal penalties and damages. Meanwhile, President Barack Obama accepted blame for not acting fast enough to ensure the safety of offshore drilling operations. The president had lifted the ban on offshore drilling in U.S. waters just weeks prior, in March, but he reinstated the ban in some places in U.S. waters at the end of his second term. In the following document, President Barack Obama updates the public in a weekly address on the status of the explosion and spill, as well as what had been done to both contain the damage and ensure another such spill would not occur.

One month ago this week, BP's Deepwater Horizon drilling rig exploded off Louisiana's coast, killing 11 people and rupturing an underwater pipe. The resulting oil spill has not only dealt an economic blow to Americans across the Gulf Coast, it also represents an environmental disaster.

In response, we're drawing on America's best minds and using the world's best technology to stop the leak. We've deployed over 1,100 vessels, about 24,000 personnel, and more than 2 million total feet of boom to help contain it. And we're doing all we can to assist struggling fishermen and the small businesses and communities that depend on them.

Folks on the Gulf Coast and across America are rightly demanding swift action to clean up BP's mess and end this ordeal. But they're also demanding to know how this happened in the first place and how we can make sure it never happens again. That's what I'd like to spend a few minutes talking with you about.

First and foremost, what led to this disaster was a breakdown of responsibility on the part of BP and perhaps others, including Transocean and Halliburton. And we'll continue to hold the relevant companies accountable not only for being forthcoming and transparent about the facts surrounding the leak but for shutting it down, repairing the damage it does, and repaying Americans who've suffered a financial loss.

But even as we continue to hold BP accountable, we also need to hold Washington accountable. Now, this catastrophe is unprecedented in its nature, and it presents a host of new challenges we're working to address. But the question is what lessons we can learn from this disaster to make sure it never happens again.

If the laws on our books are inadequate to prevent such an oil spill or if we didn't enforce those laws, I want to know it. I want to know what worked and what didn't work in our response to the disaster and where oversight of the oil and gas industry broke down. We know, for example, that a cozy relationship between oil and gas companies and the agencies that regulate them has long been a source of concern.

Secretary of Interior Ken Salazar has taken steps to address this problem, steps that build on reforms he's been implementing since he took office. But we need to do a lot more to protect the health and safety of our people, to safeguard the quality of our air and water, and to preserve the natural beauty and bounty of America.

In recent weeks, we've taken a number of immediate measures to prevent another spill. We've ordered inspections of all deepwater operations in the Gulf of Mexico. We've announced that no permits for drilling new wells will go forward until the 30-day safety and environmental review I requested is complete. And I've called on Congress to pass a bill that would provide critical funds and tools to respond to this spill and better prepare us to confront any future spills.

But we also need to take a comprehensive look at how the oil and gas industry operates and how we regulate them. That's why on Friday, I signed an Executive order establishing the National Commission on the BP Deepwater Horizon Oil Spill and Offshore Drilling. While there are a number of ongoing investigations, including an independent review by the National Academy of Engineering, the purpose of this Commission is to consider both the root causes of the disaster and offer options on what safety and environmental precautions we need to take to prevent a similar disaster from happening again. This Commission, I'd note, is similar to one proposed by Congresswoman Capps and Senator Whitehouse.

And I've asked Democrat Bob Graham and Republican Bill Reilly to cochair this Commission. Bob served two terms as Florida's Governor and represented Florida as a United States Senator for almost two decades. During that time, he earned a reputation as a champion of the environment, leading the most extensive environmental protection effort in the State's history.

Bill Reilly is chairman emeritus of the board of the World Wildlife Fund, and he also is deeply knowledgeable about the oil and gas industry. During the Presidency of George H. W. Bush, Bill was Administrator of the Environmental Protection Agency, and his tenure encompassed the *Exxon Valdez* disaster.

I can't think of two people who will bring greater experience or better judgment to the task at hand. In the days to come, I'll appoint five other distinguished Americans, including scientists, engineers, and environmental advocates, to join them on the Commission. And I'm directing them to report back in 6 months with recommendations on how we can prevent and mitigate the impact of any future spills that result from offshore drilling.

One of the reasons I ran for President was to put America on the path to energy independence, and I've not wavered from that commitment. To achieve that goal, we must pursue clean energy and energy efficiency, and we've taken significant steps to do so. And we must also pursue domestic sources of oil and gas. Because it represents 30 percent of our oil production, the Gulf of Mexico can play an important part in securing our energy future. But we can only pursue offshore oil drilling if we have assurances that a disaster like the BP oil spill will not happen again. This Commission will, I hope, help provide those assurances so we can continue to seek a secure energy future for the United States of America.

Thanks so much.

Source: *Public Papers of the Presidents of the United States. Barack Obama: 2010, Book 1.* Washington, D.C.: Government Printing Office, 2013, 691–692.

President Barack Obama Updates Nation on Hurricane Sandy Relief Efforts, 2012

In the last days of October 2012, a tropical storm brewed in the Caribbean Sea and travelled north into the Atlantic Ocean, gaining strength as it went, until it made its final landfall as Category 1 Hurricane Sandy on the East Coast of the United States. Before then, the hurricane had traveled through the islands of the Bahamas, Cuba, the Dominican Republic, and Haiti, causing mass destruction and killing around 70 people. As the hurricane approached the United States, government agencies such as the Federal Emergency Management Agency (FEMA) and other relief organizations such as the Red Cross anticipated an emergency. As Hurricane Sandy hit the American mainland in New Jersey, major coastal cities such as New York City were flooded and battered by the heavy rain and wind. Mass power outages ensued, and hundreds of thousands of homes were destroyed in New York and New Jersey altogether. Though relief efforts had been organized ahead of time by President Barack Obama and others (and were generally praised by disaster experts), Hurricane Sandy still caused an estimated $65 billion in damage and claimed around 150 lives. The following document is a transcript of President Obama's remarks on Hurricane Sandy relief efforts on October 30, 2012.

The President. First of all, I want to thank Gail and Charlie who are on the scene doing work every time we have a disaster here in the United States of America. But obviously, the Red Cross is doing outstanding work internationally, so we want to thank them for their outstanding work.

A few things that I want to emphasize to the public at the top. This storm is not yet over. We've gotten briefings from the National Hurricane Center. It is still moving north. There are still communities that could be affected. And so I want to emphasize there are still risks of flooding, there are still risks of downed power lines, risks of high winds. And so it is very important for the public to continue to monitor the situation in your local community, listen to your State and local officials, follow instructions. The more you follow instructions, the easier it is for our first responders to make sure that they are dealing with true emergency situations. So the better prepared individual families are for the situation, the easier it is going to be for us to deal with it.

Next, obviously, I want to talk about the extraordinary hardship that we've seen over the last 48 hours. Our thoughts and prayers go out to all the families who have lost loved ones. Unfortunately, there have been fatalities as a consequence of Hurricane Sandy, and it's not clear that we've counted up all the fatalities at this point. And obviously, this is something that is heartbreaking for the entire Nation. And we certainly feel profoundly for all the families whose lives have been upended and are going to be going through some very tough times over the next several days, perhaps several weeks and months.

The most important message I have for them is that America is with you. We are standing behind you, and we are going to do everything we can to help you get back on your feet.

Earlier today I had a conversation with the Governors and many of the mayors in the affected areas, including Governor Christie, Governor Cuomo, and Mayor Bloomberg. I want to praise them for the extraordinary work that they have done. Sadly, we are getting more experience with these kinds of big-impact storms along the East Coast, and the preparation shows. Were it not for the outstanding work that they and their teams have already done and will continue to do in the affected regions, we could have seen more deaths and more property damage. So they have done extraordinary work working around the clock. The coordination between the State, local, and Federal governments has been outstanding.

Obviously, we're now moving into the recovery phase in a lot of the most severely affected areas. New Jersey, New York, in particular, have been pounded by this storm. Connecticut has taken a big hit. Because of some of the work that had been done ahead of time, we've been able to get over a thousand FEMA officials in place, pre-positioned. We've been able to get supplies, food, medicine, water, emergency generators to ensure that hospitals and law enforcement offices are able to stay up and running as they are out there responding.

We are going to continue to push as hard as we can to make sure that power is up throughout the region. And obviously, this is mostly a local responsibility, and the private utilities are going to have to lean forward, but we are doing everything we can to provide them additional resources so that we can expedite getting power up and running in many of these communities.

There are places like Newark, New Jersey, for example, where you've got 80, 90 percent of the people without power. We can't have a situation where that lasts for days on end. And so my instructions to the Federal agency has been, do not figure out why we can't do something; I want you to figure out how we do something. I want you to cut through red tape. I want you to cut through bureaucracy. There's no excuse for inaction at this point; I want every agency to lean forward and to make sure that we are getting the resources where they need—where they're needed as quickly as possible.

So I want to repeat my message to the Federal Government: No bureaucracy, no redtape. Get resources where they're needed as fast as possible, as hard as possible, and for the duration, because the recovery process obviously in a place like

New Jersey is going to take a significant amount of time. The recovery process in a lower Manhattan is going to take a lot of time.

And part of what we're trying to do here is also to see where some resources that can be brought to bear that maybe traditionally are not used in these kind of disaster situations. For example, there may be military assets that allow us to help move equipment to ensure that pumping and getting the flooding out of New York subway systems can proceed more quickly. There may be resources that we can bring to bear to help some of the private utilities get their personnel and their equipment in place more swiftly so that we can get power up and running as soon as possible.

So my message to the Governors and the mayors and, through them, to the communities that have been hit so hard is that we are going to do everything we can to get resources to you and make sure that any unmet need that is identified, we are responding to it as quickly as possible. And I told the mayors and the Governors, if they're getting no for an answer somewhere in the Federal Government, they can call me personally at the White House.

Now, obviously, the State, local, Federal response is important, but what we do as a community—what we do as neighbors and as fellow citizens—is equally important. So a couple of things that I want the public to know they can do.

First of all, because our local law enforcement, our first responders are being swamped, to the extent that everybody can be out there looking out for their neighbors, especially older folks, I think that's really important. If you've got a neighbor nearby, you're not sure how they're handling a power outage, flooding, et cetera, go over, visit them, knock on their door, make sure that they're doing okay. That can make a big difference. The public can be the eyes and ears in terms of identifying unmet needs.

Second thing, the reason we're here is because the Red Cross knows what it's doing when it comes to emergency response. And so, for people all across the country who have not been affected, now is the time to show the kind of generosity that makes America the greatest nation on Earth. And a good place to express that generosity is by contributing to the Red Cross.

Obviously, you can go on their website. The Red Cross knows what they're doing. They're in close contact with Federal, State, and local officials. They will make sure that we get the resources to those families as swiftly as possible. And again, I want to thank everybody here who is doing such a great job when it comes to the disaster response.

The final message I'd just say is, during the darkness of the storm, I think we also saw what's brightest in America. I think all of us obviously have been shocked by the force of Mother Nature as we watch it on television. At the same time, we've also seen nurses at NYU hospital carrying fragile newborns to safety. We've seen incredibly brave firefighters in Queens, waist-deep in water, battling infernos and rescuing people in boats.

One of my favorite stories is down in North Carolina, the Coast Guard going out to save a sinking ship. They sent a rescue swimmer out, and the rescue swimmer said: "Hi, I'm Dan. I understand you guys need a ride." That kind of spirit of resilience and strength, but most importantly, looking out for one another, that's why we always bounce back from these kinds of disasters.

This is a tough time for a lot of people: millions of folks all across the Eastern Seaboard. But America is tougher, and we're tougher because we pull together. We leave nobody behind. We make sure that we respond as a nation and remind ourselves that whenever an American is in need, all of us stand together to make sure that we're providing the help that's necessary.

So I just want to thank the incredible response that we've already seen, but I do want to remind people this is going to take some time. It is not going to be easy for a lot of these communities to recover swiftly, and so it's going to be important that we sustain that spirit of resilience, that we continue to be good neighbors for the duration until everybody is back on their feet.

Thank you very much, everybody. Thank you, Red Cross.

Source: *Public Papers of the Presidents of the United States. Barack Obama: 2012, Book 2.* Washington, D.C.: Government Printing Office, 2017, 1671–1674.

President Donald Trump Tweets about U.S. Response to Hurricane Maria in Puerto Rico, 2018

Toward the end of September 2017, Hurricane Maria raged through the Caribbean Sea and its many islands, including the U.S. territory of Puerto Rico, where it made landfall as a Category 4 hurricane. Though the country's infrastructure and government were not well-equipped to withstand such damage at the time the hurricane hit, federal relief efforts committed to Puerto Rico were also sparse, compared to previous relief efforts provided to the states in the event of a hurricane of such a high scale. One of the most severe consequences to Puerto Rico was that almost the entire island was left without power, as almost all power lines had been destroyed and would need to be rebuilt. To complicate matters further, two earlier hurricanes, Irma and Harvey, had preoccupied government relief agencies such as the Federal Emergency Management Agency (FEMA), leaving relatively few supplies or resources for Puerto Rico. However, Puerto Rico's government had been in billions of dollars' worth of debt for years, and it could not afford to provide for those affected by the storm, let alone rebuild the island. In despair, Puerto Rico's government requested $94 billion in aid from the United States in the hurricane's aftermath. President Trump responded via Twitter that the request was an attempt to pay off Puerto Rico's debt. Though Congress had approved some relief funding to be put toward Puerto Rico, it is unclear how much of the funding actually reached Puerto Rico. In addition to the debacle over relief spending for the U.S. citizens of Puerto Rico, President Trump refused to acknowledge well-documented reports about the high death toll in Puerto Rico due to the storm. At several points, he instead made false claims that the numbers were fabricated by the Democratic Party or Puerto Rican officials. The following two tweets, written on September 13, 2018, represent the president's communication to the public about the aftermath of Hurricane Maria and its impact on Puerto Rico.

3000 people did not die in the two hurricanes that hit Puerto Rico. When I left the Island, AFTER the storm had hit, they had anywhere from 6 to 18 deaths. As time went by it did not go up by much. Then, a long time later, they started to report really large numbers, like 3000. . . .

. . . This was done by the Democrats in order to make me look as bad as possible when I was successfully raising Billions of Dollars to help rebuild Puerto Rico. If a person died for any reason, like old age, just add them onto the list. Bad politics. I love Puerto Rico!

Source: https://twitter.com/realDonaldTrump/status/1040217897703026689; https://twitter.com/realDonaldTrump/status/1040220855400386560.

President Donald Trump Tweets about Wildfires in California, 2018

On November 8, 2018, the Hill, Woolsey, and Camp Fires ignited and grew to massive proportions, scorching both the Northern and Southern parts of California. The fires proved to be some of the biggest and costliest on record, consuming more than 200,000 acres and billions of dollars worth of buildings and other structures. The Camp Fire alone caused 86 people to perish and over 10,000 homes to be destroyed. Hundreds were reported missing, and some were never found. Immense amounts of smoke clogged the air in both California and across the United States to the East Coast. All in all, the fires painted a hellish scene, and the nation sought answers as to how the fires began and how they could be prevented. Though the smallest and least destructive of the three was caused by human activity, major utility companies in the state were sued for their potential roles in the Woolsey Fire. Yet the Camp Fire, the largest and deadliest of all, began as a brush fire. While numerous scientific studies have found that global climate change can have a direct correlation to larger and deadlier wildfires (such as by worsening droughts that turn forests into virtual tinder boxes), President Donald Trump insisted that mismanagement of the state's wildlands was to blame. Just two days after the fires had combusted, on November 10, 2018, President Trump used Twitter to address the public about the fires in one of his first statements about the crisis.

There is no reason for these massive, deadly and costly forest fires in California except that forest management is so poor. Billions of dollars are given each year, with so many lives lost, all because of gross mismanagement of the forests. Remedy now, or no more Fed payments!

Source: https://twitter.com/realDonaldTrump/status/1061168803218948096.

4

Political Scandals and Tragedies

INTRODUCTION

When the delegates to the Constitutional Convention met in Philadelphia during the summer of 1787, they faced a challenging task in designing the world's first popularly elected executive office: the American presidency. Among the most pressing difficulties were three related issues: whether the executive should be one person, or a plural executive; what powers should be conferred to that office; and what constraints should be placed upon the presidency. Having just thrown off a monarchy, the concentration of executive authority in one person was a matter of tremendous consequence for the Framers. At the same time, many recognized the importance and value of a single executive—elected by the people to pursue the nation's interests with energy and dispatch. Placing the office with a single person would also have the additional virtue, according to Alexander Hamilton, of making individuals holding the office "more narrowly watched and more readily suspected." If one was concerned about the executive power being placed in one person alone (as several delegates were), the constitutional powers to be conferred might be more limited, and the constraints imposed might be more stringent than if it were an office held by multiple executives who would check each other's power.

The framers resolved the dilemma by establishing a single executive whose power was circumscribed by a shortened term of office (and the positive inducement of reappointment) and grants of authority to Congress that created the interdependence of institutional exercises of power, including appointments, war powers, treaties, and lawmaking, among others. And, of course, the possibility of impeachment was introduced; this mechanism, its supporters insisted, would act as a constraint on abuses of power by an executive.

The constitutional structure designed by the framers is only part of the larger *constitutional order* in which executives operate. That is, the constitutional order is a political as well as a legal construction. In the United States, the Constitution binds political actors, including presidents, to a set of constraints that we generally understand to comprise the rule of law. A constitutional system, then, takes certain things "off the table." Targeting religious or ethnic minorities and waging unilateral war, for instance, are beyond the constitutional powers of the president. But those constraints are only as effective as other political actors are willing to impose them. All presidents have the incentive to press against the vague boundaries of their Article II powers to their advantage, and many, particularly in the modern era, have done so.

In the aftermath of Watergate, presidential historian Arthur Schlesinger Jr. noted that the Richard Nixon presidency was a "culmination, not an aberration." What Schlesinger meant was that the seeds of the extra-constitutional actions by the president exposed in the Watergate scandal, and the crisis in confidence in the institutions of government that resulted, were sown long before 1972. Those seeds were nurtured, Schlesinger argued, by an enfeebled Congress and "considerably debilitated" constitutional constraints on the president. Consider the example of the impeachment provision of Article II as a relevant example of this interplay of law and politics in constraining presidents. Only two presidents, Andrew Johnson and Bill Clinton, have been convicted in the House of Representatives on charges of impeachment "for high crimes and misdemeanors." However, the possibility of the commission of impeachable offenses has emerged at others times as a threat to the presidencies of Richard Nixon and, more recently, Donald Trump. The determination that a president has committed an impeachable offense is a political judgment, not a strictly legal judgment.

It is therefore meaningful to examine under what conditions and by what mechanisms political actors police the constitutional order. Political scientists have long recognized that the institutional structures that shape political behavior are used, abused, ignored, or applied by individuals and groups seeking to shape political outcomes. Thus, there is no nonpolitical or neutral arbiter of when or how to apply the constraints of the constitutional system. One might be inclined to suggest that federal and state courts play the role of independent arbiter of constitutional meaning, and that would be a reasonable observation. But the courts are themselves beset with the similar difficulties of discerning and applying constitutional principles. Insofar as judges are confronted with the task of applying constitutional limits on executive branch officials, they "may be surprised at the poverty of really useful and unambiguous authority applicable to concrete problems of executive power as they actually present themselves" (Justice Jackson, *Youngstown Sheet and Tube v. Sawyer*, 1952).

In the absence of "unambiguous authority," judges apply a number of different approaches to interpreting what the Constitution means. Even on the same court, different methods can be applied, which can lead to different results in the same hard cases. Decades of political science and legal scholarship on this dynamic has led observers to a key conclusion about judicial decision making: an action of government is not unconstitutional because it conflicts with the Constitution; it is unconstitutional because it conflicts with a doctrine *developed by judges for interpreting* the Constitution (Ducat 2009, 83). And very often the doctrine to which judges adhere is shaped by their views of the proper role of government and the degree to which the text, precedent, framer intent, policy outcomes, and context, for example, matter in their decisions. In short, constitutional meaning and, by extension, the willingness of courts to apply its constraints is predicated on judicial choice, however defensible. Moreover, judicial decisions are very often only part—albeit a meaningful part—of the ongoing constitutional "dialogue" among participants in shaping the constitutional order. A judicial decision can be the last word on an issue, but it can also face reversal in Congress, amendment proceedings, presidential "foot-dragging" in implementing its order, or other means of noncompliance. Recent research reveals that judges are aware of the interdependent and contingent nature of their authority and behave accordingly, often strategically, to achieve their goals for particular cases. In other words, judges are similar to legislators in that they have no nonpolitical purchase from which they deploy constitutional constraints upon other political actors.

An example, included in this chapter, is the case of Andrew Jackson's refusal to comply with the U.S. Supreme Court's ruling in *Worcester v. Georgia* (1832), which struck down state laws that authorized the forced removal of Cherokee Indians. Without Jackson's support to uphold and implement the Court's decision, Cherokee rights were not protected, leading to their forced removal in 1838 and resulting in the death of 4,000 Cherokee on the Trail of Tears. As this case reveals, by not complying with the Court's decision in the Cherokee cases, President Jackson asserted a key power of the presidency while underscoring the limits of the Judiciary's institutional authority and its dependency on other political branches to have policy reflect its decisions.

Constitutionalism and the rule of law are—in their application—fundamentally political ideas as much as legal concepts. Law and politics are therefore deeply connected. Executive actions that push the boundaries of the Constitution or violate congressional statute are judged not simply in terms of the text of the Constitution or the statute, but in terms of what the political order will permit in light of the relevant law and the political context—and we all comprise that constitutional order. As Schlesinger noted in the midst of the Watergate scandal, "the great institutions—Congress, the courts, the executive establishment, the press, the universities, public opinion—have to reclaim their own dignity and meet their own responsibilities" to assert constitutional limits on the executive (Schlesinger 1973).

Just how those "great institutions" have responded in moments of scandal and national tragedy has, of course, varied. At times, Congress has appeared to overcome its lassitude by actively overseeing executive agencies and instituting meaningful changes in its rules or passing statutes, like the Pendleton Act, the Hatch Act, or the War Powers Act, which seek to rein in executive power. At other times, Congress simply ignored potential abuses or extralegal actions or was unable to overcome bicameralism and political differences to assert its authority to police the boundaries of executive overreach. Still other Congresses have explicitly authorized the president to take the actions *after* the fact, to endow the executive with the authority and to dispel concerns about the appropriateness of the action.

In the context of separation-of-powers cases, courts tend to take a backseat to the legislative branch. They would prefer that Congress provide the necessary oversight, budgetary control, statutory constraint, and other means necessary to place appropriate limits on executive power. However, here, too, there are exceptions. During the Nixon administration, for example, the federal courts rejected the president's claim of executive privilege and directed the White House to produce tapes that confirmed the president had approved the Watergate cover-up, an action that precipitated Nixon's resignation. And in *Ex Parte Milligan* (1866), the U.S. Supreme Court invalidated the president's use of a military tribunal to try a civilian during the Civil War.

Even within an administration, there are examples of agency and White House staff who balance their professional obligations against principles they value. Some agencies, like the Department of State and the U.S. Agency for International Development, provide a formal mechanism for public officials to express serious concerns about actions and policies directly to the Office of the Secretary, serving as an important internal constraint on the executive branch. As an example, the Department of State's Dissent Channel "is a serious policy channel reserved only for consideration of responsible dissenting and alternative views on substantive foreign policy issues that cannot be communicated in a full and timely manner through regular operating channels and procedures" (https://www.afsa.org /dissent-channel). In addition, other internal constraints are at work on the executive branch through Inspectors General, the Governmental Accountability Office, the Office of Personnel Management, and many others.

The press has also played an important "watchdog" role. The biggest political scandals of the modern era were brought to light by good reporting on a key element of that scandal. The Iran Contra affair, for instance, began as the press followed a lead about the downing of a C-123 cargo plane in Nicaragua. They soon discovered that one of the survivors of the crash was a mercenary connected to the Central Intelligence Agency and the Reagan Administration. As the media pulled on that thread, the whole "arms for hostages" story unraveled through investigations by congressional committees and Independent Counsel Lawrence Walsh.

Representatives of civil society—nongovernmental organizations, colleges and universities, individual citizens, and interest groups—have also played a part in constraining executive power. Time after time in American history, citizens have taken direct action to protest what they perceive to be misconduct by an administration. Examples include the mass student protests that erupted on college campuses and city streets during the Vietnam War, the widespread and rapid reaction by thousands of protesters upon the Trump Administration's declaration of the so-called "Muslim travel ban" in 2017, and the Bonus Marchers who descended on Washington, D.C., in 1932 to seek payment for their military service.

The events depicted in this chapter on scandals and tragedies reflect the degree to which these "great institutions" of the democratic system were able to use the scandal or tragedy to reshape presidential power. As the protectors of the constitutional order, the press, the public, Congress, the bureaucracy, and the courts have all been key players in these events. At times, the scandal was a crucible for significant institutional changes; at other times, the events were considered aberrational, thus not implicating policy. But often, the political context is such that even when many in those "great institutions" seek to impose constitutional or statutory limits on presidential power, their efforts are stymied. In many instances, it appears that the more powerful the legal constraint sought to be imposed on the presidency, the more difficult it is to achieve politically. In exploring the following events and documents, consider the braided role of law and politics in the scandal or tragedy in question. Are tragedies like school shootings independent of politics and the law, or are they deeply linked? When scandals occur, how are they resolved—and by whom? And in what sense is a resolution in a particular case adequate without safeguards to address the conditions that gave rise to the scandal? These questions, and many more, can help deepen understanding of the legal and political dynamics that shape political institutions' responses to moments of great tragedy and national scandal.

President Andrew Johnson Removes Edwin M. Stanton as Secretary of War, 1868

The following Executive Order was given on February 21, 1868, by President Andrew Johnson. It was also the legislative action that that would spur the president's impeachment three days later as a violation of the Tenure of Office Act, which stated that Congress must give permission of the dismissal. Edwin Stanton had guided the Union toward success during the Civil War. Yet Johnson attempted to use Stanton as a pawn against Congress after Congress overruled his vetoes for the Reconstruction Acts and the Tenure of Office Act a few months prior. President Johnson's intentions were to prompt a legal action in which the constitutionality of the Tenure of Office Act could be questioned. He knew that an executive order would bar Congress from its ability to overrule it. However, Stanton did not step down, Congress was inflamed, and Andrew Johnson became the first U.S. president to be impeached soon thereafter. The Tenure of Office Act was repealed in 1887, and it was, ironically, suggested to be unconstitutional by the Supreme Court decades later in 1926.

SIR: By virtue of the power and authority vested in me as President by the Constitution and laws of the United States, you are hereby removed from office as Secretary for the Department of War, and your functions as such will terminate upon the receipt of this communication.

You will transfer to Brevet Major-General Lorenzo Thomas, Adjutant-General of the Army, who has this day been authorized and empowered to act as Secretary of War *ad interim*, all records, books, papers, and other public property now in your custody and charge.

Respectfully, yours,
ANDREW JOHNSON.

Source: Richardson, James D. *A Compilation of the Messages and Papers of the Presidents 1789–1897.* Volume 9. New York: Bureau of National Literature, 1897, 3908.

President Theodore Roosevelt Announces the Death of President William McKinley, 1901

On September 6, 1901, fairgoers had lined up to meet William McKinley at the World Fair in Buffalo, New York. President McKinley welcomed the opportunity to greet the public, despite the fact that two of his predecessors had been assassinated. The train ride to the fairgrounds had already been eventful. City personnel had organized a 21-shot cannon salute for the commander in chief upon his arrival at the station, but they had miscalculated their distance from the tracks and blew out the car's windows. Nobody had been hurt. President McKinley's advisors were surely on edge and had more than once attempted to cancel the president's visitation at the fair. However, an anarchist named Leon Czolgosz had lined up for his encounter with the president with a loaded revolver hidden under a handkerchief. When it was Czolgosz's turn to approach, he met President McKinley with two bullets. The president was rushed to the hospital, where he died about a week later on September 14, 1901, having only spent about six months in office. Czolgosz was sentenced to the electric chair on October 21, 1901.

The following document is the proclamation of President McKinley's death, announced on September 14, 1901, by McKinley's former vice president, Theodore Roosevelt, who had been sworn in as America's 26th president earlier that same day.

To the people of the United States:
A terrible bereavement has befallen our people. The President of the United States has been struck down; a crime not only against the Chief Magistrate, but against every law-abiding and liberty-loving citizen.

President McKinley crowned a life of largest love for his fellow men, of earnest endeavor for their welfare, by a death of Christian fortitude; and both the way in which he lived his life and the way in which, in the supreme hour of trial, he met his death will remain forever a precious heritage of our people.

It is meet that we as a nation express our abiding love and reverence for his life, our deep sorrow for his untimely death.

Now, Therefore, I, Theodore Roosevelt, President of the United States of America, do appoint Thursday next, September 19, the day in which the body of the dead President will be laid in its last earthly resting place, as a day of mourning and prayer throughout the United States. I earnestly recommend all the people to assemble on that day in their respective places of divine worship, there to bow down in submission to the will of Almighty God, and to pay out of full hearts the homage of love and reverence to the memory of the great and good President, whose death has so sorely smitten the nation.

In Witness Whereof, I have hereunto set my hand and caused the seal of the United States to be affixed.

Done at the city of Washington, the fourteenth day of September, A.D. 1901, and of the Independence of the United States the one hundred and twenty-sixth.

Source: Richardson, James D. *A Compilation of the Messages and Papers of the Presidents 1789–1897.* Volume 14. New York: Bureau of National Literature, 1897, 6639.

President Woodrow Wilson Creates Committee on Public Information during Red Scare, 1917

The following executive order issued by President Woodrow Wilson was a symptom of unstable times in the United States. The Bolshevik Revolution had ushered in the creation of a communist regime in Russia, and the president and other officials believed that communism was a threat to the United States, which had become entangled in World War I. Wilson and many other lawmakers worried that Americans were vulnerable to communist propaganda, as many had opposed involvement in the war to begin with. On April 13, 1917, the president created the Committee on Public Information, which was instrumental in crafting propaganda to build public support for the war effort—and to counter public opposition to the war, which was especially visible in some newspapers. Yet President Wilson took the opposition as an excuse to claim a breach of trust between citizens and government. The committee and the federal government crusaded to expose those who could not be trusted due to their political beliefs or who had the potential to turn against the country. This fed into the public's anxiety and created the first Red Scare. Under the direction of committee chairman George Creel, himself a former journalist, the committee's various divisions generated huge volumes of press releases, posters, pamphlets, brochures, books, and other materials, all designed to boost support for the war—and cast suspicion on those who opposed American involvement in the conflict.

I hereby create a Committee on Public Information, to be composed of the Secretary of State, the Secretary of War, the Secretary of the Navy, and a civilian who shall be charged with the executive direction of the Committee.

As Civilian Chairman of this Committee, I appoint Mr. George Creel. The Secretary of State, the Secretary of War, and the Secretary of the Navy are authorized each to detail an officer or officers to the work of the Committee.

Source: Congressional Record, Vol. LVI, 65th Congress, 2nd Session, House, June 17, 1918. Washington, D.C.: Government Printing Office, 1918, 7907.

President Harry Truman Fires General Douglas MacArthur, 1951

President Harry Truman reacted quickly when Soviet-supported Northern Korea invaded South Korea. Concerned about the spread of communism, he sent U.S. troops to the South to help stave off the attack. U.S. and South Korean troops were able to push Northern forces back to the previously established border between the two nations, which was Truman's primary goal. Once North Korean forces were pushed out of the South, General Douglas MacArthur, who was in charge of the Korean command, pressed his military advantage and invaded the North. But this move led China to unleash its own military forces down into the Korean Peninsula, and MacArthur was forced to retreat. By mid-1951 the war had settled into a stalemate, with both sides occupying much the same territory that they had at the outset of the conflict. Truman wanted to pursue a diplomatic settlement, but MacArthur became increasingly outspoken about his support for using bombs and other violent strategies to rid the region of communist influences altogether. Though the American public supported this position at the time, President Truman was not pleased that his general so openly dissented with the United States' official policy. Angered by MacArthur's increasingly brazen insubordination, Truman relieved MacArthur of his duties on April 11, 1951, to the outrage of the public. The following document is the Statement and Order by the President on Relieving General MacArthur of His Commands.

[1.] Statement by the President:

With deep regret I have concluded that General of the Army Douglas MacArthur is unable to give his wholehearted support to the policies of the United States Government and of the United Nations in matters pertaining to his official duties. In view of the specific responsibilities imposed upon me by the Constitution of the United States and the added responsibility which has been entrusted to me by the United Nations, I have decided that I must make a change of command in the Far East. I have, therefore, relieved General MacArthur of his commands and have designated Lt. Gen. Matthew B. Ridgway as his successor.

Full and vigorous debate on matters of national policy is a vital element in the constitutional system of our free democracy. It is fundamental, however, that military commanders must be governed by the policies and directives issued to them in the manner provided by our laws and Constitution. In time of crisis, this consideration is particularly compelling.

General MacArthur's place in history as one of our greatest commanders is fully established. The Nation owes him a debt of gratitude for the distinguished and exceptional service which he has rendered his country in posts of great responsibility. For that reason I repeat my regret at the necessity for the action I feel compelled to take in his case.

[2.] Order by the President to General MacArthur:

I deeply regret that it becomes my duty as President and Commander in Chief of the United States military forces to replace you as Supreme Commander, Allied Powers; Commander in Chief, United Nations Command; Commander in Chief, Far East; and Commanding General, U.S. Army, Far East.

You will turn over your commands, effective at once, to Lt. Gen. Matthew B. Ridgway. You are authorized to have issued such orders as are necessary to complete desired travel to such place as you select.

My reasons for your replacement will be made public concurrently with the delivery to you of the foregoing order, and are contained in the next following message.

Source: *Public Papers of the Presidents of the United States. Harry S. Truman, 1951.* Washington, D.C.: Government Printing Office, 1965, 222–227.

President Harry Truman Attempts to Discredit McCarthyism, 1952

President Harry Truman addressed the Eastern Parkway Arena in Brooklyn, New York, on October 18, 1952, less than a month before the next presidential election, which pitted Democratic candidate Adlai Stevenson against Republican nominee Dwight D. Eisenhower, a famous World War II commander. Truman took the stage at a time when many Americans were consumed with paranoid fears that a communist takeover of the country was imminent. Such fears were further inflamed by Wisconsin senator Joseph McCarthy, a Republican who claimed that a secret group of left-leaning politicians were attempting to push a communist agenda on America. He accused hundreds and even thousands of public and private citizens of supporting communism and betraying America. The McCarran Act, which

President Truman references in the following document, was created in 1950 and gave the government the power to surveille those who were thought to be communists. The bill all but endorsed McCarthy's serious claims. President Truman had initially vetoed the act, but he was overruled.

Fed up with McCarthy's spectacle and what he saw as Republican fearmongering for political advantage, Truman endorsed Stevenson. But he also railed against Eisenhower for not speaking out against McCarthy and his allies. The following excerpt from Truman's address exemplifies how deep the partisan divide had become—and how much McCarthyism had influenced politics at the time.

Let me say at the outset, I have the deepest sympathy for those who desire a rebirth of the Republican Party. It would be good for the country. It would be good for the Democratic Party to have some real competition in working for the welfare of the average citizen.

A lot of people hoped for such a rebirth this year. They didn't get it. Instead, all they got was a new paint job.

The first thing the Republicans did this year was to pull one of the oldest tricks in the political book. That is to take a successful general—a man whose whole career stands for nonpartisan patriotism—and put him up as a candidate to hide their own bad partisan record.

In every case in our history, where this was done, the general turned out to be a figurehead—and usually a pitiful figurehead—for the interests using his name and reputation.

Now what has happened in this case?

Has this General come forward with a single, new constructive program? Has his leadership done a single thing to change the policies of the Republican Party? Take civil rights for example.

Here is an issue on which new leadership might try to bring the Republican Party back to its great—but almost forgotten—tradition of freedom and human rights. But nothing like that has happened. The Republican candidate has just uttered crafty equivocations designed to win the votes—and the contributions—of the Dixiecrat millionaires. He is still opposed to using the powers of the federal Government for an effective fair employment practices law.

Take the issue of refugees and displaced persons—the great question of whether we shall amend our immigration and naturalization laws in such a way as to aid and strengthen the brave peoples of Europe, and build up our own country.

Of course, the Republican platform is silent on this issue, but we are entitled to ask: What has the Republican candidate done about it?

At this 11th hour, he has come out for rewriting the McCarran Act, in words very similar to my veto message of that unfair and un-American law. I am glad he has done so, because I welcome support of every American in the fight to get that law changed. Do you suppose that he would have taken this stand—do you suppose his advisers would even have told him about this issue—if I had not begun the fight, and if I had not carried that fight to the people? How do you think we managed to get this belated "me too" out of the Republican candidate?

Now I am being criticized for what I have said about the General on this issue, and as usual my words are being distorted in the press. I have not sought to reflect on the General's military accomplishments in the great fight against the forces of Hitler in Germany. What I have said, and what I shall continue to say, is that the General, as a political candidate, cannot have this issue both ways.

He cannot go down to West Virginia or to Indiana or to Wisconsin, and put his arm around men like Revercomb and Jenner and McCarthy, and endorse them for reelection—and to ask the people to send them to Washington to help him in his "great crusade"—and then come back here to New York, and expect the people to believe that he is going to do away with the kind of injustice that is represented by that terrible McCarran law.

The apologists for the General say that he has to endorse such people in order to help the unity of the Republican Party. That, my friends, is the only kind of unity it does help. It certainly doesn't help national unity. It certainly doesn't help our unity as a great people of many origins, living up to the principles of our Constitution, and believing in the equality of man.

Indeed, as you look at this campaign, you see the Republican candidate, in his efforts to get votes and unify his party, saying the same things as those who have long been trying to pull our country apart.

For example, the Republican candidate is saying the same things about economic conditions in this country that the Communists are saying. He is asserting that our economic gains are not real—that they are due to war or to the threat of war.

This charge is utterly untrue, of course. In fact, it is the reverse of the truth. If it were not for the necessity of devoting a large part of our production to defense purposes, we could produce more civilian goods and raise our standard of living even higher than it is now.

The Republican candidate knows this—or he should know it, if he doesn't. But he is making his charges to spread fear of the future and distrust of the Government. And it is for exactly these same reasons that the Communists in this country and in Moscow are making the same charges.

Another reckless thing the Republican candidate is doing that will tear our country apart is spreading false and slanderous charges that the Democratic Party is soft on communism. In the face of the record we have made fighting against communism at home and abroad, these charges are fantastic. But because he thinks it is a way to get votes he is smearing his Government, and its civilian leaders, for the whole period of his own career under them.

These wild political charges about communism are no help to our strength and unity—or to our efforts to defeat communism. They divide us, setting American against American. You all know that that is true. There are even some Republicans who know it. Two years ago, seven Republican Senators joined in a statement declaring that this technique—if unchecked—and I quote: "will surely end what we have come to cherish as the American way of life."

If there is any doubt that this smear technique is a dangerous and destructive way to get votes, it can be dispelled if we know what the Communists think of it. They do not fear it. They are in favor of it. Listen to the words of a man who spent

9 years in the Communist Party as a volunteer counterspy for the FBI. His name is Herbert Philbrick, and he said—and I am going to quote him:

"According to leaders of the Communist Party, McCarthy has helped them a great deal. The kind of attacks he has made do three things that his comrades like: They add greatly to the confusion, putting up a smoke screen for the party and making it more difficult than ever for people to discern just who is a Communist and who is not; they make the party appear a lot stronger than it is; and they do considerable damage to some of the 'stupid liberals' whom the party hates."

There you have it. McCarthyism does not hurt the Communists—it helps them. Its purpose, like theirs, is to divide and confuse the Nation. But it is one of the weapons that the Republican Party, under its new leadership, is using in its drive for votes in November.

Now there is another field in which the Republican candidate has adopted tactics that divide and injure the Nation. That, my friends, is our struggle for peace in Korea. As I explained in Lawrence, Massachusetts, yesterday, the Republican candidate is leading people to think that he can pull all our troops out of Korea.

Now, the General is a professional soldier. I have arranged for him to receive, during this campaign, top secret reports on the fighting in Korea. He knows what the situation is there. He knows that if we pulled out of Korea it would mean a complete victory for the Communists, and would wreck our whole defense against Communist aggression in the far East.

Yet he has been going around this country implying that he has some easy patented solution. This is simply playing a cheap and cruel hoax on the mothers and wives of our men in Korea, and I have called him on it—I hope he stops it. Because it's not only a shameless cruelty for our women, and an injury to our morale, but it's also just what the Communists want.

Now, I made General Eisenhower Chief of Staff of the United States Army. I appointed him commander of NATO in Europe of our allies who are getting themselves strong enough to resist communism. He has been on my military advisers staff ever since I have been President of the United States, and if he knows any sure, quick way to wind up the Korean situation, he should have told me and not used it for a political purpose. It would be much, much easier, if he knows a quick way to end this situation, than to save it he is using it for political purposes, to get himself into office so he can stop it. He can't do it, and it's simply a political trick.

The Communists have been saying all along that we ought to get out of Korea and stay out of Korea. They have been doing everything possible to get the people of this country to think that Korea is a useless sacrifice. Their purpose is to get us out of the fight so they can take over Korea. And they have certainly been greatly helped by what the Republican candidate has been saying around the country in recent days.

Now, when I think of all these things, I challenge any Republican, or any Republican newspaper (and that includes most of them) to stand up and say that the Republican Party and the Republican candidate have waged a high-level campaign—or even ever intended to wage a high-level campaign. They haven't done it. Theirs is one of the lowest, gutter campaigns that I have ever seen. And if there had been an ordinary politician at the head of it, instead of a general of the Army, the Republicans would never have dared to put it on.

Now, I have pointed out that this gutter campaign follows the line of the Communists in several respects. This is not because the Republican Party and the Republican candidate believe in communism, or that they are sympathetic with it. It is quite the opposite. It is because the propaganda of the extreme reactionaries, and of the lunatic fringe on the right—the lunatic fringe that the candidate wants to keep in his unified Republican Party—includes the same elements of disruption and distrust as the propaganda of the Communists. Now, if the Republicans stoop to this kind of propaganda, we have a right to call it what it really is.

Communism and the lunatic fringe of extreme reaction tell the people the same lies—because they have the same aim—to weaken and confuse and divide the people as a means of achieving power.

In the sad and tortured history of our times, we have seen many bitter examples of this political technique. Dictatorships have risen to power in foreign lands on the basis of it. At the bottom of these movements are the appeals to prejudice and panic. At the top is the figure of a leader, usually in uniform or with a military background. All the followers are required to have a deep personal faith in the leader, to believe that he will do miracles, if he comes to power. He answers no questions—he is above questioning. He will change everything that is wrong, but it is blasphemous to ask him how he is going to do it.

Now, I don't for a moment suggest that the Republican candidate wants to be a dictator—or that the Republican Party is planning to set up a dictatorship. But the public relations experts and the advertising agencies who are masterminding the Republican campaign have introduced these foreign techniques to sell their political product. And what I am saying is, that these foreign techniques have no place in American political life.

We do not want a man on horseback. When a man gets into politics, he has to get off his high horse. With us, a candidate is supposed to take a stand on the issues, and tell us where he stands. Anybody is entitled to question his views.

Our political life is colorful and exciting—and nobody knows that better than I do—but it is based on reason and debate and considered judgment. And we want to keep it that way.

So don't be pressured—don't be fooled—don't be divided by fear or panic. The people run this country. And the people can trust one another as they always have.

Think over the issues. Pray over your decision. Decide on the basis of reason and judgment. I hope you will vote Democratic—and I believe you will, because the Democratic Party stands on what it has done—and is honest with the people about the issues before us. The Democratic Party has always been the party of the people. The Democratic Party has always had a heart. The Republican Party has been for the special interests, and not for the people. The Republican Party has a calculating machine for a heart. I want you to think these things over. Think them carefully, now. Vote in your own interests.

If you think them carefully, and think of your own interests, and think of the welfare of this great Nation of ours—the greatest Republic in the history of the world—and think of the welfare of the free world as a whole, you can't do anything else but vote the Democratic ticket. And if you do that, Adlai Stevenson will be the President of the United States for the next 4 years.

Source: *Public Papers of the Presidents of the United States. Harry S. Truman, 1952–53.* Washington, D.C.: Government Printing Office, 1966, 886–890.

President Lyndon B. Johnson Declares National Day of Mourning for President John F. Kennedy, 1963

On November 22, 1963, President John F. Kennedy and First Lady Jacqueline Kennedy appeared in Dallas, Texas, in an effort to garner support for the president's second term as president. A motorcade had been arranged for the pair, who were accompanied by the governor of Texas, John Connally, and his wife, Nellie Connally. As the topless limousine rode slowly down its course through the city, President Kennedy was struck by two bullets from the back, once in the head and once in the neck, by a man named Lee Harvey Oswald (Oswald was later shot and killed by a man named Jack Ruby before his trial could take place). Secret Service agent Clint Hill jumped into the vehicle and attempted to shield Jacqueline Kennedy and the president, but the president had been fatally wounded. President Kennedy was the fourth president to be assassinated in U.S. history. Less than two hours later, Lyndon B. Johnson, his vice president, was sworn in on Air Force One before its takeoff to Washington. President Kennedy's body was onboard in a casket. The following document details one of Johnson's first actions as president: to proclaim a national day of mourning for the fallen president on the day of his funeral, November 25, 1963, where Kennedy would be buried in Arlington National Cemetery in Virginia.

To the People of the United States:
John Fitzgerald Kennedy, 35th President of the United States, has been taken from us by an act which outrages decent men everywhere.

He upheld the faith of our fathers, which is freedom for all men. He broadened the frontiers of that faith, and backed it with the energy and the courage which are the mark of the Nation he led.

A man of wisdom, strength, and peace, he moulded and moved the power of our Nation in the service of a world of growing liberty and order. All who love freedom will mourn his death.

As he did not shrink from his responsibilities, but welcomed them, so he would not have us shrink from carrying on his work beyond this hour of national tragedy.

He said it himself: "The energy, the faith, the devotion which we bring to this endeavor will light our country and all who serve it-and the glow from that fire can truly light the world."

Now, Therefore, I, Lyndon B. Johnson, President of the United States of America, do appoint Monday next, November 25, the day of the funeral service of President Kennedy, to be a national day of mourning throughout the United States. I earnestly recommend the people to assemble on that day in their respective places of divine worship, there to bow down in submission to the will of Almighty God, and to pay their homage of love and reverence to the memory of a great and good man. I invite the people of the world who share our grief to join us in this day of mourning and rededication.

In Witness Whereof, I have hereunto set my hand and caused the Seal of the United States of America to be affixed.

DONE at the City of Washington this twenty-third day of November in the year of our Lord nineteen hundred and sixty-three, and of the Independence of the United States of America the one hundred and eighty-eighth.

Source: *Public Papers of the Presidents of the United States. Lyndon B. Johnson, 1963–64, Book 1.* Washington, D.C.: Government Printing Office, 1965, 2.

President Lyndon B. Johnson Makes Statement about Assassination of Dr. Martin Luther King Jr., 1968

On the evening of April 4, 1968, Dr. Martin Luther King Jr., famed leader of the civil rights movement and a proponent of nonviolent protest in the United States and across the world, was shot and killed on the balcony of a motel in Memphis, Tennessee. King was 39 years old, and had been in Memphis to lead local strikers in a march. His assassination shocked the nation and rioting broke out in several cities. In an effort to recognize King's impact on the civil rights movement and the United States as a whole—and to calm the many Americans grieving his loss—President Johnson made the following statement to the public within hours of King's murder.

AMERICA is shocked and saddened by the brutal slaying tonight of Dr. Martin Luther King.

I ask every citizen to reject the blind violence that has struck Dr. King, who lived by nonviolence.

I pray that his family can find comfort in the memory of all he tried to do for the land he loved so well.

I have just conveyed the sympathy of Mrs. Johnson and myself to his widow, Mrs. King.

I know that every American of good will joins me in mourning the death of this outstanding leader and in praying for peace and understanding throughout this land.

We can achieve nothing by lawlessness and divisiveness among the American people. It is only by joining together and only by working together that we can continue to move toward equality and fulfillment for all of our people.

I hope that all Americans tonight will search their hearts as they ponder this most tragic incident.

I have canceled my plans for the evening. I am postponing my trip to Hawaii until tomorrow.

Thank you.

Source: *Public Papers of the Presidents of the United States. Lyndon B. Johnson, 1968–69, Book 1.* Washington, D.C.: Government Printing Office, 1970, 493.

President Richard Nixon Announces Resignation after Watergate Scandal, 1974

Although Republican President Richard Nixon was reelected to office in November of 1972, the public was not yet aware of the illegal activities he and his administration had been involved with in the months and even years prior. In June of that year, five burglars were caught by security as they attempted to steal documents, tap phones, and engage in other political espionage at Washington, D.C.'s Watergate hotel complex, where the Democratic National Committee (DNC) headquarters were located. As investigators looked deeper into the burglary, it became apparent that the crimes were part of a large scheme, including a coverup coordinated by the most powerful man in the country—President Nixon himself. His involvement became apparent after a set of tapes were obtained by investigators (after the Supreme Court ordered in United States v. Nixon *that President Nixon forfeit them) which contained strong enough evidence to indict him. Further evidence and information were secretly provided to* Washington Post *journalists Bob Woodward and Carl Bernstein by a whistleblower, Mark Felt, former associate director of the Federal Bureau of Investigation (FBI). As more and more news broke over the next two years, the public became further horrified at the deception and abuse of power that had transpired in the White House. The Watergate Scandal propelled the country into a state of deep disillusionment about the presidency and the government overall. Facing impeachment, President Nixon opted to resign from office on August 8, 1974, the first president to ever do so. The following document is a transcript of his resignation speech, addressed to the nation. President Nixon was pardoned for his crimes by his successor, President Gerald Ford.*

Good evening:

This is the 37th time I have spoken to you from this office, where so many decisions have been made that shaped the history of this Nation. Each time I have done so to discuss with you some matter that I believe affected the national interest.

In all the decisions I have made in my public life, I have always tried to do what was best for the Nation. Throughout the long and difficult period of Watergate, I have felt it was my duty to persevere, to make every possible effort to complete the term of office to which you elected me.

In the past few days, however, it has become evident to me that I no longer have a strong enough political base in the Congress to justify continuing that effort. As long as there was such a base, I felt strongly that it was necessary to see the constitutional process through to its conclusion, that to do otherwise would be unfaithful to the spirit of that deliberately difficult process and a dangerously destabilizing precedent for the future.

But with the disappearance of that base, I now believe that the constitutional purpose has been served, and there is no longer a need for the process to be prolonged.

I would have preferred to carry through to the finish, whatever the personal agony it would have involved, and my family unanimously urged me to do so. But the interests of the Nation must always come before any personal considerations.

From the discussions I have had with Congressional and other leaders, I have concluded that because of the Watergate matter, I might not have the support of the Congress that I would consider necessary to back the very difficult decisions and carry out the duties of this office in the way the interests of the Nation will require.

I have never been a quitter. To leave office before my term is completed is abhorrent to every instinct in my body. But as President, I must put the interests of America first. America needs a full-time President and a full-time Congress, particularly at this time with problems we face at home and abroad.

To continue to fight through the months ahead for my personal vindication would almost totally absorb the time and attention of both the President and the Congress in a period when our entire focus should be on the great issues of peace abroad and prosperity without inflation at home.

Therefore, I shall resign the Presidency effective at noon tomorrow. Vice President Ford will be sworn in as President at that hour in this office.

As I recall the high hopes for America with which we began this second term, I feel a great sadness that I will not be here in this office working on your behalf to achieve those hopes in the next 2½ years. But in turning over direction of the Government to Vice President Ford, I know, as I told the Nation when I nominated him for that office 10 months ago, that the leadership of America will be in good hands.

In passing this office to the Vice President, I also do so with the profound sense of the weight of responsibility that will fall on his shoulders tomorrow and, therefore, of the understanding, the patience, the cooperation he will need from all Americans.

As he assumes that responsibility, he will deserve the help and the support of all of us. As we look to the future, the first essential is to begin healing the wounds of this Nation, to put the bitterness and divisions of the recent past behind us and to rediscover those shared ideals that lie at the heart of our strength and unity as a great and as a free people.

By taking this action, I hope that I will have hastened the start of that process of healing which is so desperately needed in America.

I regret deeply any injuries that may have been done in the course of the events that led to this decision. I would say only that if some of my judgments were wrong—and some were wrong—they were made in what I believed at the time to be the best interest of the Nation.

To those who have stood with me during these past difficult months—to my family, my friends, to many others who joined in supporting my cause because they believed it was right—I will be eternally grateful for your support.

And to those who have not felt able to give me your support, let me say I leave with no bitterness toward those who have opposed me, because all of us, in the final analysis, have been concerned with the good of the country, however our judgments might differ.

So, let us all now join together in affirming that common commitment and in helping our new President succeed for the benefit of all Americans.

I shall leave this office with regret at not completing my term, but with gratitude for the privilege of serving as your President for the past 5½ years. These years have been a momentous time in the history of our Nation and the world. They have been a time of achievement in which we can all be proud, achievements that represent the shared efforts of the Administration, the Congress, and the people.

But the challenges ahead are equally great, and they, too, will require the support and the efforts of the Congress and the people working in cooperation with the new Administration.

We have ended America's longest war, but in the work of securing a lasting peace in the world, the goals ahead are even more far-reaching and more difficult. We must complete a structure of peace so that it will be said of this generation, our generation of Americans, by the people of all nations, not only that we ended one war but that we prevented future wars.

We have unlocked the doors that for a quarter of a century stood between the United States and the People's Republic of China.

We must now ensure that the one quarter of the world's people who live in the People's Republic of China will be and remain not our enemies, but our friends.

In the Middle East, 100 million people in the Arab countries, many of whom have considered us their enemy for nearly 20 years, now look on us as their friends. We must continue to build on that friendship so that peace can settle at last over the Middle East and so that the cradle of civilization will not become its grave.

Together with the Soviet Union, we have made the crucial breakthroughs that have begun the process of limiting nuclear arms. But we must set as our goal not just limiting but reducing and, finally, destroying these terrible weapons so that they cannot destroy civilization and so that the threat of nuclear war will no longer hang over the world and the people.

We have opened the new relation with the Soviet Union. We must continue to develop and expand that new relationship so that the two strongest nations of the world will live together in cooperation, rather than confrontation.

Around the world in Asia, in Africa, in Latin America, in the Middle East—there are millions of people who live in terrible poverty, even starvation. We must keep as our goal turning away from production for war and expanding production for peace so that people everywhere on this Earth can at last look forward in their children's time, if not in our own time, to having the necessities for a decent life.

Here in America, we are fortunate that most of our people have not only the blessings of liberty but also the means to live full and good and, by the world's standards, even abundant lives. We must press on, however, toward a goal, not only of more and better jobs but of full opportunity for every American and of what we are striving so hard right now to achieve, prosperity without inflation.

For more than a quarter of a century in public life, I have shared in the turbulent history of this era. I have fought for what I believed in. I have tried, to the best of my ability, to discharge those duties and meet those responsibilities that were entrusted to me.

Sometimes I have succeeded and sometimes I have failed, but always I have taken heart from what Theodore Roosevelt once said about the man in the arena, "whose face is marred by dust and sweat and blood, who strives valiantly, who errs and comes short again and again because there is not effort without error and shortcoming, but who does actually strive to do the deed, who knows the great enthusiasms, the great devotions, who spends himself in a worthy cause, who at the best knows in the end the triumphs of high achievements and who at the worst, if he fails, at least fails while daring greatly."

I pledge to you tonight that as long as I have a breath of life in my body, I shall continue in that spirit. I shall continue to work for the great causes to which I have been dedicated throughout my years as a Congressman, a Senator, Vice President, and President, the cause of peace, not just for America but among all nations-prosperity, justice, and opportunity for all of our people.

There is one cause above all to which I have been devoted and to which I shall always be devoted for as long as I live.

When I first took the oath of office as President 5½ years ago, I made this sacred commitment: to "consecrate my office, my energies, and all the wisdom I can summon to the cause of peace among nations."

I have done my very best in all the days since to be true to that pledge. As a result of these efforts, I am confident that the world is a safer place today, not only for the people of America but for the people of all nations, and that all of our children have a better chance than before of living in peace rather than dying in war.

This, more than anything, is what I hoped to achieve when I sought the Presidency. This, more than anything, is what I hope will be my legacy to you, to our country, as I leave the Presidency.

To have served in this office is to have felt a very personal sense of kinship with each and every American. In leaving it, I do so with this prayer: May God's grace be with you in all the days ahead.

Source: *Public Papers of the Presidents of the United States. Richard Nixon, 1974.* Washington, D.C.: Government Printing Office, 1975, 626–629.

President Gerald R. Ford Grants Pardon to Richard Nixon, 1974

When President Richard Nixon resigned from office due to the Watergate scandal on August 8, 1974, he became the first president ever to leave office in such a manner. His vice president, Gerald R. Ford, was sworn in as president of the United States just minutes after the disgraced Nixon left the White House for good. President Ford was the first president technically appointed to the position without being elected as part (either president or vice president) of a presidential ticket. Ford had been tapped as Nixon's vice president when Spiro Agnew, who had been Nixon's vice president since 1969, was forced to resign in connection to other illegal activities in 1973.

President Gerald Ford was given the colossal task of mending a country that had lost so much of its faith and hope in the government, in justice, and, most of all, in the presidency. While President Nixon awaited trial, President Ford deliberated how to best move forward. In the end, he decided to pardon President Nixon, which marked the first time a president had ever been pardoned. The decision inspired bitterness from the public, who felt the pardon was not deserved. The following document is a transcript of the remarks President Gerald Ford made upon signing the pardon proclamation. In it, he justifies his decision and comments on the overall state of affairs in the country. Public opinion polls at the time indicate that Ford's decision was so unpopular that it might have contributed to his loss to Democratic nominee Jimmy Carter in the 1976 presidential election. As the years passed, however, a majority of Americans came to feel that Ford's pardon was the best thing for the nation.

Ladies and gentlemen:

I have come to a decision which I felt I should tell you and all of my fellow American citizens, as soon as I was certain in my own mind and in my own conscience that it is the right thing to do.

I have learned already in this office that the difficult decisions always come to this desk. I must admit that many of them do not look at all the same as the hypothetical questions that I have answered freely and perhaps too fast on previous occasions.

My customary policy is to try and get all the facts and to consider the opinions of my countrymen and to take counsel with my most valued friends. But these seldom agree, and in the end, the decision is mine. To procrastinate, to agonize, and to wait for a more favorable turn of events that may never come or more compelling external pressures that may as well be wrong as right, is itself a decision of sorts and a weak and potentially dangerous course for a President to follow.

I have promised to uphold the Constitution, to do what is right as God gives me to see the right, and to do the very best that I can for America.

I have asked your help and your prayers, not only when I became President but many times since. The Constitution is the supreme law of our land and it governs our actions as citizens. Only the laws of God, which govern our consciences, are superior to it.

As we are a nation under God, so I am sworn to uphold our laws with the help of God. And I have sought such guidance and searched my own conscience with special diligence to determine the right thing for me to do with respect to my predecessor in this place, Richard Nixon, and his loyal wife and family.

Theirs is an American tragedy in which we all have played a part. It could go on and on and on, or someone must write the end to it. I have concluded that only I can do that, and if I can, I must.

There are no historic or legal precedents to which I can turn in this matter, none that precisely fit the circumstances of a private citizen who has resigned the Presidency of the United States. But it is common knowledge that serious allegations and accusations hang like a sword over our former President's head, threatening his health as he tries to reshape his life, a great part of which was spent in the service of this country and by the mandate of its people.

After years of bitter controversy and divisive national debate, I have been advised, and I am compelled to conclude that many months and perhaps more years will have to pass before Richard Nixon could obtain a fair trial by jury in any jurisdiction of the United States under governing decisions of the Supreme Court.

I deeply believe in equal justice for all Americans, whatever their station or former station. The law, whether human or divine, is no respecter of persons; but the law is a respecter of reality.

The facts, as I see them, are that a former President of the United States, instead of enjoying equal treatment with any other citizen accused of violating the law, would be cruelly and excessively penalized either in preserving the presumption of his innocence or in obtaining a speedy determination of his guilt in order to repay a legal debt to society.

During this long period of delay and potential litigation, ugly passions would again be aroused. And our people would again be polarized in their opinions. And the credibility of our free institutions of government would again be challenged at home and abroad.

In the end, the courts might well hold that Richard Nixon had been denied due process, and the verdict of history would even more be inconclusive with respect to those charges arising out of the period of his Presidency, of which I am presently aware.

But it is not the ultimate fate of Richard Nixon that most concerns me, though surely it deeply troubles every decent and every compassionate person. My concern is the immediate future of this great country.

In this, I dare not depend upon my personal sympathy as a long-time friend of the former President, nor my professional judgment as a lawyer, and I do not.

As President, my primary concern must always be the greatest good of all the people of the United States whose servant I am. As a man, my first consideration is to be true to my own convictions and my own conscience.

My conscience tells me clearly and certainly that I cannot prolong the bad dreams that continue to reopen a chapter that is closed. My conscience tells me that only I, as President, have the constitutional power to firmly shut and seal this book. My conscience tells me it is my duty, not merely to proclaim domestic tranquility but to use every means that I have to insure it.

I do believe that the buck stops here, that I cannot rely upon public opinion polls to tell me what is right.

I do believe that right makes might and that if I am wrong, 10 angels swearing I was right would make no difference.

I do believe, with all my heart and mind and spirit, that I, not as President but as a humble servant of God, will receive justice without mercy if I fail to show mercy.

Finally, I feel that Richard Nixon and his loved ones have suffered enough and will continue to suffer, no matter what I do, no matter what we, as a great and good nation, can do together to make his goal of peace come true.

[At this point, the President began reading from the proclamation granting the pardon.]

Now, therefore, I, Gerald R. Ford, President of the United States, pursuant to the pardon power conferred upon me by Article II, Section 2, of the Constitution, have granted and by these presents do grant a full, free, and absolute pardon unto Richard Nixon for all offenses against the United States which he, Richard Nixon, has committed or may have committed or taken part in during the period from July (January) 20, 1969 through August 9, 1974.

[The President signed the proclamation and then resumed reading.]
In witness whereof, I have hereunto set my hand this eighth day of September, in the year of our Lord nineteen hundred and seventy-four, and of the Independence of the United States of America the one hundred and ninety ninth.

Source: *Public Papers of the Presidents of the United States. Gerald R. Ford, 1974.* Washington, D.C.: Government Printing Office, 1975, 101–103.

President Ronald Reagan Denies Illegal Involvement in Iran-Contra Scandal, 1987

The Iran-Contra scandal was characterized by complex international relations and secret deals. Iran and Iraq were at war in 1985, and the United States had not lifted sanctions imposed on Iran after the 1979 hostage crisis, in which 52 American citizens and diplomats had been held by Iranian fundamentalists for more than a year. That crisis had its genesis in the 1979 overthrow of Mohammad Reza Shah, an authoritarian monarch who had long been supported by the United States.

In 1985 the United States was informed of another hostage situation—this time in Lebanon, where seven Americans were being held by Iranian terrorists. In prior weeks, Iran had requested to purchase weapons from the United States in secret to continue fighting its war against Iraq. An illegal deal was made: the Reagan administration agreed to trade arms for the return of hostages from Lebanon. At the same time, anticommunist Contra forces were fighting against the communist Sandinista government in Nicaragua. President Reagan, facing pressure to continue the fight against communism, wanted to aid Contra forces, despite the fact that much of their funding came from illegal drug trafficking. The Democratic-controlled House and Senate were aware of the president's attempt to intervene using special forces from the Central Intelligence Agency (CIA) and took several measures to curb his actions, including passing the Boland Amendment. Yet when President Reagan's secret deal with Iran came to light in 1986, another facet of the deal was uncovered. Investigators learned that the U.S. government had been funneling a portion of the millions of dollars made from arms sales to Iran into funding the Contras in Nicaragua. Few believed that Reagan was unaware of these secret maneuverings, but his involvement was never proven. The following document is an excerpt of an exchange between President Reagan and reporters about the ongoing Iran-Contra scandal on May 19, 1987.

Mr. Powell. Can I ask you one quick one? I know I shouldn't, but the Iran-Contra hearings started again today. If there is any evidence down the road that you did do something illegal, is there any consideration whatsoever of resigning if it turns out that something was done illegally on your part?

The President. Well, I have to tell you, I know absolutely that I did nothing illegal. As a matter of fact, I have, over and over again, told the Washington press corps and told the leaders of Congress that the only thing about which I have no answer is the apparent funds in the Swiss bank accounts supposedly that came from our shipment of arms to Iran. Now, we got our money for that shipment and the only thing that we can figure is that somebody—in the go-betweens there between us and Iran—must have put an additional price on it and got more money from Iran than we were asking. And who did that, where the money came from or where it has gone, we absolutely have no knowledge of that, and I'm still waiting to find out who did it and what was done.

As far as just helping the contras, no, there's never been any restriction on my ability to speak publicly, as I have, in urging support for the contras. We did not violate any rules when the Congress, after appropriating money for help and then called that off after it had been used and refused to issue a new appropriation—we haven't violated that in any way. And I never solicited a foreign country, although under the Boland amendment—one of the versions of it, there are about five—actually authorized the Secretary of State, who is certainly my appointee, to solicit other countries, democratic countries, to do as we were doing and try to aid the freedom fighters down there.

So I—as I say, I never solicited anyone directly. And the one thing that has been mentioned—I, myself, have told it—and that is when King Fahd of Saudi Arabia was present in a meeting here—that was never discussed in the meeting. And he simply made mention as he was leaving that he was going to increase the contribution that he had been making to the freedom fighters.

Source: *Public Papers of the Presidents of the United States. Ronald Reagan, 1987, Book 1.* Washington, D.C.: Government Printing Office, 1989, 534–536.

President Bill Clinton Gives Remarks Prior to Vote on First Article of Impeachment, 1998

On December 11, 1998, three articles of impeachment were approved by the Republican-led House of Representatives against President Bill Clinton, though only two would be brought against him—for perjury and obstruction of justice. President Clinton was embroiled in two major scandals which led to his impeachment trial. In 1994, he was sued by Paula Jones, who alleged that in 1991, when President Clinton was the governor of Arkansas, he had harassed Jones in a private hotel room. As investigations into Jones's accusations ensued, independent prosecutor Kenneth Starr discovered that the president might have had an affair with a White House intern, Monica Lewinsky, around 1995. Lewinsky was moved to the Pentagon in 1996. Proceedings for the Jones case began in 1997, after President Clinton's claim that as a sitting president he was immune to civil suits was rejected by the Supreme Court. When Kenneth Starr asked the president whether he had an affair with Monica Lewinsky, the president denied it under oath. When Lewinsky was subpoenaed as part of the trial, she too denied the affair, but one of her coworkers at the Pentagon had taped their conversations about the affair in secret. The tapes were submitted to Starr, and Lewinsky was offered immunity for her testimony. In August of 1998, both the president and Lewinsky admitted their affair, and the story broke to the public. The following document is President Clinton's remarks prior to the vote on the first article of impeachment, where he expresses his remorse. The president would later be acquitted on both articles in 1999.

Good afternoon. As anyone close to me knows, for months I have been grappling with how best to reconcile myself to the American people, to acknowledge my own wrongdoing, and still to maintain my focus on the work of the Presidency.

Others are presenting my defense on the facts, the law, and the Constitution. Nothing I can say now can add to that. What I want the American people to know, what I want the Congress to know, is that I am profoundly sorry for all I have done wrong in words and deeds. I never should have misled the country, the Congress, my friends, or my family. Quite simply, I gave in to my shame.

I have been condemned by my accusers with harsh words. And while it's hard to hear yourself called deceitful and manipulative, I remember Ben Franklin's admonition that our critics are our friends, for they do show us our faults.

Mere words cannot fully express the profound remorse I feel for what our country is going through and for what members of both parties in Congress are now forced to deal with.

These past months have been a tortuous process of coming to terms with what I did. I understand that accountability demands consequences, and I'm prepared to accept them. Painful though the condemnation of the Congress would be, it would pale in comparison to the consequences of the pain I have caused my family. There is no greater agony.

Like anyone who honestly faces the shame of wrongful conduct, I would give anything to go back and undo what I did. But one of the painful truths I have to live with is the reality that that is simply not possible. An old and dear friend of mine recently sent me the wisdom of a poet, who wrote:

The Moving Finger writes; and, having writ,
Moves on: nor all your piety nor wit
Shall lure it back to cancel half a line,
Nor all your tears wash out a word of it.

So nothing, not piety, nor tears, nor wit, nor torment, can alter what I have done. I must make my peace with that. I must also be at peace with the fact that the public consequences of my actions are in the hands of the American people and their Representatives in the Congress. Should they determine that my errors of word and deed require their rebuke and censure, I am ready to accept that.

Meanwhile, I will continue to do all I can to reclaim the trust of the American people and to serve them well. We must all return to the work, the vital work, of strengthening our Nation for the new century. Our country has wonderful opportunities and daunting challenges ahead. I intend to seize those opportunities and meet those challenges with all the energy and ability and strength God has given me.

That is simply all I can do: the work of the American people.

Thank you very much.

Source: *Public Papers of the Presidents of the United States. William J. Clinton: 1998, Book 2.* Washington, D.C.: Government Printing Office, 1999–2000, 2158.

President Donald Trump Makes Statement during United States–Russia Summit in Helsinki, 2018

The United States–Russia summit was arranged in part to discuss trade and policies, such as oil pipelines in Europe and the countries' nuclear weapons, as well as to diminish widespread speculation that President Donald Trump's campaign might have been involved in Russia's proven interference in the U.S. 2016 presidential election. During the press conference that followed a private meeting between himself and Russian President Vladimir Putin, President Trump claimed that he did not believe Russia had interfered with his election—despite U.S. investigations carried out by his own intelligence agencies that proved otherwise. The following document is a transcript of the remarks President Trump gave as he stood next to Putin after their brief conference, issued by the White House on July 16, 2018.

PRESIDENT TRUMP: Thank you. Thank you very much.

Thank you. I have just concluded a meeting with President Putin on a wide range of critical issues for both of our countries. We had direct, open, deeply productive dialogue. It went very well.

Before I begin, I want to thank President Niinistö of Finland for graciously hosting today's summit. President Putin and I were saying how lovely it was and what a great job they did.

I also want to congratulate Russia and President Putin for having done such an excellent job in hosting the World Cup. It was really one of the best ever and your team also did very well. It was a great job.

I'm here today to continue the proud tradition of bold American diplomacy. From the earliest days of our republic, American leaders have understood that diplomacy and engagement is preferable to conflict and hostility. A productive dialogue is not only good for the United States and good for Russia, but it is good for the world.

The disagreements between our two countries are well known, and President Putin and I discussed them at length today. But if we're going to solve many of the problems facing our world, then we are going to have to find ways to cooperate in pursuit of shared interests.

Too often, in both recent past and long ago, we have seen the consequences when diplomacy is left on the table. We've also seen the benefits of cooperation. In the last century, our nations fought alongside one another in the Second World War. Even during the tensions of the Cold War, when the world looked much different than it does today, the United States and Russia were able to maintain a strong dialogue.

But our relationship has never been worse than it is now. However, that changed as of about four hours ago. I really believe that. Nothing would be easier politically than to refuse to meet, to refuse to engage. But that would not accomplish anything. As President, I cannot make decisions on foreign policy in a futile effort to appease partisan critics or the media, or Democrats who want to do nothing but resist and obstruct.

Constructive dialogue between the United States and Russia affords the opportunity to open new pathways toward peace and stability in our world. I would rather take a political risk in pursuit of peace than to risk peace in pursuit of politics. As President, I will always put what is best for America and what is best for the American people.

During today's meeting, I addressed directly with President Putin the issue of Russian interference in our elections. I felt this was a message best delivered in person. We spent a great deal of time talking about it, and President Putin may very well want to address it, and very strongly—because he feels very strongly about it, and he has an interesting idea.

We also discussed one of the most critical challenges facing humanity: nuclear proliferation. I provided an update on my meeting last month with Chairman Kim on the denuclearization of North Korea. And after today, I am very sure that President Putin and Russia want very much to end that problem. They're going to work with us, and I appreciate that commitment.

The President and I also discussed the scourge of radical Islamic terrorism. Both Russia and the United States have suffered horrific terrorist attacks, and we have agreed to maintain open communication between our security agencies to protect our citizens from this global menace.

Last year, we told Russia about a planned attack in St. Petersburg, and they were able to stop it cold. They found them. They stopped them. There was no doubt about it. I appreciated President Putin's phone call afterwards to thank me.

I also emphasized the importance of placing pressure on Iran to halt its nuclear ambitions and to stop its campaign of violence throughout the area, throughout the Middle East.

As we discussed at length, the crisis in Syria is a complex one. Cooperation between our two countries has the potential to save hundreds of thousands of lives. I also made clear that the United States will not allow Iran to benefit from our successful campaign against ISIS. We have just about eradicated ISIS in the area.

We also agreed that representatives from our national security councils will meet to follow up on all of the issues we addressed today and to continue the progress we have started right here in Helsinki.

Today's meeting is only the beginning of a longer process. But we have taken the first steps toward a brighter future and one with a strong dialogue and a lot of thought. Our expectations are grounded in realism but our hopes are grounded in America's desire for friendship, cooperation, and peace. And I think I can speak on behalf of Russia when I say that also.

President Putin, I want to thank you again for joining me for these important discussions and for advancing open dialogue between Russia and the United States. Our meeting carries on a long tradition of diplomacy between Russia and the United States, for the greater good of all.

And this was a very constructive day. This was a very constructive few hours that we spent together. It's in the interest of both of our countries to continue our conversation, and we have agreed to do so.

I'm sure we'll be meeting again in the future often, and hopefully we will solve every one of the problems that we discussed today.

So, again, President Putin, thank you very much.

Source: The President's News Conference with President Vladimir Vladimirovich Putin of Russia in Helsinki, Finland. July 16, 2018. *Compilation of Presidential Documents.* DCPD-201800488. Available online at https://www.govinfo.gov /content/pkg/DCPD-201800488/html/DCPD-201800488.htm.

5

War and Conflict

INTRODUCTION

When presidents are inclined to take action to resolve a crisis, it is not always clear that they have either the constitutional or statutory authority they require to do so. Without such clear authority, some presidents have felt constrained in their ability to act; many more, however, have understood their power to extend beyond the explicit authority derived from the Constitution or Congress. In responding to national security crises like terrorist attacks, the Constitution provides no clear authorization. Sometimes, presidents are able to cite congressional grants of authority in announcing new policies or actions. But even when congressional approval and constitutional power are absent, presidents have taken actions they deemed necessary to meet the crises.

There is a concern, of course, that once these emergency powers are exercised, they could become regularized and embedded as a constitutional norm, rather than remain aberrational. Indeed, such actions have lain about, as Justice Jackson noted, "as a loaded weapon," setting precedents for future extraconstitutional action by other presidents when a national emergency arises. Sometimes there are crises—like imminent threats to national security—that do require Lockean prerogative powers not deemed appropriate, or even legal, during ordinary times. The challenge, though, is whether the U.S. system of constitutionalism, characterized by limited governmental power and the rule of law, is able to meaningfully constrain executives in those moments of great insecurity and concentrated power. This is all the more consequential a challenge when the crisis has no clearly distinguishable end, such as threats like terrorism that seem likely to exist indefinitely.

From Lincoln's actions during the Civil War, to Franklin D. Roosevelt during World War II, Truman in the Korean War, Nixon during Vietnam and the Watergate era, and to Bush and Obama in the age of international terrorism, the powers taken by presidents in times of grave crisis often do not have clear constitutional or statutory authority. As presidents push the limits of their Article II authority and take actions that exceed that authority, the response of the constitutional order often governs future expressions of presidential power. That order is conditioned by separate institutions sharing powers in a contested, evolutive process. At times, the constitutional order that dominates a given era appears to defer to presidential prerogative; at other times, Congress or courts respond in ways that either authorize executive actions after the fact or attempt to constrain presidential authority in specific contexts. Each institution has particular claims made upon it that mitigate its willingness to impose constraints during moments of crisis. Given the public's interest in security and national defense, for instance, Congress may be hampered in its ability to constrain the executive due to members' electoral concerns. And when faced with legal challenges to presidential actions, the federal courts can shape the constitutional order in important ways, but they are typically not determinative in constraining the president. Over time, and across a range of emergency contexts, this exchange among institutions takes place. How previous challenges were resolved (or left unresolved) sets the expectations and frames the parameters of what powers are available to the president during the next crisis. In this respect, we can understand the emergency actions taken by Presidents Bush and Obama, for example, as deriving from precedents set by prior exchanges. They can thereby be interpreted as expressions of the accumulation of power rather than aberrant exercises of emergency power.

The evolutive quality of this dynamic was illustrated by Justice Robert H. Jackson in his famous dissent in *Korematsu v. U.S.* (1944). On December 7, 1941, Japanese forces attacked Pearl Harbor, destroying the United States Pacific Fleet. This attack sparked widespread fears that the West Coast of the United States was facing an imminent invasion. The West Coast also happened to be home to more than 100,000 persons of Japanese ancestry, most of whom were U.S. citizens. Concerned that their allegiance was not to the United States but to the emperor of Japan, U.S. military authorities sought to limit their ability to engage in sabotage or spying by detaining and removing all "Japanese and other subversive persons" from the region. President Franklin Delano Roosevelt issued Executive Order 9066, forcibly evacuating and relocating to detention centers (internment camps) all Japanese Americans. None of the detainees were found to have been engaged in espionage, but all were nonetheless suspected of being likely to be subversive by virtue of their race. The military order was challenged by Fred Korematsu, who refused to be evacuated and was subsequently convicted for violating the order. The U.S. Supreme Court upheld the order, which it deemed to be a military necessity in a time of war. In Justice Jackson's dissent, he rejects both the clear racism of the military order, but also the danger that judicial approval of such an action portends. Jackson wrote:

> Much is said of the danger to liberty from the Army program for deporting and detaining these citizens of Japanese extraction. But a judicial construction of the due process clause that will sustain this order is a far more subtle blow to liberty than the promulgation of the order itself. A military order, however unconstitutional, is not apt to last longer than the military emergency. But once a judicial opinion rationalizes such an order to show that it conforms to the Constitution, or rather rationalizes the Constitution to show that the Constitution sanctions such an order, the Court for all time has validated the principle. The principle then lies about like a loaded weapon, ready for the hand of any authority that can bring forward a

plausible claim of an urgent need. Every repetition imbeds that principle more deeply in our law and thinking and expands it to new purposes. A military commander may overstep the bounds of constitutionality, and it is an incident. But if we review and approve, that passing incident becomes the doctrine of the Constitution. There it has a generative power of its own, and all that it creates will be in its own image.

Jackson's concerns proved to be prescient. There has been a generative power to the discrete exercise of presidential emergency powers. The actions of presidents taken under "plausible claim of urgent need" and their subsequent validation and repetition have generated an accumulation of an expansive set of emergency powers available to contemporary presidents. If, in claiming prerogative or emergency power at a time of urgent need, presidential actions are validated by the constitutional order, there may be no meaningful limit to executive prerogative. That is not to say that emergency powers taken by presidents have not generated reactions from other institutional actors, however. As this chapter demonstrates, the actions of Truman during the Korean War, Johnson and Nixon's actions in Vietnam, and Bush's detainee policies were each challenged and, in some cases, limited in important respects. Thus, the president's ability to take particular actions is conditioned by the willingness and ability of Congress and the courts to constrain the president. If Congress lacks the incentive or capacity to restrain executives, or courts refuse to impose constraints or are unable to enforce their rulings, the unlimited emergency powers of a president can pose dramatic challenges to a system of limited government under the rule of law. Closer examination of key events in U.S. history may be helpful in understanding the significance of the tensions facing those who seek to constrain executive power in times of crisis.

During the Civil War, President Lincoln took several actions that even he recognized might lie beyond his constitutional and statutory authority, such as imposing a naval blockade on Southern ports and seizing several confederate and foreign ships without Congress authorizing the action. In the *Prize Cases* (1863), the U.S. Supreme Court declared that the president may take military action in defense of the nation without congressional approval. The Court ruled that "the President was bound to meet [war] in the shape it presented itself; without waiting for Congress to baptize it with a name." Thus, the ruling in the *Prize Cases* reflects the principle that the president can use extralegal means to defend against an attack by a foreign nation (or, in this case, domestic insurrectionists) in the absence of congressional action.

Lincoln also suspended the writ of *habeas corpus* (a legal protection granting those who have been detained by government the right to challenge their detention in court) during the Civil War. Suspension of the writ, however, is understood to be a power reserved to Congress by Article I, not the president. In *Ex Parte Milligan* (1866), a case that arose just after the war ended, the Court invalidated the president's detention and trial of a civilian by a military commission. The Court determined that the writ of *habeas corpus* had not been suspended by Congress. Moreover, the Court reasoned, the president has no constitutional authority to detain and try a civilian by means of a military commission in areas where the civil courts of the U.S. are open and functioning. "Martial rule," the Court said, "can never exist where the courts are open and in the proper and unobstructed exercise of their jurisdiction. It is also confined to the locality of actual war." With this decision, the Court limited the ability of presidents to use military commissions to try civilians in areas where the domestic courts are open. However, Congress could presumably authorize the use of such tribunals under certain conditions. In fact, the issue of congressionally authorized military commissions has arisen several times since the Civil War, notably with Nazi saboteurs during World War II and again more recently with respect to detainees held at Guantanamo Bay, Cuba, and elsewhere.

Almost a century later, when North Korea invaded South Korea, the United States sent troops to defend South Korea. There was no declaration of war by the U.S. Congress; rather, this was a "police action" taken under the authority of the United Nations Security Council. Nonetheless, President Truman and Congress placed the nation on war footing by initiating a series of measures meant to stabilize the domestic economy. In addition to the severe inflation that accompanied the onset of hostilities, Truman expressed grave concern about an impending labor strike by steel workers that would immediately jeopardize and imperil the national security of the United States in a time of war. To prevent the strike, Truman issued an executive order instructing Secretary of Commerce Charles Sawyer to nationalize the steel industry and ensure the continued production of steel—building material that was key to the production lines of tanks and armaments. The order was based on no statute, precedent, or any explicit or implied constitutional provision. Truman, however, claimed he had the inherent authority to act in a time of national emergency. In *Youngstown Sheet and Tube Co. v. Sawyer* (1952), the Court struck down the president's action, dealing a blow to presidential claims of inherent unilateral authority and confirming Congress's central role during wartime. However, the effect of the *Youngtown* decision was rather limited. As scholars have noted:

> Congress no longer sees itself as a constitutional check on presidential warmaking. . . . If members of Congress fail to assert their prerogatives over war and peace, federal judges are unwilling to fill the breach left open by lawmakers. At the time of Youngstown, Congress's failure to act was aberrational. . . . Today, Congress's general practice is to acquiesce, not challenge, presidential war-making. With Congress retreating in war powers, courts too have backed away. (Devins and Fisher 2002, 76)

In the nation's history, Congress has only declared war five times. Presidents, however, have exercised their war powers on hundreds of occasions without a formal congressional declaration of war. And while the *Youngstown* decision confirms congressional centrality and judicial circumspection with respect to presidential war-making, the nature of military conflicts has changed. No longer is it likely that Congress will have the opportunity to express a formal declaration of war prior to the onset of hostilities. Rather, rapid responses in the form of airstrikes, drone strikes, and covert action typifies military action in the contemporary context. The evolution of military conflict has thus left Congress far less equipped to exercise its constitutional authority to declare war. The changing nature of contemporary military conflict, though, is not the entire story. Congress has also taken steps to grant broad discretion to the executive to exercise military force even without a formal declaration of war. The Gulf of Tonkin Resolution in 1964 and the 2001 Authorization for the Use of Military Force are both broad authorizations for executive military action—war-making—in the absence of specific declarations of war.

In recognition of the failure of Congress to constrain presidents who take military action under such a broad grant of authority (specifically, the Gulf of Tonkin Resolution), Congress passed the War Powers Resolution of 1973. The resolution limited military actions by the president to those exercised under expressed authorization or in defense of an attack on the United States. In addition, the act required the president to report to Congress within 48 hours of the onset of military action. Another provision of the resolution required that after 60 days, the military action must end unless Congress voted to extend it. The difficulty, of course, is that Congress would be hard pressed to not extend a military action once the hostilities had begun. No member of Congress wants to be perceived as unsupportive of American troops in harm's way. In addition, 60 (or often more) days is ample time for a limited, minor action to expand into a larger military engagement from which Congress would likely be reluctant to disengage. Moreover, in practice, presidents have largely not complied with the resolution, either by delaying their initial reporting to Congress or through other means.

As one example, consider President Obama's actions with respect to military involvement in Libya. Even when his own Office of Legal Counsel in the Department of Justice determined that the War Powers Act obligated him to seek approval from Congress for the continuation of hostilities in Libya, he chose to ignore their legal guidance. Instead, the president determined that the United States was only playing a supporting role in a NATO action against Libyan leader Colonel Muammar Qaddafi, and therefore was not engaged in hostilities within the meaning of the War Powers Act. In this sense, the precedent Obama established to circumvent the Department of Justice's guidance would grant future presidents the basis to undermine what had for several decades been a key limit on the exercise of executive power. As one might expect, even when presidents acknowledge the need for congressional authorizations for military action, a president's decision to seek congressional approval is typically made in terms of whether the authorization would be politically expedient rather than legally required. Without congressional reaction to specific episodes of presidential prerogative and war-making, courts have been reluctant to step in to assert authority Congress has not taken for itself. The predictable result is unfettered presidential dominance in war-making.

The consequence of this congressional acquiescence and judicial reluctance was made most clear in the wake of the 2001 al Qaeda attacks on U.S. soil. Within days of the attacks, President George W. Bush declared a "war on terror." By labeling the attacks on New York and the Pentagon as acts of war, rather than criminal acts, President Bush was able to draw upon broad emergency powers in order to defend the country in the "Global War on Terror." The decision to fight terrorism militarily (and for an unlimited amount of time) rather than through the existing criminal codes and civilian courts created a context for an expansive array of presidential powers that remains with us today. Relying on a vast reserve of inherent and emergency powers as commander in chief, Bush was able to centralize and insulate executive authority from congressional review. When Congress did act, such as in the passage of the Authorization for the Use of Military Force or the USA PATRIOT Act, it was in coordination and conjunction with the president (even, as in the case of the AUMF, passing without substantive review legislation drafted entirely by the White House). Subsequent actions taken by the president in this new counterterror context, including the torture or "enhanced interrogation" of detainees and the use of warrantless wiretaps, fit this larger pattern. There were, however, exceptions to the president's claims of unilateral authority. In a 2004 case, *Hamdi v. Rumsfeld*, dealing with the detention and legal status of detainees, the Court declared that the president does not have the authority to hold in indefinite detention a U.S. citizen in violation of the Due Process protections of the Fifth and Fourteenth Amendments. The lone holdout in that case was Justice Thomas, who argued that the president enjoys such broad authority as commander in chief that it proscribes judicial review of executive decision-making during wartime.

It is important to note that the view articulated by Justice Thomas in the *Hamdi* case is consistent with a view of executive power that does not necessarily rely or even build upon on the gradual accumulation over time of presidential war-making authority. Rather, the approach is reflective of an orientation to executive power as the singular, unified, or unitary purview of the executive—free from congressional or even judicial interference. That was the view shared by President Bush and his advisers, and it was given particular emphasis in the context of an ongoing war on terror. The logic of that view, however, needn't be limited to that set of circumstances. It could extend well beyond emergency or wartime authority of the presidency, to the executive power generally, and be wielded in most any context. In reviewing the cases in this chapter, it will be worth reflecting on the gradual accumulation and concentration of executive power during wartime. Justice Jackson's warning that legitimizing such extralegal action would "lay about like a loaded weapon" surely remains prophetic, and historians agree that there has been something of a steady upward trajectory in executive power (with sporadic punctuations) over time. But this most recent shift—toward the unitary executive, insulated from the imposition of congressional or judicial constraints—suggests that a robust unilateralism was there all along; certain presidents simply felt more constrained than others to put the full scope of the powers of their office to use.

President George Washington Issues Neutrality Proclamation in the War between England and France, 1793

The Neutrality Proclamation was authorized by George Washington on April 22, 1793, in response to the heightening war between England and France. Although France had helped the United States win the war for its independence against England, Washington decided that the war in progress was a war with only European interests at stake. This logic would have a lasting effect on U.S. foreign policy moving forward. Neutrality was controversial at the time, and matters were complicated when President George Washington did not seek the council of Congress before the proclamation was made. He instead used his executive power to set the proclamation in motion. This added to the unease of some who believed that the United States should go to war and that the country still had a responsibility to France regardless of what the United States would stand to gain or lose. Nonetheless, the following document was binding and indicated consequences for any American who attempted to take part in the conflict and thus forgo the United States' position.

WHEREAS it appears that a state of war exists between Austria, Prussia, Sardinia, Great-Britain, and the United Netherlands, of the one part, and France on the other, and the duty and interest of the United States require, that they should with sincerity and good faith adopt and pursue a conduct friendly and impartial toward the belligerent powers:

I have therefore thought fit by these presents to declare the disposition of the United States to observe the conduct aforesaid towards those powers respectively; and to exhort and warn the citizens of the United States carefully to avoid all acts and proceedings whatsoever, which may in any manner tend to contravene such disposition.

And I do hereby also make known that whosoever of the citizens of the United States shall render himself liable to punishment or forfeiture under the law of nations, by committing, aiding or abetting hostilities against any of the said powers, or by carrying to any of them those articles, which are deemed contraband by the *modern* usage of nations, will not receive the protection of the United States, against such punishment or forfeiture: and further, that I have given instructions to those officers, to whom it belongs, to cause prosecutions to be instituted against all persons, who shall, within the cognizance of the courts of the United States, violate the Law of Nations, with respect to the powers at war, or any of them.

IN TESTIMONY WHEREOF I have caused the Seal of the United States of America to be affixed to these presents, and signed the same with my hand. Done at the city of Philadelphia, the twenty-second day of April, one thousand seven hundred and ninety-three, and of the Independence of the United States of America the seventeenth.

Source: National Archives, Record Group 46, Third Congress, 1793–1795, Senate Records of Legislative Proceedings, President's Messages.

President John Adams Wrestles over War with France after Passage of Alien and Sedition Acts, 1798

On December 8, 1798, President John Adams gave his Second Annual Address to Congress as the second president of the United States. War had broken out overseas between France and Great Britain, but the United States had adopted a position of neutrality under former president George Washington. In the midst of the war, Washington signed the Jay Treaty with Britain in 1794, which had tied up loose ends between the two countries since the Treaty of Paris in 1783. Yet France saw the move as a betrayal of trust and of the states' promise to be neutral. President Adams took office shortly thereafter, and sent delegates to discuss the United States' stance on the war. The delegates were met with a hefty price to pay before any discussion could begin, including a request for a $10 million loan. This confrontation became known as the XYZ affair. When the delegates refused to pay, and word spread of France's attempted bribe, Americans called for a war with France, abandoning any sentiment to remain neutral. Fear grew within the government that foreigners living in the United States would be sympathetic toward the French cause amid the outrage or that French spies would infiltrate the United States. Congress responded to these fears by passing the Alien and Sedition Acts, a series of acts designed to limit foreign citizenship; give the federal government the ability to arrest and deport any suspicious male, foreign citizens; and even outlaw publications from expressing any dissenting opinion from that of the government or of the government itself. The acts only stirred up stronger opinions, however, and led to President Adams' downfall in the next election. The following excerpt demonstrates how President Adams continued to conform to the United States' policy of neutrality, though he calls to prepare for war.

The course of the transactions in relation to the United States and France which have come to my knowledge during your recess will be made the subject of a future communication. That communication will confirm the ultimate failure of the measures which have been taken by the Government of the United States toward an amicable adjustment of differences with that power. You will at the same time perceive that the French Government appears solicitous to impress the opinion that it is averse to a rupture with this country, and that it has in a qualified manner declared itself willing to receive a minister from the United States for the purpose of restoring a good understanding. It is unfortunate for professions of this kind that they should be expressed in terms which may countenance the inadmissible pretension of a right to prescribe the qualifications which a minister from the United States should possess, and that while France is asserting the existence of a disposition on her part to conciliate with sincerity the differences which have arisen, the sincerity of a like disposition on the part of the United States, of which so many demonstrative proofs have been given, should even be indirectly questioned.

It is also worthy of observation that the decree of the Directory alleged to be intended to restrain the depredations of French cruisers on our commerce has not given, and can not give, any relief. It enjoins them to conform to all the laws of France relative to cruising and prizes, while these laws are themselves the sources of the depredations of which we have so long, so justly, and so fruitlessly complained.

The law of France enacted in January last, which subjects to capture and condemnation neutral vessels and their cargoes if any portion of the latter are of British fabric or produce, although the entire property belong to neutrals, instead of being rescinded has lately received a confirmation by the failure of a proposition for its repeal. While this law, which is an unequivocal act of war on the commerce of the nations it attacks, continues in force those nations can see in the French Government only a power regardless of their essential rights, of their independence and sovereignty; and if they possess the means they can reconcile nothing with their interest and honor but a firm resistance.

Hitherto, therefore, nothing is discoverable in the conduct of France which ought to change or relax our measures of defense. On the contrary, to extend and invigorate them is our true policy. We have no reason to regret that these measures have been thus far adopted and pursued, and in proportion as we enlarge our view of the portentous and incalculable situation of Europe we shall discover new and cogent motives for the full development of our energies and resources.

But in demonstrating by our conduct that we do not fear war in the necessary protection of our rights and honor we shall give no room to infer that we abandon the desire of peace. An efficient preparation for war can alone insure peace. It is peace that we have uniformly and perseveringly cultivated, and harmony between us and France may be restored at her option. But to send another minister without more determinate assurances that he would be received would be an act of humiliation to which the United States ought not to submit. It must therefore be left with France (if she is indeed desirous of accommodation) to take the requisite steps.

The United States will steadily observe the maxims by which they have hitherto been governed. They will respect the sacred rights of embassy; and with a sincere disposition on the part of France to desist from hostility, to make reparation for the injuries heretofore inflicted on our commerce, and to do justice in future, there will be no obstacle to the restoration of a friendly intercourse.

In making to you this declaration I give a pledge to France and the world that the Executive authority of this country still adheres to the humane and pacific policy which has invariably governed its proceedings, in conformity with the wishes of the other branches of the Government and of the people of the United States. But considering the late manifestations of her policy toward foreign nations, I deem it a duty deliberately and solemnly to declare my opinion that whether we negotiate with her or not, vigorous preparations for war will be alike indispensable. These alone will give to us an equal treaty and insure its observance.

Source: Richardson, James D. *A Compilation of the Messages and Papers of the Presidents, 1789–1897.* Volume 1. Washington, D.C.: Government Printing Office, 1896, 271–275.

President Thomas Jefferson Responds to British Provocations during the Napoleonic War, 1807

In Proclamation 14—Requiring Removal of British Armed Vessels from United States Ports and Waters—authorized by President Thomas Jefferson on July 2, 1807, the president chose to impose sanctions against Great Britain in response to transgressions against the United States during the Napoleonic Wars. Both Britain and France were becoming desperate for supplies following the trade restrictions that they had imposed on each other. However, neutral U.S. ships were abundant with resources, and they often crossed paths with the British and French naval forces. One British ship, the HMS Leopard, sought to make an example of the United States' neutral stance. It suspected that a passing U.S. warship, the USS Chesapeake, was harboring British deserters. When the Leopard intercepted the Chesapeake and was denied permission to board, the British ship opened fire, killing and wounding many Americans. President Jefferson ignored the cries for war against Britain after the confrontation and instead imposed the sanctions on the British whose vessels were stationed at U.S. ports. This event emboldened further British provocation toward U.S. ships at port in Britain and led President Jefferson to sign the Embargo Act of 1807 in December of that year. The following proclamation is the first inkling of President Jefferson's strategy to remain neutral while also demonstrating that there would be consequences for nations that did not respect that stance of neutrality.

During the wars which for some time have unhappily prevailed among the powers of Europe the United States of America, firm in their principles of peace, have endeavored, by justice, by a regular discharge of all their national and social duties, and by every friendly office their situation has admitted, to maintain with all the belligerents their accustomed relations of friendship, hospitality, and commercial intercourse. Taking no part in the questions which animate these powers against each other, nor permitting themselves to entertain a wish but for the restoration of general peace, they have observed with good faith the neutrality they assumed, and they believe that no instance of a departure from its duties can be justly imputed to them by any nation. A free use of their harbors and waters, the means of refitting and of refreshment, of succor to their sick and suffering, have at all times and on equal principles been extended to all, and this, too, amidst a constant recurrence of acts of insubordination to the laws, of violence to the persons, and of trespasses on the property of our citizens committed by officers of one of the belligerent parties received among us. In truth, these abuses of the laws of hospitality have, with few exceptions, become habitual to the commanders of the British armed vessels hovering on our coasts and frequenting our harbors. They have been the subject of repeated representations to their Government. Assurances have been given that proper orders should restrain them within the limits of the rights and of the respect due to a friendly nation; but those orders and assurances have been without effect—no instance of punishment for past wrongs has taken place. At length a deed transcending all we have hitherto seen or suffered brings the public sensibility to a serious crisis and our forbearance to a necessary pause. A frigate of the United States, trusting to a state of peace, and leaving her harbor on a distant service, has been surprised and attacked by a British vessel of superior force—one of a squadron then lying in our waters and covering the transaction—and has been disabled from service, with the loss of a number of men killed and wounded. This enormity was not only without provocation or justifiable cause, but was committed with the avowed purpose of taking by force from a ship of war of the United States a part of her crew; and that no circumstance might be wanting to mark its character, it had been previously ascertained that the seamen demanded were native citizens of the United States. Having effected her purpose, she returned to anchor with her squadron within our jurisdiction. Hospitality under such circumstances ceases to be a duty, and a continuance of it with such uncontrolled abuses would tend only, by multiplying injuries and irritations, to bring on a rupture between the two nations. This extreme resort is equally opposed to the interests of both, as it is to assurances of the most friendly dispositions on the part of the British Government, in the midst of which this outrage has been committed. In this light the subject can not but present itself to that Government and strengthen the motives to an honorable reparation of the wrong which has been done, and to that effectual control of its naval commanders which alone can justify the Government of the United States in the exercise of those hospitalities it is now constrained to discontinue.

In consideration of these circumstances and of the right of every nation to regulate its own police, to provide for its peace and for the safety of its citizens, and consequently to refuse the admission of armed vessels into its harbors or waters, either in such numbers or of such descriptions as are inconsistent with these or with the maintenance of the authority of the laws, I have thought proper, in pursuance of the authorities specially given by law, to issue this my proclamation, hereby requiring all armed vessels bearing commissions under the Government of Great Britain now within the harbors or waters of the United States immediately and without any delay to depart from the same, and interdicting the entrance of all the said harbors and waters to the said armed vessels and to all others bearing commissions under the authority Of the British Government.

And if the said vessels, or any of them, shall fall to depart as aforesaid, or if they or any others so interdicted shall hereafter enter the harbors or waters aforesaid, I do in that case forbid all intercourse with them, or any of them, their officers or crews, and do prohibit all supplies and aid from being furnished to them, or any of them.

And I do declare and make known that if any person from or within the jurisdictional limits of the United States shall afford any aid to any such vessel contrary to the prohibition contained in this proclamation, either in repairing any such vessel or in furnishing her, her officers or crew, with supplies of any kind or in any manner whatsoever; or if any pilot shall assist in navigating any of the said armed vessels, unless it be for the purpose of carrying them in the first instance beyond the limits and jurisdiction of the United States, or unless it be in the case of a vessel forced by distress or charged with public dispatches, as hereinafter provided for, such person or persons shall on conviction suffer all the pains and penalties by the laws provided for such offenses.

And I do hereby enjoin and require all persons bearing office, civil or military, within or under the authority of the United States, and all others citizens or inhabitants thereof, or being within the same, with vigilance and promptitude to exert their respective authorities and to be aiding and assisting to the carrying this proclamation and every part thereof into full effect.

Provided, nevertheless, that if any such vessel shall be forced into the harbors or waters of the United States by distress, by the dangers of the sea, or by the pursuit of an enemy, or shall enter them charged with dispatches or business from their Government, or shall be a public packet for the conveyance of letters and dispatches, the commanding officer, immediately reporting his vessel to the collector of the district, stating the object or causes of entering the said harbors or waters, and conforming himself to the regulations in that case prescribed under the authority of the laws, shall be allowed the benefit of such regulations respecting repairs, supplies, stay, intercourse, and departure as shall be permitted under the same authority.

In testimony whereof I have caused the seal of the United States to be affixed to these presents, and signed the same.

Given at the city of Washington, the 2d day of July, A. D. 1807, and of the Sovereignty and Independence of the United States the thirty-first.

Source: Richardson, James D. *A Compilation of the Messages and Papers of the Presidents.* Volume 1, Part 3. New York: Bureau of National Literature, 1897, 410–412.

President James Madison Calls All Citizens to Unite in Defense of the District of Columbia, 1814

The War of 1812 between the United States and Britain and their respective allies lasted for three years, ending only after the Treaty of Ghent was signed in 1815. Even then, however, conflict continued. In what was perhaps the climax of the war between the United States, the United Kingdom, Canada (which was not yet independent from the United Kingdom), and several Native American groups, the British managed to breach various national landmarks, including the Capitol building in Washington, D.C., and set fire to them in August of 1814. Several U.S. militias fought against the scores of British troops that had encroached, but they were eventually overpowered. Critical documents such as the Declaration of Independence were saved from the White House with minutes to spare before the building was seized and burned, and President James Madison and his wife, Dolly, were forced to flee to Maryland. Yet in the following days, a torrential storm overtook the ransacking and not only doused the fires but also forced British troops to retreat. The following document, issued on September 1, 1814, is the first proclamation issued by President James Madison after the British occupation of Washington, D.C.

Whereas the enemy by a sudden incursion have succeeded in invading the capital of the nation, defended at the moment by troops less numerous than their own and almost entirely of the militia, during their possession of which, though for a single day only, they wantonly destroyed the public edifices, having no relation in their structure to operations of war nor used at the time for military annoyance, some of these edifices being also costly monuments of taste and of the arts, and others depositories of the public archives, not only precious to the nation as the memorials of its origin and its early transactions, but interesting to all nations as contributions to the general stock of historical instruction and political science; and

Whereas advantage has been taken of the loss of a fort more immediately guarding the neighboring town of Alexandria to place the town within the range of a naval force too long and too much in the habit of abusing its superiority wherever it can be applied to require as the alternative of a general conflagration an undisturbed plunder of private property, which has been executed in a manner peculiarly distressing to the inhabitants, who had inconsiderately cast themselves upon the justice and generosity of the victor; and

Whereas it now appears by a direct communication from the British commander on the American station to be his avowed purpose to employ the force under his direction "in destroying and laying waste such towns and districts upon the coast as may be found assailable," adding to this declaration the insulting pretext that it is in retaliation for a wanton destruction committed by the army of the United States in Upper Canada, when it is notorious that no destruction has been committed, which, notwithstanding the multiplied outrages previously committed by the enemy was not unauthorized, and promptly shown to be so, and that the United States have been as constant in their endeavors to reclaim the enemy from such outrages by the contrast of their own example as they have been ready to terminate on reasonable conditions the war itself; and

Whereas these proceedings and declared purposes, which exhibit a deliberate disregard of the principles of humanity and the rules of civilized warfare, and which must give to the existing war a character of extended devastation and barbarism at the very moment of negotiations for peace, invited by the enemy himself, leave no prospect of safety to anything within the reach of his predatory and incendiary operations but in manful and universal determination to chastise and expel the invader:

Now, therefore, I, James Madison. President of the United States, do issue this my proclamation, exhorting all the good people thereof to unite their hearts and hands in giving effect to the ample means possessed for that purpose. I enjoin it on all officers, civil and military, to exert themselves in executing the duties with which they are respectively charged; and more especially I require the officers commanding the respective military districts to be vigilant and alert in providing for the defense thereof, for the more effectual accomplishment of which they are authorized to call to the defense of exposed and threatened places portions of the militia most convenient thereto, whether they be or be not parts of the quotas detached for the service of the United States under requisitions of the General Government.

On an occasion which appeals so forcibly to the proud feelings and patriotic devotion of the American people none will forget what they owe to themselves, what they owe to their country and the high destinies which await it, what to the glory acquired by their fathers in establishing the independence which is now to be maintained by their sons with the augmented strength and resources with which time and Heaven had blessed them.

In testimony whereof I have hereunto set my hand and caused the seal of the United States to be affixed to these presents.

Done at the city of Washington, the 1st day of September, A.D. 1814, and of the Independence of the United States the thirty-ninth.

Source: Richardson, James D. *A Compilation of the Messages and Papers of the Presidents.* Volume 2. New York: Bureau of National Literature, 1897, 530–531.

President James Monroe Ratifies Missouri as a Slave State with the Missouri Compromise, 1821

As pioneers continued to settle farther west, and new territories grew in population, Congress needed to decide how to admit states without disrupting the numerical balance of states that would allow slavery and states that would not. When Missouri applied for statehood, there was a bitter debate over whether or not it would adopt slavery. Alabama had been admitted as a slave state in 1819 and had thus equalized the ratio of slave to free staves. Missouri threatened to upend the temporary equilibrium. The bill that would grant Missouri its statehood originally included an amendment that prohibited slavery in the state, and it was indeed passed by the House in 1819, to the outrage of many. Yet, a year later, a bill that granted Maine its statehood was passed by the House despite the inclusion of a provision that prohibited slavery in the territory. Lawmakers saw the dual bills as an opportunity to provide equality between slave and free states yet again. They thus brought them to the Senate as one—but without the amendment that would ratify Missouri as a free state. Instead, the amendment would be replaced with a provision that effectively outlawed slavery in the rest of the territory above the southern border of Missouri, but not in Missouri itself. The bills then passed the Senate as separate entities in 1820, when Maine was admitted, and 1821, when Missouri was admitted. This so-called Missouri Compromise, which was crafted in large part by Senator Henry Clay of Kentucky, was touted by proponents as an example of political fairness and a skillful maneuver to push the United States' final day of reckoning over slavery into the hazy future. The following document is Proclamation 28 in which President James Monroe ratifies Missouri as a state on August 10, 1821.

Whereas the Congress of the United States, by a joint resolution of the 2d day of March last, entitled "Resolution providing for the admission of the State of Missouri into the Union on a certain condition," did determine and declare "that Missouri should be admitted into this Union on an equal footing with the original States in all respects whatever upon the fundamental condition that the fourth clause of the twenty-sixth section of the third article of the constitution submitted on the part of said State to Congress shall never be construed to authorize the passage of any law, and that no law shall be passed in conformity thereto, by which any citizen of either of the States of this Union shall be excluded from the enjoyment of any of the privileges and immunities to which such citizen is entitled under the Constitution of the United States: *Provided*, That the legislature of said State, by a solemn public act, shall declare the assent of the said State to the said fundamental condition, and shall transmit to the President of the United States on or before the first Monday in November next an authentic copy of said act, upon the receipt whereof the President, by proclamation, shall announce the fact, whereupon, and without any further proceeding on the part of Congress, the admission of the said State into this Union shall be considered as complete;" and

Whereas by a solemn public act of the assembly of said State of Missouri, passed on the 26th of June, in the present year, entitled "A solemn public act declaring the assent of this State to the fundamental condition contained in a resolution passed by the Congress of the United States providing for the admission of the State of Missouri into the Union on a certain condition," an authentic copy whereof has been communicated to me, it is solemnly and publicly enacted and declared that that State has assented, and does assent, that the fourth clause of the twenty-sixth section of the third article of the constitution of said State "shall never be construed to authorize the passage of any law, and that no law shall be passed in conformity thereto, by which any citizen of either of the United States shall be excluded from the enjoyment of any of the privileges and immunities to which such citizens are entitled under the Constitution of the United States":

Now, therefore, I, James Monroe, President of the United States, in pursuance of the resolution of Congress aforesaid, have issued this my proclamation, announcing the fact that the said State of Missouri has assented to the fundamental condition required by the resolution of Congress aforesaid, whereupon the admission of the said State of Missouri into this Union is declared to be complete.

In testimony whereof I have caused the seal of the United States of America to be affixed to these presents, and signed the same with my hand.

Done at the city of Washington, the 10th day of August, A.D. 1821, and of the Independence of the said United States of America the forty-sixth.

Source: Richardson, James D. *A Compilation of the Messages and Papers of the Presidents.* Volume 2, Part 1. New York: Bureau of National Literature, 1897, 664–665.

President Andrew Jackson Praises the Indian Removal Act, 1830

This excerpt from President Andrew Jackson's Second Annual Message to Congress, given on December 6, 1830, represents the position taken by the United States government as it prepared to relocate all Native American tribes from their lands in the Southeast to land west of the Mississippi River. The Indian Removal Act, which was passed on May 28, 1830, gave President Jackson the power to use whatever means he deemed fit to negotiate land-ownership treaties with tribes. Though the treaties were meant to be fair, and tribes were meant to volunteer their land, the "exchanges" did not often reflect the law. The language used by President Jackson in this message underscored his belief that Native peoples were uncivilized and suggested that their presence was nothing more than a nuisance to Southern settlers who wanted to use their lands to till crops. In the following decade, tens of thousands of Native peoples were forcibly removed from their lands, and many perished on the arduous westward journey. These forced relocations came to be collectively known as the Trail of Tears, and that time remains one of the darkest chapters in U.S. history. The reality of their experience was a stark contrast to the often cheery tone Jackson presented in the following passage.

It gives me pleasure to announce to Congress that the benevolent policy of the Government, steadily pursued for nearly 30 years, in relation to the removal of the Indians beyond the white settlements is approaching to a happy consummation. Two important tribes have accepted the provision made for their removal at the last session of Congress, and it is believed that their example will induce the remaining tribes also to seek the same obvious advantages.

The consequences of a speedy removal will be important to the United States, to individual States, and to the Indians themselves. The pecuniary advantages which it promises to the Government are the least of its recommendations. It puts an end to all possible danger of collision between the authorities of the General and State Governments on account of the Indians. It will place a dense and civilized population in large tracts of country now occupied by a few savage hunters. By opening the whole territory between Tennessee on the north and Louisiana on the south to the settlement of the whites it will incalculably strengthen the SW frontier and render the adjacent States strong enough to repel future invasions without remote aid. It will relieve the whole State of Mississippi and the western part of Alabama of Indian occupancy, and enable those States to advance rapidly in population, wealth, and power. It will separate the Indians from immediate contact with settlements of whites; free them from the power of the States; enable them to pursue happiness in their own way and under their own rude institutions; will retard the progress of decay, which is lessening their numbers, and perhaps cause them gradually, under the protection of the Government and through the influence of good counsels, to cast off their savage habits and become an interesting, civilized, and Christian community. These consequences, some of them so certain and the rest so probable, make the complete execution of the plan sanctioned by Congress at their last session an object of much solicitude.

Toward the aborigines of the country no one can indulge a more friendly feeling than myself, or would go further in attempting to reclaim them from their wandering habits and make them a happy, prosperous people. I have endeavored to impress upon them my own solemn convictions of the duties and powers of the General Government in relation to the State authorities. For the justice of the laws passed by the States within the scope of their reserved powers they are not responsible to this Government. As individuals we may entertain and express our opinions of their acts, but as a Government we have as little right to control them as we have to prescribe laws for other nations.

With a full understanding of the subject, the Choctaw and the Chickasaw tribes have with great unanimity determined to avail themselves of the liberal offers presented by the act of Congress, and have agreed to remove beyond the Mississippi River. Treaties have been made with them, which in due season will be submitted for consideration. In negotiating these treaties they were made to understand their true condition, and they have preferred maintaining their independence in the Western forests to submitting to the laws of the States in which they now reside. These treaties, being probably the last which will ever be made with them, are characterized by great liberality on the part of the Government. They give the Indians a liberal sum in consideration of their removal, and comfortable subsistence on their arrival at their new homes. If it be their real interest to maintain a separate existence, they will there be at liberty to do so without the inconveniences and vexations to which they would unavoidably have been subject in Alabama and Mississippi.

Humanity has often wept over the fate of the aborigines of this country, and Philanthropy has been long busily employed in devising means to avert it, but its progress has never for a moment been arrested, and one by one have many powerful tribes disappeared from the earth. To follow to the tomb the last of his race and to tread on the graves of extinct nations excite melancholy reflections. But true philanthropy reconciles the mind to these vicissitudes as it does to the extinction of one generation to make room for another. In the monuments and fortifications of an unknown people, spread over the extensive regions of the West, we behold the memorials of a once powerful race, which was exterminated or has disappeared to make room for the existing savage tribes. Nor is there any thing in this which, upon a comprehensive view of the general interests of the human race, is to be regretted. Philanthropy could not wish to see this continent restored to the condition in which it was found by our forefathers. What good man would prefer a country covered with forests and ranged by a few thousand savages to our extensive Republic, studded with cities, towns, and prosperous farms, embellished with all the improvements which art can devise or industry execute, occupied by more than 12,000,000 happy people, and filled with all the blessings of liberty, civilization, and religion?

The present policy of the Government is but a continuation of the same progressive change by a milder process. The tribes which occupied the countries now constituting the Eastern States were annihilated or have melted away to make room for the whites. The waves of population and civilization are rolling to the westward, and we now propose to acquire the countries occupied by the red men of the South and West by a fair exchange, and, at the expense of the United States, to send them to a land where their existence may be prolonged and perhaps made perpetual.

Doubtless it will be painful to leave the graves of their fathers; but what do they more than our ancestors did or than our children are now doing? To better their condition in an unknown land our forefathers left all that was dear in earthly objects. Our children by thousands yearly leave the land of their birth to seek new homes in distant regions. Does Humanity weep at these painful separations from every thing, animate and inanimate, with which the young heart has become entwined? Far from it. It is rather a source of joy that our country affords scope where our young population may range unconstrained in body or in mind, developing the power and faculties of man in their highest perfection.

These remove hundreds and almost thousands of miles at their own expense, purchase the lands they occupy, and support themselves at their new homes from the moment of their arrival. Can it be cruel in this Government when, by events which it can not control, the Indian is made discontented in his ancient home to purchase his lands, to give him a new and extensive territory, to pay the expense of his removal, and support him a year in his new abode? How many thousands of our own people would gladly embrace the opportunity of removing to the West on such conditions! If the offers made to the Indians were extended to them, they would be hailed with gratitude and joy.

And is it supposed that the wandering savage has a stronger attachment to his home than the settled, civilized Christian? Is it more afflicting to him to leave the graves of his fathers than it is to our brothers and children? Rightly considered, the policy of the General Government toward the red man is not only liberal, but generous. He is unwilling to submit to the laws of the States and mingle with their population. To save him from this alternative, or perhaps utter annihilation, the General Government kindly offers him a new home, and proposes to pay the whole expense of his removal and settlement.

In the consummation of a policy originating at an early period, and steadily pursued by every Administration within the present century—so just to the States and so generous to the Indians—the Executive feels it has a right to expect the cooperation of Congress and of all good and disinterested men. The States, moreover, have a right to demand it. It was substantially a part of the compact which made them members of our Confederacy. With Georgia there is an express contract; with the new States an implied one of equal obligation. Why, in authorizing Ohio, Indiana, Illinois, Missouri, Mississippi, and Alabama to form constitutions and become separate States, did Congress include within their limits extensive tracts of Indian lands, and, in some instances, powerful Indian tribes? Was it not understood by both parties that the power of the States was to be coextensive with their limits, and that with all convenient dispatch the General Government should extinguish the Indian title and remove every obstruction to the complete jurisdiction of the State governments over the soil? Probably not one of those States would have accepted a separate existence—certainly it would never have been granted by Congress—had it been understood that they were to be confined for ever to those small portions of their nominal territory the Indian title to which had at the time been extinguished.

It is, therefore, a duty which this Government owes to the new States to extinguish as soon as possible the Indian title to all lands which Congress themselves have included within their limits. When this is done the duties of the General Government in relation to the States and the Indians within their limits are at an end. The Indians may leave the State or not, as they choose. The purchase of their lands does not alter in the least their personal relations with the State government. No act of the General Government has ever been deemed necessary to give the States jurisdiction over the persons of the Indians. That they possess by virtue of their sovereign power within their own limits in as full a manner before as after the purchase of the Indian lands; nor can this Government add to or diminish it.

May we not hope, therefore, that all good citizens, and none more zealously than those who think the Indians oppressed by subjection to the laws of the States, will unite in attempting to open the eyes of those children of the forest to their true condition, and by a speedy removal to relieve them from all the evils, real or imaginary, present or prospective, with which they may be supposed to be threatened.

Source: Richardson, James D. *A Compilation of the Messages and Papers of the Presidents.* Volume 3, Part 1. New York: Bureau of National Literature, 1897, 1063–1092.

President James Polk Prepares for War against Mexico, 1846

President James Polk gave this special message to Congress on May 11, 1846, days before he issued a proclamation of war against Mexico. When the United States annexed the Republic of Texas in 1844, the relationship between Mexico and the United States was compromised. Mexico had vowed it would go to war with the United States if it went through with its plans, but the United States did not heed Mexico's threat and admitted Texas to the Union as a state in 1845. In 1846, President Polk sent delegates to Mexico to settle its claims against the United States and to reopen negotiations for other Mexican-held territories. When Mexico refused to entertain the visit, Polk sent troops to disputed territories between Mexico and the United States. He then set about trying to enlist Congressional support for going to war against Mexico.

The grievous wrongs perpetrated by Mexico upon our citizens throughout a long period of years remain unredressed, and solemn treaties pledging her public faith for this redress have been disregarded. A government either unable or unwilling to enforce the execution of such treaties fails to perform one of its plainest duties.

Our commerce with Mexico has been almost annihilated. It was formerly highly beneficial to both nations, but our merchants have been deterred from prosecuting it by the system of outrage and extortion which the Mexican authorities have pursued against them, whilst their appeals through their own Government for indemnity have been made in vain. Our forbearance has gone to such an extreme as to be mistaken in its character. Had we acted with vigor in repelling the insults and redressing the injuries inflicted by Mexico at the commencement, we should doubtless have escaped all the difficulties in which we are now involved.

Instead of this, however, we have been exerting our best efforts to propitiate her good will. Upon the pretext that Texas, a nation as independent as herself, thought proper to unite its destinies with our own she has affected to believe that we have severed her rightful territory, and in official proclamations and manifestoes has repeatedly threatened to make war upon us for the purpose of reconquering Texas.

In the meantime we have tried every effort at reconciliation. The cup of forbearance had been exhausted even before the recent information from the frontier of the Del Norte. But now, after reiterated menaces, Mexico has passed the boundary of the United States, has invaded our territory and shed American blood upon the American soil. She has proclaimed that hostilities have commenced, and that the two nations are now at war.

As war exists, and, notwithstanding all our efforts to avoid it, exists by the act of Mexico herself, we are called upon by every consideration of duty and patriotism to vindicate with decision the honor, the rights, and the interests of our country.

Anticipating the possibility of a crisis like that which has arrived, instructions were given in August last, "as a precautionary measure" against invasion or threatened invasion, authorizing General Taylor, if the emergency required, to accept volunteers, not from Texas only, but from the States of Louisiana, Alabama, Mississippi, Tennessee, and Kentucky, and corresponding letters were addressed to the respective governors of those States. These instructions were repeated, and in January last, soon after the incorporation of "Texas into our Union of States," General Taylor was further "authorized by the President to make a requisition upon the executive of that State for such of its militia force as may be needed to repel invasion or to secure the country against apprehended invasion." On the 2d day of March he was again reminded, "in the event of the approach of any considerable Mexican force, promptly and efficiently to use the authority with which he was clothed to call to him such auxiliary force as he might need." War actually existing and our territory having been invaded, General Taylor, pursuant to authority vested in him by my direction, has called on the governor of Texas for four regiments of State troops, two to be mounted and two to serve on foot, and on the governor of Louisiana for four regiments of infantry to be sent to him as soon as practicable.

In further vindication of our rights and defense of our territory, I invoke the prompt action of Congress to recognize the existence of the war, and to place at the disposition of the Executive the means of prosecuting the war with vigor, and thus hastening the restoration of peace. To this end I recommend that authority should be given to call into the public service a large body of volunteers to serve for not less than six or twelve months unless sooner discharged. A volunteer force is beyond question more efficient than any other description of citizen soldiers, and it is not to be doubted that a number far beyond that required would readily rush to the field upon the call of their country. I further recommend that a liberal provision be made for sustaining our entire military force and furnishing it with supplies and munitions of war.

The most energetic and prompt measures and the immediate appearance in arms of a large and overpowering force are recommended to Congress as the most certain and efficient means of bringing the existing collision with Mexico to a speedy and successful termination.

In making these recommendations I deem it proper to declare that it is my anxious desire not only to terminate hostilities speedily, but to bring all matters in dispute between this Government and Mexico to an early and amicable adjustment; and in this view I shall be prepared to renew negotiations whenever Mexico shall be ready to receive propositions or to make propositions of her own.

I transmit herewith a copy of the correspondence between our envoy to Mexico and the Mexican minister for foreign affairs, and so much of the correspondence between that envoy and the Secretary of State and between the Secretary of War and the general in command on the Del Norte as is necessary to a full understanding of the subject.

Source: Richardson, James D. *A Compilation of the Messages and Papers of the Presidents 1789–1897.* Volume 5. New York: Bureau of National Literature, 1897, 2287–2293.

President Millard Fillmore Addresses Congress about the Compromise of 1850

Just as the Compromise of 1820 averted a potential imbalance of slave and free states admitted to the Union, so the Compromise of 1850 avoided another such skirmish. In President Millard Fillmore's First Annual Message to the Senate and House of Representatives on December 6, 1850, he discussed how the latter compromise would facilitate the admission of new territories acquired in the Mexican War as slave or free states. Under the 1850 compromise (composed largely by Senator Henry Clay of Kentucky, who also crafted the 1820 compromise), the slave trade was abolished in Washington, D.C. But the legislation also introduced the contested Fugitive Slave Act, in which all freed or runaway slaves were to be captured and returned to their slave owners.

The act, passed at your last session, making certain propositions to Texas for settling the disputed boundary between that State and the Territory of New Mexico was, immediately on its passage, transmitted by express to the governor of Texas, to be laid by him before the general assembly for its agreement thereto. Its receipt was duly acknowledged, but no official information has yet been received of the action of the general assembly thereon. It may, however, be very soon expected, as, by the terms of the propositions submitted they were to have been acted upon on or before the first day of the present month.

It was hardly to have been expected that the series of measures passed at your last session with the view of healing the sectional differences which had sprung from the slavery and territorial questions should at once have realized their beneficent purpose. All mutual concession in the nature of a compromise must necessarily be unwelcome to men of extreme opinions. And though without such concessions our Constitution could not have been formed, and can not be permanently sustained, yet we have seen them made the subject of bitter controversy in both sections of the Republic. It required many months of discussion and deliberation to secure the concurrence of a majority of Congress in their favor. It would be strange if they had been received with immediate approbation by people and States prejudiced and heated by the exciting controversies of their representatives. I believe those measures to have been required by the circumstances and condition of the country. I believe they were necessary to allay asperities and animosities that were rapidly alienating one section of the country from another and destroying those fraternal sentiments which are the strongest supports of the Constitution. They were adopted in the spirit of conciliation and for the purpose of conciliation. I believe that a great majority of our fellow citizens sympathize in that spirit and that purpose, and in the main approve and are prepared in all respects to sustain these enactments. I can not doubt that the American people, bound together by kindred blood and common traditions, still cherish a paramount regard for the Union of their fathers, and that they are ready to rebuke any attempt to violate its integrity, to disturb the compromises on which it is based, or to resist the laws which have been enacted under its authority.

The series of measures to which I have alluded are regarded by me as a settlement in principle and substance—a final settlement of the dangerous and exciting subjects which they embraced. Most of these subjects, indeed, are beyond your reach, as the legislation which disposed of them was in its character final and irrevocable. It may be presumed from the opposition which they all encountered that none of those measures was free from imperfections, but in their mutual dependence and connection they formed a system of compromise the most conciliatory and best for the entire country that could be obtained from conflicting sectional interests and opinions.

For this reason I recommend your adherence to the adjustment established by those measures until time and experience shall demonstrate the necessity of further legislation to guard against evasion or abuse.

By that adjustment we have been rescued from the wide and boundless agitation that surrounded us, and have a firm, distinct, and legal ground to rest upon. And the occasion, I trust, will justify me in exhorting my countrymen to rally upon and maintain that ground as the best, if not the only, means of restoring peace and quiet to the country and maintaining inviolate the integrity of the Union.

Source: Richardson, James D. *A Compilation of the Messages and Papers of the Presidents 1789–1897.* Volume 6. New York: Bureau of National Literature, 1897, 2613–2630.

President Franklin Pierce Intervenes in "Bleeding Kansas," 1856

Proclamation 66—Law and Order in the Territory of Kansas—was issued by President Franklin Pierce in February of 1856 as a warning to those involved in the border conflict wracking that state. Kansas had voted on whether or not it would join the Union as a free or slave state, and while it was expected to join as a free state, the vote was believed to be rigged to support a proslavery position. Separate governing bodies within the state were formed as result. Violence ensued, and the Bleeding Kansas crisis began, foreshadowing the Civil War. Pierce's proclamation, which emphasized that it was the constitutional responsibility of the individual states to account for their own elections, was ineffective in ending the violence in the state. Kansas would attempt to adopt an antislavery constitution in 1859, but its federal ratification was stalled until 1861, when Southern secession had already occurred.

Whereas indications exist that public tranquility and the supremacy of law in the Territory of Kansas are endangered by the reprehensible acts or purposes of persons, both within and without the same, who propose to direct and control its political organization by force. It appearing that combinations have been formed therein to resist the execution of the Territorial laws, and thus in effect subvert by violence all present constitutional and legal authority; it also appearing that persons residing without the Territory, but near its borders, contemplate armed intervention in the affairs thereof; it also appearing that other persons, inhabitants of remote States, are collecting money, engaging men, and providing arms for the same purpose; and it further appearing that combinations within the Territory are endeavoring, by the agency of emissaries and otherwise, to induce individual States of the Union to intervene in the affairs thereof, in violation of the Constitution of the United States; and

Whereas all such plans for the determination of the future institutions of the Territory, if carried into action from within the same, will constitute the fact of insurrection, and if from without that of invasive aggression, and will in either case justify and require the forcible interposition of the whole power of the General Government, as well to maintain the laws of the Territory as those of the Union:

Now, therefore, I, Franklin Pierce, President of the United States, do issue this my proclamation to command all persons engaged in unlawful combinations against the constituted authority of the Territory of Kansas or of the United States to disperse and retire peaceably to their respective abodes, and to warn all such persons that any attempted insurrection in said Territory or aggressive intrusion into the same will be resisted not only by the employment of the local militia, but also by that of any available forces of the United States, to the end of assuring immunity from violence and full protection to the persons, property, and civil rights of all peaceable and law-abiding inhabitants of the Territory.

If, in any part of the Union, the fury of faction or fanaticism, inflamed into disregard of the great principles of popular sovereignty which, under the Constitution, are fundamental in the whole structure of our institutions is to bring on the country the dire calamity of an arbitrament of arms in that Territory, it shall be between lawless violence on the one side and conservative force on the other, wielded by legal authority of the General Government.

I call on the citizens, both of adjoining and of distant States, to abstain from unauthorized intermeddling in the local concerns of the Territory, admonishing them that its organic law is to be executed with impartial justice, that all individual acts of illegal interference will incur condign punishment, and that any endeavor to intervene by organized force will be firmly withstood.

I invoke all good citizens to promote order by rendering obedience to the law, to seek remedy for temporary evils by peaceful means, to discountenance and repulse the counsels and the instigations of agitators and of disorganizers, and to testify their attachment to their country, their pride in its greatness, their appreciation of the blessings they enjoy, and their determination that republican institutions shall not fail in their hands by cooperating to uphold the majesty of the laws and to vindicate the sanctity of the Constitution.

In testimony whereof I have hereunto set my hand and caused the seal of the United States to be affixed to these presents.

Done at the city of Washington, the 11th day of February, A.D. 1856, and of the Independence of the United States the eightieth.

Source: Richardson, James D. *A Compilation of the Messages and Papers of the Presidents.* Volume 7. New York: Bureau of National Literature, 1897, 2923–2924.

President Abraham Lincoln Issues the Emancipation Proclamation, 1863

Proclamation 95—Regarding the Status of Slaves in States Engaged in Rebellion Against the United States—is one of the most important documents in the history of the United States. Also known as the Emancipation Proclamation, this proclamation from President Abraham Lincoln eliminated slavery in all rebel states. The proclamation did not apply to slaveholding states that were not in active rebellion against the Union, however, or to Confederate territories under Northern control. President Abraham Lincoln asserted that the proclamation would go into effect in the midst of the war on January 1, 1863, if rebel states did not lay down arms before then. The Confederacy remained defiant, and millions of slaves were freed in the South as a result.

With the Emancipation Proclamation, the issue of slavery became even more central to the Civil War. President Lincoln understood that if strategizing was essential to the Union's victory, then the emancipation of slaves would be the vehicle through which it would occur. As the National Archives and Records Administration (NARA) noted, "although the Emancipation Proclamation did not end slavery in the nation, it captured the hearts and imagination of millions of Americans and fundamentally transformed the character of the war. After January 1, 1863, every advance of federal troops expanded the domain of freedom. Moreover, the Proclamation announced the acceptance of black men into the Union Army and Navy, enabling the liberated to become liberators." The following is a full transcript of Lincoln's Emancipation Proclamation.

Whereas on the 22d day of September, A.D. 1862, a proclamation was issued by the President of the United States. containing, among other things, the following, to wit:

That on the 1st day of January, A.D. 1863, all persons held as slaves within any State or designated part of a State the people whereof shall then be in rebellion against the United States shall be then, thenceforward, and forever free; and the executive government of the United States, including the military and naval authority thereof, will recognize and maintain the freedom of such persons and will do no act or acts to repress such persons, or any of them, in any efforts they may make for their actual freedom.

That the Executive will on the 1st day of January aforesaid, by proclamation, designate the States and parts of States, if any, in which the people thereof, respectively, shall then be in rebellion against the United States; and the fact that any State or the people thereof shall on that day be in good faith represented in the Congress of the United States by members chosen thereto at elections wherein a majority of the qualified voters of such States shall have participated shall, in the absence of strong countervailing testimony, be deemed conclusive evidence that such State and the people thereof are not then in rebellion against the United States.

Now, therefore, I, Abraham Lincoln, President of the United States, by virtue of the power in me vested as Commander in Chief of the Army and Navy of the United States in time of actual armed rebellion against the authority and Government of the United States, and as a fit and necessary war measure for suppressing said rebellion, do, on this 1st day of January, A.D. 1863, and in accordance with my purpose so to do, publicly proclaimed for the full period of one hundred days from the day first above mentioned, order and designate as the States and parts of States wherein the people thereof, respectively, are this day in rebellion against the United States the following, to wit:

Arkansas, Texas, Louisiana (except the parishes of St. Bernard, Plaquemines, Jefferson, St. John, St. Charles, St. James, Ascension, Assumption, Terrebonne, Lafourche, St. Mary, St. Martin, and Orleans, including the city of New Orleans), Mississippi, Alabama, Florida, Georgia, South Carolina, North Carolina, and Virginia (except the forty-eight counties designated as West Virginia, and also the counties of Berkeley, Accomac, Northampton, Elizabeth City, York, Princess Anne, and Norfolk, including the cities of Norfolk and Portsmouth), and which excepted parts are for the present left precisely as if this proclamation were not issued.

And by virtue of the power and for the purpose aforesaid, I do order and declare that all persons held as slaves within said designated States and parts of States are and henceforward shall be free, and that the executive government of the United States, including the military and naval authorities thereof, will recognize and maintain the freedom of said persons.

And I hereby enjoin upon the people so declared to be free to abstain from all violence, unless in necessary self-defense; and I recommend to them that in all cases when allowed they labor faithfully for reasonable wages.

And I further declare and make known that such persons of suitable condition will be received into the armed service of the United States to garrison forts, positions, stations, and other places and to man vessels of all sorts in said service.

And upon this act, sincerely believed to be an act of justice, warranted by the Constitution upon military necessity, I invoke the considerate judgment of mankind and the gracious favor of Almighty God.

In witness whereof I have hereunto set my hand and caused the seal of the United States to be affixed.

Done at the city of Washington, this 1st day of January, A.D. 1863, and of the Independence of the United States of America the eighty-seventh.

Source: Abraham Lincoln, Emancipation Proclamation, January 1, 1863, Presidential Proclamations, 1791–1991, Record Group 11, General Records of the United States Government, National Archives.

President Abraham Lincoln Delivers the Gettysburg Address, 1863

The Battle of Gettysburg in Pennsylvania was a success for the Union, but it also marked the most violent engagement of the American Civil War. Confederate General Robert E. Lee was optimistic as he directed his troops north into Pennsylvania following a substantial victory in Virginia. He hoped that in addition to gaining important strategic ground, another military success on Northern soil would have tremendous symbolic value and perhaps even convince the North to let the Confederate states secede in peace. Union General George G. Meade had other plans, however, and he maneuvered Union forces to meet Lee. The battle was joined on July 1, 1863, and it continued for three days. The Confederate troops were forced to retreat after being hit with a barrage of attacks, and Lee's defeat at Gettysburg is regarded by military historians as one of the decisive turning points of the war.

On November 19, 1863, a few months after the battle had taken place, President Abraham Lincoln traveled to Gettysburg to dedicate a National Cemetery to the fallen soldiers at the battlefield. Though the speech contained fewer than three hundred words, it spoke volumes to the sacrifices that a country or people make for freedom. The following document is one of the most famous speeches in U.S. history.

Four score and seven years ago our fathers brought forth on this continent, a new nation, conceived in Liberty, and dedicated to the proposition that all men are created equal.

Now we are engaged in a great civil war, testing whether that nation, or any nation so conceived and so dedicated, can long endure. We are met on a great battle-field of that war. We have come to dedicate a portion of that field, as a final resting place for those who here gave their lives that that nation might live. It is altogether fitting and proper that we should do this.

But, in a larger sense, we can not dedicate—we can not consecrate—we can not hallow—this ground. The brave men, living and dead, who struggled here, have consecrated it, far above our poor power to add or detract. The world will little note, nor long remember what we say here, but it can never forget what they did here. It is for us the living, rather, to be dedicated here to the unfinished work which they who fought here have thus far so nobly advanced. It is rather for us to be here dedicated to the great task remaining before us—that from these honored dead we take increased devotion to that cause for which they gave the last full measure of devotion—that we here highly resolve that these dead shall not have died in vain—that this nation, under God, shall have a new birth of freedom—and that government of the people, by the people, for the people, shall not perish from the earth.

> **Source:** Abraham Lincoln. Transcript of the "Nicolay Copy" of the Gettysburg Address, 1863. Library of Congress.

President Abraham Lincoln Ponders the Future of Slavery and Citizenship in America, 1863

As President Abraham Lincoln gave his Third Annual Message to Congress on December 8 of 1863, the country was gearing up for another year of war. Both the public and government officials were concerned about the fast pace at which slavery seemed to be dismantling, and many expressed anxiety about the possible consequences of complete emancipation—a possibility set in motion by Lincoln's earlier Emancipation Proclamation. In his message, Lincoln continued to align himself with the Union cause and offered a positive assessment of the war's progress. But he also addressed looming questions that were on the minds of his audience. Hundreds of thousands of freed slaves had become soldiers for his armies; would they become citizens? How should the executive branch interpret the Constitution, given the shifting legal terrain concerning slavery? The following document foreshadows the ideas that President Lincoln would continue to wrestle with until his assassination in 1865, mere days after the war had ended with a Union victory.

Of those who were slaves at the beginning of the rebellion full 100,000 are now in the United States military service, about one-half of which number actually bear arms in the ranks, thus giving the double advantage of taking so much labor from the insurgent cause and supplying the places which otherwise must be filled with so many white men. So far as tested, it is difficult to say they are not as good soldiers as any. No servile insurrection or tendency to violence or cruelty has marked the measures of emancipation and arming the blacks. These measures have been much discussed in foreign countries, and, contemporary with such discussion, the tone of public sentiment there is much improved. At home the same measures have been fully discussed, supported, criticised, and denounced, and the annual elections following are highly encouraging to those whose official duty it is to bear the country through this great trial. Thus we have the new reckoning. The crisis which threatened to divide the friends of the Union is past.

Looking now to the present and future, and with reference to a resumption of the national authority within the States wherein that authority has been suspended, I have thought fit to issue a proclamation, a copy of which is herewith transmitted. On examination of this proclamation it will appear, as is believed, that nothing will be attempted beyond what is amply justified by the Constitution. True, the form of an oath is given, but no man is coerced to take it. The man is only promised a pardon in case he voluntarily takes the oath. The Constitution authorizes the Executive to grant or withhold the pardon at his own absolute discretion, and this includes the power to grant on terms, as is fully established by judicial and other authorities.

It is also proffered that if in any of the States named a State government shall be in the mode prescribed set up, such government shall be recognized and guaranteed by the United States, and that under it the State shall, on the constitutional conditions, be protected against invasion and domestic violence. The constitutional obligation of the United States to guarantee to every State in the Union a republican form of government and to protect the State in the cases stated is explicit and full. But why tender the benefits of this provision only to a State government set up in this particular way? This section of the Constitution contemplates a case wherein the element within a State favorable to republican government in the Union may be too feeble for an opposite and hostile element external to or even within the State, and such are precisely the cases with which we are now dealing.

An attempt to guarantee and protect a revived State government, constructed in whole or in preponderating part from the very element against whose hostility and violence it is to be protected, is simply absurd. There must be a test by which to separate the opposing elements, so as to build only from the sound; and that test is a sufficiently liberal one which accepts as sound whoever will make a sworn recantation of his former unsoundness.

But if it be proper to require as a test of admission to the political body an oath of allegiance to the Constitution of the United States and to the Union under it, why also to the laws and proclamations in regard to slavery? Those laws and proclamations were enacted and put forth for the purpose of aiding in the suppression of the rebellion. To give them their fullest effect there had to be a pledge for their maintenance. In my judgment, they have aided and will further aid the cause for which they were intended. To now abandon them would be not only to relinquish a lever of power, but would also be a cruel and an astounding breach of faith. I may add at this point that while I remain in my present position I shall not attempt to retract or modify the emancipation proclamation, nor shall I return to slavery any person who is free by the terms of that proclamation or by any of the acts of Congress. For these and other reasons it is thought best that support of these measures shall be included in the oath, and it is believed the Executive may lawfully claim it in return for pardon and restoration of forfeited rights, which he has clear constitutional power to withhold altogether or grant upon the terms which he shall deem wisest for the public interest. It should be observed also that this part of the oath is subject to the modifying and abrogating power of legislation and supreme judicial decision.

The proposed acquiescence of the National Executive in any reasonable temporary State arrangement for the freed people is made with the view of possibly modifying the confusion and destitution which must at best attend all classes by a total revolution of labor throughout whole States. It is hoped that the already deeply afflicted people in those States may be somewhat more ready to give up the cause of their affliction if to this extent this vital matter be left to themselves, while no power of the National Executive to prevent an abuse is abridged by the proposition.

The suggestion in the proclamation as to maintaining the political framework of the States on what is called reconstruction is made in the hope that it may do good without danger of harm. It will save labor and avoid great confusion.

But why any proclamation now upon this subject? This question is beset with the conflicting views that the step might be delayed too long or be taken too soon. In some States the elements for resumption seem ready for action. but remain inactive apparently for want of a rallying point—a plan of action, Why shall A adopt the plan of B rather than B that of A? And if A and B should agree, how can they know but that the General Government here will reject their plan? By the proclamation a plan is presented which may be accepted by them as a rallying point, and which they are assured in advance will not be rejected here. This may bring them to act sooner than they otherwise would. The objections to a premature presentation of a plan by the National Executive consist in the danger of committals on points which could be more safely left to further developments. Care has been taken to so shape the document as to avoid embarrassments from this source. Saying that on certain terms certain classes will be pardoned with rights restored, it is not said that other classes or other terms will never be in included. Saying that reconstruction will be accepted if presented in a specified way, it is not said it will never be accepted in any other way.

The movements by State action for emancipation in several of the States not included in the emancipation proclamation are matters of profound gratulation. And while I do not repeat in detail what I have heretofore so earnestly urged upon this subject, my general views and feelings remain unchanged; and I trust that Congress will omit no fair opportunity of aiding these important steps to a great consummation. In the midst of other cares, however important, we must not lose sight of the fact that the war power is still our main reliance. To that power alone can we look yet for a time to give confidence to the people in the contested regions that the insurgent power will not again overrun them. Until that confidence shall be established little can be done anywhere for what is called reconstruction. Hence our chiefest care must still be directed to the Army and Navy, who have thus far borne their harder part so nobly and well; and it may be esteemed fortunate that in giving the greatest efficiency to these indispensable arms we do also honorably recognize the gallant men, from commander to sentinel, who compose them, and to whom more than to others the world must stand indebted for the home of freedom disenthralled, regenerated, enlarged, and perpetuated.

Source: Richardson, James D. *A Compilation of the Messages and Papers of the Presidents 1789–1897.* Volume 8. New York: Bureau of National Literature, 1897, 3380–3392.

President William McKinley Facilitates Occupation of the Philippines, 1898

The brief but bloody Spanish-American War of 1898 formally ended with the signing of a peace treaty in Paris in December of 1898. According to the terms of the treaty, the United States acquired the territories of Cuba, Puerto Rico, and the

Philippines, which were previously under Spanish control. President William McKinley decided that these territories were not bound to the United States Constitution in the same way that the states were, but he did find that additional support was necessary as the territories transitioned leadership. In this executive order, the president acknowledges the destruction of Manila by American forces, acknowledges the "absolute and supreme" power of the states' military occupation, acknowledges that he will seize all monies belonging to the Philippines' government and tax the people, and yet promises that as long as the people cooperate, they will be rewarded with freedom. The actions outlined here provide insight as to how the acquisition of territories was handled under President McKinley's direction.

SIR: The destruction of the Spanish fleet at Manila, followed by the taking of the naval station at Cavite, the paroling of the garrisons, and the acquisition of the control of the bay, has rendered it necessary, in the further prosecution of the measures adopted by this Government for the purpose of bringing about an honorable and durable peace with Spain, to send an army of occupation to the Philippines for the twofold purpose of completing the reduction of the Spanish power in that quarter and of giving order and security to the islands while in the possession of the United States. For the command of this expedition I have designated Major-General Wesley Merritt, and it now becomes my duty to give instructions as to the manner in which the movement shall be conducted.

The first effect of the military occupation of the enemy's territory is the severance of the former political relations of the inhabitants and the establishment of a new political power. Under this changed condition of things the inhabitants, so long as they perform their duties, are entitled to security in their persons and property and in all their private rights and relations. It is my desire that the people of the Philippines should be acquainted with the purpose of the United States to discharge to the fullest extent its obligations in this regard. It will therefore be the duty of the commander of the expedition, immediately upon his arrival in the islands, to publish a proclamation declaring that we come not to make war upon the people of the Philippines, nor upon any party or faction among them, but to protect them in their homes, in their employments, and in their personal and religious rights. All persons who, either by active aid or by honest submission, co-operate with the United States in its efforts to give effect to this beneficent purpose will receive the reward of its support and protection. Our occupation should be as free from severity as possible.

Though the powers of the military occupant are absolute and supreme and immediately operate upon the political condition of the inhabitants, the municipal laws of the conquered territory, such as affect private rights of person and property and provide for the punishment of crime, are considered as continuing in force, so far as they are compatible with the new order of things, until they are suspended or superseded by the occupying belligerent; and in practice they are not usually abrogated, but are allowed to remain in force and to be administered by the ordinary tribunals substantially as they were before the occupation.

This enlightened practice is, so far as possible, to be adhered to on the present occasion. The judges and the other officials connected with the administration of justice may, if they accept the authority of the United States, continue to administer the ordinary law of the land as between man and man under the supervision of the American commander-in-chief. The native constabulary will, so far as may be practicable, be preserved. The freedom of the people to pursue their accustomed occupations will he abridged only when it may be necessary to do so.

While the rule of conduct of the American commander-in-chief will be such as has just been defined, it will be his duty to adopt measures of a different kind if, unfortunately, the course of the people should render such measures indispensable to the maintenance of law and order. He will then possess the power to replace or expel the native officials in part or altogether, to substitute new courts of his own constitution for those that now exist, or to create such new or supplementary tribunals as may be necessary. In the exercise of these high powers the commander must be guided by his judgment and his experience and a high sense of justice.

One of the most important and most practical problems with which the commander of the expedition will have to deal is that of the treatment of property and the collection and administration of the revenues. It is conceded that all public funds and securities belonging to the government of the country in its own right and all arms and supplies and other movable property of such government may be seized by the military occupant and converted to the use of this Government. The real property of the state he may hold and administer, at the same time enjoying the revenues thereof; but he is not to destroy it save in the case of military necessity. All public means of transportation, such as telegraph lines, cables, railways, and boats belonging to the state may be appropriated to his use, but unless in case of military necessity they are not to be destroyed. All churches and buildings devoted to religious worship and to the arts and sciences, all schoolhouses, are, so far as possible, to be protected, and all destruction or intentional defacement of such places, of historical monuments or archives, or of works of science or art is prohibited save when required by urgent military necessity.

Private property, whether belonging to individuals or corporations, is to be respected, and can be confiscated only as hereafter indicated. Means of transportation, such as telegraph lines and cables, railways, and boats, may, although they belong to private individuals or corporations, be seized by the military occupant, but unless destroyed under military necessity, are not to be retained.

While it is held to be the right of a conqueror to levy contributions upon the enemy in their seaports, towns, or provinces which may be in his military possession by conquest, and to apply the proceeds to defray the expenses of the war, this right is to be exercised within such limitations that it may not savor of confiscation. As the result of military occupation the taxes and duties payable by the inhabitants to the former government become payable to the military occupant, unless he sees fit to substitute for them other rates or modes of contribution to the expenses of the government. The moneys so collected are to be used for the purpose of paying expenses of government under the military occupation, such as the salaries of the judges and the police, and for the payment of the expenses of the army.

Private property taken for the use of the army is to be paid for when possible in cash at a fair valuation, and when payment in cash is not possible receipts are to be given.

In order that there may be no conflict of authority between the army and the navy in the administration of affairs in the Philippines you are instructed to confer with the Secretary of the Navy so far as necessary for the purpose of devising measures to secure the harmonious action of those two branches of the public service.

I will give instructions to the Secretary of the Treasury to make a report to me upon the subject of the revenues of the Philippines, with a view to the formulation of such revenue measures as may seem expedient. All ports and places in the Philippines which may be in the actual possession of our land and naval forces will be opened, while our military occupation may continue, to the commerce of all neutral nations, as well as our own, in articles not contraband of war, and upon payment of the prescribed rates of duty which may be in force at the time of the importation.

> **Source:** Richardson, James D. *A Compilation of the Messages and Papers of the Presidents 1789–1897.* Volume 13. New York: Bureau of National Literature, 1897, 6571–6572.

President Woodrow Wilson Seeks Peace during World War I, 1918

The following document is Woodrow Wilson's Address to a Joint Session of Congress on the Conditions of Peace, also known as the Fourteen Points speech, given on January 8, 1918. This speech outlines the foundations of what would become the Treaty of Versailles, the peace agreement that would end World War I almost a year later. The United States had positioned itself on the fringe of the war when it had first broken out across Europe in 1914, and President Wilson was in favor of remaining neutral. The public was also reluctant to interfere. Yet Germany's aggression toward the United States became progressively more violent and daring. President Wilson finally requested a proclamation of war against Germany and the action went into effect on April 6, 1917. It took just about seven months for the United States' debut in the war to end it. The country's large, drafted military presence and heavy armament in Europe halted the advancement of Germany and the other Central Powers with which it was allied, and it ultimately proved pivotal in defeating Germany.

President Wilson explained to Congress his hopes and fears the future of the United States' relationship with the Central Powers, and those of the United States' allies. He recognized that a new world order was imminent, and he was determined to maintain the United States' high status within it. He also knew that the security of the United States had become more intermingled with the security of the world than ever before, and so he proposed the League of Nations to maintain balance between powers. This league would later become the United Nations.

Gentlemen of the Congress:

Once more, as repeatedly before, the spokesmen of the Central Empires have indicated their desire to discuss the objects of the war and the possible bases of a general peace. Parleys have been in progress at Brest-Litovsk between Russian representatives and representatives of the Central Powers to which the attention of all the belligerents has been invited for the purpose of ascertaining whether it may be possible to extend these parleys into a general conference with regard to terms of peace and settlement. The Russian representatives presented not only a perfectly definite statement of the principles upon which they would be willing to conclude peace but also an equally definite program of the concrete application of those principles. The representatives of the Central Powers, on their part, presented an outline of settlement which, if much less definite, seemed susceptible of liberal interpretation until their specific program of practical terms was added. That program proposed no concessions at all either to the sovereignty of Russia or to the preferences of the populations with whose fortunes it dealt, but meant, in a word, that the Central Empires were to keep every foot of territory their armed forces had occupied,—every province, every city, every point of vantage,—as a permanent addition to their territories and their power. It is a reasonable conjecture that the general principles of settlement which they at first suggested originated with the more liberal statesmen of Germany and Austria, the men who have begun to feel the force of their own peoples' thought and purpose, while the concrete terms of actual settlement came from the military leaders who have no thought but to keep what they have got. The negotiations have been broken off. The Russian representatives were sincere and in earnest. They cannot entertain such proposals of conquest and domination.

The whole incident is full of significance. It is also full of perplexity. With whom are the Russian representatives dealing? For whom are the representatives of the Central Empires speaking? Are they speaking for the majorities of their respective parliaments or for the minority parties, that military and imperialistic minority which has so far dominated their whole policy and controlled the affairs of Turkey and of the Balkan states which have felt obliged to become their associates in this war? The Russian representatives have insisted, very justly, very wisely, and in the true spirit of modern democracy, that the conferences they have been holding with the Teutonic and Turkish statesmen should be held within open, not closed, doors, and all the world has been audience, as was desired. To whom have we been listening, then? To those who speak the spirit and intention of the Resolutions of the German Reichstag of the ninth of July last, the spirit and intention of the liberal leaders and parties of Germany, or to those who resist and defy that spirit and intention and insist upon conquest and subjugation? Or are we listening, in fact, to both, unreconciled and in open and hopeless contradiction? These are very serious and pregnant questions. Upon the answer to them depends the peace of the world.

But, whatever the results of the parleys at Brest-Litovsk, whatever the confusions of counsel and of purpose in the utterances of the spokesmen of the Central Empires, they have again attempted to acquaint the world with their objects in the war and have again challenged their adversaries to say what their objects are and what sort of settlement they would deem just and satisfactory. There is no good reason why that challenge should not be responded to, and responded to with the utmost candor. We did not wait for it. Not once, but again and again, we have laid our whole thought and purpose before the world, not in general terms only, but each time with sufficient definition to make it clear what sort of definitive terms of settlement must necessarily spring out of them. Within the last week Mr. Lloyd George has spoken with admirable candor and in admirable spirit for the people and Government of Great Britain. There is no confusion of counsel among the adversaries of the Central Powers, no uncertainty of principle, no vagueness of detail. The only secrecy of counsel, the only lack of fearless frankness, the only failure to make definite statement of the objects of the war, lies with Germany and her Allies. The issues of life and death hang upon these definitions. No statesman who has the least conception of his responsibility ought for a moment to permit himself to continue this tragical and appalling outpouring of blood and treasure unless he is sure beyond a peradventure that the objects of the vital sacrifice are part and parcel of the very life of society and that the people for whom he speaks think them right and imperative as he does.

There is, moreover, a voice calling for these definitions of principle and of purpose which is, it seems to me, more thrilling and more compelling than any of the many moving voices with which the troubled air of the world is filled. It is the voice of the Russian people. They are prostrate and all but helpless, it would seem, before the grim power of Germany, which has hitherto known no relenting and no pity. Their power, apparently, is shattered. And yet their soul is not subservient. They will not yield either in principle or in action. Their conception of what is right, of what it is humane and honorable for them to accept, has been stated with a frankness, a largeness of view, a generosity of spirit, and a universal human sympathy which must challenge the admiration of every friend of mankind; and they have refused to compound their ideals or desert others that they themselves may be safe. They call to us to say what it is that we desire, in what, if in anything, our purpose and our spirit differ from theirs; and I believe that the people of the United States would wish me to respond, with utter simplicity and frankness. Whether their present leaders believe it or not, it is our heartfelt desire and hope that some way may be opened whereby we may be privileged to assist the people of Russia to attain their utmost hope of liberty and ordered peace.

It will be our wish and purpose that the processes of peace, when they are begun, shall be absolutely open and that they shall involve and permit henceforth no secret understandings of any kind. The day of conquest and aggrandizement is gone by; so is also the day of secret covenants entered into in the interest of particular governments and likely at some unlooked-for moment to upset the peace of the world. It is this happy fact, now clear to the view of every public man whose thoughts do not still linger in an age that is dead and gone, which makes it possible for every nation whose purposes are consistent with justice and the peace of the world to avow now or at any other time the objects it has in view.

We entered this war because violations of right had occurred which touched us to the quick and made the life of our own people impossible unless they were corrected and the world secured once for all against their recurrence. What we demand in this war, therefore, is nothing peculiar to ourselves. It is that the world be made fit and safe to live in; and particularly that it be made safe for every peace-loving nation which, like our own, wishes to live its own life, determine its own institutions, be assured of justice and fair dealing by the other peoples of the world as against force and selfish aggression. All the peoples of the world are in effect partners in this interest, and for our own part we see very clearly that unless justice be done to others it will not be done to us. The program of the world's peace, therefore, is our program; and that program, the only possible program, as we see it, is this:

I. Open covenants of peace, openly arrived at, after which there shall be no private international understandings of any kind, but diplomacy shall proceed always frankly and in the public view.

II. Absolute freedom of navigation upon the seas, outside territorial waters, alike in peace and in war, except as the seas may be closed in whole or in part by international action for the enforcement of international covenants.

III. The removal, so far as possible, of all economic barriers and the establishment of an equality of trade conditions among all the nations consenting to the peace and associating themselves for its maintenance.

IV. Adequate guarantees given and taken that national armaments will be reduced to the lowest point consistent with domestic safety.

V. A free, open-minded, and absolutely impartial adjustment of all colonial claims, based upon a strict observance of the principle that in determining all such questions of sovereignty the interests of the populations concerned must have equal weight with the equitable claims of the government whose title is to be determined.

VI. The evacuation of all Russian territory and such a settlement of all questions affecting Russia as will secure the best and freest cooperation of the other nations of the world in obtaining for her an unhampered and unembarrassed opportunity for the independent determination of her own political development and national policy and assure her of a sincere welcome into the society of free nations under institutions of her own choosing; and, more than a welcome, assistance also of every kind that she may need and may herself desire. The treatment accorded Russia by her sister nations in the months to come will be the acid test of their good will, of their comprehension of her needs as distinguished from their own interests, and of their intelligent and unselfish sympathy.

VII. Belgium, the whole world will agree, must be evacuated and restored, without any attempt to limit the sovereignty which she enjoys in common with all other free nations. No other single act will serve as this will serve to restore confidence among the nations in the laws which they have themselves set and determined for the government of their relations with one another. Without this healing act the whole structure and validity of international law is forever impaired.

VIII. All French territory should be freed and the invaded portions restored, and the wrong done to France by Prussia in 1871 in the matter of Alsace-Lorraine, which has unsettled the peace of the world for nearly fifty years, should be righted, in order that peace may once more be made secure in the interest of all.

IX. A readjustment of the frontiers of Italy should be effected along clearly recognizable lines of nationality.

X. The peoples of Austria-Hungary, whose place among the nations we wish to see safeguarded and assured, should be accorded the freest opportunity of autonomous development.

XI. Rumania, Serbia, and Montenegro should be evacuated; occupied territories restored; Serbia accorded free and secure access to the sea; and the relations of the several Balkan states to one another determined by friendly counsel along historically established lines of allegiance and nationality; and international guarantees of the political and economic independence and territorial integrity of the several Balkan states should be entered into.

XII. The Turkish portions of the present Ottoman Empire should be assured a secure sovereignty, but the other nationalities which are now under Turkish rule should be assured an undoubted security of life and an absolutely unmolested opportunity of autonomous development and the Dardanelles should be permanently opened as a free passage to the ships and commerce of all nations under international guarantees.

XIII. An independent Polish state should be erected which should include the territories inhabited by indisputably Polish populations, which should be assured a free and secure access to the sea, and whose political and economic independence and territorial integrity should be guaranteed by international covenant.

XIV. A general association of nations must be formed under specific covenants for the purpose of affording mutual guarantees of political independence and territorial integrity to great and small states alike.

In regard to these essential rectifications of wrong and assertions of right we feel ourselves to be intimate partners of all the governments and peoples associated together against the Imperialists. We cannot be separated in interest or divided in purpose. We stand together until the end.

For such arrangements and covenants we are willing to fight and to continue to fight until they are achieved; but only because we wish the right to prevail and desire a just and stable peace such as can be secured only by removing the chief provocations to war, which this program does remove. We have no jealousy of German greatness, and there is nothing in this program that impairs it. We grudge her no achievement or distinction of learning or of pacific enterprise such as have made her record very bright and very enviable. We do not wish to injure her or to block in any way her legitimate influence or power. We do not wish to fight her either with arms or with hostile arrangements of trade if she is willing to associate herself with us and the other peace-loving nations of the world in covenants of justice and law and fair dealing. We wish her only to accept a place of equality among the peoples of the world,—the new world in which we now live,—instead of a place of mastery.

Neither do we presume to suggest to her any alteration or modification of her institutions. But it is necessary, we must frankly say, and necessary as a preliminary to any intelligent dealings with her on our part, that we should know whom her spokesmen speak for when they speak to us, whether for the Reichstag majority or for the military party and the men whose creed is imperial domination.

We have spoken now, surely, in terms too concrete to admit of any further doubt or question. An evident principle runs through the whole program I have outlined. It is the principle of justice to all peoples and nationalities, and their right to live on equal terms of liberty and safety with one another, whether they be strong or weak. Unless this principle be made its foundation no part of the structure of international justice can stand. The people of the United States could act upon no other principle; and to the vindication of this principle they are ready to devote their lives, their honor, and everything that they possess. The moral climax of this the culminating and final war for human liberty has come, and they are ready to put their own strength, their own highest purpose, their own integrity and devotion to the test.

Source: President Wilson's Message to Congress, January 8, 1918; Records of the United States Senate: Record Group 4; Records of the United States Senate; National Archives.

President Franklin D. Roosevelt Declares War against Japan, 1941

The United States had struggled to remain exempt from World War II since its commencement in 1939, but on December 7, 1941, the United States shifted its position when Japan bombed a naval base in Pearl Harbor, Hawaii. Thousands of U.S. soldiers and civilians perished as a result of the surprise attack, and President Franklin D. Roosevelt requested that Congress declare war against Japan the next day. In the week that followed, the United States also declared war with Germany and Italy, Japan's allies in World War II. The following Address to Congress Requesting a Declaration of War with Japan is often called the "Infamy Speech," due to the president's use of the word and the harrowing nature of his tone.

Mr. Vice President, and Mr. Speaker, and Members of the Senate and House of Representatives:

Yesterday, December 7, 1941—a date which will live in infamy—the United States of America was suddenly and deliberately attacked by naval and air forces of the Empire of Japan.

The United States was at peace with that Nation and, at the solicitation of Japan, was still in conversation with its Government and its Emperor looking toward the maintenance of peace in the Pacific. Indeed, one hour after Japanese air squadrons had commenced bombing in the American Island of Oahu, the Japanese

Ambassador to the United States and his colleague delivered to our Secretary of State a formal reply to a recent American message. And while this reply stated that it seemed useless to continue the existing diplomatic negotiations, it contained no threat or hint of war or of armed attack.

It will be recorded that the distance of Hawaii from Japan makes it obvious that the attack was deliberately planned many days or even weeks ago. During the intervening time the Japanese Government has deliberately sought to deceive the United States by false statements and expressions of hope for continued peace.

The attack yesterday on the Hawaiian Islands has caused severe damage to American naval and military forces. I regret to tell you that very many American lives have been lost. In addition American ships have been reported torpedoed on the high seas between San Francisco and Honolulu.

Yesterday the Japanese Government also launched an attack against Malaya.

Last night Japanese forces attacked Hong Kong.

Last night Japanese forces attacked Guam.

Last night Japanese forces attacked the Philippine Islands.

Last night the Japanese attacked Wake Island. And this morning the Japanese attacked Midway Island.

Japan has, therefore, undertaken a surprise offensive extending throughout the Pacific area. The facts of yesterday and today speak for themselves. The people of the United States have already formed their opinions and well understand the implications to the very life and safety of our Nation.

As Commander in Chief of the Army and Navy I have directed that all measures be taken for our defense.

But always will our whole Nation remember the character of the onslaught against us.

No matter how long it may take us to overcome this premeditated invasion, the American people in their righteous might will win through to absolute victory. I believe that I interpret the will of the Congress and of the people when I assert that we will not only defend ourselves to the uttermost but will make it very certain that this form of treachery shall never again endanger us.

Hostilities exist. There is no blinking at the fact that our people, our territory, and our interests are in grave danger.

With confidence in our armed forces—with the unbounding determination of our people—we will gain the inevitable triumph—so help us God.

I ask that the Congress declare that since the unprovoked and dastardly attack by Japan on Sunday, December 7, 1941, a state of war has existed between the United States and the Japanese Empire.

Source: U.S. Department of State. *Peace and War: United States Foreign Policy, 1931–1941.* Washington, D.C.: U.S. Government Printing Office, 1943, 838–839.

President Franklin D. Roosevelt Gives State of the Union Address during World War II, 1944

The following document is Franklin D. Roosevelt's State of the Union Address, given on January 11, 1944, by radio. The country was still embroiled in World

War II, and the president advises in his address that Congress secure its tax, food, labor, and war contract policies, among other recommendations. In addition to discussion of political matters, President Roosevelt also offers moral advice to the American people. He communicates about the nature of the war and its emotional demands, and he is blunt about the enemies that the United States faces. He maintains a conversational style in keeping with the regular "Fireside Chats" that had proven so popular with the American public during the 1930s.

President Roosevelt did not live to see the United States and its allies win the war, as he passed away on April 12, 1945. Less than five months later, on September 2, 1945, the war came to an official end with Japan's surrender.

Ladies and Gentlemen:

Today I sent my Annual Message to the Congress, as required by the Constitution. It has been my custom to deliver these Annual Messages in person, and they have been broadcast to the Nation. I intended to follow this same custom this year.

But, like a great many other people, I have had the "flu" and, although I am practically recovered, my Doctor simply would not permit me to leave the White House to go up to the Capitol.

Only a few of the newspapers of the United States can print the Message in full, and I am anxious that the American people be given an opportunity to hear what I have recommended to the Congress for this very fateful year in our history—and the reasons for those recommendations. Here is what I said:

This Nation in the past two years has become an active partner in the world's greatest war against human slavery.

We have joined with like-minded people in order to defend ourselves in a world that has been gravely threatened with gangster rule.

But I do not think that any of us Americans can be content with mere survival. Sacrifices that we and our Allies are making impose upon us all a sacred obligation to see to it that out of this war we and our children will gain something better than mere survival.

We are united in determination that this war shall not be followed by another interim which leads to new disaster—that we shall not repeat the tragic errors of ostrich isolationism.

When Mr. Hull went to Moscow in October, when I went to Cairo and Teheran in November, we knew that we were in agreement with our Allies in our common determination to fight and win this war. There were many vital questions concerning the future peace, and they were discussed in an atmosphere of complete candor and harmony.

In the last war such discussions, such meetings, did not even begin until the shooting had stopped and the delegates began to assemble at the peace table. There had been no previous opportunities for man-to-man discussions which lead to meetings of minds. And the result was a peace which was not a peace.

And right here I want to address a word or two to some suspicious souls who are fearful that Mr. Hull or I have made "commitments" for the future which might pledge this Nation to secret treaties, or to enacting the role of a world Santa Claus.

Of course, we made some commitments. We most certainly committed ourselves to very large and very specific military plans which require the use of all allied forces to bring about the defeat of our enemies at the earliest possible time.

But there were no secret treaties or political or financial commitments.

The one supreme objective for the future, which we discussed for each nation individually, and for all the United Nations, can be summed up in one word: Security.

And that means not only physical security which provides safety from attacks by aggressors. It means also economic security, social security, moral security—in a family of nations.

In the plain down-to-earth talks that I had with the Generalissimo and Marshal Stalin and Prime Minister Churchill, it was abundantly clear that they are all most deeply interested in the resumption of peaceful progress by their own peoples—progress toward a better life.

All our Allies have learned by experience—bitter experience that real development will not be possible if they are to be diverted from their purpose by repeated wars—or even threats of war.

The best interests of each nation, large and small, demand that all freedom-loving nations shall join together in a just and durable system of peace. In the present world situation, evidenced by the actions of Germany, and Italy and Japan, unquestioned military control over the disturbers of the peace is as necessary among nations as it is among citizens in any community. And an equally basic essential to peace—permanent peace—is a decent standard of living for all individual men and women and children in all nations. Freedom from fear is eternally linked with freedom from want.

There are people who burrow—burrow through the nation like unseeing moles, and attempt to spread the suspicion that if other nations are encouraged to raise their standards of living, our own American standard of living must of necessity be depressed.

The fact is the very contrary. It has been shown time and again that if the standard of living of any country goes up, so does its purchasing power—and that such a rise encourages a better standard of living in neighboring countries with whom it trades. That is just plain common sense—and is the kind of plain common sense that provided the basis for our discussions at Moscow, and Cairo and Teheran.

Returning from my journeying, I must confess to a sense of being "let down" when I found many evidences of faulty perspectives here in Washington. The faulty perspective consists in over-emphasizing lesser problems and thereby under-emphasizing the first and greatest problem.

The overwhelming majority of our people have met the demands of this war with magnificent courage and a great deal of understanding. They have accepted inconveniences; they have accepted hardships; they have accepted tragic sacrifices.

However, while the majority goes on about its great work without complaint, we all know that a noisy minority maintains an uproar, an uproar of demands for special favors for special groups. There are pests who swarm through the lobbies of the Congress and the cocktail bars of Washington, representing these special groups as opposed to the basic interests of the Nation as a whole. They have come to look upon the war primarily as a chance to make profits for themselves at the expense of their neighbors—profits in money or profits in terms of political or social preferment.

Such selfish agitation can be and is highly dangerous in wartime. It creates confusion. It damages morale. It hampers our national effort. It prolongs the war.

In this war, we have been compelled to learn how interdependent upon each other are all groups and sections of the whole population of America.

Increased food costs, for example, will bring new demands for wage increases from all war workers, which will in turn raise all prices of all things including those things which the farmers themselves have to buy. Increased wages or prices will each in turn produce the same results. They all have a particularly disastrous result on all fixed income groups.

And I hope you will remember that all of us in this Government, including myself, represent the fixed income group just as much as we represent business owners, or workers or farmers. This group of fixed-income people include: teachers, and clergy, and policemen, and firemen, and widows and minors who are on fixed incomes, wives and dependents of our soldiers and sailors, and old age pensioners. They and their families add up to more than a quarter of our one hundred and thirty million people. They have few or no high pressure representatives at the Capitol. And in a period of gross inflation they would be the worst sufferers. Let us give them an occasional thought.

If ever there was a time to subordinate individual or group selfishness for the national good, that time is now. Disunity at home, and bickering, self-seeking partisanship, stoppages of work, inflation, business as usual, politics as usual, luxury as usual—and sometimes a failure to tell the whole truth—these are the influences which can undermine the morale of the brave men ready to die at the front for us here.

Those who are doing most of the complaining, I do not think that they are deliberately striving to sabotage the national war effort. They are laboring under the delusion that the time is past when we must make prodigious sacrifices—that the war is already won and we can begin to slacken off. But the dangerous folly of that point of view can be measured by the distance that separates our troops from their ultimate objectives in Berlin and Tokyo—and by the sum of all the perils that lie along the way.

Over confidence and complacency are among our deadliest of all enemies.

And that attitude on the part of anyone—Government or management or labor—can lengthen this war. It can kill American boys.

Let us remember the lessons of 1918. In the summer of that year the tide turned in favor of the Allies. But this Government did not relax, nor did the American people. In fact, our nation's effort was stepped up. In August, 1918, the draft age limits were broadened from 21 to 31 all the way to 18 to 45. The President called for "force to the utmost," and his call was heeded. And in November, only three months later, Germany surrendered.

That is the way to fight and win a war—all out and not with half-an-eye on the battlefronts abroad and the other eye-and-a-half on personal selfish, or political interests here at home.

Therefore, in order to concentrate all of our energies, all of our resources on winning this war, and to maintain a fair and stable economy at home, I recommend that the Congress adopt:

First, A realistic and simplified tax law—which will tax all unreasonable profits, both individual and corporate, and reduce the ultimate cost of the war to our sons and our daughters. The tax bill now under consideration by the Congress does not begin to meet this test.

Secondly, A continuation of the law for the renegotiations of war contracts—which will prevent exorbitant profits and assure fair prices to the Government. For two long years I have pleaded with the Congress to take undue profits out of war.

Third, A cost of food law—which will enable the Government to place a reasonable floor under the prices the farmer may expect for his production; and to place a ceiling on the prices the consumer will have to pay for the necessary food he buys. This should apply, as I have intimated, to necessities only; and this will require public funds to carry it out. It will cost in appropriations about one percent of the present annual cost of the war.

Fourth, An early re-enactment of the stabilization statute of October, 1942. This expires this year, June 30th, 1944, and if it is not extended well in advance, the country might just as well expect price chaos by summertime.

We cannot have stabilization by wishful thinking. We must take positive action to maintain the integrity of the American dollar.

And fifth, A national service law—which, for the duration of the war, will prevent strikes, and, with certain appropriate exceptions, will make available for war production or for any other essential services every able-bodied adult in this whole Nation.

These five measures together form a just and equitable whole. I would not recommend a national service law unless the other laws were passed to keep down the cost of living, to share equitably the burdens of taxation, to hold the stabilization line, and to prevent undue profits.

The Federal Government already has the basic power to draft capital and property of all kinds for war purposes on a basis of just compensation.

And, as you know, I have for three years hesitated to recommend a national service act. Today, however, with all the experience we have behind us and with us, I am convinced of its necessity. Although I believe that we and our Allies can win the war without such a measure, I am certain that nothing less than total mobilization of all our resources of manpower and capital will guarantee an earlier victory, and reduce the toll of suffering and sorrow and blood.

As some of my advisers wrote me the other day:

> When the very life of the nation is in peril the responsibility for service is common to all men and women. In such a time there can be no discrimination between the men and women who are assigned by the Government to its

defense at the battlefront and the men and women assigned to producing the vital materials that are essential to successful military operations. A prompt enactment of a National Service Law would be merely an expression of the universality of this American responsibility.

I believe the country will agree that those statements are the solemn truth.

National service is the most democratic way to wage a war. Like selective service for the armed forces, it rests on the obligation of each citizen to serve his nation to his utmost where he is best qualified.

It does not mean reduction in wages. It does not mean loss of retirement and seniority rights and benefits. It does not mean that any substantial numbers of war workers will be disturbed in their present jobs. Let this fact be wholly clear.

There are millions of American men and women who are not in this war at all. That is not because they do not want to be in it. But they want to know where they can best do their share. National service provides that direction.

I know that all civilian war workers will be glad to be able to say many years hence to their grandchildren: "Yes, I, too, was in service in the great war. I was on duty in an airplane factory, and I helped to make hundreds of fighting planes. The Government told me that in doing that I was performing my most useful work in the service of my country."

It is argued that we have passed the stage in the war where national service is necessary. But our soldiers and sailors know that this is not true. We are going forward on a long, rough road—and, in all journeys, the last miles are the hardest. And it is for that final effort—for the total defeat of our enemies—that we must mobilize our total resources. The national war program calls for the employment of more people in 1944 than in 1943.

And it is my conviction that the American people will welcome this win-the-war measure which is based on the eternally just principle of "fair for one, fair for all."

It will give our people at home the assurance that they are standing four-square behind our soldiers and sailors. And it will give our enemies demoralizing assurance that we mean business—that we, one hundred and thirty million Americans, are on the march to Rome, and Berlin and Tokyo.

I hope that the Congress will recognize that, although this is a political year, national service is an issue which transcends politics. Great power must be used for great purposes.

As to the machinery for this measure, the Congress itself should determine its nature—as long as it is wholly non-partisan in its make-up.

Several alleged reasons have prevented the enactment of legislation which would preserve for our soldiers and sailors and marines the fundamental prerogative of citizenship—in other words, the right to vote. No amount of legalistic argument can becloud this issue in the eyes of these ten million American citizens. Surely the signers of the Constitution did not intend a document which, even in wartime, would be construed to take away the franchise of any of those who are fighting to preserve the Constitution itself.

Our soldiers and sailors and marines know that the overwhelming majority of them will be deprived of the opportunity to vote, if the voting machinery is left exclusively to the States under existing State laws—and that there is no likelihood of these laws being changed in time to enable them to vote at the next election. The Army and Navy have reported that it will be impossible effectively to administer forty-eight different soldier-voting laws. It is the duty of the Congress to remove this unjustifiable discrimination against the men and women in our armed forces—and to do it just as quickly as possible.

It is our duty now to begin to lay the plans and determine the strategy. More than the winning of the war, it is time to begin plans and determine the strategy for winning a lasting peace and the establishment of an American standard of living higher than ever known before.

This Republic had its beginning, and grew to its present strength, under the protection of certain inalienable political rights—among them the right of free speech, free press, free worship, trial by jury, freedom from unreasonable searches and seizures. They were our rights to life and liberty.

We have come to a clear realization of the fact, however, that true individual freedom cannot exist without economic security and independence. "Necessitous men are not free men." People who are hungry, people who are out of a job are the stuff of which dictatorships are made.

In our day these economic truths have become accepted as self-evident. We have accepted, so to speak, a second Bill of Rights under which a new basis of security and prosperity can be established for all—regardless of station, or race or creed.

Among these are:

The right to a useful and remunerative job in the industries, or shops or farms or mines of the nation;

The right to earn enough to provide adequate food and clothing and recreation;

The right of farmers to raise and sell their products at a return which will give them and their families a decent living;

The right of every business man, large and small, to trade in an atmosphere of freedom from unfair competition and domination by monopolies at home or abroad;

The right of every family to a decent home;

The right to adequate medical care and the opportunity to achieve and enjoy good health;

The right to adequate protection from the economic fears of old age, and sickness, and accident and unemployment;

And finally, the right to a good education.

All of these rights spell security. And after this war is won we must be prepared to move forward, in the implementation of these rights, to new goals of human happiness and well-being.

America's own rightful place in the world depends in large part upon how fully these and similar rights have been carried into practice for all our citizens. For unless there is security here at home there cannot be lasting peace in the world.

One of the great American industrialists of our day—a man who has rendered yeoman service to his country in this crisis—recently emphasized the grave dangers of "rightist reaction" in this Nation. Any clear-thinking business men share that concern. Indeed, if such reaction should develop—if history were to repeat itself and we were to return to the so-called "normalcy" of the 1920s—then it is certain that even though we shall have conquered our enemies on the battlefields abroad, we shall have yielded to the spirit of fascism here at home.

I ask the Congress to explore the means for implementing this economic bill of rights—for it is definitely the responsibility of the Congress so to do, and the country knows it. Many of these problems are already before committees of the Congress in the form of proposed legislation. I shall from time to time communicate with the Congress with respect to these and further proposals. In the event that no adequate program of progress is evolved, I am certain that the Nation will be conscious of the fact.

Our fighting men abroad—and their families at home—expect such a program and have the right to insist on it. It is to their demands that this Government should pay heed, rather than to the whining demands of selfish pressure groups who seek to feather their nests while young Americans are dying.

I have often said that there are no two fronts for America in this war. There is only one front. There is one line of unity that extends from the hearts of people at home to the men of our attacking forces in our farthest outposts. When we speak of our total effort, we speak of the factory and the field and the mine as well as the battlefield—we speak of the soldier and the civilian, the citizen and his Government.

Each and every one of them has a solemn obligation under God to serve this Nation in its most critical hour—to keep this Nation great—to make this Nation greater in a better world.

Source: Franklin D. Roosevelt Presidential Library and Museum. Available online at http://www.fdrlibrary.marist.edu/archives/address_text.html.

President Harry Truman Drops Atomic Bomb on Hiroshima, Japan, 1945

On August 6, 1945, President Harry Truman gave an order to drop the first atomic bomb over Hiroshima, Japan. The entire world was shocked by the bomb, not only because of its incredible destructive force but because the bomb's very existence had been a secret—even to Truman himself when he was vice president. Franklin Roosevelt had begun work on the nuclear bomb in 1939 in confidence with the British and a scant few other U.S. intelligence officials. The bomb, dubbed "Little Boy," was dropped by a B-29 plane and killed around 100,000 people. Another atomic bomb was dropped over the Japanese city of Nagasaki three days later. The Japanese surrendered on August 15, ending the war. The following document is a "Statement by the President Announcing the Use of the A-Bomb at Hiroshima," released the same day the bomb was dropped. Much of it was a virtual tutorial for the American people on the history and scientific underpinnings of the fearsome new weapon, while the rest sought to provide justification for its use against Japan.

SIXTEEN HOURS AGO an American airplane dropped one bomb on Hiroshima, an important Japanese Army base. That bomb had more power than 20,000 tons of T.N.T. It had more than two thousand times the blast power of the British "Grand Slam" which is the largest bomb ever yet used in the history of warfare.

The Japanese began the war from the air at Pearl Harbor. They have been repaid many fold. And the end is not yet. With this bomb we have now added a new and revolutionary increase in destruction to supplement the growing power of our armed forces. In their present form these bombs are now in production and even more powerful forms are in development.

It is an atomic bomb. It is a harnessing of the basic power of the universe. The force from which the sun draws its power has been loosed against those who brought war to the Far East.

Before 1939, it was the accepted belief of scientists that it was theoretically possible to release atomic energy. But no one knew any practical method of doing it. By 1942, however, we knew that the Germans were working feverishly to find a way to add atomic energy to the other engines of war with which they hoped to enslave the world. But they failed. We may be grateful to Providence that the Germans got the V-1s and V-2s late and in limited quantities and even more grateful that they did not get the atomic bomb at all.

The battle of the laboratories held fateful risks for us as well as the battles of the air, land and sea, and we have now won the battle of the laboratories as we have won the other battles.

Beginning in 1940, before Pearl Harbor, scientific knowledge useful in war was pooled between the United States and Great Britain, and many priceless helps to our victories have come from that arrangement. Under that general policy the research on the atomic bomb was begun. With American and British scientists working together we entered the race of discovery against the Germans.

The United States had available the large number of scientists of distinction in the many needed areas of knowledge. It had the tremendous industrial and financial resources necessary for the project and they could be devoted to it without undue impairment of other vital war work. In the United States the laboratory work and the production plants, on which a substantial start had already been made, would be out of reach of enemy bombing, while at that time Britain was exposed to constant air attack and was still threatened with the possibility of invasion. For these reasons Prime Minister Churchill and President Roosevelt agreed that it was wise to carry on the project here. We now have two great plants and many lesser works devoted to the production of atomic power. Employment during peak construction numbered 125,000 and over 65,000 individuals are even now engaged in operating the plants. Many have worked there for two and a half years. Few know what they have been producing. They see great quantities of material going in and they see nothing coming out of these plants, for the physical size of the explosive charge is exceedingly small. We have spent two billion dollars on the greatest scientific gamble in history—and won.

But the greatest marvel is not the size of the enterprise, its secrecy, nor its cost, but the achievement of scientific brains in putting together infinitely complex pieces of knowledge held by many men in different fields of science into a workable plan. And hardly less marvelous has been the capacity of industry to design, and of labor to operate, the machines and methods to do things never done before so that the brain child of many minds came forth in physical shape and performed as it was supposed to do. Both science and industry worked under the direction of the United States Army, which achieved a unique success in managing so diverse a problem in the advancement of knowledge in an amazingly short time. It is doubtful if such another combination could be got together in the world. What has been done is the greatest achievement of organized science in history. It was done under high pressure and without failure.

We are now prepared to obliterate more rapidly and completely every productive enterprise the Japanese have above ground in any city. We shall destroy their docks, their factories, and their communications. Let there be no mistake; we shall completely destroy Japan's power to make war.

It was to spare the Japanese people from utter destruction that the ultimatum of July 26 was issued at Potsdam. Their leaders promptly rejected that ultimatum. If they do not now accept our terms they may expect a rain of ruin from the air, the like of which has never been seen on this earth. Behind this air attack will follow sea and land forces in such numbers and power as they have not yet seen and with the fighting skill of which they are already well aware.

The Secretary of War, who has kept in personal touch with all phases of the project, will immediately make public a statement giving further details.

His statement will give facts concerning the sites at Oak Ridge near Knoxville, Tennessee, and at Richland near Pasco, Washington, and an installation near Santa Fe, New Mexico. Although the workers at the sites have been making materials to be used in producing the greatest destructive force in history they have not themselves been in danger beyond that of many other occupations, for the utmost care has been taken of their safety.

The fact that we can release atomic energy ushers in a new era in man's understanding of nature's forces. Atomic energy may in the future supplement the power that now comes from coal, oil, and falling water, but at present it cannot be produced on a basis to compete with them commercially. Before that comes there must be a long period of intensive research.

It has never been the habit of the scientists of this country or the policy of this Government to withhold from the world scientific knowledge. Normally, therefore, everything about the work with atomic energy would be made public.

But under present circumstances it is not intended to divulge the technical processes of production or all the military applications, pending further examination of possible methods of protecting us and the rest of the world from the danger of sudden destruction.

I shall recommend that the Congress of the United States consider promptly the establishment of an appropriate commission to control the production and use of atomic power within the United States. I shall give further consideration and make further recommendations to the Congress as to how atomic power can become a powerful and forceful influence towards the maintenance of world peace.

> **Source:** *Public Papers of the Presidents of the United States, Harry S. Truman, 1945–1953*. Washington, D.C.: United States Government Printing Office, 1966.

President Harry Truman Nationalizes Steel Industry during Korean War, 1952

As the Korean War continued without an end in sight, President Harry Truman believed it was necessary to secure the United States' economy and labor force. The Wage Stabilization Board, armed with the legislation of the Defense Production Act passed in 1950, was able to fix price ceilings on certain products in an effort to keep workers happy and costs stable. However, President Truman's plan backfired when steel laborers, knowing their worth in wartime, demanded wages higher than the law allowed. Negotiations between corporations and the Board ensued, and they concluded that workers would not receive pay increases. On April 4, 1952, steel unions across the country voted to strike. The president was tasked with a critical choice, knowing that the country's efforts in Korea would be crippled without consistent steel production. He could either force the workers back to their jobs under the authority of the Taft-Hartley Act or seize the steel industry using an executive order. On April 8, 1952, President Truman signed Executive Order 10340—Directing the Secretary of Commerce to Take Possession and Operate the Plants and Facilities of Certain Steel Companies. Workers were outraged at Truman's move, which they knew closed off any possibility of securing wage increases. But the Trump administration pointed out that similar action had been taken by past presidents in other wartime scenarios. Steel companies filed lawsuits against the president as well, however, and in the Supreme Court case Youngstown Sheet & Tube Co. v. Sawyer, *the Supreme Court ruled that the president's actions had violated the Constitution. Workers went on to strike for almost two months. Below is an excerpt of President Truman's order.*

WHEREAS on December 16, 1950, I proclaimed the existence of a national emergency which requires that the military, naval, air, and civilian defenses of this country be strengthened as speedily as possible to the end that we may be able to repel any and all threats against our national security and to fulfill our responsibilities in the efforts being made throughout the United Nations and otherwise to bring about a lasting peace; and

WHEREAS American fighting men and fighting men of other nations of the United Nations are now engaged in deadly combat with the forces of aggression in Korea, and forces of the United States are stationed elsewhere overseas for the purpose of participating in the defense of the Atlantic Community against aggression; and

WHEREAS the weapons and other materials needed by our armed forces and by those joined with us in the defense of the free world are produced to a great extent in this country, and steel is an indispensable component of substantially all of such weapons and materials; and

WHEREAS steel is likewise indispensable to the carrying out of programs of the Atomic Energy Commission of vital importance to our defense efforts; and

WHEREAS a continuing and uninterrupted supply of steel is also indispensable to the maintenance of the economy of the United States, upon which our military strength depends; and

WHEREAS a controversy has arisen between certain companies in the United States producing and fabricating steel and the elements thereof and certain of their workers represented by the United Steel Workers of America, CIO, regarding terms and conditions of employment; and

WHEREAS the controversy has not been settled through the processes of collective bargaining or through the efforts of the Government, including those of the Wage Stabilization Board, to which the controversy was referred on December 22, 1951, pursuant to Executive Order No. 10233, and a strike has been called for 12:01 A.M., April 9, 1952; and

WHEREAS a work stoppage would immediately jeopardize and imperil our national defense and the defense of those joined with us in resisting aggression, and would add to the continuing danger of our soldiers, sailors, and airmen engaged in combat in the field; and

WHEREAS in order to assure the continued availability of steel and steel products during the existing emergency, it is necessary that the United States take possession of and operate the plants, facilities, and other property of the said companies as hereinafter provided:

NOW, THEREFORE, by virtue of the authority vested in me by the Constitution and laws of the United States, and as President of the United States and Commander in Chief of the armed forces of the United States, it is hereby ordered as follows:

1. The Secretary of Commerce is hereby authorized and directed to take possession of all or such of the plants, facilities, and other property of the companies named in the list attached hereto, or any part thereof, as he may deem necessary in the interests of national defense; and to operate or to arrange for the operation thereof and to do all things necessary for, or incidental to, such operation.
2. In carrying out this order the Secretary of Commerce may act through or with the aid of such public or private instrumentalities or persons as he may designate; and all Federal agencies shall cooperate with the Secretary of Commerce to the fullest extent possible in carrying out the purposes of this order.
3. The Secretary of Commerce shall determine and prescribe terms and conditions of employment under which the plants, facilities, and other properties possession of which is taken pursuant to this order shall be operated. The Secretary of Commerce shall recognize the rights of workers to bargain collectively through representatives of their own choosing and to engage in concerted activities for the purpose of

collective bargaining, adjustment of grievances, or other mutual aid or protection, provided that such activities do not interfere with the operation of such plants, facilities, and other properties.

4. Except so far as the Secretary of Commerce shall otherwise provide from time to time, the managements of the plants, facilities, and other properties possession of which is taken pursuant to this order shall continue their functions, including the collection and disbursement of funds in the usual and ordinary course of business in the names of their respective companies and by means of any instrumentalities used by such companies.

5. Except so far as the Secretary of Commerce may otherwise direct, existing rights and obligations of such companies shall remain in full force and effect, and there may be made, in due course, payments of dividends on stock, and of principal, interest, sinking funds, and all other distributions upon bonds, debentures, and other obligations, and expenditures may be made for other ordinary corporate or business purposes.

6. Whenever in the judgment of the Secretary of Commerce further possession and operation by him of any plant, facility, or other property is no longer necessary or expedient in the interest of national defense, and the Secretary has reason to believe that effective future operation is assured, he shall return the possession and operation of such plant, facility or other property to the company in possession and control thereof at the time possession was taken under this order.

7. The Secretary of Commerce is authorized to prescribe and issue such regulations and orders not inconsistent herewith as he may deem necessary or desirable for carrying out the purposes of this order; and he may delegate and authorize subdelegation of such of his functions under this order as he may deem desirable.

Source: Executive Order 10340—Directing the Secretary of Commerce to Take Possession of and Operate the Plants and Facilities of Certain Steel Companies. 3 CFR, 1949-1953 Comp., 861.

President Dwight D. Eisenhower Warns about the Implications of Russia's Sputnik Space Satellite, 1958

The Soviet Union's successful launch of the world's first space satellite, Sputnik, on October 4, 1957, came as a grim surprise to the U.S. government and public. The launch emphasized the Soviet Union's growing power in technical and scientific fields, and cast a shadow over the related achievements of the United States. As the Cold War continued between the two superpowers, the added element of space exploration created further tension. Sputnik's implications struck fear in Americans, who could imagine the raised stakes of missile and nuclear warfare from space. Almost exactly one year later, on October 1, 1958, President Dwight

D. Eisenhower held a press conference in which he fielded questions about the Soviets' intentions and the United States' military capabilities. In the following excerpt, he reassures reporters of the United States' military readiness and of its dedication to strengthening its space programs.

Q. Edward W. O'Brien, St. Louis Globe-Democrat: Saturday, sir, will be the first anniversary of the launching of the first Russian Sputnik. Could you discuss with us the evolution of our military position in the past year in relation to that of Russia; and as a somewhat related matter, could you tell us, sir, if we have the military power in the Far Pacific that is adequate for our possible needs in that area?

THE PRESIDENT. These guns are getting about three barreled, rather than two. [Laughter]

With respect to the Sputnik incidents of the Russians, I should say they represent, as the whole world recognizes, remarkable achievements, and they are additional evidence of the quality of the top Russian scientists right down the whole field.

Our committees that come back to the United States, our electrical committee, the steel committee and the others, they come back and they report very great, tremendous advances in the scientific character of all of their steel-making facilities and everything else. In one or two instances it has been said to me, "You know, these people in one or two kinds of items are ahead of us, even in quality, and you might say, in the height of the scientific ingenuity that has been displayed."

Now, we have, I believe in the last 7 months, put four satellites in orbit. Our plan was devised, as I pointed out before, with an entirely different purpose from that that the Soviets had.

We started it as a part of the Geophysical Year. It was our responsibility that we voluntarily assumed. When it comes to the weaponry, I point it out to you again, the Russians started with their German scientists that they had secured right after 1945.

Our own interest in this particular field was not very great. We went into long-range weapons, missiles, but they were aerodynamic. They were not the ballistic missiles. In other words, we didn't go at all into the IRBM and the ICBMs.

So, when I came in here, I got two successive scientific committees to go into this thing and find out what was going on, what we should be doing, and it took them quite a long time. But, along about a year and a half after the first committee was organized, we believed that we knew what we should do. That was the first time that anything was really dedicated—any sizable sum—to ballistic missiles of a long range. And the whole project was now put on first priority, over every other expenditure.

But, remember, with our curve starting over here, and theirs here, we had to get a very steep one. I think we have constructed a very steep curve of accomplishment but, naturally, with that length of time, there are going to be some incidents here and there where we are not satisfied with our results.

But they are going ahead, and I believe we have the biggest, strongest, finest body of scientists amply armed with money to do the job, and that's that.

Now, in the Far East, I think our weaponry is in very good shape, and our forces are in good shape.

Marvin L. Arrowsmith, Associated Press: Thank you, Mr. President.

Source: *Public Papers of the Presidents of the United States. Dwight D. Eisenhower, 1958.* Washington, D.C.: Government Printing Office, 1959, 712–722.

President Dwight D. Eisenhower Addresses the Press about U-2 Plane Incident, 1960

As the Cold War and space race roiled on between the United States and the Soviet Union, U.S. military and intelligence agencies engaged in a wide range of covert operations against the Soviets and their geopolitical allies. But in May 1960, one of the United States' secret espionage operations was revealed after the Soviet military shot down an American U-2 spy plane and captured its pilot, who was sentenced to prison. President Dwight D. Eisenhower was left to answer not just the Soviet Union's angry condemnations but also an uneasy general public that wondered if the incident might trigger more active engagement between the two countries. The president delivered these remarks at a press conference shortly after the incident was brought to light. He justified the espionage and reassured reporters and the public that secret operations were worth it because they protected the people. The following is an excerpt from that conference on May 11, 1960. The U-2 spy plane incident remained a thorn in the side of U.S.–Soviet relations for months to come, but it finally faded in importance after Eisenhower traded a captured Soviet agent for the U-2 pilot on February 10, 1962.

THE PRESIDENT [reading]. I have made some notes from which I want to talk to you about this U-2 incident.

A full statement about this matter has been made by the State Department, and there have been several statesmanlike remarks by leaders of both parties.

For my part, I supplement what the Secretary of State has had to say, with the following four main points. After that I shall have nothing further to say—for the simple reason I can think of nothing to add that might be useful at this time.

The first point is this: the need for intelligence-gathering activities.

No one wants another Pearl Harbor. This means that we must have knowledge of military forces and preparations around the world, especially those capable of massive surprise attacks.

Secrecy in the Soviet Union makes this essential. In most of the world no large-scale attack could be prepared in secret, but in the Soviet Union there is a fetish of secrecy and concealment. This is a major cause of international tension and uneasiness today. Our deterrent must never be placed in jeopardy. The safety of the whole free world demands this.

As the Secretary of State pointed out in his recent statement, ever since the beginning of my administration I have issued directives to gather, in every feasible way, the information required to protect the United States and the free world against surprise attack and to enable them to make effective preparations for defense.

My second point: the nature of intelligence-gathering activities.

These have a special and secret character. They are, so to speak, "below the surface" activities.

They are secret because they must circumvent measures designed by other countries to protect secrecy of military preparations.

They are divorced from the regular visible agencies of government which stay clear of operational involvement in specific detailed activities.

These elements operate under broad directives to seek and gather intelligence short of the use of force—with operations supervised by responsible officials within this area of secret activities.

We do not use our Army, Navy, or Air Force for this purpose, first, to avoid any possibility of the use of force in connection with these activities, and second, because our military forces, for obvious reasons, cannot be given latitude under broad directives but must be kept under strict control in every detail.

These activities have their own rules and methods of concealment which seek to mislead and obscure—just as in the Soviet allegations there are many discrepancies. For example, there is some reason to believe that the plane in question was not shot down at high altitude. The normal agencies of our Government are unaware of these specific activities or of the special efforts to conceal them.

Third point: how should we view all of this activity?

It is a distasteful but vital necessity.

We prefer and work for a different kind of world—and a different way of obtaining the information essential to confidence and effective deterrents. Open societies, in the day of present weapons, are the only answer.

This was the reason for my "open skies" proposal in 1955, which I was ready instantly to put into effect—to permit aerial observation over the United States and the Soviet Union which would assure that no surprise attack was being prepared against anyone. I shall bring up the "open skies" proposal again at Paris—since it is a means of ending concealment and suspicion.

My final point is that we must not be distracted from the real issues of the day by what is an incident or a symptom of the world situation today.

This incident has been given great propaganda exploitation. The emphasis given to a flight of an unarmed nonmilitary plane can only reflect a fetish of secrecy.

The real issues are the ones we will be working on at the summit-disarmament, search for solutions affecting Germany and Berlin, and the whole range of East-West relations, including the reduction of secrecy and suspicion.

Frankly, I am hopeful that we may make progress on these great issues. This is what we mean when we speak of "working for peace."

And as I remind you, I will have nothing further to say about this matter. [Ends reading]

Source: *Public Papers of the Presidents of the United States. Dwight D. Eisenhower, 1960–61.* Washington, D.C.: Government Printing Office, 1961, 403–404.

President John F. Kennedy Speaks about the Bay of Pigs Fiasco, 1961

By the break of day on April 19, 1961, John F. Kennedy's plan to invade Fidel Castro's Cuba, a communist regime closely allied with the Soviet Union, with 1,400 troops at Cuba's Bay of Pigs was already a failure. Fighter planes were late, and some were shot down by Castro's forces. American paratroopers made inaccurate landings onto the island. Ground troops were outnumbered and unprepared and captured. In a particularly humiliating turn, an American-trained brigade of Cubans, called Brigade 2506, exiled from Cuba after Castro came to power, also surrendered to Cuban forces.

The failed invasion at the Bay of Pigs is often referred to as a disaster for the United States and for President Kennedy himself, who had inherited the plan from President Dwight D. Eisenhower. The U.S. government had been seeking to remove Castro ever since he overthrew Cuba's previous leader, American ally Fulgencio Batista, in 1959.

In the following document, the president addresses the American Society of Newspaper Editors the day after the Bay of Pigs attack had transpired. He justifies his attempts and warns again of the dangers of communism, while assuring the public that the United States will not let Cuba become a threat.

Mr. Catledge, members of the American Society of Newspaper Editors, ladies and gentlemen:

The President of a great democracy such as ours, and the editors of great newspapers such as yours, owe a common obligation to the people: an obligation to present the facts, to present them with candor, and to present them in perspective. It is with that obligation in mind that I have decided in the last 24 hours to discuss briefly at this time the recent events in Cuba.

On that unhappy island, as in so many other arenas of the contest for freedom, the news has grown worse instead of better. I have emphasized before that this was a struggle of Cuban patriots against a Cuban dictator. While we could not be expected to hide our sympathies, we made it repeatedly clear that the armed forces of this country would not intervene in any way.

Any unilateral American intervention, in the absence of an external attack upon ourselves or an ally, would have been contrary to our traditions and to our international obligations. But let the record show that our restraint is not inexhaustible. Should it ever appear that the inter-American doctrine of non-interference merely conceals or excuses a policy of nonaction—if the nations of this Hemisphere should fail to meet their commitments against outside Communist penetration—then I want it clearly understood that this Government will not hesitate in meeting its primary obligations which are to the security of our Nation!

Should that time ever come, we do not intend to be lectured on "intervention" by those whose character was stamped for all time on the bloody streets of Budapest! Nor would we expect or accept the same outcome which this small band of gallant Cuban refugees must have known that they were chancing, determined as they were against heavy odds to pursue their courageous attempts to regain their Island's freedom.

But Cuba is not an island unto itself; and our concern is not ended by mere expressions of nonintervention or regret. This is not the first time in either ancient or recent history that a small band of freedom fighters has engaged the armor of totalitarianism.

It is not the first time that Communist tanks have rolled over gallant men and women fighting to redeem the independence of their homeland. Nor is it by any means the final episode in the eternal struggle of liberty against tyranny, anywhere on the face of the globe, including Cuba itself.

Mr. Castro has said that these were mercenaries. According to press reports, the final message to be relayed from the refugee forces on the beach came from the rebel commander when asked if he wished to be evacuated. His answer was: "I will never leave this country." That is not the reply of a mercenary. He has gone now to join in the mountains countless other guerrilla fighters, who are equally determined that the dedication of those who gave their lives shall not be forgotten, and that Cuba must not be abandoned to the Communists. And we do not intend to abandon it either!

The Cuban people have not yet spoken their final piece. And I have no doubt that they and their Revolutionary Council, led by Dr. Cardona—and members of the families of the Revolutionary Council, I am informed by the Doctor yesterday, are involved themselves in the Islands—will continue to speak up for a free and independent Cuba.

Meanwhile we will not accept Mr. Castro's attempts to blame this nation for the hatred which his onetime supporters now regard his repression. But there are from this sobering episode useful lessons for us all to learn. Some may be still obscure, and await further information. Some are clear today.

First, it is clear that the forces of communism are not to be underestimated, in Cuba or anywhere else in the world. The advantages of a police state—its use of mass terror and arrests to prevent the spread of free dissent—cannot be overlooked by those who expect the fall of every fanatic tyrant. If the self-discipline of the free cannot match the iron discipline of the mailed fist—in economic, political, scientific and all the other kinds of struggles as well as the military—then the peril to freedom will continue to rise.

Secondly, it is clear that this Nation, in concert with all the free nations of this hemisphere, must take an ever closer and more realistic look at the menace of external Communist intervention and domination in Cuba. The American people are not complacent about Iron Curtain tanks and planes less than 90 miles from their shore. But a nation of Cuba's size is less a threat to our survival than it is a base for subverting the survival of other free nations throughout the hemisphere. It is not primarily our interest or our security but theirs which is now, today, in the greater peril. It is for their sake as well as our own that we must show our will.

The evidence is clear—and the hour is late. We and our Latin friends will have to face the fact that we cannot postpone any longer the real issue of survival of freedom in this hemisphere itself. On that issue, unlike perhaps some others, there can be no middle ground. Together we must build a hemisphere where freedom can flourish; and where any free nation under outside attack of any kind can be assured that all of our resources stand ready to respond to any request for assistance.

Third, and finally, it is clearer than ever that we face a relentless struggle in every corner of the globe that goes far beyond the clash of armies or even nuclear armaments. The armies are there, and in large number. The nuclear armaments are there. But they serve primarily as the shield behind which subversion, infiltration, and a host of other tactics steadily advance, picking off vulnerable areas one by one in situations which do not permit our own armed intervention.

Power is the hallmark of this offensive-power and discipline and deceit. The legitimate discontent of yearning people is exploited. The legitimate trappings of self-determination are employed. But once in power, all talk of discontent is repressed, all self-determination disappears, and the promise of a revolution of hope is betrayed, as in Cuba, into a reign of terror. Those who on instruction staged automatic "riots" in the streets of free nations over the efforts of a small group of young Cubans to regain their freedom should recall the long roll call of refugees who cannot now go back—to Hungary, to North Korea, to North Viet-Nam, to East Germany, or to Poland, or to any of the other lands from which a steady stream of refugees pours forth, in eloquent testimony to the cruel oppression now holding sway in their homeland.

We dare not fail to see the insidious nature of this new and deeper struggle. We dare not fail to grasp the new concepts, the new tools, the new sense of urgency we will need to combat it—whether in Cuba or South Viet-Nam. And we dare not fail to realize that this struggle is taking place every day, without fanfare, in thousands of villages and markets—day and night—and in classrooms all over the globe.

The message of Cuba, of Laos, of the rising din of Communist voices in Asia and Latin America—these messages are all the same. The complacent, the self-indulgent the soft societies are about to be swept away with the debris of history. Only the strong, only the industrious, only the determined, only the courageous, only the visionary who determine the real nature of our struggle can possibly survive.

No greater task faces this country or this administration. No other challenge is more deserving of our every effort and energy. Too long we have fixed our eyes on traditional military needs, on armies prepared to cross borders, on missiles poised for flight. Now it should be clear that this is no longer enough—that our security may be lost piece by piece, country by country, without the firing of a single missile or the crossing of a single border.

We intend to profit from this lesson. We intend to reexamine and reorient our forces of all kinds—our tactics and our institutions here in this community. We intend to intensify our efforts for a struggle in many ways more difficult than war, where disappointment will often accompany us.

For I am convinced that we in this country and in the free world possess the necessary resource, and the skill, and the added strength that comes from a belief in the freedom of man. And I am equally convinced that history will record the fact that this bitter struggle reached its climax in the late 1950s and the early 1960s. Let me then make clear as the President of the United States that I am determined upon our system's survival and success, regardless of the cost and regardless of the peril!

Source: *Public Papers of the Presidents of the United States. John F. Kennedy, 1961.* Washington, D.C.: Government Printing Office, 1962, 304–306.

President John F. Kennedy Warns Soviet Union about Actions in Berlin, 1961

As a new decade commenced, the United States continued its occupation of West Berlin. Berlin had been divided after World War II, with its western side under the joint control of the United States, the United Kingdom, and France and its eastern jurisdictions in the power of the Soviet Union, which had been led by Soviet Premier Nikita Khrushchev since 1958. President John F. Kennedy considered the United States' presence in West Berlin to be of critical, strategic importance in the country's efforts to halt the spread of communism and in the Cold War overall. When Kennedy and Khrushchev met at a diplomatic summit in 1961, the two leaders did not reach an agreement on the confrontational situation in Berlin. Instead, Khrushchev renewed his demand for the United States and its allies to withdraw from the city. President Kennedy instead bulked the presence of U.S. armed forces in West Berlin in preparation for potentially escalated circumstances, and on August 13, 1961, Khrushchev responded by installing a barbed-wire fence across East Berlin's western border; this structure was later strengthened and enlarged and became known as the Berlin Wall. This action was meant to inhibit the movement of Eastern Berliners into West Berlin, where the free movement of Berliners had been a vital aspect of the two countries' previous agreements. The following document is President Kennedy's August 24, 1961, response to the actions the Soviet Union had taken in the city.

THE SOVIET NOTE of August 23, 1961, is dearly but one more step in a deliberate campaign of deception and attempted intimidation designed to distract attention from failures of the Soviet Government and to heighten world tensions.

The charges and allegations contained in this note with respect to the United States and its allies are false, as the Soviet Government well knows. That such statements should be made with respect to activities in the free Western sectors of Berlin at the very moment when the Soviet Government is sealing off the Eastern sector of the city is an act of cynicism and irresponsibility. This act is also a direct violation of the Soviet Government's commitment to "the economic and political unity of Germany" and the pledged word of the Soviet Government to cooperate with the Allied Governments "to mitigate the effects of the administrative division of Germany and Berlin" by "facilitation of the movement of persons and goods and the exchange of information" throughout Germany, including Berlin.

The slanderous remarks of the Soviet Government about the legitimate activities of free men in West Berlin suggest that somehow the Soviet Government supposes the United States to share the Soviet view that subservience to dictator-ship is the proper mode of German life. The peaceful commitment to freedom of the people of West Berlin and the restraint of their leaders under great provocation have never been demonstrated more plainly than in recent days. Moreover, it is strange that the Soviet Government should protest against relations between West Germany and West Berlin at a time when it is insisting upon the identity of East Berlin with East Germany.

These charges and allegations can thus not be taken seriously. What must be taken seriously by the whole world, however, is the scarcely veiled threat of aggression against the Allied air routes to and from West Berlin. The United States must serve a solemn warning to the Soviet Union that any interference by the Soviet Government or its East German regime with free access to West Berlin would be an aggressive act for the consequences of which the Soviet Government would bear full responsibility.

Source: *Public Papers of the Presidents of the United States. John F. Kennedy, 1961.* Washington, D.C.: Government Printing Office, 1962, 568–569.

President John F. Kennedy Gives Report on Cuban Missile Crisis, 1962

When Fidel Castro displaced Fulgencio Batista as the leader of Cuba in 1959, the United States lost an important ally and trade partner. The Soviet Union, led by Premier Nikita Khrushchev, seized the opportunity to align itself with the island both economically and politically. While the alliance raised alarm from the out-set, especially as Cuba was located only a little more than 100 miles from main-land Florida, it became an existential threat to the United States to many military and intelligence officials when they learned that Cuba had given permission for the Soviet Union to install nuclear missiles on Cuban land. Castro believed that the missiles would serve as a deterrent to future invasion from the United States, President John F. Kennedy saw it as a deadly threat to the nation. He responded by creating a blockade around the island and engaging in tense negotiations with Khrushchev to halt the missiles' construction. Khrushchev proposed to remove the missiles on two conditions: that the United States abstain from another Cuban invasion and that it remove missiles stationed in Turkey that had the capacity to reach targets inside the Soviet Union. The first proposition was agreed to pub-licly, but the second was agreed to privately, and that part of the agreement remained a secret for decades to come. The Cuban Missile Crisis lasted 13 days, from October 16, 1962, to October 28, 1962. The following document is a tran-script of the radio and television address President Kennedy gave to the American public on October 22, 1962—the midpoint of the crisis. His grim remarks created widespread fear across the nation that nuclear war with the Soviet Union might actually become a reality. Indeed, President Kennedy uses foreboding language in the address, describing the Soviet Union as an empire intent on world domination.

Good evening, my fellow citizens:

This Government, as promised, has maintained the closest surveillance of the Soviet military buildup on the island of Cuba. Within the past week, unmistakable evidence has established the fact that a series of offensive missile sites is now in preparation on that imprisoned island. The purpose of these bases can be none other than to provide a nuclear strike capability against the Western Hemisphere.

Upon receiving the first preliminary hard information of this nature last Tuesday morning at 9 a.m., I directed that our surveillance be stepped up. And having now confirmed and completed our evaluation of the evidence and our decision on a course of action, this Government feels obliged to report this new crisis to you in fullest detail.

The characteristics of these new missile sites indicate two distinct types of installations. Several of them include medium range ballistic missiles, capable of carrying a nuclear warhead for a distance of more than 1,000 nautical miles. Each of these missiles, in short, is capable of striking Washington, D.C., the Panama Canal, Cape Canaveral, Mexico City, or any other city in the southeastern part of the United States, in Central America, or in the Caribbean area.

Additional sites not yet completed appear to be designed for intermediate range ballistic missiles—capable of traveling more than twice as far—and thus capable of striking most of the major cities in the Western Hemisphere, ranging as far north as Hudson Bay, Canada, and as far south as Lima, Peru. In addition, jet bombers, capable of carrying nuclear weapons, are now being uncrated and assembled in Cuba, while the necessary air bases are being prepared.

This urgent transformation of Cuba into an important strategic base—by the presence of these large, long-range, and clearly offensive weapons of sudden mass destruction—constitutes an explicit threat to the peace and security of all the Americas, in flagrant and deliberate defiance of the Rio Pact of 1947, the traditions of this Nation and hemisphere, the joint resolution of the 87th Congress, the Charter of the United Nations, and my own public warnings to the Soviets on September 4 and 13. This action also contradicts the repeated assurances of Soviet spokesmen, both publicly and privately delivered, that the arms buildup in Cuba would retain its original defensive character, and that the Soviet Union had no need or desire to station strategic missiles on the territory of any other nation.

The size of this undertaking makes clear that it has been planned for some months. Yet only last month, after I had made clear the distinction between any introduction of ground-to-ground missiles and the existence of defensive antiaircraft missiles, the Soviet Government publicly stated on September 11 that, and I quote, "the armaments and military equipment sent to Cuba are designed exclusively for defensive purposes," that, and I quote the Soviet Government, "there is no need for the Soviet Government to shift its weapons. . . . For a retaliatory blow to any other country, for instance Cuba," and that, and I quote their government, "the Soviet Union has so powerful rockets to carry these nuclear warheads that there is no need to search for sites for them beyond the boundaries of the Soviet Union." That statement was false.

Only last Thursday, as evidence of this rapid offensive buildup was already in my hand, Soviet Foreign Minister Gromyko told me in my office that he was instructed to make it clear once again, as he said his government had already done, that Soviet assistance to Cuba, and I quote, "pursued solely the purpose of contributing to the defense capabilities of Cuba," that, and I quote him, "training by Soviet specialists of Cuban nationals in handling defensive armaments was by no means offensive, and if it were otherwise," Mr. Gromyko went on, "the Soviet Government would never become involved in rendering such assistance." That statement also was false.

Neither the United States of America nor the world community of nations can tolerate deliberate deception and offensive threats on the part of any nation, large or small. We no longer live in a world where only the actual firing of weapons represents a sufficient challenge to a nation's security to constitute maximum peril. Nuclear weapons are so destructive and ballistic missiles are so swift, that any substantially increased possibility of their use or any sudden change in their deployment may well be regarded as a definite threat to peace.

For many years, both the Soviet Union and the United States, recognizing this fact, have deployed strategic nuclear weapons with great care, never upsetting the precarious status quo which insured that these weapons would not be used in the absence of some vital challenge. Our own strategic missiles have never been transferred to the territory of any other nation under a cloak of secrecy and deception; and our history—unlike that of the Soviets since the end of World War II— demonstrates that we have no desire to dominate or conquer any other nation or impose our system upon its people. Nevertheless, American citizens have become adjusted to living daily on the bull's-eye of Soviet missiles located inside the U.S.S.R. or in submarines.

In that sense, missiles in Cuba add to an already clear and present danger— although it should be noted the nations of Latin America have never previously been subjected to a potential nuclear threat.

But this secret, swift, and extraordinary buildup of Communist missiles—in an area well known to have a special and historical relationship to the United States and the nations of the Western Hemisphere, in violation of Soviet assurances, and in defiance of American and hemispheric policy—this sudden, clandestine decision to station strategic weapons for the first time outside of Soviet soil—is a deliberately provocative and unjustified change in the status quo which cannot be accepted by this country, if our courage and our commitments are ever to be trusted again by either friend or foe.

The 1930s taught us a clear lesson: aggressive conduct, if allowed to go unchecked and unchallenged, ultimately leads to war. This nation is opposed to war. We are also true to our word. Our unswerving objective, therefore, must be to prevent the use of these missiles against this or any other country, and to secure their withdrawal or elimination from the Western Hemisphere.

Our policy has been one of patience and restraint, as befits a peaceful and powerful nation, which leads a worldwide alliance. We have been determined not to be diverted from our central concerns by mere irritants and fanatics. But now further action is required—and it is under way; and these actions may only be the beginning. We will not prematurely or unnecessarily risk the costs of worldwide nuclear war in which even the fruits of victory would be ashes in our mouth—but neither will we shrink from that risk at any time it must be faced.

Acting, therefore, in the defense of our own security and of the entire Western Hemisphere, and under the authority entrusted to me by the Constitution as endorsed by the resolution of the Congress, I have directed that the following initial steps be taken immediately:

First: To halt this offensive buildup, a strict quarantine on all offensive military equipment under shipment to Cuba is being initiated. All ships of any kind bound for Cuba from whatever nation or port will, if found to contain cargoes of offensive weapons, be turned back. This quarantine will be extended, if needed, to other types of cargo and carriers. We are not at this time, however, denying the necessities of life as the Soviets attempted to do in their Berlin blockade of 1948.

Second: I have directed the continued and increased close surveillance of Cuba and its military buildup. The foreign ministers of the OAS, in their communique of October 6, rejected secrecy on such matters in this hemisphere. Should these offensive military preparations continue, thus increasing the threat to the hemisphere, further action will be justified. I have directed the Armed Forces to prepare for any eventualities; and I trust that in the interest of both the Cuban people and the Soviet technicians at the sites, the hazards to all concerned of continuing this threat will be recognized.

Third: It shall be the policy of this Nation to regard any nuclear missile launched from Cuba against any nation in the Western Hemisphere as an attack by the Soviet Union on the United States, requiring a full retaliatory response upon the Soviet Union.

Fourth: As a necessary military precaution, I have reinforced our base at Guantanamo, evacuated today the dependents of our personnel there, and ordered additional military units to be on a standby alert basis.

Fifth: We are calling tonight for an immediate meeting of the Organ of Consultation under the Organization of American States, to consider this threat to hemispheric security and to invoke articles 6 and 8 of the Rio Treaty in support of all necessary action. The United Nations Charter allows for regional security arrangements—and the nations of this hemisphere decided long ago against the military presence of outside powers. Our other allies around the world have also been alerted.

Sixth: Under the Charter of the United Nations, we are asking tonight that an emergency meeting of the Security Council be convoked without delay to take action against this latest Soviet threat to world peace. Our resolution will call for the prompt dismantling and withdrawal of all offensive weapons in Cuba, under the supervision of U.N. observers, before the quarantine can be lifted.

Seventh and finally: I call upon Chairman Khrushchev to halt and eliminate this clandestine, reckless, and provocative threat to world peace and to stable relations between our two nations. I call upon him further to abandon this course of world domination, and to join in an historic effort to end the perilous arms race and to transform the history of man. He has an opportunity now to move the world back from the abyss of destruction—by returning to his government's own words that it had no need to station missiles outside its own territory, and withdrawing these weapons from Cuba by refraining from any action which will widen or deepen the present crisis—and then by participating in a search for peaceful and permanent solutions.

This Nation is prepared to present its case against the Soviet threat to peace, and our own proposals for a peaceful world, at any time and in any forum—in the OAS, in the United Nations, or in any other meeting that could be useful—without limiting our freedom of action. We have in the past made strenuous efforts to limit the spread of nuclear weapons. We have proposed the elimination of all arms and military bases in a fair and effective disarmament treaty. We are prepared to discuss new proposals for the removal of tensions on both sides—including the possibilities of a genuinely independent Cuba, free to determine its own destiny. We have no wish to war with the Soviet Union—for we are a peaceful people who desire to live in peace with all other peoples.

But it is difficult to settle or even discuss these problems in an atmosphere of intimidation. That is why this latest Soviet threat—or any other threat which is made either independently or in response to our actions this week—must and will be met with determination. Any hostile move anywhere in the world against the safety and freedom of peoples to whom we are committed-including in particular the brave people of West Berlin—will be met by whatever action is needed.

Finally, I want to say a few words to the captive people of Cuba, to whom this speech is being directly carried by special radio facilities. I speak to you as a friend, as one who knows of your deep attachment to your fatherland, as one who shares your aspirations for liberty and justice for all. And I have watched and the American people have watched with deep sorrow how your nationalist revolution was betrayed—and how your fatherland fell under foreign domination. Now your leaders are no longer Cuban leaders inspired by Cuban ideals. They are puppets and agents of an international conspiracy which has turned Cuba against your friends and neighbors in the Americas—and turned it into the first Latin American country to become a target for nuclear war—the first Latin American country to have these weapons on its soil.

These new weapons are not in your interest. They contribute nothing to your peace and well-being. They can only undermine it. But this country has no wish to cause you to suffer or to impose any system upon you. We know that your lives and land are being used as pawns by those who deny your freedom.

Many times in the past, the Cuban people have risen to throw out tyrants who destroyed their liberty. And I have no doubt that most Cubans today look forward to the time when they will be truly free—free from foreign domination, free to choose their own leaders, free to select their own system, free to own their own land, free to speak and write and worship without fear or degradation. And then shall Cuba be welcomed back to the society of free nations and to the associations of this hemisphere.

My fellow citizens: let no one doubt that this is a difficult and dangerous effort on which we have set out. No one can foresee precisely what course it will take or what costs or casualties will be incurred. Many months of sacrifice and self-discipline lie ahead—months in which both our patience and our will be tested—months in which many threats and denunciations will keep us aware of our dangers. But the greatest danger of all would be to do nothing.

The path we have chosen for the present is full of hazards, as all paths are—but it is the one most consistent with our character and courage as a nation and our commitments around the world. The cost of freedom is always high—but Americans have always paid it. And one path we shall never choose, and that is the path of surrender or submission.

Our goal is not the victory of might, but the vindication of right—not peace at the expense of freedom, but both peace and freedom, here in this hemisphere, and, we hope, around the world. God willing, that goal will be achieved.

Thank you and good night.

Source: *Public Papers of the Presidents of the United States. John F. Kennedy, 1962.* Washington, D.C.: Government Printing Office, 1963, 806–809.

President Lyndon B. Johnson Vows Continued Support for South Vietnam in Letter to General Minh, 1964

In the following letter (written on New Year's Eve, 1963, and publicly released the following day), President Lyndon B. Johnson pledges his allegiance to South Vietnam's cause, which is to maintain its independence in the face of threats from communist North Vietnam and communist guerrillas based in South Vietnam (known as Viet Cong). Johnson's letter was addressed to General Duong Van Minh, who had taken control of the country in a military coup (that may have been covertly assisted by the United States) in November 1963. Just weeks after Minh received this letter, however, he himself was overthrown in a coup led by General Nguyen Khanh. This trend of violent coups and general political turmoil continued to destabilize South Vietnam until its eventual demise in 1975—two years after the last American troops were withdrawn—when North Vietnam launched a successful invasion.

Dear General Minh:

As we enter the New Year of 1964, I want to wish you, your Revolutionary Government, and your people full success in the long and arduous war which you are waging so tenaciously and bravely against the Viet Cong forces directed and supported by the Communist regime in Hanoi. Ambassador Lodge and Secretary McNamara have told me about the serious situation which confronts you and of the plans which you are developing to enable your armed forces and your people to redress this situation.

This new year provides a fitting opportunity for me to pledge on behalf of the American Government and people a renewed partnership with your government and people in your brave struggle for freedom. The United States will continue to furnish you and your people with the fullest measure of support in this bitter fight. We shall maintain in Vietnam American personnel and material as needed to assist you in achieving victory.

Our aims are, I know, identical with yours: to enable your government to protect its people from the acts of terror perpetrated by Communist insurgents from the north. As the forces of your government become increasingly capable of dealing with this aggression, American military personnel in South Vietnam can be progressively withdrawn.

The U.S. Government shares the view of your government that "neutralization" of South Vietnam is unacceptable. As long as the Communist regime in North Vietnam persists in its aggressive policy, neutralization of South Vietnam would only be another name for a Communist takeover. Peace will return to your country just as soon as the authorities in Hanoi cease and desist from their terrorist aggression.

Thus, your government and mine are in complete agreement on the political aspects of your war against the forces of enslavement, brutality, and material misery. Within this framework of political agreement we can confidently continue and improve our cooperation.

I am pleased to learn from Secretary McNamara about the vigorous operations which you are planning to bring security and an improved standard of living to your people.

I wish to congratulate you particularly on your work for the unity of all your people, including the Hoa Hao and Cao Dai, against the Viet Cong. I know from my own experience in Vietnam how warmly the Vietnamese people respond to a direct human approach and how they have hungered for this in their leaders. So again I pledge the energetic support of my country to your government and your people.

We will do our full part to ensure that under your leadership your people may win a victory—a victory for freedom and justice and human welfare in Vietnam.

Source: *Public Papers of the Presidents of the United States. Lyndon B. Johnson, 1963–64, Book 1.* Washington, D.C.: Government Printing Office, 1965, 106.

President Lyndon B. Johnson Gives Report on Gulf of Tonkin Incident, 1964

By the spring of 1964, U.S. military involvement in the Vietnam War was deepening but remained limited to military equipment and armaments and a training/advisory role to the South Vietnamese Army. That summer, however, a strange and mysterious encounter off the coast of Vietnam triggered a dramatic escalation in U.S. involvement in the war—including the first deployments of U.S. ground troops in March 1965.

The mysterious clash in the Gulf of Tonkin took place on August 2, when the U.S.S. Maddox, *a Navy destroyer, fended off an unprovoked attack from three North Vietnamese patrol torpedo (PT) boats with assistance from a nearby U.S. aircraft carrier. One day later, a second American destroyer, the U.S.S.* Turner Joy *joined the* Maddox. *On August 4, the* Maddox *once again reported that it was under attack, citing suspicious radar sightings and intercepted North Vietnamese radio communications. The destroyers and the aircraft carrier—the U.S.S.*

Ticonderoga—subsequently fired in the direction of the radar images. They also alerted military commanders of the clash, who informed President Lyndon B. Johnson that U.S. forces in the Gulf were under attack again. Johnson saw the August 4 incident as an opportunity to expand America's involvement in the Vietnam War. He ordered a robust military response to the second attack, approving a military strike that destroyed much of North Vietnam's PT boat fleet and damaged an oil storage installation. He also made a formal statement on national television to the American people (reprinted below) describing the encounters in the Tonkin Gulf. The following day—August 5—he asked Congress to approve a resolution (which came to known as the Gulf of Tonkin Resolution) giving him expansive authority to expand American involvement in the war. It passed the Senate by an 88-2 vote and was approved unanimously by the House of Representatives. American involvement in the Vietnam War expanded rapidly in the months following passage of the Gulf of Tonkin Resolution, even though many historians now believe that the event that precipitated the resolution—the second wave of attacks on American ships on the evening of August 4—never actually took place. They believe that storms in the region, inexperienced military personnel, and heightened emotions all combined to generate a false alarm about a second attack.

My fellow Americans:

As President and Commander in Chief, it is my duty to the American people to report that renewed hostile actions against United States ships on the high seas in the Gulf of Tonkin have today required me to order the military forces of the United States to take action in reply.

The initial attack on the destroyer Maddox, on August 2, was repeated today by a number of hostile vessels attacking two U.S. destroyers with torpedoes. The destroyers and supporting aircraft acted at once on the orders I gave after the initial act of aggression. We believe at least two of the attacking boats were sunk. There were no U.S. losses.

The performance of commanders and crews in this engagement is in the highest tradition of the United States Navy. But repeated acts of violence against the Armed Forces of the United States must be met not only with alert defense, but with positive reply. That reply is being given as I speak to you tonight. Air action is now in execution against gunboats and certain supporting facilities in North Viet-Nam which have been used in these hostile operations.

In the larger sense this new act of aggression, aimed directly at our own forces, again brings home to all of us in the United States the importance of the struggle for peace and security in southeast Asia. Aggression by terror against the peaceful villagers of South Viet-Nam has now been joined by open aggression on the high seas against the United States of America.

The determination of all Americans to carry out our full commitment to the people and to the government of South Viet-Nam will be redoubled by this outrage. Yet our response, for the present, will be limited and fitting. We Americans know, although others appear to forget, the risks of spreading conflict. We still seek no wider war.

I have instructed the Secretary of State to make this position totally clear to friends and to adversaries and, indeed, to all. I have instructed Ambassador Stevenson to raise this matter immediately and urgently before the Security Council of the United Nations. Finally, I have today met with the leaders of both parties in the Congress of the United States and I have informed them that I shall immediately request the Congress to pass a resolution making it clear that our Government is united in its determination to take all necessary measures in support of freedom and in defense of peace in southeast Asia.

I have been given encouraging assurance by these leaders of both parties that such a resolution will be promptly introduced, freely and expeditiously debated, and passed with overwhelming support. And just a few minutes ago I was able to reach Senator Goldwater and I am glad to say that he has expressed his support of the statement that I am making to you tonight.

It is a solemn responsibility to have to order even limited military action by forces whose overall strength is as vast and as awesome as those of the United States of America, but it is my considered conviction, shared throughout your Government, that firmness in the right is indispensable today for peace; that firmness will always be measured. Its mission is peace.

Source: *Public Papers of the Presidents of the United States. Lyndon B. Johnson, 1963–64, Book 2.* Washington, D.C.: Government Printing Office, 1965, 927–928.

President Jimmy Carter Gives Statement on Iran Hostage Crisis, 1979

On November 4, 1979, 52 U.S. citizens were taken hostage at the U.S. Embassy in Tehran, Iran, by students who were protesting what they perceived to be the Westernization of their country. The roots of this incident could be traced back to January 1979, when rioting and pressure from nationalist groups forced Iran's longtime authoritarian ruler, Mohammad Reza Shah, to flee the country. That opened the door for militant religious leader Ayatollah Khomeini to take over the country and further inflame resentment for Americans. When the Shah was later permitted to enter the United States for cancer treatment, student protestors raided the U.S. Embassy. A few of the building's inhabitants were able to escape, but most were captured.

In mid-November, the students released 13 captives, a mix of women and African Americans and another captive due to his health complications. The remaining captives were held hostage for 444 days in poor conditions. The American public was frightened for the hostages and humiliated by the United States' seeming helplessness. They demanded that President Jimmy Carter take action, but Carter chose to prioritize patience and poise, to the public's frustration. Meanwhile, the next presidential campaign was fast approaching, and Republican nominee Ronald Reagan ultimately cruised to a decisive victory. On the day that President Reagan was inaugurated, the hostages were released and flown to Germany after billions of dollars in assets were exchanged on January 20, 1981. President Carter flew to Germany to welcome them back to safety. The following document is of a few remarks given by President Carter at a news conference in the early days of the hostage crisis, in which he details the support of the United Nations and his dedication to the safe return of the hostages.

THE PRESIDENT. For the last 24 days our Nation's concern has been focused on our fellow Americans being held hostage in Iran. We have welcomed some of them home to their families and their friends. But we will not rest nor deviate from our efforts until all have been freed from their imprisonment and their abuse. We hold the Government of Iran fully responsible for the well-being and the safe return of every single person.

I want the American people to understand the situation as much as possible, but there may be some questions tonight which I cannot answer fully, because of my concern for the well-being of the hostages.

First of all, I would like to say that I am proud of this great Nation, and I want to thank all Americans for their prayers, their courage, their persistence, their strong support and patience. During these past days our national will, our courage, and our maturity have all been severely tested, and history will show that the people of the United States have met every test.

In the days to come, our determination may be even more sorely tried, but we will continue to defend the security, the honor, and the freedom of Americans everywhere. This Nation will never yield to blackmail. For all Americans, our constant concern is the well-being and the safety of our fellow citizens who are being held illegally and irresponsibly hostage in Iran.

The actions of Iran have shocked the civilized world. For a government to applaud mob violence and terrorism, for a government actually to support and, in effect, participate in the taking and the holding of hostages is unprecedented in human history. This violates not only the most fundamental precepts of international law but the common ethical and religious heritage of humanity. There is no recognized religious faith on Earth which condones kidnaping. There is no recognized religious faith on Earth which condones blackmail. There is certainly no religious faith on Earth which condones the sustained abuse of innocent people.

We are deeply concerned about the inhuman and degrading conditions imposed on the hostages. From every corner of the world, nations and people have voiced their strong revulsion and condemnation of Iran and have joined us in calling for the release of the hostages.

Last night, a statement of support was released and was issued by the President of the United Nations General Assembly, the Security Council, on behalf of all of its members. We expect a further Security Council meeting on Saturday night, at which more firm and official action may be taken to help in obtaining the release of the American hostages. Any claims raised by government officials of Iran will ring hollow while they keep innocent people bound and abused and threatened.

We hope that this exercise of diplomacy and international law will bring a peaceful solution, because a peaceful solution is preferable to the other remedies available to the United States. At the same time, we pursue such a solution with grim determination. The Government of Iran must recognize the gravity of the situation, which it has itself created, and the grave consequences which will result if harm comes to any of the hostages.

I want the American people to know and I want the world to know that we will persist in our efforts, through every means available, until every single American has been freed. We must also recognize now, as we never have before, that it is our entire Nation which is vulnerable, because of our overwhelming and excessive dependence on oil from foreign countries. We have got to accept the fact that this dependence is a direct physical threat to our national security, and we must join together to fight for our Nation's energy freedom.

We know the ways to win this war: more American energy and the more efficient use of what we have. The United States Congress is now struggling with this extremely important decision. The way to victory is long and difficult, but we have the will, and we have the human and the natural resources of our great Nation.

However hard it might be to see into the future, one thing tonight is clear: We stand together. We stand as a nation unified, a people determined to protect the life and the honor of every American. And we are determined to make America an energy-secure nation once again. It is unthinkable that we will allow ourselves to be dominated by any form of overdependence at home or any brand of terrorism abroad. We are determined that the freest nation on Earth shall protect and enhance its freedom.

I'd be glad to answer questions.

Source: *Public Papers of the Presidents of the United States. Jimmy Carter, 1979, Book 2.* Washington, D.C.: Government Printing Office, 1980, 2167–2174.

President Ronald Reagan Addresses Bombing of U.S. Military Barracks in Beirut, 1983

On October 23, 1983, two men drove two trucks full of explosives into U.S. and French barracks located at the Beirut International Airport and another building two miles down the road. The terrorist attack killed over 200 American service members and nearly 100 French troops. The groups were stationed in Lebanon as part of the U.S.-led Multinational Peacekeeping Force (MNF), which sought to bring political and religious peace to Lebanon, then in the midst of a civil war, and its neighboring countries. However, divides in the region were fierce. To complicate matters, some Lebanese believed that the United States' alliance with Israel reflected an anti-Muslim bias on the part of the United States, which further inflamed tensions in areas with U.S. presence. Six months before in April, the U.S. Embassy in Beirut was also attacked by a suicide bomber, and almost twenty Americans were killed.

Much of the American public wanted to know why President Reagan was involved in the conflict in the Middle East in the first place. Others did not understand why it was necessary to continue to maintain a military presence there after so many American casualties. In the following document, President Reagan addresses the nation on October 27, 1983, about the violent events that had transpired in recent months, as well as his plan of action going forward. He also attempts to clarify the strategic importance of Lebanon in the Middle East. In the address, the president seems committed to the MNF and its mission, but in February 1984, he withdrew all U.S. troops from the region.

My fellow Americans:

Some 2 months ago we were shocked by the brutal massacre of 269 men, women, and children, more than 60 of them Americans, in the shooting down of a Korean airliner. Now, in these past several days, violence has erupted again, in Lebanon and Grenada.

In Lebanon, we have some 1,600 marines, part of a multinational force that's trying to help the people of Lebanon restore order and stability to that troubled land. Our marines are assigned to the south of the city of Beirut, near the only airport operating in Lebanon. Just a mile or so to the north is the Italian contingent and not far from them, the French and a company of British soldiers.

This past Sunday, at 22 minutes after 6 Beirut time, with dawn just breaking, a truck, looking like a lot of other vehicles in the city, approached the airport on a busy, main road. There was nothing in its appearance to suggest it was any different than the trucks or cars that were normally seen on and around the airport. But this one was different. At the wheel was a young man on a suicide mission.

The truck carried some 2,000 pounds of explosives, but there was no way our marine guards could know this. Their first warning that something was wrong came when the truck crashed through a series of barriers, including a chain-link fence and barbed wire entanglements. The guards opened fire, but it was too late. The truck smashed through the doors of the headquarters building in which our marines were sleeping and instantly exploded. The four-story concrete building collapsed in a pile of rubble.

More than 200 of the sleeping men were killed in that one hideous, insane attack. Many others suffered injury and are hospitalized here or in Europe.

This was not the end of the horror. At almost the same instant, another vehicle on a suicide and murder mission crashed into the headquarters of the French peacekeeping force, an eight-story building, destroying it and killing more than 50 French soldiers.

Prior to this day of horror, there had been several tragedies for our men in the multinational force. Attacks by snipers and mortar fire had taken their toll.

I called bereaved parents and/or widows of the victims to express on behalf of all of us our sorrow and sympathy. Sometimes there were questions. And now many of you are asking: Why should our young men be dying in Lebanon? Why is Lebanon important to us?

Well, it's true, Lebanon is a small country, more than five-and-a-half thousand miles from our shores on the edge of what we call the Middle East. But every President who has occupied this office in recent years has recognized that peace in the Middle East is of vital concern to our nation and, indeed, to our allies in Western Europe and Japan. We've been concerned because the Middle East is a powderkeg; four times in the last 30 years, the Arabs and Israelis have gone to war. And each time, the world has teetered near the edge of catastrophe.

The area is key to the economic and political life of the West. Its strategic importance, its energy resources, the Suez Canal, and the well-being of the nearly 200 million people living there—all are vital to us and to world peace. If that key should fall into the hands of a power or powers hostile to the free world, there would be a direct threat to the United States and to our allies.

We have another reason to be involved. Since 1948 our Nation has recognized and accepted a moral obligation to assure the continued existence of Israel as a nation. Israel shares our democratic values and is a formidable force an invader of the Middle East would have to reckon with.

For several years, Lebanon has been torn by internal strife. Once a prosperous, peaceful nation, its government had become ineffective in controlling the militias that warred on each other. Sixteen months ago, we were watching on our TV screens the shelling and bombing of Beirut which was being used as a fortress by PLO bands. Hundreds and hundreds of civilians were being killed and wounded in the daily battles.

Syria, which makes no secret of its claim that Lebanon should be a part of a Greater Syria, was occupying a large part of Lebanon. Today, Syria has become a home for 7,000 Soviet advisers and technicians who man a massive amount of Soviet weaponry, including SS-21 ground-to-ground missiles capable of reaching vital areas of Israel.

A little over a year ago, hoping to build on the Camp David accords, which had led to peace between Israel and Egypt, I proposed a peace plan for the Middle East to end the wars between the Arab States and Israel. It was based on U.N. resolutions 242 and 338 and called for a fair and just solution to the Palestinian problem, as well as a fair and just settlement of issues between the Arab States and Israel.

Before the necessary negotiations could begin, it was essential to get all foreign forces out of Lebanon and to end the fighting there. So, why are we there? Well, the answer is straightforward: to help bring peace to Lebanon and stability to the vital Middle East. To that end, the multinational force was created to help stabilize the situation in Lebanon until a government could be established and a Lebanese army mobilized to restore Lebanese sovereignty over its own soil as the foreign forces withdrew. Israel agreed to withdraw as did Syria, but Syria then reneged on its promise. Over 10,000 Palestinians who had been bringing ruin down on Beirut, however, did leave the country.

Lebanon has formed a government under the leadership of President Gemayal, and that government, with our assistance and training, has set up its own army. In only a year's time, that army has been rebuilt. It's a good army, composed of Lebanese of all factions.

A few weeks ago, the Israeli army pulled back to the Awali River in southern Lebanon. Despite fierce resistance by Syrian-backed forces, the Lebanese army was able to hold the line and maintain the defensive perimeter around Beirut.

In the year that our marines have been there, Lebanon has made important steps toward stability and order. The physical presence of the marines lends support to both the Lebanese Government and its army. It allows the hard work of diplomacy to go forward. Indeed, without the peacekeepers from the U.S., France,

Italy, and Britain, the efforts to find a peaceful solution in Lebanon would collapse.

As to that narrower question—what exactly is the operational mission of the marines—the answer is, to secure a piece of Beirut, to keep order in their sector, and to prevent the area from becoming a battlefield. Our marines are not just sitting in an airport. Part of their task is to guard that airport. Because of their presence, the airport has remained operational. In addition, they patrol the surrounding area. This is their part—a limited, but essential part—in the larger effort that I've described.

If our marines must be there, I'm asked, why can't we make them safer? Who committed this latest atrocity against them and why?

Well, we'll do everything we can to ensure that our men are as safe as possible. We ordered the battleship New Jersey to join our naval forces offshore. Without even firing them, the threat of its 16-inch guns silenced those who once fired down on our marines from the hills, and they're a good part of the reason we suddenly had a ceasefire. We're doing our best to make our forces less vulnerable to those who want to snipe at them or send in future suicide missions.

Secretary Shultz called me today from Europe, where he was meeting with the Foreign Ministers of our allies in the multinational force. They remain committed to our task. And plans were made to share information as to how we can improve security for all our men.

We have strong circumstantial evidence that the attack on the marines was directed by terrorists who used the same method to destroy our Embassy in Beirut. Those who directed this atrocity must be dealt justice, and they will be. The obvious purpose behind the sniping and, now, this attack was to weaken American will and force the withdrawal of U.S. and French forces from Lebanon. The clear intent of the terrorists was to eliminate our support of the Lebanese Government and to destroy the ability of the Lebanese people to determine their own destiny.

To answer those who ask if we're serving any purpose in being there, let me answer a question with a question. Would the terrorists have launched their suicide attacks against the multinational force if it were not doing its job? The multinational force was attacked precisely because it is doing the job it was sent to do in Beirut. It is accomplishing its mission.

Now then, where do we go from here? What can we do now to help Lebanon gain greater stability so that our marines can come home? Well, I believe we can take three steps now that will make a difference.

First, we will accelerate the search for peace and stability in that region. Little attention has been paid to the fact that we've had special envoys there working, literally, around the clock to bring the warring factions together. This coming Monday in Geneva, President Gemayel of Lebanon will sit down with other factions from his country to see if national reconciliation can be achieved. He has our firm support. I will soon be announcing a replacement for Bud McFarlane, who was preceded by Phil Habib. Both worked tirelessly and must be credited for much if not most of the progress we've made.

Second, we'll work even more closely with our allies in providing support for the Government of Lebanon and for the rebuilding of a national consensus.

Third, we will ensure that the multinational peace-keeping forces, our marines, are given the greatest possible protection. Our Commandant of the Marine Corps, General Kelley, returned from Lebanon today and will be advising us on steps we can take to improve security. Vice President Bush returned just last night from Beirut and gave me a full report of his brief visit.

Beyond our progress in Lebanon, let us remember that our main goal and purpose is to achieve a broader peace in all of the Middle East. The factions and bitterness that we see in Lebanon are just a microcosm of the difficulties that are spread across much of that region. A peace initiative for the entire Middle East, consistent with the Camp David accords and U.N. resolutions 242 and 338, still offers the best hope for bringing peace to the region.

Let me ask those who say we should get out of Lebanon: If we were to leave Lebanon now, what message would that send to those who foment instability and terrorism? If America were to walk away from Lebanon, what chance would there be for a negotiated settlement, producing a unified democratic Lebanon?

If we turned our backs on Lebanon now, what would be the future of Israel? At stake is the fate of only the second Arab country to negotiate a major agreement with Israel. That's another accomplishment of this past year, the May 17th accord signed by Lebanon and Israel.

If terrorism and intimidation succeed, it'll be a devastating blow to the peace process and to Israel's search for genuine security. It won't just be Lebanon sentenced to a future of chaos. Can the United States, or the free world, for that matter, stand by and see the Middle East incorporated into the Soviet bloc? What of Western Europe and Japan's dependence on Middle East oil for the energy to fuel their industries? The Middle East is, as I've said, vital to our national security and economic well-being.

Brave young men have been taken from us. Many others have been grievously wounded. Are we to tell them their sacrifice was wasted? They gave their lives in defense of our national security every bit as much as any man who ever died fighting in a war. We must not strip every ounce of meaning and purpose from their courageous sacrifice.

We're a nation with global responsibilities. We're not somewhere else in the world protecting someone else's interests; we're there protecting our own.

I received a message from the father of a marine in Lebanon. He told me, "In a world where we speak of human rights, there is a sad lack of acceptance of responsibility. My son has chosen the acceptance of responsibility for the privilege of living in this country. Certainly in this country one does not inherently have rights unless the responsibility for these rights is accepted." Dr. Kenneth Morrison said that while he was waiting to learn if his son was one of the dead. I was thrilled for him to learn today that his son Ross is alive and well and carrying on his duties in Lebanon.

Let us meet our responsibilities. For longer than any of us can remember, the people of the Middle East have lived from war to war with no prospect for any other future. That dreadful cycle must be broken. Why are we there? Well, a

Lebanese mother told one of our Ambassadors that her little girl had only attended school 2 of the last 8 years. Now, because of our presence there, she said her daughter could live a normal life.

With patience and firmness, we can help bring peace to that strife-torn region—and make our own lives more secure. Our role is to help the Lebanese put their country together, not to do it for them.

Source: *Public Papers of the Presidents of the United States: Ronald Reagan, 1983, Book 2.* Washington, D.C.: Government Printing Office, 1985, 1517–1522.

President George H. W. Bush Discusses the Persian Gulf Crisis, 1990

Saddam Hussein deposed Iraq's president from power in the summer of 1979 and began to work toward his goal of the unification of Arab countries using often aggressive and violent means. Despite having been through a recent war and ceasefire with Iran, Hussein decided to invade oil-rich Kuwait on August 2, 1990, ordering hundreds of thousands of Iraqi troops to the border between the two nations. The United Nations (UN) intervened at once, and ordered that Iraq disengage from Kuwait before January 15 of 1991. In the interim, the United States and other countries from the UN took up arms against Hussein and prepared themselves for war. When the deadline was ignored, the United States launched a barrage of attacks against Iraq. The attacks lasted for less than two months before Iraq was forced out of Kuwait, and a ceasefire was signed that both maintained sanctions on Iraq, and halted the development of its chemical weapons programs. The Gulf War is often cited as the catalyst to the Iraq War which would begin in 2003. The following document is a transcript of President George H. W. Bush's remarks on the budding Gulf War during a news conference held on November 8, 1990.

The President. I have a brief statement, and I'd be glad to take a couple of questions and then turn to Secretary Cheney, who will take some questions. And then he will go over to the Pentagon for more of an in-depth briefing.

On August 6th, in response to the unprovoked Iraqi invasion of Kuwait, I ordered the deployment of U.S. military forces to Saudi Arabia and the Persian Gulf to deter further Iraqi aggression and to protect our interests in the region. What we've done is right, and I'm happy to say that most Members of Congress and the majority of Americans agree.

Before the invasion in August, we had succeeded in the struggle for freedom in Eastern Europe, and we'd hopefully begun a new era that offered the promise of peace. Following the invasion, I stated that if history had taught us any lesson it was that we must resist aggression or it would destroy our freedom. Just ask the people of Kuwait and the foreign nationals in hiding there and the staffs of the remaining Embassies who have experienced the horrors of Iraq's illegal occupation, its systematic dismantling of Kuwait, and its abuse of Kuwaitis and other citizens.

The world community also must prevent an individual clearly bent on regional domination from establishing a chokehold on the world's economic lifeline. We're seeing global economic stability and growth already at risk as, each day, countries around the world pay dearly for Saddam Hussein's [President of Iraq] aggression.

From the very beginning, we and our coalition partners have shared common political goals: the immediate, complete, and unconditional withdrawal of Iraqi forces from Kuwait; restoration of Kuwait's legitimate government; protection of the lives of citizens held hostage by Iraq both in Kuwait and Iraq; and restoration of security and stability in the Persian Gulf region.

To achieve these goals, we and our allies have forged a strong diplomatic, economic, and military strategy to force Iraq to comply with these objectives. The framework of this strategy is laid out in 10 United Nations resolutions, overwhelmingly supported by the United Nations Security Council. In 3 months, the U.S. troop contribution to the multinational force in Saudi Arabia has gone from 10,000 to 230,000 as part of Operation Desert Shield. General Schwarzkopf [commander of the U.S. forces in the Persian Gulf] reports that our forces, in conjunction with other coalition forces, now have the capability to defend successfully against any further Iraqi aggression.

After consultation with King Fahd [of Saudi Arabia] and our other allies, I have today directed the Secretary of Defense to increase the size of U.S. forces committed to Desert Shield to ensure that the coalition has an adequate offensive military option should that be necessary to achieve our common goals. Toward this end, we will continue to discuss the possibility of both additional allied force contributions and appropriate United Nation actions.

Iraq's brutality, aggression, and violations of international law cannot be allowed to succeed. Secretary Baker has been consulting with our key partners in the coalition. He's met with the Amirs of Bahrain ['Isa bin Salman Al Khalifa] and Kuwait [Jabir al-Ahmad al-Jabir al-Sabah], King Fahd, President Mubarak [of Egypt], as well as the Chinese Foreign Minister [Qian Qichen], President Ozal [of Turkey], [Soviet] Foreign Minister Shevardnadze, President Gorbachev. He also will be meeting with Prime Minister Thatcher [of the United Kingdom] and President Mitterrand [of France]. I've been heartened by Jim's appraisal of the strong international solidarity and determination to ensure that Iraq's aggression does not stand and is not rewarded.

But right now, Kuwait is struggling for survival. And along with many other nations, we've been called upon to help. The consequences of our not doing so would be incalculable because Iraq's aggression is not just a challenge to the security of Kuwait and other Gulf nations but to the better world that we all have hoped to build in the wake of the Cold War. And therefore, we and our allies cannot and will not shirk our responsibilities. The state of Kuwait must be restored, or no nation will be safe and the promising future we anticipate will indeed be jeopardized.

Let me conclude with a word to the young American GI's deployed in the Gulf. We are proud of each and every one of you. I know you miss your loved ones and want to know when you'll be coming home. We won't leave you there any longer than necessary. I want every single soldier out of there as soon as possible. And we're all grateful for your continued sacrifice and your commitment.

Now, with no further ado, I'd be glad to take a couple of questions. And when I leave, Dick, take some questions and then go over to the Pentagon.

Source: *Public Papers of the Presidents of the United States. George Bush, 1990, Book 2.* Washington, D.C.: Government Printing Office, 1991, 1580–1585.

President Bill Clinton Addresses Military Efforts in Somalia after Ambush in Mogadishu, 1993

In the fall of 1993, after the United Nations (UN) determined that millions of Somalis were at risk of death due to a lack of resources and violence, a humanitarian coalition was organized to provide aid. Operation Provide Relief, as it was called, was stationed in Mogadishu, the nation's capital, after a ceasefire arrangement was crafted between two powerful Somalian warlords. However, the ceasefire was not respected in all of Mogadishu, and militia groups continued to fight, making relief efforts difficult and often perilous for troops. President Bill Clinton decided to target the source, and ordered a few hundred troops to capture one of Somalia's dangerous warlords, Muhammed Farah Aydid. On October 3, 1993, as troops approached a hotel in Mogadishu that was believed to house their target, the troops were ambushed. Two Black Hawk helicopters were shot down, troops were met with gunfire from all sides, and, after almost 24 hours of continuous violence, 18 American troops had been killed. Close to 100 other U.S. soldiers were wounded, as well as several hundred Somali fighters and civilians. In the following document, President Clinton addresses the nation on events in Somalia on October 7, 1993. Though the president seems determined to follow through with the humanitarian effort in Somalia, he withdrew all remaining troops soon thereafter.

Today I want to talk with you about our Nation's military involvement in Somalia. A year ago, we all watched with horror as Somali children and their families lay dying by the tens of thousands, dying the slow, agonizing death of starvation, a starvation brought on not only by drought, but also by the anarchy that then prevailed in that country.

This past weekend we all reacted with anger and horror as an armed Somali gang desecrated the bodies of our American soldiers and displayed a captured American pilot, all of them soldiers who were taking part in an international effort to end the starvation of the Somali people themselves. These tragic events raise hard questions about our effort in Somalia. Why are we still there? What are we trying to accomplish? How did a humanitarian mission turn violent? And when will our people come home?

These questions deserve straight answers. Let's start by remembering why our troops went into Somalia in the first place. We went because only the United States could help stop one of the great human tragedies of this time. A third of a million people had died of starvation and disease. Twice that many more were at risk of dying. Meanwhile, tons of relief supplies piled up in the capital of Mogadishu because a small number of Somalis stopped food from reaching their own countrymen.

Our consciences said, enough. In our Nation's best tradition, we took action with bipartisan support. President Bush sent in 28,000 American troops as part of a United Nations humanitarian mission. Our troops created a secure environment so that food and medicine could get through. We saved close to one million lives. And throughout most of Somalia, everywhere but in Mogadishu, life began returning to normal. Crops are growing. Markets are reopening. So are schools and hospitals. Nearly a million Somalis still depend completely on relief supplies, but at least the starvation is gone. And none of this would have happened without American leadership and America's troops.

Until June, things went well, with little violence. The United States reduced our troop presence from 28,000 down to less than 5,000, with other nations picking up where we left off. But then in June, the people who caused much of the problem in the beginning started attacking American, Pakistani, and other troops who were there just to keep the peace.

Rather than participate in building the peace with others, these people sought to fight and to disrupt, even if it means returning Somalia to anarchy and mass famine. And make no mistake about it, if we were to leave Somalia tomorrow, other nations would leave, too. Chaos would resume. The relief effort would stop, and starvation soon would return.

That knowledge has led us to continue our mission. It is not our job to rebuild Somalia's society or even to create a political process that can allow Somalia's clans to live and work in peace. The Somalis must do that for themselves. The United Nations and many African states are more than willing to help. But we, we in the United States must decide whether we will give them enough time to have a reasonable chance to succeed.

We started this mission for the right reasons, and we're going to finish it in the right way. In a sense, we came to Somalia to rescue innocent people in a burning house. We've nearly put the fire out, but some smoldering embers remain. If we leave them now, those embers will reignite into flames, and people will die again. If we stay a short while longer and do the right things, we've got a reasonable chance of cooling off the embers and getting other firefighters to take our place.

We also have to recognize that we cannot leave now and still have all our troops present and accounted for. And I want you to know that I am determined to work for the security of those Americans missing or held captive. Anyone holding an American right now should understand, above all else, that we will hold them strictly responsible for our soldiers' well-being. We expected them to be well-treated, and we expect them to be released.

So now we face a choice. Do we leave when the job gets tough, or when the job is well done? Do we invite a return of mass suffering, or do we leave in a way that gives the Somalis a decent chance to survive?

Recently, General Colin Powell said this about our choices in Somalia: "Because things get difficult, you don't cut and run. You work the problem and try to find a correct solution." I want to bring our troops home from Somalia. Before the events of this week, as I said, we had already reduced the number of our troops there from 28,000 to less than 5,000. We must complete that withdrawal soon, and I will. But we must also leave on our terms. We must do it right. And here is what I intend to do.

This past week's events make it clear that even as we prepare to withdraw from Somalia, we need more strength there. We need more armor, more air power, to ensure that our people are safe and that we can do our job. Today I have ordered 1,700 additional Army troops and 104 additional armored vehicles to Somalia to protect our troops and to complete our mission. I've also ordered an aircraft carrier and two amphibious groups with 3,600 combat Marines to be stationed offshore. These forces will be under American command.

Their mission, what I am asking these young Americans to do, is the following:

First, they are there to protect our troops and our bases. We did not go to Somalia with a military purpose. We never wanted to kill anyone. But those who attack our soldiers must know they will pay a very heavy price.

Second, they are there to keep open and secure the roads, the port, and the lines of communication that are essential for the United Nations and the relief workers to keep the flow of food and supplies and people moving freely throughout the country so that starvation and anarchy do not return.

Third, they are there to keep the pressure on those who cut off relief supplies and attacked our people, not to personalize the conflict but to prevent a return to anarchy.

Fourth, through their pressure and their presence, our troops will help to make it possible for the Somali people, working with others, to reach agreements among themselves so that they can solve their problems and survive when we leave. That is our mission.

I am proposing this plan because it will let us finish leaving Somalia on our own terms and without destroying all that two administrations have accomplished there. For, if we were to leave today, we know what would happen. Within months, Somali children again would be dying in the streets. Our own credibility with friends and allies would be severely damaged. Our leadership in world affairs would be undermined at the very time when people are looking to America to help promote peace and freedom in the post-cold-war world. And all around the world, aggressors, thugs, and terrorists will conclude that the best way to get us to change our policies is to kill our people. It would be open season on Americans.

That is why I am committed to getting this job done in Somalia, not only quickly but also effectively. To do that, I am taking steps to ensure troops from other nations are ready to take the place of our own soldiers. We've already withdrawn some 20,000 troops, and more than that number have replaced them from over two dozen other nations. Now we will intensify efforts to have other countries deploy more troops to Somalia to assure that security will remain when we're gone.

And we'll complete the replacement of U.S. military logistics personnel with civilian contractors who can provide the same support to the United Nations. While we're taking military steps to protect our own people and to help the U.N. maintain a secure environment, we must pursue new diplomatic efforts to help the Somalis find a political solution to their problems. That is the only kind of outcome that can endure.

For fundamentally, the solution to Somalia's problems is not a military one, it is political. Leaders of the neighboring African states, such as Ethiopia and Eritrea, have offered to take the lead in efforts to build a settlement among the Somali people that can preserve order and security. I have directed my representatives to pursue such efforts vigorously. And I've asked Ambassador Bob Oakley, who served effectively in two administrations as our representative in Somalia, to travel again to the region immediately to advance this process.

Obviously, even then there is no guarantee that Somalia will rid itself of violence and suffering. But at least we will have given Somalia a reasonable chance. This week some 15,000 Somalis took to the streets to express sympathy for our losses, to thank us for our effort. Most Somalis are not hostile to us but grateful. And they want to use this opportunity to rebuild their country.

It is my judgment and that of my military advisers that we may need up to 6 months to complete these steps and to conduct an orderly withdrawal. We'll do what we can to complete the mission before then. All American troops will be out of Somalia no later than March the 31st, except for a few hundred support personnel in noncombat roles.

If we take these steps, if we take the time to do the job right, I am convinced we will have lived up to the responsibilities of American leadership in the world. And we will have proved that we are committed to addressing the new problems of a new era.

When out troops in Somalia came under fire this last weekend, we witnessed a dramatic example of the heroic ethic of our American military. When the first Black Hawk helicopter was downed this weekend, the other American troops didn't retreat although they could have. Some 90 of them formed a perimeter around the helicopter, and they held that ground under intensely heavy fire. They stayed with their comrades. That's the kind of soldiers they are. That's the kind of people we are.

So let us finish the work we set out to do. Let us demonstrate to the world, as generations of Americans have done before us, that when Americans take on a challenge, they do the job right.

Let me express my thanks and my gratitude and my profound sympathy to the families of the young Americans who were killed in Somalia. My message to you is, your country is grateful, and so is the rest of the world, and so are the vast majority of the Somali people. Our mission from this day forward is to increase our strength, do our job, bring our soldiers out, and bring them home.

Thank you, and God bless America.

Source: *Public Papers of the Presidents of the United States. William J. Clinton, 1993, Book 2.* Washington, D.C.: Government Printing Office, 1994, 1703–1706.

President Bill Clinton Responds to Terrorist Attack on USS *Cole*, 2000

On October 12, 2000, two suicide bombers in a small boat full of explosives crashed into the side of the USS Cole, *a guided missile destroyer anchored at the Port of Aden in Yemen for refueling. The blast killed 17 U.S. sailors, injuring scores more. The attack was orchestrated by Al Qaeda, and believed to have been aided by the Sudanese government. The following excerpt is President Bill Clinton's radio address to the American people following the deadly attack.*

Good morning. This week an apparent terrorist attack claimed the lives of brave American sailors off the coast of Yemen, and new violence erupted between Israelis and Palestinians in the Middle East.

Our sailors aboard the U.S.S. *Cole* were simply doing their duty, but a dangerous duty, standing guard for peace. Yesterday I spoke to the captain of the *Cole*, Commander Kirk Lippold. On behalf of all Americans, I expressed our deepest sympathies and commended him and his crew for the great job they're doing at this very difficult time.

To our sailors' families, let me say we hold you in our prayers. We will never know your loved ones as you did or remember them as you will, but we join you in grief. For your loss is America's loss, and we bow our heads to God in gratitude for the lives and service of your loved ones.

In their honor, I have ordered that flags be flown at halfstaff in the United States, our territories, our Embassies, military bases, and naval vessels until sunset on Monday. As we see the flag this weekend, we should think of the families and the sacrifice they have made for America.

This tragic loss should remind us all that even when America is not at war, the men and women of our military risk their lives every day in places where comforts are few and dangers are many. No one should think for a moment that the strength of our military is less important in times of peace, because the strength of our military is a major reason we are at peace. History will record our triumphs on the battlefield, but no one can ever write a full account of the wars never fought, the losses never suffered, the tears never shed because the men and women of our military were risking their lives for peace. We should never, ever forget that.

Our military power is not all people see when ships of the United States enter a foreign port. When U.S. sailors head down the brow of the ship or our troops set foot on foreign soil, our hosts see in the uniform of the United States men and women of every race, creed, and color who trace their ancestry to every region on Earth, yet are bound together by a common commitment to freedom and a common pride in being Americans.

That image of unity amidst diversity must confound the minds of the hate-filled cowards who killed our sailors. They can take innocent life, they can cause tears and anguish, but they can never heal or build harmony or bring people together. That is work only free, law-abiding people can do.

And that is why we will do whatever it takes, for as long as it takes, to find those who killed our sailors and hold them accountable, and why we will never let the enemies of freedom and peace stop America from seeking peace, fighting terrorism, and promoting freedom. For only by defending our people, our interests, and our values will we redeem the lives of our sailors and ruin the schemes of their killers.

That includes, of course, our efforts to promote peace in the Middle East. The conflict between Israelis and Palestinians is one of the greatest tragedies of our time and one of the very hardest problems to solve. Every step forward has been

284 The Presidency in Times of Crisis and Disaster

marked with pain. Each time the forces of reconciliation have reached out, the forces of destruction have lashed out. The violence we've seen there demonstrates beyond a shadow of a doubt that the alternative to peace is unacceptable, and that no one will gain from an endless contest of inflicting and absorbing pain.

Ending the violence and getting people of the Middle East back to dialog will be hard after what has happened. But no matter how difficult that task may be, no matter how terrible the images of this week's violence, the effort must continue, with America's strong support. We must do so because we have a profound national interest in peace in the Middle East and a very special bond to the State of Israel. As in all the world's troubled places, our efforts do not guarantee success. But not to try is to guarantee failure.

So today I ask your prayers for our men and women in uniform, for the families of our fallen sailors, and for all those here and everywhere who hope and work for a world at peace.

Thanks for listening.

Source: *Public Papers of the Presidents of the United States. William J. Clinton: 2000–2001, Book 3.* Washington, D.C.: Government Printing Office, 2001–2002, 2176–2177.

President George W. Bush Addresses the Nation after 9/11 Terror Attacks, 2001

On September 11, 2001, 19 terrorists boarded four separate planes with a combined 265 passengers for the purpose of hijacking them and flying them into the World Trade Center (WTC) in New York and the Pentagon and White House in Washington, D.C. Although three planes were successful in reaching their targets, the plane designated to crash into the White House crashed into a field as its passengers and crew attempted to retake its control. Close to 3,000 men, women, and children were killed in the attack after crashing into the Pentagon and the North and South Towers of the WTC, both of which collapsed. The attacks were the deadliest terrorist event ever to hit the United States, and they marked a new era of the "War on Terrorism," as President George W. Bush said in a later speech. Investigators later determined that the terrorists had acted on the orders of Al Qaeda leader Osama bin Laden, who had orchestrated previous acts of terror against the United States both within the country (such as the bombing of the WTC in 1993) and overseas (such as the ambush against U.S. servicemen in Mogadishu). The following are President George W. Bush's first remarks to the public after the attacks took place.

Good evening. Today our fellow citizens, our way of life, our very freedom came under attack in a series of deliberate and deadly terrorist acts. The victims were in airplanes or in their offices: secretaries, business men and women, military and Federal workers, moms and dads, friends and neighbors. Thousands of lives were suddenly ended by evil, despicable acts of terror.

The pictures of airplanes flying into buildings, fires burning, huge structures collapsing have filled us with disbelief, terrible sadness, and a quiet, unyielding anger. These acts of mass murder were intended to frighten our Nation into chaos and retreat, but they have failed. Our country is strong.

A great people has been moved to defend a great nation. Terrorist attacks can shake the foundations of our biggest buildings, but they cannot touch the foundation of America. These acts shattered steel, but they cannot dent the steel of American resolve. America was targeted for attack because we're the brightest beacon for freedom and opportunity in the world. And no one will keep that light from shining.

Today our Nation saw evil, the very worst of human nature. And we responded with the best of America, with the daring of our rescueworkers, with the caring for strangers and neighbors who came to give blood and help in any way they could.

Immediately following the first attack, I implemented our Government's emergency response plans. Our military is powerful, and it's prepared. Our emergency teams are working in New York City and Washington, DC, to help with local rescue efforts.

Our first priority is to get help to those who have been injured and to take every precaution to protect our citizens at home and around the world from further attacks.

The functions of our Government continue without interruption. Federal agencies in Washington which had to be evacuated today are reopening for essential personnel tonight and will be open for business tomorrow. Our financial institutions remain strong, and the American economy will be open for business as well.

The search is underway for those who are behind these evil acts. I've directed the full resources of our intelligence and law enforcement communities to find those responsible and to bring them to justice. We will make no distinction between the terrorists who committed these acts and those who harbor them.

I appreciate so very much the Members of Congress who have joined me in strongly condemning these attacks. And on behalf of the American people, I thank the many world leaders who have called to offer their condolences and assistance.

America and our friends and allies join with all those who want peace and security in the world, and we stand together to win the war against terrorism.

Tonight I ask for your prayers for all those who grieve, for the children whose worlds have been shattered, for all whose sense of safety and security has been threatened. And I pray they will be comforted by a power greater than any of us, spoken through the ages in Psalm 23: "Even though I walk through the valley of the shadow of death, I fear no evil, for You are with me."

This is a day when all Americans from every walk of life unite in our resolve for justice and peace. America has stood down enemies before, and we will do so this time. None of us will ever forget this day. Yet, we go forward to defend freedom and all that is good and just in our world.

Thank you. Good night, and God bless America.

Source: *Public Papers of the Presidents of the United States. George W. Bush: 2001, Book 2.* Washington, D.C.: Government Printing Office, 2002, 1099–1100.

President Barack Obama Makes Statement on Attack on U.S. Embassy in Benghazi, 2012

On the night of September 11, 2012, Al Qaeda affiliates attacked American diplomats and workers in Benghazi, Libya. First, over 100 Al Qaeda affiliates set fire to the U.S. diplomatic facility and killed two American citizens, including Chris Stevens, the U.S. ambassador for Libya. Stevens had been in the country for a few months on assignment as revolts in Libya remained steady against militant leader Muammar Gaddafi. Such uprisings marked the beginning of the Arab Spring, in which ordinary people in countries such as Tunisia, Morocco, Egypt, Syria, and others revolted against their governments' oppressive regimes. Two other attacks were attempted that night by the same group on the Central Intelligence Agency (CIA) compound in Benghazi, and two American security officers were killed in the second attempt. Republican critics of the Obama administration charged that the four deaths were avoidable, and they blamed President Barack Obama and his secretary of state, Hillary Clinton, for failing to keep them safe. The situation remained a subject of political contention even after an investigation was completed, due to the confusion and misinformation (much of it politically motivated) that circulated following the events. The following document is President Obama's initial statement on the attacks, given on September 12, 2012.

I strongly condemn the outrageous attack on our diplomatic facility in Benghazi, which took the lives of four Americans, including Ambassador Chris Stevens. Right now the American people have the families of those we lost in our thoughts and prayers. They exemplified America's commitment to freedom, justice, and partnership with nations and people around the globe and stand in stark contrast to those who callously took their lives.

I have directed my administration to provide all necessary resources to support the security of our personnel in Libya and to increase security at our diplomatic posts around the globe. While the United States rejects efforts to denigrate the religious beliefs of others, we must all unequivocally oppose the kind of senseless violence that took the lives of these public servants.

On a personal note, Chris was a courageous and exemplary representative of the United States. Throughout the Libyan revolution, he selflessly served our country and the Libyan people at our mission in Benghazi. As Ambassador in Tripoli, he has supported Libya's transition to democracy. His legacy will endure wherever human beings reach for liberty and justice. I am profoundly grateful for his service to my administration and deeply saddened by this loss.

The brave Americans we lost represent the extraordinary service and sacrifices that our civilians make every day around the globe. As we stand united with their families, let us now redouble our own efforts to carry their work forward.

Source: *Public Papers of the Presidents of the United States. Barack Obama: 2012, Book 2.* Washington, D.C.: Government Printing Office, 2017, 1360.

Bibliography

Baumgartner, Frank R., and Bryan D. Jones. 1993. *Agendas and Instability in American Politics*. Chicago, IL: University of Chicago Press.

Devins, Neal, and Louis Fisher. 2002. "The Steel Seizure Case: One of a Kind?" *Constitutional Commentary* 19, no. 1: 63–86.

Ducat, Craig R. 2009. *Constitutional Interpretation*. 10th ed. Boston, MA: Wadsworth.

Edwards, George C. III, and Stephen J. Wayne. 1999. *Presidential Leadership*. New York, NY: St. Martin's Press.

Epstein, David, and Sharyn O'Halloran. 1999. *Delegating Powers*. Cambridge, UK: Cambridge University Press.

Ford, Paul Leicester. 1898. *The Federalist: A Commentary on the Constitution of the United States by Alexander Hamilton, James Madison and John Jay*. New York, NY: Henry Holt and Company.

Gormley, William T. 1986. "Regulatory Issue Networks in a Federal System." *Polity* 18, no. 4: 595–620.

Kernell, Samuel. 1997. *Going Public: New Strategies of Presidential Leadership*. Washington, D.C.: CQ Press.

Kingdon, John W. 1995. *Agendas, Alternatives, and Public Policies*. 2nd ed. New York, NY: Harper Collins.

Light, Paul. 1991. *The President's Agenda: Domestic Policy Choice from Kennedy to Reagan*. Baltimore, MD: Johns Hopkins University Press.

Locke, John. 1955. *Of Civil Government, Second Treatise*. Chicago, IL: Henry Regnery.

Mayhew, David. 1974. *Congress: The Electoral Connection*. New Haven, CT: Yale University Press.

Moe, Terry M., and William G. Howell. 1999. "Unilateral Action and Presidential Power: A Theory." *Presidential Studies Quarterly* 29: 850–873.

Moe, Terry M., and William G. Howell. 2016. *Relic: How Our Constitution Undermines Effective Government and Why We Need a More Powerful Presidency*. New York, NY: Basic Books.

Neustadt, Richard E. 1962. *Presidential Power: The Politics of Leadership*. New York, NY: John Wiley and Sons.

Roosevelt, Theodore. 1926. *Theodore Roosevelt, An Autobiography*. In *The Works of Theodore Roosevelt*. Vol. 20. New York, NY: Charles Scribner's Sons.

Schlesinger, Arthur, Jr. 1973. "Dealing with an Out-of-Control President, in 1973." *Atlantic Monthly*. https://www.theatlantic.com/politics/archive/1973/11/dealing-with-an-out-of-control-president-in-1973/569845

Taft, William Howard. 1916. *Our Chief Magistrate and His Powers*. New York, NY: Columbia University Press.

Urofsky, Melvin I., ed. 1989. *Documents of American Constitutional and Legal History*. Vol. 1. New York, NY: Knopf.

Index

on possibility of withholding funds, 176

Tyler, John, vetoes bill to create a national bank, 1841 (primary document), 104–108

on federal monopoly, 107

on public revenue as a corporation, 105–106

and resignation of most of Tyler's cabinet, 104

U-2 plane incident, 256–257

United States-Russia summit, 201–203

United States v. Nixon, 192

USA PATRIOT Act, 210

USS *Cole* attack, 282–285

Van Buren, Martin, addresses Congress during economic panic of 1837 (primary document), 97–104

on banks' use of deposited money for their own benefit, 103

on bills of exchange, 99

on constitutional role of government in domestic and foreign exchange, 100

on effect of a national bank, 98–99

on employment of local banks, 101–102

on late deposit system, 103

on purchase of public lands, 103

on transference of funds, 100

War of 1812, 94, 95, 216

War Powers Act, 179, 209

War powers of presidency, 208–209, 233

Washington, D.C., destruction of, 216–218

Washington, George, authorization of military intervention to confront the Whiskey Rebellion, 1794 (primary document), 7–8

announcement that force has already been dispatched, 8

on intelligence received, 8

on need for militia, 8

reasons for decision, 7–8

warning against aiding and abetting insurgents, 8

Washington, George, issues Neutrality Proclamation in war between England and France, 1793 (primary document), 211

on punishment or forfeiture for taking part in the conflict, 211

warning to citizens to avoid acts of contravening, 211

Watergate scandal

and crisis in confidence, 59, 63, 178

Ford, Gerald R., pardon of Nixon, 192–195

institutional response to, 179–180

Nixon, Richard, announcement of resignation, 192–195

Whiskey Rebellion, 7–8. *See also* Washington, George, authorization of military intervention to confront the Whiskey Rebellion, 1794 (primary document)

Wilson, Woodrow, creates committee on public information during Red Scare, 1917 (primary document), 183–184

and Bolshevik Revolution, 183

on Committee members, 184

on creation of Committee on Public Information, 184

Wilson, Woodrow, endorses Nineteenth Amendment, 1918 (primary document), 28–31

on justice to women as contributors to the war effort, 29

on keeping the trust of world nations, 29–30

on need for sympathy, insight, and moral instinct of women after the war, 30–31

on women's suffrage as necessary for success in the war, 28

Wilson, Woodrow, seeks peace during World War I, 1918 (primary document), 236–241

on Fourteen Points, 239–240

on perplexity of Russian representatives, 237

on reasons for entering the war, 238–239

on voice of the Russian people, 238

Worcester v. Georgia, 179

XYZ affair, 212

Youngstown Sheet and Tube Co. v. Sawyer, 178, 208, 252